ETHEL WILSON
A CRITICAL BIOGRAPHY

ETHEL WILSON

A CRITICAL BIOGRAPHY

David Stouck

UNIVERSITY OF TORONTO PRESS

Toronto Buffalo London

© University of Toronto Press Incorporated 2003
Toronto Buffalo London
Printed in Canada

ISBN 0-8020-8741-8 (cloth)

Printed on acid-free paper

National Library of Canada Cataloguing in Publication

Stouck, David, 1940–
Ethel Wilson : a critical biography / David Stouck.

Includes bibliographical references and index.
ISBN 0-8020-8741-8

1. Wilson, Ethel, 1888–1980. 2. Novelists, Canadian (English) –
20th century – Biography. I. Title.

PS8545.I62Z87 2003   c813'.54   c2002-905869-4
PR9199.3.W4984Z87 2003

University of Toronto Press acknowledges the financial assistance to its
publishing program of the Canada Council for the Arts and the
Ontario Arts Council.

This book has been published with the help of a grant from the Humanities
and Social Sciences Federation of Canada, using funds provided by the
Social Sciences and Humanities Research Council of Canada.

University of Toronto Press acknowledges the financial support for its
publishing activities of the Government of Canada through the Book
Publishing Industry Development Program (BPIDP).

For Mary-Ann

No verbal humour ... wouldn't it be *awful* to live in such solemnity.
— Ethel Wilson to Alan Crawley

Truth ... is opinion, of course.
— Ethel Wilson to John Gray

Do we always live on a brink, then, said Nora to herself,
lying there in the dark. Yes, I believe we do.
— *Love and Salt Water*

Contents

Illustrations follow page 174

Preface

I first heard of Ethel Wilson in 1966, when my wife and I were preparing to take academic positions in British Columbia. We were eager to learn about our new home, and our curiosity eventually led us to the six works of fiction by Ethel Wilson. Some of my family had been living in British Columbia for many years: one of my grandmother's brothers had settled on Quadra Island with the Lekwiltok people in the 1890s, another at Mission a few years later. In Ontario my grandparents had a cupboard filled with letters from the 'west,' but the vivid accounts of logging and fishing in those letters, even the horns and antlers sent for our walls, lacked substance beside the luminous accounts of British Columbia in the writings of Ethel Wilson. So, as we drove into the mountains, past stump ranches and fishing camps, through landscapes that seemed as fresh as the day of creation, I was seeing this world through Ethel Wilson's eyes. And coming into Vancouver for the first time was coming into a city that had been mapped for me, one I already knew.

It happened that we soon met Joy McDonagh, a family acquaintance who turned out to be a close friend to Ethel Wilson's housekeeper. When I expressed a wish to meet the novelist, however, I was told she had recently been widowed and was in seclusion. Two university colleagues who were acquainted with the Wilsons told the same story, that Ethel Wilson was in mourning and should not be disturbed. At one point they said she was near death. So I taught her novels and stories, wrote an essay about her work, and kept a respectful distance from Killarney Manor. But, nearly ten years later, I learned that she was still living, now in a nursing home, and that her caregivers welcomed visitors to help pass the hours. At that time, two exceptional graduate students, Barbara Wild and Janet Giltrow, began working within my sphere of interests, and both found in Ethel Wilson's writing a sophistication of vision and style that set her work apart from other Canadian novelists they were reading. Barbara Wild would eventually conduct the first extensive research into the Malkin and Bryant genealogies, laying the groundwork for subsequent biographical research into Ethel Wilson's family history and English origins.

With Janet Giltrow, who was drawn to the motif of travel in literature, I made my first visit to Ethel Wilson in December 1975. Young and unthinking, we went to the Arbutus Private Hospital in the evening and found her lying prone on a bed with metal sides raised – in Janet's words, 'like a sarcophagus.' She was only barely awake, evidently sedated for the night. It was depressing to see the elegant writer we greatly admired so diminished by circumstances and we hurried away, promising ourselves and a staff attendant that we would return another day. But the paraphernalia and ambiance of a nursing home – or perhaps just the glimpse of an arborite table with a little plastic Christmas tree and some tattered issues of the *Reader's Digest* in the hallway – discouraged us from going back any time soon.

But when we did return, on a spring morning, having arranged the visit in advance, we found Ethel Wilson fresh from the hair salon in a smartly tailored dress, ready with her nurse's assistance to entertain visitors for tea. There was little conversation with the author, who at eighty-eight was profoundly deaf – the nurse talked instead – but there was poise and self-possession in Ethel Wilson's august, watchful presence. I went by myself one afternoon in 1977 and enjoyed dry sherry and biscuits, and Ethel Wilson watched me closely with her piercing blue eyes; during that visit, she pointed to her husband's photo and told me it was her father. Did I try to correct her? I have wondered since.

There was one more visit, three years later, this time with Barbara Wild. Ethel Wilson was now ninety-two and had suffered several cerebral haemorrhages, which had erased almost all evidence of the person who had once inhabited the body. The nurse insisted that she had selected the blue dress herself to wear for company, but Ethel Wilson remained silent and her opaque stare gave little sign of a knowing presence. Later that year, at the funeral service and reception, I noted that no one exhibited the grief that comes from a loss, aunt and cousin having long departed.

Why have I chosen to write a biography of Ethel Wilson? She largely shunned the autobiographical herself, preferring analytical forms of fiction and deploring the *Bildungsroman* or 'growing up' story. I had arrived, moreover, too late in Vancouver to be able to talk with her about her life. Literary theory has made us aware that no matter how well researched any history of a life may be, it will always be imprinted with the biographer's view of the world as much as the subject's, and that with an artist subject especially the creative spirit or essence of that subject will remain elusive, uninterpretable. Yet certain facts – dates, places, marriage records, letters, photographs – have incontrovertible substance, and their preservation in a narrative form remains a solid contribution. In 1988 Mary McAlpine, who had known Ethel Wilson in her later years, published a book titled *The Other Side of Silence*, which she subtitled *A Life of Ethel Wilson*. Better described as a memoir, McAlpine's book combines scenes from the author's life, as remembered by family and friends, with a patchwork of often lengthy passages quoted from Wilson's writings. But there is little evidence of archival research in this volume and almost no scholarly reporting. When I read the book, I was aware of egregious errors and great gaps in the life. In the opinion of many reviewers, the book was poorly written, and I was disappointed that Ethel Wilson had been served in this way. It was clear that a full-scale biography, to at least set the record straight, was yet to be written.

But the main reason I have returned to Ethel Wilson again, thirty-six years after first driving through British Columbia, is because her writing has never ceased to engage me. She asks the difficult questions: Does the essence of all custom and virtue perish? That is, are all individual efforts and accomplishments finally lost or forgotten? Is charity possible, or is it just another form of power? What is truth? Is it wholly contextual? What is around us that we cannot see? Is civilization just a thin veneer over irrationality and violent forms of behaviour? Is existence itself all just a trick of light? Her texts are riven by epistemological and ethical uncertainties rooted in language – its materiality, and its contingencies – for, as she sometimes quoted from Lewis Carroll about words, 'their meaning depends on who is the master.' The forms of her writings are likewise uncertain – novel? novella? short story? These classifications by genre become inadequate as descriptions of her work.

Ethel Wilson's writing has a contemporary cast in another respect. Unlike most of her fellow writers in the 1950s and '60s, she did not subscribe to a nationalist program for the arts in Canada. If the writing (or painting or musical composition) was good, that was what mattered, not a Canadian theme. Some of her writing was set outside the country – in England, Europe, Egypt – and in this respect prefigures the work of writers like Michael Ondaatje, Rohinton Mistry, or Anne Michaels, who, at the outset of the twenty-first century, set their novels in places far from Canada, or who write novels set in Canada but whose characters come from somewhere else. Strangers, migrants, and mingled homes are part of Wilson's fiction as much as they are of the writing of a post-national era.

In this vein, Ethel Wilson's powerful evocations of landscape (and what she called the 'genius' of place) haunt the sensitive traveller who knows that place is always displacement and there is no such place as home. Her writings are prized for their descriptions of the British Columbia landscape and for what she called 'the formidable power of geography that determines the character and performance of a people.' At the same time, she viewed this landscape as an outsider and remembered the anxiety of her own arrival 'with an urgency that remained in [her] heart' thereafter. Ethel Wilson is often described as a 'writer's writer,' an incisive and elegant stylist, but she is also a traveller's writer, and so, as another traveller to British Columbia, I have taken up the task of trying to illuminate the life history and art of Ethel Wilson, who liked to quote from Edwin Muir that 'life is "a difficult country and our home."'

Acknowledgments

The research and writing of this book could not have been done without assistance from many people and institutions. I want first to acknowledge three researchers whose work in relation to this book truly merits that complimentary tag *sine qua non*. Barbara Wild's careful recording of the Edge, Malkin, and Bryant genealogies has provided a solid backbone for this biography of Ethel Wilson, which is also the story of an extended family. Irene Howard's splendid essays on the Malkins and Vancouver's West End, and her interviews with people who knew Ethel Wilson in the early part of the twentieth century, have been an invaluable source of information for this book. The meticulous researches of Bonnie Martyn McComb, in compiling the first comprehensive bibliography of writings by and about Ethel Wilson, have saved this writer many hours of searching for materials and references. My relations with another study of Ethel Wilson are of a different kind. The late Mary McAlpine was not a friend to this book, but her memoir, *The Other Side of Silence: A Life of Ethel Wilson*, challenged me to set the record straight and to expand the knowledge we can have of Wilson's life and art. I am grateful for some of the information and anecdotes McAlpine's book has preserved.

For their confidence in me and for their generosity in sharing stories, photographs, and memorabilia, I want to thank these members of the Malkin and Wilson families whom I came to know: Ethel Wilson's first cousins Ursula Malkin, James Malkin, and Nancy Malkin Rowell, who patiently answered many questions; Peter Malkin, who revived this project with a timely phone call; Bill Malkin, who showed me around Point Cowan; and David Malkin, English grandson of Sydney Malkin, who provided several items from the family archive. Wallace Wilson's cousins were also close friends of this project: I thank Sylvia and Colin Graham Jr and Joan and Angus Kenning for their stories of Ethel Wilson, their permission to use photographs in their possession, and for their hospitality. In 1990 I travelled to England and visited Audrey Butler, the Wilsons' 'evacuee' daughter. In conversation and correspondence, she has generously supplied a wealth of information for this book and a unique view of its subject. Here I especially want to thank Mary Buckerfield White, the Wilsons' niece, who has befriended this project longer than she realizes. The archival items from her family's estate and her stories of the art scene in Vancouver have been an invaluable resource, and her enthusiasm for this project has been unwavering and invigorating.

Over the years, several of Canada's distinguished writers and editors have shared with me their memories of, and ideas about, Ethel Wilson. I want to acknowledge the contributions of Earle Birney, Roy Daniells, Northrop Frye, Margaret Laurence, Dorothy Livesay, Joyce Marshall, William McConnell, Alice Munro, P.K. Page, Malcolm Ross, Jane Rule, and Robert Weaver. I thank here especially my colleague George Bowering, whose glowing admiration for Ethel Wilson's literary craft has confirmed this project's worth. I want to thank Lorraine McMullen, who invited me to present a report on UBC Library's Wilson archive at a symposium in Ottawa. I also thank those who have made suggestions and provided items of information for this book – Esther Birney, Miemie Brink, Jocelyn Cannon, Nan Cheney, Bea Corbett, Michael Crawley, Theodora Dowsley, Sandra Djwa, Carole Gerson, Lynn Henry, Joy McDonagh, Nicolette McIntosh, Kathy Mezei, Bruce Robertson, Phyllis Rochfort, Lynn Simpson, Meg Stainsby, Theo Tufts, Glenn Wolfe, Donez Xiques – and I thank my mother, Winnifred Stouck, for preparing some of the illustrations.

A book of this kind, with its critical assessment of a writer's art, owes much to those who have written on the subject before. Here I acknowledge, in particular, the work of Desmond Pacey, Helen Sonthoff, W.H. New, P.M. Hinchcliffe, R.D. MacDonald, Heather Murray, Brent Thompson, and, most recently, Katherine Ashenburg, who has kept Ethel Wilson's name alive in the media. Two distinguished critics from outside the country have confirmed for us that Ethel Wilson has a significant place in international as well as Canadian literature. I thank my good friends Blanche H. Gelfant, Dartmouth College, New Hampshire, and Anjali Bhelande, Ramnarain Ruia College, University of Bombay, for their luminous and wholly original readings of Ethel Wilson.

Special thanks goes to Thomas Woods, who reviewed *Ethel Wilson: Stories, Essays, and Letters* in 1988 and urged me in the pages of the *Globe and Mail* to write this book; and to Gerald Hallowell, who followed up that suggestion with an invitation to do so from University of Toronto Press. I thank Siobhan McMenemy for carrying this project through the process of publication so expeditiously.

I am grateful to the staff of libraries and archives across the country who have considerately provided materials when requested. I acknowledge especially Anne Goddard and Wilma MacDonald of the National Archives of Canada, Carl Spadoni, McMaster University Library, Edna Hajnal, Thomas Fisher Rare Book Library, and Jane Everett at McGill University. I thank George Brandak, who has made the Special Collections room at University of British Columbia Library a friendly place in which to work, and there especially I thank Rachel Chan, who for two years fetched and carried for me many heavy boxes of Wilson and Macmillan papers. Finally I thank François Ricard for permission to quote materials from the fonds Gabrielle Roy, Montreal, and University of British Columbia Library, Rare Book and Special Collections, for permission to quote from the Ethel Wilson Papers.

ETHEL WILSON
A CRITICAL BIOGRAPHY

CHAPTER ONE

Child

1888–1898

Missionaries / Edge-ware / South Africa / Death / The Bryants /
Happiness / An orphan

When Ethel Wilson was born on a hot summer day, 20 January 1888, there were no members of her large extended family to welcome her into the world. Her father, alone, anxiously christened the baby and named her for his wife's youngest sister, who had died five years before at the age of twelve. His concern was for his wife, who was tubercular and scarcely had strength to undergo childbirth. Would she survive? The families were in England, seven thousand nautical miles from Port Elizabeth, South Africa, and it would be some weeks before they had news of the baby's arrival. Ethel Wilson began life tenuously, on a margin, far from the centre of her parents' world and the place that her families called home; and, eventually orphaned, she would live most of her life on another margin, British Columbia, Canada. In her writing, she would always be negotiating the idea of 'home' and would tell us that, whether we recognize it or not, we are always living 'on a brink.'

Ethel Wilson's parents, Lila and Robert Bryant, were Methodist missionaries. They met when Robert, who had already been eleven years in Africa, was on six months' leave in England and was invited to preach at the Wesleyan Chapel in Burslem, Staffordshire. Lila was a tall, serious, and deeply religious woman who devoted her time to charity among the people of her town. She and Robert were not in their first youth when they met – they would both be thirty-one that year – which may be why their courtship proceeded quickly. They were married 14 April 1887, before the end of Robert's leave. Robert was certainly attracted to Lila's deep devotion to the Methodist cause and by the refinement of her manners, but he also could not have helped being impressed by her social standing in the town.

Lila's full name was Eliza Davis Malkin (her maiden name would one day be well known in Vancouver, British Columbia), and she was a member of a large and prominent family that was distinguished especially by the enterprise of her maternal grandfather, Joseph Edge. In partnership with his son-in-law, James Malkin, Edge was one of the town's leading earthenware manufacturers whose factory made all kinds of encaustic tile and pottery, from dinner platters to chamber pots. While his products would never be as famous as those of Staffordshire potter Josiah Wedgwood, Grandfather Edge, nonetheless, according to the 1861 census, had 325 workers in his employ,[1] and by 1887 the Edge-Malkin business had grown even larger. This is the family (see Appendix) that Ethel Wilson would describe faithfully and in loving, comic detail in her autobiographical novel, *The Innocent Traveller*. Wilson stated unequivocally in a public address at University of British Columbia that *The Innocent Traveller* was 'about real, not imaginary people,'[2] and Malkin family members have repeatedly confirmed 'it was all true,' so that I will use the novel, in spite of its 'names changed,' to suggest the broad outlines of the family's history. In that book, the oldest of Joseph and Eliza Edge's nine children, Ann Elizabeth, would be the author's grandmother, called Annie Hastings or 'the Grandmother,' while Ann's unmarried sister, Eliza Phillips Edge, would be presented fictionally as Aunt Topaz Edgeworth. The Edges' youngest son, John Wilcox, appears in Wilson's fiction as fastidious, handsome Uncle John, who accompanies his flighty sister Topaz on a trip to Italy,[3] and in old age escorts her to Buckingham Palace to meet the Queen. Vignettes of all the Edge children are presented in the opening chapter to *The Innocent Traveller* during a formal dinner visit from an enlightened young educator, Matthew Arnold.

According to a little history set down by Eliza Edge (Aunt Topaz) when she was an old lady,[4] the Edges were an ancient and distinguished Staffordshire family, a baronet under James I among their numbers. The name was spelled *del Each* in 1338, later Egge. The seat of their property was at Horton,[5] but it had been lost or dissipated by the close of the eighteenth century, its owner having lived a fairly riotous life. One story that came down in the family was that Horton had been unlawfully taken away by a will that was signed by a 'dead hand.' Two unscrupulous friends arrived at the deathbed of great-grandfather Edge, hoping to persuade him to sign over his property to them, but he had already expired. To be able to swear there was still life in the body, they placed a living fly in the nose of the corpse; one held the nostril closed, while the other guided the hand to sign a will in their favour.

The deceased's disinherited son, William Edge, came to Burslem while still in his teens with two shillings sixpence in his pocket to work in a pottery. There he came under the influence of the Methodists and married Ann Wilcox, the daughter of a potter and a Methodist lay minister who was appointed by John Wesley, the founder of the faith himself. It was William's son, Joseph (Ethel Wilson's great-grandfather), who renewed the family's material fortunes through his pottery works, and his wife, Eliza Davis, descended from the Milletts, added to the family pedigree with a list of admirals and generals among her family's ranks. One of Eliza's cousins was Sir Humphry Davy, a distinguished British scientist in the mid-nineteenth century, best known for his invention of the miner's lamp.

Working for Joseph Edge at the pottery was his son-in-law, James Malkin, who was married to Ann Elizabeth and who also fathered nine children, the oldest being Lila, Ethel Wilson's mother. James' father, Elijah Malkin, was buried at St Paul's churchyard in Burslem, but little is known about this side of the family otherwise. Ethel Wilson would describe her mother's family as serious people, Methodist dissenters earnestly dedicated to the social gospel, and constrained by an overpowering sense of custom and propriety. A strictly pious form of Wesleyan Methodism prevailed in Burslem, which took great pride in being the fourth congregation to be founded *in the world*.[6] The Edges and Malkins enjoyed a life of material privilege in Burslem, but the high seriousness of their spiritual and social commitments gave a formal and rather dour cast to their lives. This is strongly suggested by the photograph taken at the wedding of Lila Malkin and Robert Bryant, in which twenty-seven very sombre-looking people are presented standing or seated outdoors against the brick wall of a large house. The women, bonneted and tightly corseted, modestly avert their eyes downward or to one side, while most of the men are bearded and stand tall in dark suits. Joseph Edge, in his eighties, stares grimly into the camera, his morning coat buttoned up to his whiskers, his top hat between his knees. James Malkin, with his sharply refined features, has a slightly bemused air about him, but in the windows one can perceive dimly the faces of three servants in stiff white caps and a boy in a lace collar, all of whom look as if they have just witnessed an accident in the street.[7]

While the smokestacks and the grime and poverty of a Midlands industrial town may not seem like a romantic setting for a wedding, the event would always be viewed by Ethel Wilson as a magical one for, as she would insist, her parents made a 'love marriage.'[8] That day was enhanced in Wilson's imagination by her understanding that her parents were married by Fred Macdonald, the uncle of writer Rudyard Kipling and brother-in-law of the painter Edward Burne-Jones.[9] Family lore, in fact, holds that James and Annie Malkin introduced Kipling's parents to each other at a picnic at Rudyard Lake, a beauty spot in North Staffordshire.[10] Macdonald himself was one of the most distinguished ministers of the Wesleyan Methodist Church, and Lila and Robert gave him a copy of the Bible in French.[11] In turn, he gave the couple one of Burne-Jones's drawings as a wedding gift, which Ethel Wilson would eventually bring to Canada and leave to the Art Gallery of Victoria.[12]

The marriage of the oldest daughter of Burslem's principal employer was an important event in the life of the town and included the local member of parliament as an honorary guest.[13] The evening before the wedding, a reception was held in one of the large rooms of the pottery works, where the working people presented the couple with a tea and coffee service and a number of songs were performed by the work choir. The following morning, such a large number of people arrived to attend the wedding that they filled the chapel and the chapel-yard, and some stood outside the gates. Lila Malkin was dressed in gold satin and wore a Honiton lace veil; on entering the chapel-yard, she passed under a 'triumphal arch of holly, interspersed with fresh flowers [that] had been erected in the very early hours of the morning.' Lila's cousin, Edna Edge, known as the beauty in the family, was an elegantly attired bridesmaid. The service was choral, and the congregation as well as the choir sang 'The voice that breathed o'er Eden' and 'Saviour let Thy sanction rest.'

Robert and Lila left on the voyage to South Africa three weeks after their wedding. Lila, who had never travelled very far beyond Burslem, was apprehensive about the journey, and her fears were well grounded for she would never see England again. It took nearly a month to reach Cape Town, and by then Lila was already pregnant with the future author. The colour and clamour of Cape Town with its large number of indigenous inhabitants would likely have been unsettling to a nervous and fastidious Englishwoman. In spite of herself and her missionary purpose, she may have experienced some of Anthony Trollope's negative feelings when he described Cape Town as 'a poor niggery, yellow-faced, half-bred sort of place with an ugly Dutch flavour about it.'[14] But their destination was Port Elizabeth further east, a small attractive English port on the cliffs overlooking the white beaches of Algoa Bay. Port Elizabeth was in size like Burslem, about fifteen thousand, the second largest European settlement in the Cape colony. It possessed all the advantages of a well-appointed English town – churches, schools, newspapers, a good library – and was in close communication with England by means of cable service and the weekly arrival of steamships. Port Elizabeth was where David Livingstone in 1841 had preached his first sermon in Africa. The town was well established and 'settled,' but gold and diamonds were being found in the open lands beyond the town and all kinds of people were pouring in from many parts of the world to make their fortunes. Robert Bryant had an especially strong sense of his purpose as a preacher of the gospel in this part of the world.

Robert William Bryant had first come to South Africa eleven years earlier, in 1876, on the advice of his doctor, who had diagnosed the young man of twenty with a dormant form of tuberculosis. He believed the warmth and dry air of an African climate would keep his patient alive longer than the cold and damp of England. Robert had been born and raised in the Lincolnshire village of Stickney, the second of his father's eleven children by two wives. His father was a grocer and draper, but he was also a Methodist lay minister (a class leader), and by the time Robert was twenty he had decided, after a year at the Methodist College in Belfast, to become an ordained minister in the faith himself. His first trip to South Africa lasted for ten years, and he gives a lively account of his experiences during that time in a narrative which appears to have been composed for a Methodist audience about twenty years later.[15] He tells of making the port of Durban his first destination, where he was met by a friend of his father's, who was also the mayor of the town. He describes relaxing there on the lush, almost tropical coast, but he did not get well and, since his 'immediate object in going to South Africa was health,' he said good-bye to his father's friend and journeyed inland, first to Pietermaritzburg, and then three hundred miles into the interior through 'country over-run by huge herds of game.' He continued by ox-cart and horse until he reached his pre-arranged destination, the small town of Bethlehem on the flat grass plains of the Orange Free State. In the drier climate, his health improved quickly, and he stayed there for nearly three years. But Bethlehem was a depressing small town – one jail, one hotel, six stores, and two hundred Europeans, chiefly Boers – and its isolation seemed to accentuate the problems of maintaining some kind of moral code and spiritual life. It was a difficult place for an earnest young man of the Church. In his journal narrative, Robert referred to the drinking and gambling that 'weighed heavily upon [his] heart' and that were such a 'hindrance to the work of God.' In a letter to a friend, Thomas Lockyer, dated 1 June 1877, he wrote, 'Bethlehem is a very wicked place. From all I can hear, nearly every young man who has come into the place has gone wrong. But by God's help, I mean to do what I can to rescue and save the young men of the place.'[16] He saw himself being tested, and a year later he was able to write optimistically, 'I do believe ... that there is no training like trouble for future usefulness. If I am worth anything at all, thanks to affliction for it.' He earned a transfer in 1879 to Pietermaritzburg, where, though it was still a small settlement, he 'felt [he] was in the world once more.' Indeed, he felt that the colonists of Natal, who were English, were the freest, friendliest, and most lovable people on earth. In Pietermaritzburg, Robert completed his lay service and was ordained as a Wesleyan Methodist minister.

In an unpublished manuscript titled 'Duchess,' Ethel Wilson tells the story (a 'true story') about a tailor in South Africa, Jan Mortimer, who made clothes for a doll, and in this little narrative we are given a glimpse of the author's parents in Port Elizabeth and of her own early days as a small child.[17] Living in South Africa was hard for Robert's humourless bride. She was homesick for England and grew increasingly unwell and unable to perform the duties of a minister's wife as her pregnancy continued. Robert hired a 'Kaffir'[18] girl to do housework at the parsonage, but she did not have the training to keep an English home. Lila survived the birth of her child – who was named Ethel for the sister who had not lived long and Davis for her maternal great-grandmother – but her general health continued to deteriorate. Many years later, Ethel Wilson would read a bundle of letters that Lila had written to her mother in England. In these letters, she described herself torn between her love for Robert and her desire to return home, and lamented her inadequacies as a wife and new mother. (Tears had stained some of the pages when she was writing, and Wilson, finding these letters still very painful after seventy years, had them burned.) The townspeople, seeing Mrs Bryant wheeling the baby, did not think she looked well. 'No, she is not well,' the minister said curtly. And, after nine months, she was pregnant again. This time she could not survive the ordeal and, after a hard struggle, died at the parsonage on 28 July 1889. The baby boy, christened Robert Norman, died ten days later and was buried beside her in Port Elizabeth's Russell Road Cemetery.

In her story about her parents, Wilson tells of the difficult time that followed; how her father tried to perform his duties as a minister and also look after his child, how 'he knelt beside the child's bed and prayed desperately that God would help him to bear what had descended upon him in this loss and all this misery.' In *The Innocent Traveller* she described the parallel grief of a missionary uncle in India, who writes the terrible news to his wife's family at home: 'He sat at his desk with the notepaper lying in front of him. He sat there suffering and helpless and blinded by his loss. Was it for this that he had brought [his wife] to the land that had killed her?'[19] Heaps of letters, which Robert hardly had time to read, came from England, and they all exhorted him to leave South Africa and bring the baby home. Many kind relatives offered to raise the child, but while she was Robert's greatest care, she was his only personal happiness. So he stayed in Port Elizabeth for another year, assisted by women from the chapel, and befriended by the elderly tailor, Jan Mortimer, also a widower, who unobtrusively did chores about the minister's bungalow. Robert had sermons to prepare and young people to instruct in the Christian life and a parish to bring to self-sufficiency. But he had to face the fact that when his child was sick he had no confidence in the local doctor and his housekeeper was careless and had little skill. His child was over two years old and active, and increasingly needed care and supervision. And secretly he knew he was not very strong. So in July of 1890, when he felt his parish could be connected to the neighbouring one, he made arrangements to return to England, and he and his daughter, who was two and a half, prayed for the last time over Lila's and Robert Norman's graves and left South Africa, never to return again.

Robert was stationed first at a Methodist chapel in the small village of Pembroke in Wales, then at Brighton, and finally at Acton near London. Those seven years were remembered by Ethel Wilson as perhaps the happiest in her life; certainly, they created a template in her imagination for a time in Eden where 'everything was unimaginably happy.' The parsonage and the small child were looked after by Robert's 'courtesy' aunt, Maria Riggall, and an 'angelic' servant named Mary from the Malkin household. Wilson would remember her father as tall and very handsome and wearing a small dark beard, which was suitable to a minister in those days. Photographs of Robert Bryant suggest a vigorous-looking rather than conventionally handsome man, a man with a rather craggy face, deep-set eyes, and large nose. But what Wilson especially remembered was the fun she shared with her father when 'life was luminous and merry and beloved.'[20] In the essay 'Duchess,' she describes those times and herself in the third person:

> Father and she had laughed so much together that E. used to roll on the floor with laughing. She never never laughed so much ever again. Sometimes they walked to a park to see the animals. And sometimes father had to whip her a little on the hand, for instance if she told a lie and said she had not taken the chocolate from the drawer and eaten the whole thing when she had. But her life was the happiest life that a little girl could ever have, even if she were rich, oh much better than that, with Father and Aunt Maria and the two dogs and Nigger the cat and Mary and Duchess that old Mr Mortimer had sent her.

Duchess was a doll that belonged to the lonely tailor in Port Elizabeth. He missed the lively, blue-eyed, flaxen-haired child very much after the Bryants had left, and eventually he mailed the doll to England with a complete set of clothes that he had made for her. The little girl loved the doll beyond words, and she would keep it all her life as a symbol of that 'unimaginably happy' time. Another of her happiest memories from that time is of teaching herself to read, sharing her father's study while he was at his desk working.[21] 'My father,' she once described in an interview, 'had a big library and I used to sit on the floor and try to read everything and anything. I mispronounced all over the place. "Hail most loverly verggin," quoth Ivanhoe. I read carefully and aloud and wondered what was a verggin.'[22]

It is hard to get a clear picture of Robert Bryant, but it is important to try because his daughter would idealize his memory, and his influence would remain strong throughout her life. Bryant's missionary narrative and the few lines that were published from his letters to a friend suggest a serious man who felt his religious calling strongly. That same friend, Thomas Lockyer, published a tribute in the *Wesleyan Methodist Magazine* after Robert's death, in which he wrote that '[Robert's] conversion took place at an early age in the Stickney classroom, and it became his great ambition to be a preacher. When only eleven or twelve years of age he began to write sermons ...'[23] Although Robert had a dormant form of tuberculosis, his narrative suggests nonetheless an optimistic, well-adjusted, and physically vigorous young man who rode the circuit in the veldt, preaching the gospel and doing the administrative work of the Church. He was frequently exhilarated by that work and tells about re-establishing a chapel and Sunday school that proved so attractive that children walked to it from five and six miles away. 'It was a laborious time,' he wrote, 'for the converts had to be folded and shepherded, but the joy of it all carried one through. "I wonder if we shall ever be any happier than this in Heaven," said one of my colleagues as we rode home in the night from one of the country chapels.' But he also had a highly developed social consciousness. He wrote that the Orange Free State was on the whole well governed by the Dutch except for one serious blemish; and he prophetically lamented 'that the natives were not ... allowed to own land and could never acquire the full rights of citizenship.' He was disturbed by the racism of the Europeans, their habitual 'contempt for the natives,' whereas he himself never 'experienced greater liberty or joy in preaching the gospel than in a Kaffir hut.' Bryant was clearly a hard-working man of high serious vision and commitment.

Yet Ethel Wilson would claim that her father and his family were especially remarkable for their great sense of humour and love of fun. While her mother's family were serious and stern and easily 'shocked' by any break from convention, her father's family she remembered for their unconventional, sometimes bohemian style of living, and for their 'swift perceptions and senses of humours that made life amusing whether rural or urban.'[24] Her father, she wrote, 'had a sense of joy and fun and humour that fed and lightened [his wife], and brightened young and old people.'[25] The influence on Ethel Wilson from this side of the family was likely felt from an early age: pictures from the 1890s, taken by professional photographers in places like Boston and Alford in eastern Lincolnshire, indicate that she and her father visited the Bryants there when she was a small child.

No doubt the happiness that Ethel Wilson knew as a child was safeguarded by the fact that her father did not remarry. Outside his pastoral duties, his attentions were focused on his daughter, whose sense of well-being is conveyed by her description of herself in 'Duchess' as 'healthy, and pink and white and golden, and merry, and naughty.' Robert's not remarrying was unusual, given his position in the community and his relative youth (he was only thirty-three when Lila died). Women frequently died in childbirth and their husbands as frequently remarried, often within the year: Grandfather Edge took a second wife after his first wife bore a 'last and fatal child,' and Grandfather Bryant remarried and sired five more children. Perhaps, as his daughter would suggest, his love for his wife had been too great for him to enter quickly into another union. She wrote that he 'never mentioned my Mother because

[it] was too terrible for him even to say her name,'[26] and, indeed, in his African narrative, which includes the three years in Port Elizabeth, he does not once mention the presence of his wife there with him. Perhaps he preferred greater freedom for his work and to be at home with his daughter, providing her with a childhood in which she was at the centre of the world, or perhaps it was fatigue and the knowledge of his tubercular condition that kept him celibate. Ethel Wilson tells us simply that he always overworked, and that one day he went out to preach when he had a cold and took pneumonia and died. Robert Bryant was just forty. He died at Acton near London on 19 June 1897 and was buried in Alford, Lincolnshire. Ethel Bryant was nine.

She would say years later of that time that 'the bottom dropped out of everything,'[27] and in an essay would write, 'It is not to be described how a child feels when the [parent] dies. It can never be told, and the world dies too for a long time in bewilderment.'[28] Her most vivid memory from that time was of seeing the country's national embodiment of perpetual mourning:

> I was ... carried away from the house of death, and I dried my eyes in London in time to see Queen Victoria driving in what was probably a barouche. It was a conveyance entirely suited to the rather upholstered appearance of the Queen whose extraordinary plain-ness and unattractiveness exuded magic, causing all to stand transfixed yet moved, and some to weep.[29]

Ethel spent most of the following year being passed around among the Edge and Malkin relatives in Staffordshire who came forward to claim her. She remembered most of them as being kind to her, but 'the smashed-up feeling of Father not being there was very bad.'[30] The doll from South Africa was her only companion from that happier time. She went first, by her account, to a Mrs Moon,[31] and then to her distinguished-looking and meticulously groomed Great-Uncle John, who, with his wife, Aunt Annie, were a fastidious, middle-aged couple with no children of their own. And then she went to stay with one of her mother's younger brothers, Uncle Sydney, and his wife, Edith, who had four sons, Alan, Roy, Harold, and Keith. These rambunctious young male cousins in the house remained strange to her and made her feel her homesickness and bereftness more keenly. Sydney Malkin was the ambitious son who had taken over the tile works after his father's death (the Edges retained the pottery part of the business) and was on the threshold of a distinguished business career that included extensive world travel and culminated in his becoming the highly respected mayor of Burslem.[32] But his orphaned niece did not feel comfortable in his house. Many years afterward, Ethel Wilson would write to one of her cousins in Vancouver that in spite of Uncle Sydney's 'kind hospitality and Aunt Edith's real goodness, his sarcasms frightened me very much and I became painfully shy.'[33] And she would write tellingly of one of her fictional characters that there was 'the strong taste of sorrow in her throat, and in her stomach the cold core of lead that only the desolate know.'[34]

In the meantime, when Annie Malkin, Ethel's maternal grandmother, heard about Robert's death, she was determined that her oldest daughter's girl should come and live with her. She had seen the child once, when Robert came back to England and was on his way to the church in Wales. But Annie Malkin was now living on the far west coast of Canada, in Vancouver, which was approximately the same distance from England as South Africa. Annie had been widowed with the death of James Malkin in 1894, and her family was grown and dispersed. Two of her younger sons, Fred and William Harold, had set out on an adventure to Canada in the mid-1880s, where they were joined in 1894 by Philip, the youngest of the Malkin brothers.[35] When they had all finally settled in Vancouver, they invited their widowed mother to come out and keep house for them. So Annie Malkin, a pious, diminutive woman of sixty-three, with little experience of the world beyond Burslem, had set out with two other members of the family, her unmarried sister, Eliza, and her unmarried daughter, Isabelle, to make a new life on the far shore of North America. Now she had to make a trip home to England to fetch her ten-year-old granddaughter.

For the future author, the rupture of her father's death and her eventual displacement to Canada would leave an indelible imprint on her emotional and imaginative life. In the only account we have of Ethel at this time, Isabelle Malkin in Canada writes to relatives in Australia that 'everyone says what a sweet loveable child Ethel is.'[36] While within the extended family she was a much-loved and sought-after child, her family members were nonetheless strangers to her. She had not previously known the kind Staffordshire aunts and uncles who looked after her for a year, and she did not know the pious elderly grandmother who came to take her on the long journey to Canada. She was lovingly cared for, but at the same time alone and desolate. This condition bred paradox in her imaginative life. If she was privileged all her life, living in material comfort and social ease, she always felt that security could be quickly

ched away, as had happened with her father's sudden death. In
__ า, the characters in her fiction would be women deprived of the inti-
mate bonds of family who, on their own, must establish a link with the
larger human community. They would discover that the world was not
benign and orderly, but chaotic, ruthlessly shaped by accident and
chance. On a philosophical level, Ethel Wilson would turn her insecurity into a search for a moral order that would confirm the humanistic
values of love and faith and unity, and she would transform her emotional preference for retreat, isolation, and distance into a vision of
unity and the theme of moral responsibility. But it would take a long
road to accomplish that quest.

CHAPTER TWO

Orphan
1898–1902

That is one thing that is nice about Vancouver. You are still near the beginning
of things, or your parents were. – 'Herself When Young'

Journey west / The Malkins / Miss Gordon's school /
Young Vancouver / Joe Fortes / Disreputable Vancouver /
'I Have a Father in the Promised Land'

Ethel Bryant had no memory of the grandmother who came to take her
to Canada. She and her father had lived a long distance from Staffordshire and by 1898, when Ethel was ten, Annie Malkin had already been
living in Vancouver for more than three years. The future writer is not
likely to have been intimidated by her grandmother when they first met
because the woman in widow's weeds was 'very little, very neat, and very
quiet.'[1] The girl would quickly come to recognize, however, that in the
family there was an aura around this little person, that her word was law,
and that law was God's word as interpreted by John Wesley. Annie had
come back to England in late March with her sister, Eliza, and daughter,
Isabelle, and they stayed until mid-summer visiting the families in
Burslem and environs and letting the girl get to know them. They were
sensitive to the fact that there would be another sharp break in the
child's life, as she left the only country she knew for another one six
thousand miles away.

The trip to Vancouver took sixteen days altogether, eight on the water
and another eight overland. Contemporary accounts of train travel
across Canada celebrate the amenities of an era when cars were luxuri-
ously appointed with plush seats and polished mahogany walls, and the

dining compartment glittered with white linen, silver service, and cut
glass. But in an unpublished personal essay titled 'Seen through Waves,'
Ethel Wilson, writing about herself in the third person, focuses instead
on a child's anxieties as she travels to her new home:

> 'Are there any schools in Vancouver?' asked the orphan, removing her
> gaze from the prairie which flowed past the west-bound train, and looking
> up at her Grandmother.
>
> 'Oh I think so dear,' said her Grandmother vaguely, with her finger in
> her book. 'But there is a very nice young girl called Miss Gordon who lives
> near us and she told me before I left that she is going to open a little school
> for little girls and that will be nice for you,' and the Grandmother added,
> 'she is a Girton girl.'
>
> 'Oh,' said the orphan. She did not know what kind of a girl a Girton girl
> was. (A pile of white buffalo bones flashed past).
>
> 'But is she kind?' asked the inexperienced orphan.
>
> 'Oh very very kind I should think,' said the Grandmother, 'she has fair
> hair.'[2]

The child's confusion and insecurity are suggested in her questions
about a school, in the swiftly moving train, the pile of buffalo bones, and
the grandmother's vagueness – especially the latter's mysterious identification of the teacher as a Girton girl, and her equation of kindness with
fair hair. In another autobiographical piece, Wilson describes the train
finally coming into the station in Vancouver, and how she saw for the
first time – 'with an urgency that has remained in my heart ever since'[3] –
the sparsely manned harbour, the steamers that were beginning to use
it, and the mountains so close by. But, above all, what she saw was dense
forest everywhere, surrounding the little city of 15,000. It was so very different from the cultivated shores of home.

The company of travellers was greeted warmly by the men of the family, the pioneering uncles, two of whom had already been in Canada for
fourteen years. With the newly arrived niece, all seven members of the
Malkin family,[4] all single, lived in a small frame house known as 'The
Hawthorns,' so-named for two bushes brought from England and
planted on either side of the front door. The house was located on Richards Street, in the core of the city and close to the family business on
Water Street (an area now known by its original name of Gastown). The
Malkin brothers, with a wholesale grocery business known as 'Malkin's

Best,' were already among the city's most prosperous businessmen, but their path to success had not been a direct one.

Fred and Harold Malkin had left Burslem in March of 1884, at the early ages of twenty-one and sixteen, for Canada's Northwest Territories. A note in Ethel Wilson's papers suggests they might have left because of a disagreement with their brother Sydney.[5] Although they had set out to rough it, Fred and Harold were well provisioned for their travels. Someone, possibly their mother, Annie, made a list of the things they took with them, which included for each son seventeen shirts, eight pairs of trousers, seven coats and three topcoats, five collars, and thirteen white shirt fronts. They also took sheets, pillow cases, blankets, and nine sets of towels; silver knives and forks to share, teaspoons and dessert spoons, and two tablecloths; and gifts from family and community, which included a violin 'from the work people' at the pottery, a book of poems, a picture album from Aunt Eliza, a locket from sisters Lila and Belle, and a knife and watch from Uncle John. Yet these comforts would have done little to soften the conditions that met them in Grenfell (Saskatchewan), where, while learning to ranch, they lived for a year in a little sod-roofed cabin with straw pallets for sleeping. They were granted a homestead in 1885, but a series of bad years – drought and flood and various blights – during which 'they killed and pickled and ate their one and only ox,'[6] made them reconsider the life of the rancher. 'There is only a living here for one,' Fred is reputed to have announced. Harold, accordingly, went to work in a general store in Grenfell, where he was eventually joined by Philip, the youngest of the Malkin brothers. Fred sold the homestead in 1889 and after working for a druggist in Lethbridge went on to Vancouver, where, among other jobs, he hodded bricks for the construction of the first Hotel Vancouver. Harold came out to see his brother on New Year's Day, 1895. Years later, he recalled that Vancouver then seemed to him a depressing place: 'Water Street was on stilts and [there was] a vista of stumps and water holes from Burrard Street to [False Creek].'[7] There was no certainty that a real city would develop (the Klondike hadn't opened yet, nor had significant mining operations begun in the Kootenays), and he wasn't tempted to stay. But back in the harsh winter of the Prairies he reconsidered, and in April he and Philip came out to settle permanently in Vancouver. With their background in merchandising, the brothers established, with Harold as president, a wholesale grocery business legally titled 'W.H. Malkin Co. Wholesale Grocers, Tea Blenders and Coffee Roasters.' The company went on to make preserves and pickles and to import spices, all known as 'Malkin's Best,' and quickly became the premier grocery import business in the city. Malkin products were in every household and in the packs of the Klondike miners as they toiled up the Chilkoot Pass. Well established in business, the brothers would go on to be among those who shaped the new city in a variety of ways as it moved into the twentieth century.

But to the ten-year-old girl in 1898 the shape of the future city was hardly conceivable; indeed, the immediacy of ocean and mountains was scarcely visible because everything was still obscured by high trees – the cedars, hemlocks, and Douglas firs of the temperate rainforest. Heavily forested Vancouver had been chosen as the terminus for the Canadian Pacific Railway because of its deep harbour, replacing New Westminster on the Fraser River as the centre of commerce. The West End, Kitsilano, and Point Grey were still uncut forests and so was Shaughnessy, except for a corduroy road that ran through it to the Fraser River. Wilson would remember that, because the little city then faced northward, Vancouver Island was only occasionally glimpsed from a rowboat, and that one day a bewhiskered old man claimed he had seen a 'my-rage' across the water.[8] Today's views were then unviewable.

As the family business prospered and the Malkins became leaders in the community, they moved at the beginning of the century with others to the West End, a new residential district being created between Burrard Street and Stanley Park. This was the preserve of bank and trust company presidents, officials of the Canadian Pacific Railway, mill and cannery owners, and professional men, including Charles Hibbert Tupper, a prominent lawyer and son of one of the Fathers of Confederation. Here the city's social elite were cutting down forest and building large houses in the eclectic late Empire style of Victorian architecture, houses with turrets and cupolas and gazebos. The first Malkin house in that area was on Broughton Street at the corner of Davie, and it was named 'Heatherlea,' after the family home in Burslem. It was a large house on several lots with a stable for a horse and a cow. When Fred married Julia Eldridge, he built himself and his young wife a separate home on Bute Street at Harwood overlooking English Bay, and called it 'Horton' after the Edge ancestral residence in Staffordshire. Harold decided to stay on at 'Heatherlea' when he married Marion Dougall, and built a home for his mother on Barclay Street at Jervis. It was the smallest of the Malkin homes; it had a gracious wraparound verandah, but also what Wilson would one day describe as a bastard architectural excrescence that 'resembled both a Norman turret and a pepper-pot but was neither.'[9] The importing of English culture extended to the gardens planted with roses and holly bushes brought from England and to caged canaries suspended in sunny windows. Yet directly across the water of False Creek (where the Vancouver Museum and Planetarium stand today), the native people would still gather around great bonfires at the edge of the forest, and their drumming could be heard on nights throughout the West End.

In the fall of 1898, Miss Jessie Gordon, the young woman who had attended Girton College at Cambridge, opened her school for girls on the ground floor of her parents' house on West Georgia Street, and Ethel Bryant was enrolled.[10] Miss Gordon was assisted by her sisters, Mary and Agnes. There were six pupils of different ages that first year, and the teaching was done largely by a teacher sitting beside a pupil and 'showing her how.' Most of the classes were taught by Jessie Gordon herself, but for two of Ethel's favourite subjects an expert was brought to the classroom. Art was taught by a Miss Marstrand, whose most distinctive feature for young Ethel was her fine hair filled with silver pins. More memorable was learning French, for which the pupils were grouped around a deal table near the stove and taught French words by an elderly and courteous gentleman known as Monsieur Dongour-Jouty. Fifty years later, Ethel Wilson would remember how he made the French language sound musical and exciting to the girls, showing them how the syllables flowed. And she remembered him awarding St John's Gospels in French, all the pupils receiving a prize, like the animals who each won the race in *Alice in Wonderland.* Looking back, she realized Monsieur Dongour-Jouty was something of a mystery. Where did such a man come from to a remote little place where no one spoke French, and where did he go? She had no idea, but she remembered him, as she would many older men, with much affection. Religious knowledge became part of the instruction, with classes in the Scriptures being given by the rector of Christ Church, and the girls were taught pianoforte and required to play before the mistresses and other girls once a term. But especially important, according to the school's brochure, was the 'attention paid to manners and deportment.'[11]

Miss Gordon's school prospered, and in 1901 it became a real school in new quarters on Jervis Street, with boarders (living upstairs) and monitors and uniforms, and was titled (rather grandly Ethel Wilson thought) Crofton House. One of the boarders was Marion Martin from New Westminster.[12] She was three years younger than Ethel, but they had a common bond in that Marion's mother had died and her father, a hard-working young lawyer, had remarried, sending his daughter to school in the city. (Later, he would send her to Havergal in Toronto for her high-school education.) Ethel and Marion, the latter known for her very feminine manner and striking beauty, would become fast friends and remain so all their lives, though most of the time they lived far apart. She would be fictionalized as a school friend with a name beginning with 'M' in several of Wilson's stories.

During recess break, the girls played rounders in the garden – an English game with bat and ball. But just as stimulating for Ethel Bryant as recess games was the ten-block journey to and from school.[13] In rainy weather, it meant running the long distance in an embarrassing old-fashioned mackintosh to keep dry, and taking her lunch, which consisted of bread and butter and an uncooked egg, which she carried 'safely and solemnly' to school, where Miss Gordon would boil it for her. Miss Gordon also made her a cup of hot cocoa on rainy days, because Ethel was the only child who remained in the schoolroom, where she felt 'a little lonely and a little important.' But, on fine days, she could ride her bicycle along the wooden sidewalks, or walk with a special friend, like Marion Martin or Laura Jukes, daughter of a bank manager, through the fast-rising, though still muddy, pioneer streets of the West End. That first year, when the family had moved to the corner of Broughton and the still-forested wilds of Davie Street, she had to make her way past a gang of shackled men who were employed to clear building lots for Jervis Street.[14] Their guards stood with guns cradled in their arms or sat on logs, and the child averted her gaze as she ran quickly past. Her real desire was to explore the faces of these condemned men and know why this punishment had come about. What she glimpsed on the street was so different from anything she was exposed to in the family home.

For twenty-one years (until Annie Malkin's death in 1919), Ethel Bryant's home was with her grandmother and two unmarried aunts, and her upbringing, under her grandmother's influence, was deeply religious. For a shy and insecure girl, a grandmother with such unwavering convictions was a bedrock and an anchor. She would write to a cousin years later: 'They were bent on making up for me what I had lost – which was really everything. Never did I hear a sarcastic word from any of them.'[15] The girl came to love her grandmother dearly and modelled her life to suit hers. Annie Malkin was descended from Church leaders who had known John Wesley himself, and her life was wholly guided by

her religious connections and beliefs. Many in the family had given
their lives for this faith. Her brother, Joseph Edge, was a Wesleyan minister, and her sister Mary had gone to Ceylon to marry a Wesleyan missionary and died there at an early age in childbirth. Two of her own
children died in the missionary cause: her oldest daughter, Lila, in
South Africa in 1889, and her second eldest son, Joseph Malkin, who
had been ordained in the Burslem chapel and was shipwrecked in the
Bay of Biscay en route to India in 1892. In Vancouver, Annie Malkin was
viewed as a spiritual leader, and when the Homer Street Methodist congregation set out to build a larger church at the southwest corner of
Georgia and Burrard (since destroyed), she was asked to lay the cornerstone for the new building.[16] Her words on that snowy New Year's Day of
1901 ring with the zeal of her faith: 'I am sure you will join me in strong
desire and earnest prayer that faithful men of God ... may never be wanting to preach the Gospel in the church now to be built ... and that an
influence for good may go forth from this church, not only to this city,
but to the very ends of the earth.'[17] On this same occasion, the little lady
in black was given an oaken mallet made from the tree under which
John Wesley preached his last sermon. Annie Malkin belonged to the
Women's Missionary Society and subscribed to numerous missionary
publications, and her chief pleasure and interest in old age was reading
the reports on the society's work around the world.

Annie's daughter Isabelle, known as Belle, was also committed to the
causes of the Church. The record books for St Andrew's Wesley Church
reveal that she was 'one of the indefatigable women in the Ladies' Aid
who kept the organization going, seeing to the maintenance of the parsonage, planning programs, collecting money.'[18] But her greatest
responsibility was in running the Barclay Street home and looking after
her dead sister's child. Ethel Wilson would create a complex portrait of
this plain, hard-working woman in the character of Aunt Rachel in *The
Innocent Traveller*, a sometimes frustrated but wholly disciplined woman
who sacrificed herself for her family. 'Belle was a little dour and perhaps
severe looking,' remembered a family friend, who reflected on the three
generations living in one house. 'But,' she said, 'Belle looked after them
all. Granny was known as a saint. She was absolutely good, but she did
nothing else. She simply sat there in her white cap and was good.'[19]
Belle, in fact, had the adventurous spirit of her brothers. In 1886, when
she was twenty-seven, she travelled by herself to Canada to join them on
their farm in Grenfell. She stayed for three years, keeping house for
them, until Fred sold the homestead and moved to town, at which point

she returned to England. This aspect of her life lies outside the plot of *The Innocent Traveller*, in which all the women travel to Canada for the first time together, but Wilson evokes this desire for freedom in the aunt's character when she describes the release of her spirit as the train travels across the country and her dream of living on a remote Prairie farm with a brother, not a husband or lover. Belle Malkin, however, would spend the rest of her life, not as a ranch woman, but in a city caring for her mother and aunt and her sister's daughter.

The aunt, Eliza Edge, would in fact outlive Belle. Eliza (Aunt Topaz) was fifty when she came to Canada and lived until she was ninety-eight. Vancouver historian Irene Howard suggests that this garrulous, ebullient, sometimes eccentric woman saw herself, even in Canada, as a participant in the 'grand unfolding pageant of English history.'[20] In the notes she put together for her nephews and nieces, Eliza Edge traced their ancestry back to the knights who fought at the Battle of Hastings, and during her own time she managed to be present at some of the royal family's most splendid and solemn ceremonies. She attended Queen Victoria's Jubilee, saw Edward vii crowned, and she also saw him buried. When the Duke and Duchess of York (the future George v and Queen Mary) visited Vancouver in September 1901, she was part of a delegation to welcome them, subsequently entering into a correspondence with her royal highness and organizing a Vancouver branch of the London Needlework Guild at her request. She was viewed by some (again, I summarize Howard, who writes so well on Eliza Edge) as rather vainglorious and a little ridiculous, but she was reaffirmed in her assumed role when the Queen summoned her for an interview at Buckingham Palace in 1923.

Although Eliza was a staunch royalist, her ideas and behaviours were not always traditional or conventional ones. Howard, for example, tells of a fourteen-year-old girl's dismay at arriving at the beach in a new, trend-setting, one-piece bathing suit and finding Miss Edge wearing one in exactly the same style. She was very likely to stop a complete stranger on the street on the slightest pretext and enter into a lengthy conversation. Her unpredictable behaviour exasperated her convention-bound sister and niece, but it endeared her to the future author. Her portrait of Aunt Eliza as Topaz for the most part focuses on her seemingly irresponsible, carefree nature, but in the chapter of *The Innocent Traveller* titled 'Down at English Bay,' she suggests something of the complexity of this figure, who often chaperoned her on the street and was an important part of her childhood. In this sequence there is the humour of Aunt Topaz walking everywhere with her bicycle and its sometimes coarse behaviour to her person, and her irrepressible chatter with other visitors at the beach; but her innocent simplicity and goodness also bring her to the defence of a woman who has scandalized a local society matron by taking swimming lessons from a black man. Her aunt's membership in the Local Council of Women, as well as church organizations, and her socially effective action on several occasions led the author to one of those whimsical but firm observations in the novel – that 'human beings are very strange, and there you are.'[21]

Ethel Bryant's happiest hours in the summer months were spent swimming at English Bay – initially in the arms of a black man. She was taught to swim, along with three generations of children, by Joe Fortes, who over time has achieved legendary status in Vancouver. Born and raised in Barbados, Joe Fortes (whose Christian name was actually Seraphim) was a powerful, broad-chested man of Spanish and African ancestry. At age seventeen, he shipped as a sailor to Liverpool, England, where he became a swimming instructor and received a gold medal from the city for swimming the Mersey River – three miles across. When he was twenty-two, Joe arrived in Vancouver on the schooner *Robert Kerr*, which was partially wrecked in a storm while still in the harbour. That was 1885, but the boat played a crucial role the following year when it took people on board during the great fire that completely levelled the town. Joe thus stayed in Vancouver by accident, earning his living as a labourer at a sawmill, as a bartender, and as the city's first bootblack. But from his earliest days in Vancouver, he was teaching the city's children to swim. Before the West End was logged, he would take the children through bush trails to the best swimming beach at English Bay. Eventually he made his home there in a little squatter's cottage on the water and in 1900 was made a salaried swimming instructor by the city and appointed a special constable for the area. As Wilson puts it in *The Innocent Traveller*, future judges and aldermen and cabinet ministers, and lawyers and doctors and business magnates, and grandmothers and prostitutes and burglars and Sunday school superintendents and dry-cleaners were all taught by Joe Fortes to swim. She could, of course, have added 'writer' to that list of occupations. She also recalled Joe Fortes in an article written years later about Vancouver in its earliest days. Joe would say to the children in his rotund rich voice, 'Jump! I tell you jump! If you don't jump off that raft, I'll throw you in!'[22] Sometimes he threatened to leave them there all night. And so Ethel, one of the cowardly ones, finally jumped, and she grew to love the water and to swim and dive like a seal. Water would be something she would write about with love and respect, but also with fear. And in that article she called Joe a 'heroic figure.'

But for the members of the Vancouver Morals Association at the turn of the century (and likely for some of the members of the Woman's Christian Temperance Union as well), Joe Fortes as a black man and bartender represented everything that was suspect about English Bay. It was one of Vancouver's pleasantest beaches, but it already had a boat-house and pier, a dancing pavilion and a bandstand, and a transient population accumulated there every summer, living in cottages and tents and looking for fun. The incident in *The Innocent Traveller* that illustrates Topaz's lively sense of social justice was based on an actual event (designated by local historians as 'The Great English Bay Scandal'),[23] one that the author would have heard talked over frequently as a child. In 1901 the superintendent of rescue work for the Woman's Christian Temperance Union (WCTU) went to English Bay to find a young girl who had been reported living in a tent with a married man. In retaliation, this man suggested she would do better to rescue the president of the Vancouver WCTU, who was also camping at English Bay and had been seen to 'misconduct herself while in the water with "Nigger Joe."' In those days, swimming lessons from a bartender for the president of the Woman's Christian Temperance Union was admittedly pretty incongruous, but surprisingly the Union membership did not censure their leader; rather, they expelled the rescue worker. The two women subsequently sued each other for defamation of character, and the courts pondered the libel cases for nearly two years. It was because English Bay had this kind of reputation that Annie Malkin insisted her granddaughter be accompanied there by an adult. Sunday afternoon was the preferred time for a walk to the beach because then the band was limited to playing hymns and military airs.

Ethel Wilson dramatizes another disreputable aspect of the city's early life in her 'Young Vancouver' memoir. When she went shopping with her Aunt Belle on Cordova or Water Streets (at that time the liveliest streets in the city), she saw beautiful ladies in large black hats and long black skirts, usually travelling in pairs.[24] Their cheeks were very pink, their eyes large, and they lingered as they looked about. Rough, unshaven loggers from up the coast would roll along the streets. 'Aunty Belle,' the child would say. 'Look at the lovely lady. Who is she?' And she was disappointed and a little ashamed that her aunt did not know these women or want to know them, and in this way her 'burning innocence' continued. Like Rose in *The Innocent Traveller*, she may have thought then that brothels were where broth was made. In the novel, the prostitutes on Cordova are rendered in more erotic language: 'They sauntered lazily with a swaying of opulent hips and bosom, looking softly yet alertly from lustrous eyes set in masks of rose and white.' Rachel, the guardian aunt, 'behave[s] as if she were blind and deaf.' Certainly the Malkin household, an enclave of English piety and propriety, wanted to know nothing of the wildness of Vancouver, which was still a frontier town.

Yet a denizen of that world lived in their midst. For many years, the Malkins employed a Chinese cook named Yow (as in *The Innocent Traveller*), who gambled away his evenings and his earnings in Chinatown once the family had been fed dinner. His behaviour was always suspect, and if the novel is accurate in this regard, he was frequently surly and overbearing in his relations with his employers. The grandchildren feared him, and one claimed that he tried to molest her when she was a girl of eleven or twelve.[25] However, he loved the grandmother devotedly and willingly attended family prayers when required, and his continued employment was guaranteed by the special bond that existed between them. Wilson's fictional portrait partly undercuts the stereotype of the docile, submissive Chinese servant and accords with Wayson Choy's memoir *Paper Shadows* by suggesting in Yow a three-dimensional character who inhabits a world quite different from the one in which he serves. Chinese men had already been coming to Canada for many years – to lay track for the railroads, to pan for gold, to set up laundries and restaurants, and to send home money to support their families in China. Many found employment as houseboys and cooks in Vancouver homes and hotels, in logging camps, and on boats. They were frequently unhappy men and they smoked opium, and some had second wives as was their custom in China. They did important work, yet they were viewed with suspicion by Europeans, who feared their numbers would overwhelm them. Ethel's Uncle Harold was apprehensive about the growing immigration from Asia to British Columbia and kept a scrapbook of articles published on the subject during the first decade of the century.[26]

But these were still innocent days for Ethel Bryant, graced by the sight of beautiful high-stepping horses on the streets or a 'dashing young married woman [driving] a high dog-cart, with her whip held at the correct angle.'[27] As a child, she knew nothing of crime or social ills or politics and remembered instead picnics and entertainments in the young city. To avoid the disreputable aspects of English Bay, in summer the family would sometimes be rowed by the uncles across False Creek to a beach where a logging outfit known as Jerry and Co. was working. (It would eventually be called Jericho Beach.) Or, more ambitiously, the uncles would row everyone across Burrard Inlet to picnic on the beach at the Indian reservation on the North Shore. More than once the girl passed whales at close quarters on these crossings. For the really adventurous there were outings by rowboat up the North Arm of Burrard Inlet. The natural world pressed close on all sides, but the social conventions from 'home' remained firmly in place – for example, no one, especially not a woman, went outside without a hat, not even on a picnic. Judges and doctors and gold miners and explorers wore hats, said Wilson; even robbers wore hats.[28] Many years later, she observed that a nice thing about Vancouver is that you are still near the beginning of things, yet 'there is more nostalgia in an inflated frontier town than one would think.' Remembering the spanking pairs of horses that lent the frontier town an air of elegance, she wrote: 'People lived up to the sparkling pairs – calling cards and pink candle shades, red light district and opera capes, sitting together on the verandah steps and watching night fall upon the mountains, evening dress at the theatre and no murders, gangs of chained prisoners clearing the empty lots yet an unlocked door as you came and went, "drinking" with a nice discretion in "society" and roaring drunk on the waterfront.'[29]

There is evidence in the Wilson archives at UBC that the family travelled outside the city, as well. In the summer of 1900, they went over to Vancouver Island, and Ethel did a watercolour on a postcard that she mailed to her 'Aunt' Maria Riggall, her father's housekeeper cousin in Lincolnshire. The postcard, which somehow found its way back to Wilson, was postmarked Comox, B.C., 10 July 1900. It read: 'Dear Auntie. I have been painting a good many postcards. This is nobody only a thing out of my head. It is meant to be a girl walking by the sea in a storm of wind. Much love. Ethel.'[30] With so little material evidence of the author's life in this period, a biographer is tempted to 'interpret' this sketch. Here innocent days seem shadowed by upheaval. The girl walking by the sea is struggling to keep her balance in the wind. Her face is completely covered by the upsurge of her blonde hair, and her hat is rolling along the pier. Her umbrella is also in peril of flying off. The girl is holding on for dear life. It would be exaggerating to compare the subject with one of Edvard Munch's figures, yet a sense of bleakness and foreboding is conveyed by this little sketch, suggesting perhaps something of the girl's anxiety in being away from 'home,' even on a family holiday. Comox at the turn of the century would in fact be the setting for a memorable segment of 'Lilly's Story,' where both an idyll and an abrupt transition in a small girl's life take place.

The family's life, however, was grounded very securely in Vancouver and in the Church. Uncle Fred didn't just row across Burrard Inlet for picnics; he was licensed, according to Methodist practice, as a lay preacher and rowed across the inlet to Moodyville (near the mouth of Lynn Creek) to teach Sunday school there. Uncle Harold, with his business acumen, was a member of the Church's governing board and applied himself to problems of administration. Both uncles were Church stewards. In Annie Malkin's household, Church discipline was strictly adhered to, which meant no smoking or drinking or card-playing, though dominoes were allowed. Twice a day the family was called to prayers. Methodist piety also meant suspicion of other forms of Christian worship, and when Miss Gordon added religious knowledge to her school curriculum, Annie Malkin was upset by the fact that a minister from the Church of England was in charge of the girls' instruction.

Social life outside the home was also focused primarily within the sphere of the Methodist chapel, which not only provided a steady program of evangelical instruction, but sponsored public lectures of an 'uplifting' nature. One of these was a performance by Pauline Johnson, the Mohawk poet from Ontario, who sang and recited her verses, sometimes as a native princess in costume. Wilson had a confused memory years later of 'a buxom glowing woman with an eagle's feather in her hair' and of being too shy to speak to her.[31] Johnson invited the little girl to come and visit her, but on her way home that night she knew she was too afraid to do so: '[T]he sardonic goblin,' she would write, 'who inhabits and be-devils and preserves shy people of all ages, laughed derisively. This he did daily, and I did not, could not, ring the princess's doorbell.' But she would see Pauline Johnson on the streets of Vancouver some years later, when she had come to live in the city, a sombre-looking woman grown much older and very ill (by 1913 she was dying of breast cancer), and Ethel Bryant would feel in some irrational way that her failure to pay court had caused the princess's decline.

This guilty feeling that she recalled many years later when telling about her encounters with Pauline Johnson is worthy of note here. The effect of Methodism's social gospel on an acutely sensitive girl like Ethel Bryant was to instil in her a strong sense of duty that would remain with her all her life. She would come to regard her Methodist upbringing as restricted, 'blinkered,'[32] but her love for and gratitude to the family that

took her in made her proud to be one of these people, whom she characterized as 'those rather magnificent well-read austere Nonconformists
– a great great grandfather made class leader by John Wesley.' This
upbringing, however, carried with it such 'a terrific sense of duty and of
personal responsibility that if rain fell on Dominion Day, [she experi-
enced] a slight sense of guilt.'

Another event that took place at the Homer Street church when the
author was still a young girl was more embarrassing than guilt-ridden. In
1899 a vigorous, middle-aged minister took over the pulpit at the plain
little Homer Street church and made a number of changes.[33] The Reverend E.E. Scott preached a doctrine of perfectibility and sanctification
achieved solely through spiritual self-discipline. He believed the enter-
tainment system of raising funds was an obstacle to saving souls and that
concerts and lectures, like the one given by Pauline Johnson, were
essentially allurements from the world of sinful pleasure. He expected
his congregation to support the church instead through the collection
envelopes. 'A man of untiring energy and zeal,' Scott launched a program of revival meetings to convert lost souls and renew religious
vows. In a story titled 'I Have a Father in the Promised Land,' Wilson
describes how one evening the minister's eloquence moved her to stand
and tearfully confess her sins, because she wanted to be with her dead
father in heaven some day. In fact, she was prevailed upon to testify
three times, for her mother and again for her baby brother, while the
congregation sang the hymn 'I Have a Father in the Promised Land.' As
a girl in Vancouver, Wilson attended many such services, as well as the
mid-weekly prayer meetings and Sunday morning services. She recalled
men and women rising as she had done to confess themselves sinners
and weeping with emotion, though later in life she would grow suspicious of emotion displayed so publicly and so easily managed. But for
now it was part of her duty to her beloved grandmother, and she was
willing to play her role as a devout Methodist too.

CHAPTER THREE

Pupil

1902–1906

When circumstances reduce us to being alone and unhappy, pride is a
good companion. – 'The Birds'

Staffordshire again / Trinity Hall School / A grand tour /
'The Cigar and the Poor Young Girl'

Perhaps because Ethel Bryant was a stellar pupil at Crofton House, the
family felt she should be given wider opportunities for education. Perhaps because she was suddenly a ravishingly beautiful teenage girl, the
pious grandmother and the maiden aunts felt uncertain how to guide
their charge through this growing-up time. Or, perhaps because Crofton House was Church of England in its affiliation, Annie Malkin feared
the influence on her granddaughter of the religious instruction at the
school. For whatever reason, the Malkin family decided when Ethel had
turned fourteen that she should be sent 'home' to England for the next
few years of her education. The choice, not surprisingly, was Trinity Hall
School in Southport, Lancashire, which had been established in the
1870s to educate girls from Methodist families and was attended primarily by daughters of the manse. Its educational standards were high, its
daily regimen strict, and its religious focus Wesleyan, so that it offered
schooling that was not available in Vancouver. Moreover, it would place
her with girls of her own age and background with whom she might
develop friendships. Perhaps the family was growing concerned about
her ongoing shyness and her increasing preference to spend her time at
home in the library.[1] In a sketch titled 'Vancouver Child,' Wilson put it
this way: 'She was an only child. She was an orphan. She should, then,

learn to live with other children. She should go to boarding school. She must go back to beloved and unregretted England, and go to boarding school. This was dreadful.'[2]

Mary McAlpine creates a scene,[3] which may have been described to her by the author, in which the girl comes home from school on a spring afternoon in 1902 and learns that she will be sent away for her high-school years. She knew on that day, writes McAlpine, that when she entered the parlour and kissed her grandmother there was a tension in the room, and she asked if something was wrong. Her grandmother, who was granted all the power of decision-making in the family, explained, while the others remained silent, that she would be enrolled at Trinity Hall School in England in the fall and that she would be living not so far from the relatives in Staffordshire. It would not be a great expense to the family because daughters of Methodist clergy were charged very little for their education at Trinity. As she listened, the insecure fourteen-year-old likely felt 'the bottom had dropped out of everything' again. 'She wept often and was ashamed of herself,' we are told in 'Vancouver Child.'[4] Her later writing would reflect on how 'desperately homesick' she was to become, how for a year she would not mix with other girls willingly but kept entirely to herself.[5] Again she was 'on a brink.'

Before she was admitted to Trinity School, she had to write a set of entrance examination papers in the presence of either a notary public or a pastor. Reverend E.E. Scott, the flamboyant revivalist and her grandmother's greatly admired preacher friend, was approached on this matter, and he agreed that she could write the papers under his surveillance. In 'Vancouver Child,' she describes her stomach heaving and her palms moist and sticky as she made her way to the parsonage. Was she tempted perhaps to answer the questions badly in a bid to stay in Vancouver? On the street, she was aware of a church being moved, which in turn made her think of secure homes that were suddenly made to 'walk.' At the parsonage, she followed Scott along a 'dark and dinnery hall' to his study. There she found that up close the vigorous and charismatic preacher was a coarse-grained, self-centred, somewhat ignorant man. For the reading test, he gave her a passage from the Bible, but after she had nervously finished the first sentence, he took the Bible from her hands and declaimed the passage himself in a grating, ugly voice. While she wrote papers in geography, history, and mathematics, Scott worked at the other end of the table – on a sermon perhaps? – but his mouth was uncomfortable, and presently he withdrew his false teeth.

While Ethel wrote her exams, 'the teeth sat there grinning.' As she was leaving after a long afternoon, Scott gave her a piece of advice. '"Make the most of your advantages,"' he said, reflecting on her chance to go to England, but '"remember, too much edjcation is a snare ... never let any amount of edjcation come between you and your spiritual life."' Shun doubt, he said, for it is '"of the Devil,"' and he told her how miserable it had made Thomas Carlyle. The latter, he reported, became so nervous and sour that he would say to his wife '"don't breathe s'loud."' Once again he urged Ethel, '"Don't let edjcation get the better of you."'

In the summer of 1902, the Barclay Street household boarded the train and crossed the vast expanses of Canada and the Atlantic Ocean on another of its journeys 'home.' It was by now a journey well known to all the members of the Malkin family living in Canada: the uncles and Aunt Belle had made the return trip at least once each, before deciding to remain in Vancouver, and Aunt Eliza would make several trips to England during the remainder of her long life, sustaining a lively connection with the family and her interest in the monarchy. In the meantime, Great-Aunt Annie and Great-Uncle John Edge (Annie Malkin's brother and his wife) had made the trip to Vancouver just the year before to see what was keeping members of the family 'in the colonies' so long. Now the family was bringing Ethel back for school.

There was a special occasion to attend in the summer of 1902: Annie and John were celebrating their twenty-fifth wedding anniversary and there was a large, well-photographed gathering at 'Horton,' their new home in Wolstanton, Staffordshire. Everyone would have been remembering the inauspicious beginning to that union, because John Edge had secretly married his first cousin, Annie Edge, shocking both families and creating a rupture between father and daughter which lasted twelve years. Some speculated that John married his cousin because she was already an heiress, having been left a substantial sum of money when her mother died. As a young man, John was seen as somewhat precious and effeminate, more interested in the arts and social pleasures than in the pottery works. Suffering from chronic bronchitis, he spent a year living in Italy and was known with slight mockery in the family as Giovanni. He had a close friendship with a young widower in Burslem of similar tastes and interests, and this friendship brought Eliza the experience of unrequited love as recorded in her ill-fated passion for Mr Sandbach in *The Innocent Traveller*. At age thirty-three, John married his cousin Annie; they had no children. By 1902, Uncle John was particularly concerned to make an impression with his new home, which his impressionable young niece would remember for its remarkable bath. There were, she wrote, 'red carpeted steps up to the tub, like an altar. There was no bath mat. Simply you were exhorted not to splash. My great uncle rebuked a titled guest for splashing.'[6]

When in the summer of 1902 the visiting all around had concluded, the grandmother and Aunt Belle left Ethel in the care of her Aunt Edith and Uncle Sydney (Lila's brother), who seemed always to be their first choice as guardians. Ethel's photo album from that summer[7] has a picture of their home, 'Penrhyn,' purchased in 1895 and situated at Cobridge, half-way between Burslem and Henley on the Waterloo Road. The photo album also shows a strikingly attractive Ethel Bryant in her aunt and uncle's company, as well as in pictures from the anniversary party. All these photos (at 'Horton' and 'Penrhyn') of well-groomed, fashionably dressed people give evidence of a prosperity and elevated social status that the Edge and Malkin families enjoyed as England entered the Edwardian period.

Trinity Hall School in Lancashire, however, would present a rather different face to English life in the early twentieth century.[8] In 1872 a philanthropist in Southport donated the site and funds for the building of a Methodist church and a secondary school for girls adjacent to it. Built out of grey stone in an architectural style known as Early English, Trinity Hall was an austere and imposing building with classrooms and boarding facilities that by 1902 accommodated sixty-eight girls. Its grounds were enhanced by large shade trees and lawns broken up by small flower gardens. Ethel Bryant would have first entered the school into a long wide hall on the ground floor that led directly to the communal dining room. On one side of the hall was the drawing room and the study of the headmistress, Miss Peet, and a morning room for the staff. On the other side were two gymnasia and three classrooms. In a fairly bright semi-basement there were science laboratories and a laundry room, where maids, who roomed on the third floor, did the washing for the school. When she first entered the building that September, she may have heard coming from the basement a cacophony of several pianos being played at once, for there were also music rooms in the basement and the school had ten pianos! Up from the entrance hall swept the Big Stairs, which were for the exclusive use of staff, visitors, and prefects (student monitors). The other girls used the Little Stairs at either end of the building. The upstairs featured a large, bright drawing room for the girls with settees and basket chairs and an extensive library. The bedrooms were also located here. The girls roomed together in groups of three to six, the arrangements changing every term so that they would all get to know each other and so that relationships that were becoming too close or had become quarrelsome would be broken up. For a girl who had always had her own bedroom, this lack of a private place was difficult.

A daily routine at the school was strictly followed. The rising bell was at 6:30 A.M. and there was a piano practice every other day at 7:00. Breakfast was at 7:30, and then lessons from 9:00 until 1:00 P.M. A hot lunch was the main meal of the day, followed by a piano practice or sewing and mending. Sports and games were held between 3:00 and 4:30 or, for the non-athletic, a compulsory walk in crocodile pairs through the streets of the town, with a different partner each day. Tea at 5:00 was followed by a quiet period of reading and class preparation, with a break for bread and butter and milk at 8:15. After prayers were said, lights went out at 9:00 P.M. The same routine applied on Saturdays, except that Saturday evening was for writing letters home. Sunday mornings were spent in services at Trinity Methodist Church across the street, and Sunday afternoons were for reading. Girls were allowed to choose any book they liked from the library, but were required to submit a list of all the books they had read at the end of each term. Before they left Trinity Hall, girls were expected, in addition to the routine requirements of education, to be able to play hymns at the piano, to have read widely in both the classics and contemporary writers, and to have developed social skills for the dining hall and the drawing room. At ordinary meals, no girl was allowed to help herself or to ask for anything on the table, a regulation which was meant to foster consideration for others, but which caused some difficult times for unpopular girls and for shy girls like Ethel Bryant. To behave correctly at the tea table was still a highly prized social accomplishment, and to teach these skills the headmistress would invite two or three girls at a time to Sunday afternoon tea, where they were served wafer-thin slices of bread and butter, fancy cakes, and tea to be drunk very slowly from dainty cups and saucers. Ethel Wilson would remember her boarding-school years as 'rigorous, almost spartan' ones which provided her, however, with a sound education and some raw material for her fiction.[9] That first September, the school was celebrating its thirtieth anniversary, but festive events and much of the benefit of the school were initially lost on her for she 'suffered miseries of homesickness for a year.'[10]

In a short story titled 'The Birds,' Wilson perhaps suggests how she survived that first year of being alone and afraid at boarding school. 'Let me recommend [pride],' says the narrator of the story, who has experienced an emotional trauma. 'When circumstances reduce us,' she continues, 'to being alone and unhappy, pride is a good companion.' Pride is not a religious quality, she admits, and it is only 'cold comfort,' yet it is good – it gets one through.[11] We know there was the inevitable 'nasty girl' whom Ethel Bryant was anxious about,[12] and that she passed many hours alone in the school library that first year, and that she survived. One of the authors she discovered in the library was Arnold Bennett, a distinguished contemporary novelist who at once claimed her attention because he was writing about the town of Burslem.

Burslem, one of the Five Pottery Towns, was where she spent most of the first summer in England, with her Aunt Edith and Uncle Sydney Malkin, but she was scarcely any happier there than at school. Although all her life she would acknowledge the kindness of these relatives who took her in, she apparently never felt entirely comfortable with them, perhaps because they were associated with the pain of her father's death and her feelings of being a burden to them.[13] In a letter to friends in old age, she explains how the name of the Staffordshire town Leek always recalled her sense of inferiority. The ambiance of Leek among her manufacturing relatives was superior, admired, for it was a town where Persian silks were manufactured and where the family had 'hunting' friends. 'My uncle had a gift for making young girls feel *small* – and whenever we drove to Leek I felt insignificant and was, small, inadequate, reflecting no credit on anybody.'[14]

But as Mary McAlpine suggests, correctly I think, there was another reason for her discomfort with this couple, and that was her awakening social conscience. Sydney Malkin was one of the principal employers in Burslem and a man of affairs in the world. When Ethel first came to live at 'Penrhyn,' she was made physically comfortable, with a fire in her room and hot water to wash with; but, in time, she developed a friendship with the servants in the house, and when she went to visit the maids in the morning, she found their rooms were very cold, they had no fires, and had to sleep in their undergarments to keep warm. In the town where her uncle would eventually be the mayor, she saw beggars at the street corners, and maimed people selling pencils, and others who were physically scarred or deformed with heavy goiters at their throats, people who had probably never had any medical attention. Now, as she revisited Burslem, she became increasingly ill at ease with the kind of charity practised by her Aunt Edith. The latter would drive out in her handsome carriage surrounded by hampers (Ethel would sometimes go with her), and sitting behind a glass partition, she would instruct her chauffeur through a tube to leave hampers of food and clothing at the doorsteps of the poor. This gesture seemed to Ethel to have more to do with social status than charity.

Similarly, for Ethel, there was something false in the piety exhibited by her aunt and uncle. Like Fred Malkin in Vancouver, Uncle Sydney was a lay minister, and he relished standing in the pulpit and preaching a sermon – in the same Methodist church, in fact, where Ethel's parents had been married. According to her cousin, Philip Malkin of Vancouver, Ethel would try to avoid church if she knew her uncle was preaching, but she told Philip that if she was absent Uncle Sydney would come home and summarize the sermon for her. He was a small man with a ruddy complexion, and 'he would stand before her, feet wide apart, knees bent, clenched fists out front, and he would say "Ethel, I had them weeping. I had them crying. I had them fearing the Lord."'[15] But Ethel was too aware of inconsistencies. Methodism still adhered to a strict policy of no drinking, and in public Aunt Edith wore a sprig of white heather in her lapel to indicate her purity as a teetotaller.[16] But when Sydney ran for political office – as mayor and, unsuccessfully, as the Liberal candidate for his Staffordshire riding – he would, according to McAlpine, frequent the local pubs to get votes and come home smelling of spirits.[17]

More rewarding that summer was the contact she renewed with her father's family, particularly his two half-sisters, Margaret Bryant and Hannah Atkinson, who were living in London. Margaret Bryant, who had travelled in her youth as far as South Africa, was a distinguished journalist for the *Observer*. In a summary account of her life, she is described as 'a worker and a fighter, concealing an iron will under a deceptively meek exterior, loving gay company, helping and inspiring all who came into contact with her ...' It also reports that while little of her writing was signed, the *Encyclopaedia Britannica*, the Royal Institute of International Affairs, and the League of Nations benefited from her enormous energies, and that when she went to Geneva it usually heralded an unusual burst of activity on the part of the League secretariat.[18] Many years later, Ethel Wilson described this aunt as 'a female Savonarola with a beautiful smile.'[19] The older half-sister, Hannah Waller Atkinson, was of a more dreamy, romantic nature, but in many ways no less accomplished. In her youth, she had travelled to Russia, where she had lived for a time in St Petersburg with the pianist at the Imperial Palace; she was a talented linguist and eventually translated into English Pushkin's *The Tale of the Golden Cockerel* (1936). But her most intense interest was in music, and in Germany she became Clara Schumann's last pupil. She returned to England prepared for a brilliant musical career but married a man named Atkinson. Ethel Wilson would later describe him as a 'feckless clever fellow,' who deserted his wife and their children for a woman 'who took to drink.'[20] Hannah translated into English a selection of Schumann's letters and, with Atkinson, Spengler's *Decline of the West*, but the best part of her working life was spent in straitened circumstances raising the children. Her middle name, Waller, reflected her descent on the step-side from Edmund Waller, the erratic Cavalier poet who wrote 'Go, lovely rose! Tell her that wastes her time and me.' (There was a third half-sister also living in London, whose name was Elizabeth Bryant, but she was quite different from her sisters, without imagination, and Ethel as a young woman actively disliked her.)[21]

Hannah and Margaret, who were in early middle age, captured their niece's imagination and her love. They took her to concerts and theatre in London, to art galleries and restaurants, all of which were glamorous excitements and riches for a boarding-school girl. Presumably the Bryants introduced her to Reverend Fred Macdonald, because that fall he sent her the French Bible that her parents had given him when, according to his account, he married them.[22] In 'Reflections in a Pool,' an essay about the two sides of her family, she wrote about how much she loved her father's two sisters 'for their unshockability and funniness and cleverness and musicalness.' It was their sense of humour that she would especially treasure all her life, which would sweeten austerity and 'make happiness itself more enchanting as life [went] on.'[23] But Uncle Sydney would apparently sneer at these intellectual women in London and say to Ethel, '"So you will be visiting your hoity-toity relations while the rest of us struggle along."'[24] The girl was irritated by the absurdity of this sort of remark, for the Malkins were rich and her half-aunts were not rich at all.

Although Ethel never knew her mother, she could not help developing a bias that favoured her father and her father's family. A legend of goodness and piety surrounded her mother that made her unapproachable. After Lila's death, the family had published a pamphlet titled *Eliza Davis Bryant: A Brief Memorial of a Beautiful Life*, which consisted of tributes to a beloved family member and friend, compiled by Reverend W.D. Williams of South Africa.[25] Included was part of a letter written by one of her brothers in Canada:

Dear Lila has lived for others all her life, and her influence will never die. She lived for us when we were children, and for you and father ... O how memories have revived. Talks, walking home from chapel, little acts of kindness. How loving, considerate, self-forgetful! The best of sisters, as you say – but more, a saint! The best woman I ever knew, whose goodness and utter purity have astonished me ... Can I ever forget how in utter self-forget-fulness – fearless of the danger of catching it herself [tuberculosis] – she put her arm around [sister] Ethel, and strengthened her dear little heart for the coming conflict. Now they rest together. Together they see Christ.

In an account of Lila Bryant's life, Williams writes that, next to her house, 'the sanctuary of God was her delight. Her life was consecrated to Christ ... and burning with zeal for the glory of God.' He reminds her townspeople that 'to those who needed them, she taught lessons of thrift and self-help' and pitied those who suffered. He relates that when dying at just thirty-two years of age, she was asked if she still trusted in Christ and expressed great surprise at the question, replying, 'Yes, but wish I had loved Him more singly – more singly – more singly.' During forty-eight hours of great pain, she never murmured or lost composure, he reassures her family, and concludes on behalf of the family and himself with the reassuring belief that 'He doeth all things well.'

During Ethel's second year at Trinity Hall, the routine of school life began to endear itself to her. Her skill at games drew admiration from some of the other girls and helped to penetrate her shyness. Gradually she was becoming popular. Ethel Bryant was tall (at least five feet, ten inches) and well coordinated, and became especially adept at swimming and playing tennis. Judging from Christopher Armitage's account of the school, Trinity Hall was progressive in providing girls with a varied pro-gram of physical education, which included gymnastics, field hockey, and skating, and Trinity did well in competitions. The school made use of facilities in other parts of the seacoast town – swimming, for example, took place in Southport's newly enclosed sea-water Baths. Her account of non-academic activities is fairly blunt: 'For recreation we panted up and down hockey fields in hateful pursuit of each other's shin-bones; we played every known athletic game; we whirled about on trapezes; we held debates; we produced plays staged with a few yards of cheese cloth.'[26]

Apparently, Ethel Bryant enjoyed most the games of tennis on the grass courts of the school grounds, for she would write that she returned to Canada 'with a good tennis racquet.' She also mentioned returning with chilblains, a part of her spartan existence on the north Atlantic coast of England, where cold and damp prevail, and where in winter ice would form on the water basins in the bedrooms. From the school, day and night, one could hear the cold, gray, sometimes angry-sounding Atlantic breaking on the stony beach.

Her English education took a leap forward in the summer of 1904 when she was taken by Sydney and Edith Malkin on a trip to France (Uncle Sydney attending to tile business). Great-Uncle John Edge arranged to pay for Ethel's expenses. Having no children of their own, Uncle John and Aunt Annie (she was actually known in the family as Aunt John to distinguish her from sister Annie Malkin) had interested themselves in Ethel's upbringing. Ethel had complicated feelings about her great-uncle. John Edge was only minimally involved in the pottery works himself; his interests had turned to the activities of the borough and bench, and he was an industrious public servant who cultivated many connections in London. But while he belonged to a prosperous, middle-class family on the rise, he wished he had been born into the peerage. Wilson describes him in a family narrative as a handsome, complex man 'whose finely modelled head might have looked like a portrait by Van Dyck, elegant, fastidious, well-groomed, a man of principle, a snob, a man round whom glowed romantic emanations from a bachelor year spent in Italy.'[27] Wilson was more than usually aware of her uncle's snobbery because he lamented very publicly how coarsened certain members of the family had become by living in the colonies. He trusted that a few years at an English school would 'cure' Ethel, but in the meantime he is made to say, '[W]hen I met them [particularly Eliza, Belle, and Ethel] at Liverpool ... I was almost ashamed.'[28] Although she was tempted to make fun of Uncle John's pretensions, he was at the same time romantically associated in her mind with her parents' courtship. Lila had been on holiday with Aunt and Uncle John in Aberystwith, Wales, when Robert visited her there and they became engaged.[29]

Ethel Bryant was grateful for his generous offer of travel, for it was a time of awakening in many spheres. She remembered with special vividness three experiences with Aunt Edith and Uncle Sydney. They travelled first to Paris, where they went to visit a Madame Chenier who had been a school friend of her aunt's. This lady looked at the sixteen-year-old girl and said she was pretty but lacked chic, and proceeded to scold her friend for not putting the girl in corsets. Wilson would write, 'I

blushed all the time we were in France because I had no corsets.'[30] Then
they travelled to Monte Carlo on the Riviera, where in the glittering
gambling halls, fortunes were won and lost on the turn of a wheel or
card, and where the eyes of a shy Methodist girl from Canada were
opened to a worldliness undreamed of before. Dressed in one of her
aunt's long skirts and wearing elaborate make-up in order to falsify her
age, she accompanied her aunt and uncle to one of the casinos. The
feverish scene was marked indelibly on her mind with such details as the
truly wealthy using gold and silver coins to get the attention of Lady
Luck.[31] But the experience that was most compelling to her imagination was a visit to the Louvre in Paris and seeing the *Winged Victory of
Samothrace* at the head of the stairs, a sculpture that 'lifts the hearts of
mankind and womankind' she wrote.[32] It lifted hers and made her
determined to learn Greek when she returned to school and to read all
she could find in the library about Greek history.

But, before school resumed, she had another experience she would
relate years later. When they returned to Burslem from France, her aunt
directed her to Cock's, a draper's shop at the corner of St Luke's Square
that was soon to be immortalized in Arnold Bennett's *The Old Wives' Tale*
(1908). There, alone, and not knowing her size, the blushing young
woman hurriedly selected from among the black and scarlet garments
two light gray corsets, but on the way home with the long parcel held
awkwardly under her arm, she met Arnold Bennett on the Waterloo
Road. She wanted to go down on her knees to the famous writer, who
was by then living in London, still young and smartly tailored, but she
was too embarrassed over the corsets and he appeared to be thinking of
something else, so that they passed each other on the street without
exchanging a word.[33] On a later visit, Ethel was taken by her aunt to
have tea with Bennett's sister in a neighbouring town. Emily Bennett
was at that time married to Ethel's cousin, Spencer Edge, and the three
women shared family anecdotes and confidences. Ethel especially marvelled to learn that in his absence from the Pottery Towns, Bennett
never failed to write his mother a letter every day. This information
made her ponder on the unique – perhaps transforming – power of
motherhood (something she had never known), because all she saw in
Mrs Bennett was a 'small severe old gray wrinkled woman in a black
cape and bonnet walking slowly down the Waterloo Road.'[34]

When Ethel Bryant returned to school, she did not tell the other girls
she had been to France because she knew they did not have the same
opportunities she did. She knew Trinity Hall was a good, plain, bread-

and-butter boarding school, not a young ladies' finishing school. She was becoming sensitive to the fact that perceived advantages could be the cause for fatal jealousies. Ethel had become popular during her second year at Trinity because she did well for the school in athletic competitions and perhaps because her reserve had gradually transformed into a natural warmth for others. But she was also regarded as the handsomest girl in the school (still remembered twenty-five years later by the headmistress and fellow students as 'the School Beauty'),[35] and she was winning most of the awards for excellence in academic subjects, including music, in which she had little interest.[36] She felt vulnerable to feelings of jealousy and dislike that might arise in other girls and knew herself to be without defences, so that instinctively she remained as humble as possible, a pattern of behaviour that would remain throughout her life.

She would always be thankful to Trinity Hall School for providing her with a sound education, and she would credit especially two of her teachers for grounding her in an appreciation of language that would become an important part of her life's equipment. One of these was the headmistress, Miss Peet, who had a special love of literature.[37] On the Sunday afternoons in her drawing room, she would gather a group of girls by her fire and read from Jane Austen or Dickens or the Brontës, and Ethel Bryant probably began to cultivate that appreciation for the natural beauty and sometimes appropriate ugliness of English words that would be a hallmark of the future writer. One of Miss Peet's students many years later recalled listening with rapt attention to the headmistress's quiet voice reading Francis Thompson's 'The Hound of Heaven,' at that time a new and startling poem. Miss Peet was also an art teacher and awakened in her pupil a love of painting that remained for years. A few of Ethel Wilson's watercolours have survived – amateurish pieces, but strongly suggestive nonetheless that for a time she might have wanted to be a painter.[38]

But when remembering Trinity Hall School, her special gratitude and affection were reserved for 'an uncommonly plain, elderly woman' in thick spectacles who, in a basement classroom, taught the girls Greek history. Her name was Miss Mould and she spoke in a droning voice,[39] but she filled her students with a passionate fear that Athens would fall – 'we trembled at the approach of the doom of [the city].' This teacher's extraordinary power in retelling history was a matter of language, in her use of the inevitable word. Her students felt that she really cared that Athens fell, and in her dull but poignant voice chose words – 'careful falling fateful *words*' – that made nothing so terrible or melancholy as the demise of the city: 'Athens fell, and Miss Mould walked out of the room.' Wilson would say that she returned to Canada with a good tennis racquet and chilblains, but also a passionate love for the English language. She had received, in her estimate, an 'education based largely ... on the use and study of words,' and would insist repeatedly that 'there is no substitute for the study of words and language.'

Another teacher she remembered vividly, but in her recollections never named, was the science mistress at Trinity – 'very elegant, haughty, with a flashing turquoise eye.'[40] Ethel was frightened of her, but after leaving Trinity they remained in touch, and Ethel was delighted that this woman in old age read her novels, with a map of British Columbia at hand. Very naturally, Ethel's memories would be vividly imprinted with details from her schooling. When sixty years later she saw the title of Malcolm Lowry's posthumous short story collection, *Hear Us O Lord from Heaven Thy Dwelling Place*, she remembered at once that this was the first line of 'a Manx fisherman's hymn that was almost our school hymn at Trinity Hall.' She 'often played it for evening prayers (we seniors had our days for playing, a.m. and p.m.). It had an additional 3 accompanying descending notes not in [Lowry's] book, very lovely.'[41]

The four years at Trinity Hall proved finally a valuable experience for the girl from Canada, but they would only obliquely inform the content of her fiction. In Wilson's first published novel, *Hetty Dorval*, the narrator is sent from British Columbia as a teenager to an unnamed boarding school in England, but none of the scenes of the story is laid there. Long holidays with a family on a windy Atlantic headland are as close as the novel comes to recreating the setting at Southport. The intense loneliness and homesickness that Ethel Bryant experienced at the outset of her boarding-school years might be taken as a given in much of her writing, although it is only articulated once, and that is in *Swamp Angel* when Hilda Severance remembers how she was always separated from her parents, living at a private school, dressed in uniform, and the other girls laughing at her: '"And she hasn't got a real home!" said the girls. "Hush, dear," said a teacher.'[42]

In the summer of 1906, Ethel Bryant was excited to be returning to Vancouver, whose physical beauties she would identify as part of her homesickness – a four-year 'dream of green forests, blue mountains and white-fringed ocean, halo-ed Vancouver.'[43] In England she would miss most the pleasure of spending time with her father's half-sisters, whose humour and intellectual interests were becoming a reassuring legacy. Those visits were being discouraged by the Malkin relatives, who feared that if she stayed with these emancipated women she would wind up on the stage. The Bryant sisters apparently did encourage their niece to become an actress, likely because they saw in the tall young woman not only extraordinary beauty but grace and poise and a strong feeling for the arts. The 'shockable' Methodists in Burslem would have viewed this as a terrible fate and their niece 'forever lost.'[44]

There is no record of Ethel Bryant's last days in England or of the journey home (no family letters from this period in her life have survived), but there are two autobiographical stories that suggest what might have happened. In both of these, a young woman from Vancouver receives an unwanted marriage proposal before leaving England. In 'The Mirage of Edward Pontifex,'[45] the young man who is smitten by the girl from Canada is 'the hero' of a local literary group and an admirer of Wordsworth, who writes flowery, passionate love letters to the indifferent girl. In 'The Cigar and the Poor Young Girl' (a story directly linked to *The Innocent Traveller,* though not part of that book), the girl of the title is named Rose and is on her way home to Canada in 'secret possession of an indited proposal of marriage.' While we can't be certain this happened to Ethel Bryant, there is some likelihood it did take place because these stories are part of two cycles of stories – one about Rose, the other about Lucy – both of which follow Wilson's actual life very closely. Edward Pontifex remembers seeing Lucy when she was a small girl and then when she came back to England to go to school. This would suggest an admirer in Burslem during Ethel Bryant's frequent visits over the years.

'The Cigar and the Poor Young Girl' tells us quite clearly that Ethel Bryant was accompanied home by her Uncle Fred Malkin and his young wife, Julia, who here and in *The Innocent Traveller* are called Frank and Miranda Hastings. Julia Malkin is always identified as 'the lovely and engaging Miranda,' whose physical and social composure make the younger woman feel awkward and 'unfinished.' The story is worth quoting for an intimate glimpse of how the author saw herself when she was eighteen:

> [She] was now grownup, The hatpins longer than skewers testified to this, so did her hairpins, her long skirts, a strong pair of curiously shaped whalebone corsets, and the secret possession of an indited proposal of marriage. Yet she was not grownup. Not at all. She was a miserable imitation of

grownupness, and all this business of hairpins was just a disgrace, for she remained an innocent ninny. She bumped into new and disturbing conventions from morning till night. She did not know how to cope with these matters, and blushed for all to behold at least five times a day. She could blush, often for no reason, until the tears squeezed out of her eyes, in spite of the support of hatpins longer than skewers, of hairpins, whalebone, and a proposal of marriage.[46]

The story not only comically highlights Ethel Bryant's youthful awkwardness and lack of self-confidence, but also her lifelong disposition to take things too seriously. 'Mrs Golightly and the First Convention' would be Wilson's most memorable self-portrait in that light, but 'The Cigar and the Poor Young Girl' is a worthy forerunner. While the engines of the ship plunging westward beat out 'Vancouver, Vancouver,' Rose and her aunt find a partly smoked cigar on the floor of Rose's cabin. Fearing a scandal, the high-strung girl completely misjudges social conventions and makes a fool of herself in the dining saloon. But a suave older man on the boat, who has enjoyed her company at meals, tells the distraught young woman about his own unhappiness and gives her some advice: '"Take your troubles as they come and take 'em easy, and get all the fun you can that doesn't do anyone any harm."' These were words that would take Ethel Bryant Wilson the best part of a lifetime to put into practice.

CHAPTER FOUR

Teacher

1906–1921

Proceed from the known to the unknown – like a pearl fisher. – Principal
William Burns, Vancouver Normal School

A teacher / 'Let Me Go' / Bowen Island / Art lessons / Engaged /
'A Few Years' / 'The Surprising Adventures of Peter' /
The Langham Hotel

In 'The Cigar and the Poor Young Girl,' friendly shipboard ladies who
attach themselves to the 'lovely Miranda' ask if her niece is 'Out' in society. Miranda replies, '"Not yet ... but when we get to Vancouver ..."' That
would have been the natural answer for Julia Malkin to make. She was
regarded, until she started wearing glasses, as 'the prettiest girl in Vancouver,' and in her niece's eyes 'an angel of loquacity ... and a lover of
Society,' who was not by nature inclined to strict Methodist obser-
vances;[1] but her answer did not describe the little world to which Ethel
Bryant was returning. Unlike most eighteen-year-old girls coming back
from finishing school abroad, Ethel Bryant did not have a coming-out
party to launch her into society and could not, outside the Church, take
part in social affairs that brought marriageable young men and women
together. Accordingly, it was difficult for her to meet men, and when
she did, she was strictly chaperoned. Instead of becoming part of Vancouver's leisured female class, Ethel Bryant, as an orphan, had to find a
way to earn her living.

The first Normal School for training teachers for British Columbia
had recently opened in Vancouver and held classes in three rooms on
the second floor of Lord Roberts School in the West End.[2] Ethel had

passed the Cambridge examinations and London Matriculation at Trin_
ity Hall and so took the path followed by most young women who did
well at school and applied for the teacher-training program. She was
admitted in September of 1906. Here she encountered the other great
teacher in her life who, like Miss Mould, would leave a lasting mark.
Again it was a teacher who had enormous power in the classroom
because of his solicitude about the meaning and use of words. This was
Principal William Burns, an English-born former inspector of schools,
who exercised true caustic wit and both delighted and frightened his
students – a natural bent that Wilson would eventually cultivate in herself. She could not remember any practical instruction that he gave
prospective teachers ('when we went out into an [actual classroom]
everything seemed unprecedented');[3] she credited him, instead, for
teaching them a good deal about life and human relations and especially about language, a legacy that would eventually empower her as a
writer. Another teacher at the Normal School left his mark, but in a less
positive way. She gives him no name, and it is hard to be certain about
his identity from the teacher's register in 1906, but her description of
him is more vivid than any naming: 'an ardent pale frail red-bearded
teacher who feared the intrusion of ideas beyond those provided by the
Ontario school course. Through all his narrow loving passion for
instruction his defensive ardour shone.'[4] Ethel Bryant recognized in this
man, as she had in her Great-Uncle John, a contempt, almost a fear, for
local culture, for a way of living that lay outside the control of the centre. She pitied the man's curious 'suffering' but broke away from his
dominion. It was one of her early awakenings to the importance of what
is concrete and at hand. She would argue later in her life against the
idea of a 'Canadian' novel, that instead stories were told about a specific
place and their value was in how well they were told, not whether they
had abstract national characteristics or not.

According to Mary McAlpine, the young graduate went first to Miss
Gordon to apply for a teaching position at Crofton House and stayed
there for a year.[5] However, there is no record either in the school's files
or in Ethel Wilson's two pieces of writing about her association with
Crofton House that she ever taught there. Instead there is a clear record
of her teaching in four different public schools in the city over the next
thirteen years.[6] They are Kitsilano Elementary (1907–9), the Model
School (1909–12), Lord Roberts Elementary (1914–18), and Dawson
Elementary (1918–20). Perhaps Wilson did talk to Jessie Gordon about
employment but decided in favour of the public schools because they

would pay her better. Even so, all she was paid was $47.50 per month in
the city system. McAlpine writes that she once asked Ethel Wilson about
her years as a teacher and got almost no response. In her formal remi-
niscences about her early life in Vancouver, Wilson mentions her teaching only once and that very obliquely, saying that when she taught in
Kitsilano it was still mostly forest, that a boy from further west on Point
Grey Road reported one day that he had just killed a bear that had been
at his father's pigs.[7] When McAlpine asked specifically if she had
enjoyed the experience of working with children, Wilson said firmly,
and with irritation, 'No.' However, the pupils whom McAlpine was able
to interview sixty years later had no dislike of their teacher, and their testimony seems to undercut McAlpine's conclusion that teaching had
been such a negative experience in Wilson's life.[8] One woman remembered her as 'a goddess, tall, blonde and beautiful, like a fairy princess.'
One of the male pupils in her 'Baby Class' at Lord Roberts described
her as 'beautiful and gentle. She never disciplined or teased anyone. We
all loved her.' Another student, who came to the city when she was ten,
remembered being taken to tea at Grandmother Malkin's house and
being told stories of Vancouver to help her feel at home. That student's
mother was surprised that such a well-connected and beautiful, sophisticated young woman had to make a living as a teacher, but Ethel
accepted without question family discipline and the expectation that
she earn her own living.

More likely, Wilson's negative memories of her teaching years were
related to the first school principal under whom she taught.[9] In a letter
written at least fifty years later, she describes with strong feeling the ani-
mosity she felt towards this man both personally and professionally. His
name was H.B. King and he was principal at Kitsilano Elementary. Wilson, in an uncharacteristic outburst of spleen, calls him 'a pompous
windbag' and 'the evil genius of education in British Columbia.' A man
with 'smatterings of knowledge' and an amateur psychologist, King
tried, Wilson relates, to reform educational methods in the province.
What she particularly detested was his introduction of the 'true and
false' method of examining pupils, and that, says Wilson, 'was the down-
fall of the English sentence.' A very diffident young teacher, she probably said little at the time, but she transferred to another school after two
years. Language skill as the enabling medium of all education became
an overriding principle in Wilson's later discussions of civilized life.[10]

In Wilson's early life, from the information we have, we get no
glimpse of ambition or the will to succeed. If they were strong, she kept

them secret, conforming to the social expectations for young women of her time and station in life. There was almost certainly considerable frustration for Ethel Bryant living at 1273 Barclay Street during this long stretch of her young life – from age eighteen to thirty-one. It was a closely confined female household, in which the strict forms of Method- ist piety continued to prevail. Not only were smoking and drinking of alcohol forbidden, but Church members were not allowed to go to parties where there would be dances, to attend theatre or circuses, or to play games of chance. Ethel Wilson would say in an interview many years later that she loved her grandmother dearly – Grandmother was 'kind and loving and so modest that I often wonder how she ever managed to have all those children.'[11] But she suggests a less happy aspect to life on Barclay Street when she says, 'It was not until I was married that I learned it was possible to enjoy life without first passing a moral judgment on it.' In the early years of the century there was a movement in the Methodist Church of Canada to relax rules of personal conduct, particularly regarding those amusements forbidden in the Church handbook, *The Doctrine and Discipline of the Methodist Church.* Although a liberal motion, debated at length at the Annual Conference in Toronto in 1902, was defeated, Church members gradually began tempering their views, and Methodism itself was to become the more permissive, less demanding faith of the United Church of Canada. But Annie Malkin was too old to adapt to liberal ways ('Methodism is revival of religion and spiritual edification ... and cannot speak otherwise,' decided the Conference in 1902),[12] and Ethel Wilson would say years later, in something like a footnote, 'It was almost impossible to be young in such a house.'[13]

In two articles, based chiefly on family interviews, Irene Howard describes some of the strict social conventions adhered to in the Malkin households in the West End.[14] On Sundays 'the boys' and their families came in turns to the Barclay Street house for high tea, with Annie Malkin presiding in her black dress and starched white cap trailing ribbons, a little reticule at her waist. It was a frugal meal – a tin of sardines or potted shrimp with bread and butter and seed cake – as cooking was not done on Sundays, and, further, the Barclay household lived on the limited means provided by James Malkin's Burslem estate. The tile works had not been sold on James Malkin's death (Sydney carried on the business), and its assets remained invested. Although the Malkin family in all its branches was known as one of the 'best' families in the city, all its members lived modestly at that time as Methodism prescribed. After tea, the family, grown men included, knelt together for prayers; Annie Malkin would read from the Bible, and Aunt Eliza would play hymns at the piano. The Malkin grandchildren, still dressed in their church-going clothes, in later years remembered it as 'all rather depressing,' but Wilson makes clear in *The Innocent Traveller* that it was seen very differently at Barclay Street: 'Grannie's sons and their exhilarating wives and children were the delight of this family. Their visits brought infinite pleasure and variety to this sedate household of three ageing ladies and one young girl.'[15]

Although her father's memory occupied a magical place in her heart and imagination, Ethel Wilson had enormous respect and affection for her Vancouver uncles, whom she regarded as foster-fathers.[16] They were hard-working businessmen and strict Methodists, but each had a facet to his character that fascinated and charmed the niece. Fred Malkin (1863–1950), who had been first to propose a life for the family in Canada, continued to exemplify the pioneer spirit. He had ridden horseback over the Hope-Princeton trail and, when he was older, drove a model T from Vancouver to New York City. He enjoyed blasting stumps and clearing the land on a property he owned on Bowen Island. He is described at the same time as meticulous and handsome, wearing a wing collar and glasses with black ribbon, a familiar figure in business and Church circles in Vancouver. In a youthful photograph, he has the fine, aristocratic features of his father, James Malkin. He married the much younger Julia Eldridge, 'the prettiest girl in Vancouver,' and his Methodism was tempered over the years by her easy social graces.

William Harold (1868–1959), known in the city as W.H., was a man of smaller build and of greater drive to succeed in business. He was very reserved socially, a teetotaller who adhered strictly to the regimen of his faith. In 1901 he married Marion Dougall, who had come to Vancouver with her widowed mother from Ontario. Marion had been raised an Anglican, and in one of the unpublished stories she wrote about her Malkin family (this one titled 'The Umbrella'), Ethel describes in a lightly comic style the tension over religious denominations that existed at the outset of their marriage – between Harold 'a Methodist of stern and inexorable descent' and Marion 'by tradition, training, and temperament a devout member of the Church of England.'[17] The story is told from Marion's point of view, and we learn that for six months 'with reverent mien [she] entered the ugly wooden structure of pseudo Byzantine design' that was the Wesley church, thinking all the while with nostalgia 'of the glowing windows of little St. John.' In her eyes, the

Methodists approached worship in a casual manner, lacking any form of
ritual: 'instead of Gothic charm here was crudeness and an appearance
of irreverence,' as people took their pews, smiled and nodded at each
other, and leaned forward to exchange friendly chat, without dropping
on their knees for a brief, silent dedication. Marion is described as not a
beauty, but as a little woman with something more than beauty – 'something warm and glowing ... and darkly vivid.' In the story, she makes a
fool of herself trying to assist two ladies who appear mysteriously at a
Sunday morning service, and she vows she will *never, never, never* go to
that church again.' But her vow only lasts for two weeks, dissolved by her
love for her husband, and we are told that years later she laughed to
look back on that affair. Theirs, in fact, was a strong marriage, and
Harold became one of Vancouver's most prosperous and respected
businessmen. In 1929 he was elected mayor of Vancouver on a prohibi-
tion platform, and though he did not succeed in making Vancouver a
'dry' city, he carried forward the city's business in other respects, being
best remembered eventually for building the Burrard Street bridge over
False Creek. His children in later years lamented his strictness, but Ethel
Wilson greatly admired her Uncle Harold's public spiritedness and his
modesty. He made large anonymous donations to charities like the Cancer Foundation and supported the arts generously: he was one of the
founders of the Vancouver Art Gallery, and a president of the Vancouver Symphony Society; and he donated the funds to build an outdoor
concert pavilion in Stanley Park that became known as Malkin Bowl.

Philip Malkin (1878–1952) was the much younger uncle – only ten
years older than Ethel herself – who was the sales manager for the company. The summer after she returned from England, he was married to
Georgina Grundy, another of the 'exhilarating wives,' and Aunt Edith
and Uncle Sydney came to Canada for the first time to attend the wedding. For the author there always hovered over Philip and his family an
aura of social ease and laughter, for Philip was the most gregarious of
the brothers, a man with many friends who was well liked in the community at large. Georgina, who was known in the family as 'Jo,' was only a
few years older than Ethel, and they grew to be very close. Eventually,
Ethel would dedicate one of her most popular pieces of writing ('Lilly's
Story') to this woman, who was technically her aunt, but was in fact her
near contemporary and very close friend.

On those Sunday visits, the grandchildren remembered above all how
carefully they had to behave. There was a gramophone at Grannie's
house which delighted them, but they were only allowed to play record-

ings of hymns or classical pieces. Annie Malkin frowned on laughter in her house, and the children were warned in advance that they must conduct themselves soberly. They had to wear their best clothes to visit Grannie, the same outfits they had worn to church. Any form of work was strictly forbidden, including sewing or knitting, and the family members were forbidden to read the newspapers, which were regarded as worldly. A chapter of *The Innocent Traveller* titled 'Rather Close in the Sitting-room' suggests the stuffiness of the routine observed so carefully in the Barclay Street household. Finally, in the novel, Rose slips away on Sunday evening to her bedroom to read a story about a young woman named Poppy, who lives on the veldt in 'dark, sensual, amorous Africa.' The grandmother approves, thinking it must be a book about missionaries, and Rose kisses her and goes upstairs to be alone and vicariously sensual with Poppy in the veldt country associated, for Ethel Bryant, with her father's life and the laughing Bryants.

Wilson's working title for this chapter of *The Innocent Traveller* is 'Let Me Go,' and in the first draft she deals directly with the problems for a young woman in such a restricting environment, observing that the Chinese servant had more freedom of choice than Rose did. Should we conclude accordingly that this was a period of rebelliousness and profound unhappiness in Ethel Wilson's life, or was it mostly a happy time as the overall comic tone of the novel suggests? Her younger cousins, looking back on the Barclay household of their childhood, thought it must have been terrible for a young woman growing up there. But the answer is probably somewhere in between. Knowing so well her own timidity and insecurity, Ethel Bryant treasured the safety of her grandmother's home and the extended family. Her willingness to model herself according to her grandmother's wishes was not simply repressive tolerance, but a source of pleasure in her life. To rebel in anger, with a rush of bitter words and tears such as Margaret Laurence describes for her orphan-heroine Vanessa in *A Bird in the House,* would be a remote course for someone of Ethel Wilson's character and background. Her need for security was all-pervading, and life was made tolerable, indeed very enjoyable, by a sense of humour that fed on the ironies that she perceived all around her. In an interview years later, she said, 'I am proud of my strict upbringing because as long as one feels loved, a conventional home life is salutary, gives assurance.'[18] She described occasional weekend visits with her friend Marion Martin as a fresh breeze, but one that went through what she called nonetheless her 'good kind elderly Barclay Street life.'[19]

She was less comfortable with her life at the church. When she returned from England, she was persuaded to play the hymns for the mid-week prayer meetings. There she observed people encouraged to stand up and confess themselves sinners and publicly ask God for forgiveness. The penitents were often moved to tears by their proneness to sin ('I am prone to uncharitableness, I am prone to sloth'), and one woman concluded her elaborate confessions with the words 'Oh Lord, I am liable to prone,' all of which Ethel Bryant found outwardly embarrassing, though secretly amusing. The social life of the Malkin family was entirely circumscribed by the Church. Methodist ladies visited other Methodist ladies on 'At Home' days, leaving their calling cards in turn, and young people, restricted from attending parties and dances, all joined the church choir in order to meet other young people. Years later, Ethel Wilson compared this world to an ostrich egg, a world cut off from the contemporary world at large, self-righteously confident that it was unquestionably 'The World.'[20]

Because the world was equated with the Church, it was assumed in the family that Ethel would find a husband among eligible young Methodists. In Annie Malkin's view there was an ideal candidate in the person of John Pethybridge Nicolls, a bachelor who lived with his mother, four sisters, and a niece, and who was prospering in Vancouver's booming real estate market. He had been born in Cornwall, emigrated to Vancouver in 1891, and by 1898 had established Vancouver's first real estate business in partnership with C.H. Macauley. His first home was on Seaton Street (now West Hastings), a neighbourhood then eminent and fashionable, and it had an 'exquisite view of the mountains, forest-clad Deadman Island and Stanley Park.'[21] But Nicolls was nearly twenty years older than Ethel, a short man with the build of a pouter pigeon, and though he was said to have been a student of literature and politics, there is no indication that Ethel felt any attraction to him. The fact that his mother was one of Annie Malkin's best friends and that he had known Ethel since she was a young teenager likely dulled her interest rather sharpened it.

Escape from the confines of the ostrich egg and a real breath of fresh air came in the summers when the family spent several weeks at Bowen Island in Howe Sound, a short ferry ride from Vancouver.[22] The three uncles bought property on the island, Harold and Philip owning a cottage at Point Cowan (also known in reverse as Cowan's Point). George H. Cowan (1858–1935), who sold them land for a cottage in 1906, was a Vancouver lawyer and politician who had come upon the southeastern

tip of the island before the turn of the century and over the years
bought up more than 1,000 acres, where he built a series of spacious cottages (some with as many as ten rooms) to share with his friends. Determined that his little community be as self-sufficient as possible, George
Cowan set up a twelve-acre farm at Seymour Bay on the eastern edge of
his property, where he had a large kitchen garden to supply his friends
with vegetables, a dairy, sheep and lambs, and a hen house for fresh
chicken and eggs. A caretaker lived on the farm all year round. Friends
paid a small rent each summer, but the bulk of the expenses was carried
by Cowan and his wife, who took enormous pleasure in creating this
idyllic summer retreat for their family and friends, especially the family
of S.B. Woods, deputy attorney-general of Alberta, who came for twenty-
one consecutive summers. The Malkin cottage was set in their midst and
enjoyed the sense of community that existed at the Point.

People remembering that special place in the first half of the century
recall the blue and purple vistas of ocean and islands, the green paths
through the bush, rowboat rides, fishing for salmon and rock cod, and
swimming by moonlight in the bays. But they also recall the feeling of
community provided by Saturday night dances, games, and amateur the-
atricals, and by Sunday morning church services, because Annie Malkin
with her 'gift of religion' made sure that regular services were held
under a tent for all to attend. The Cowans were actually Anglicans, as
were many of their friends, but in the lighter mood of this summer
place, denominations relaxed a little and joined together for a service
every Sunday. This was a place where Ethel Bryant mixed easily with
non-Methodists, where other young men and women came and went
during the summer months, giving her a glimpse of the world outside
the ostrich egg. She enjoyed a friendship with the Cowans' daughter
Irene, who would one day marry Ernest Rogers, a son of the B.C. Sugar
Refinery family, and with various members of the Woods family. She
also got to know the daughters of Dr and Mrs David Wilson, who owned
land near Cowan Point, and who would one day be important people in
her life. Sometimes she would bring along her special friend Marion
Martin, who was a cousin of the Woods children. She appears briefly as
Rose's beautiful friend Marcella Martin in *The Innocent Traveller* and,
strangely, as a character by the same name in *Hetty Dorval*. In her photograph albums there are a number of pictures of the future author enjoying summer activities in these rustic surroundings, or dressed in motley
and clowning for the camera.[23] She taught small children how to swim
in Trinity Bay, took part in the sports days and regattas organized by her

Uncle Philip, and attended the fancy-dress birthday parties for her Uncle Harold (costumes were decorated with leaves and flowers). Kenneth Caple, one of those children, remembered Ethel not only as a good swimmer, but as the most beautiful and vivacious young woman he had known. He remembered the stylish and rather daring swimsuit she wore – skintight black wool with a short skirt – and how she emerged from the water and let down masses of beautiful hair to dry.[24] She was both athletic and elegant, not so common at that time. There were always young cousins, her uncles' children, to play with. Uncle Fred and Aunt Julia had a property on the west side of the island, so that long hikes over rough trails to pay a visit were part of the summer's adventures for the Malkins. The idyllic pleasures of those summer holidays are partly preserved in 'The Innumerable Laughter' chapter in *The Innocent Traveller*, where the island is called Benbow and the Cowans are named Oxteds. Returning to the city every September was a narrowing of the horizons.

To broaden them, Ethel Bryant decided one fall to take painting classes. She remembered her pleasure in the drawing classes supervised by Miss Peet at Trinity, and then again at Normal School, where there had been painting classes, given first by a lecherous but charming old Scot who drank and taught oils ('"May I give you a little squeeze, Miss B.?"') and then by a charming young Scot who did not drink.[25] But in Vancouver between 1906 and 1910 there lived in an upper room on Granville Street a forthright woman who gave painting lessons whose name was Emily Carr. Wilson writes that being at that time herself 'a very immature young teacher with a private natural love for the arts, and determined to continue in drawing and painting,' she went to see Miss Carr for private lessons. 'But as the lessons consisted entirely of conversation, and as I did not recognize genius, and I earned only $47.50 a month and had no talent, I could not afford to buy conversation,' and so Miss Carr 'lost her least promising pupil.' 'Also,' she adds, 'there were things about her parrots that I did not like.'[26]

Emily Carr's presence in Vancouver at that time was anomalous. There was little real interest yet in the arts, although an Art, Scientific, and Historical Society had been formed as early as 1894, with the intention, as one of its presidents would recall, of diverting some of the people's energies away from simply making money.[27] What Ethel Wilson would remember was how very rudimentary the arts were in early Vancouver: the walls of people's homes were hung with portraits of dead relatives, and the art of painting was largely confined to china. Music fared better in that Vancouver had an Opera House on Granville Street with a good stage and elegant boxes and in the early years drew such luminaries as pianist Jan Paderewski and soprano Luisa Tettrazini.[28] It also brought actresses of the calibre of Ellen Terry and writers and thinkers like theosophist Annie Besant and Indian poet Rabindranath Tagore. The theatre was restricted to Methodists, but if *The Innocent Traveller* is actual history in this respect, Ethel Wilson did see a stage production of Shakespeare at the Opera House at least once when she was a very young woman. She remembered that some women wore tiaras and pearl necklaces, or 'fascinators' over their heads.[29] But for most Methodists, Shakespeare meant a reading group in a home. The Malkins were like many other English families that had brought with them the accoutrements of their civilization and a quiescent devotion to the arts. And she would remember that 'there was music in the homes of Vancouver. Evenings were not complete without a song, or piano, or violin, not music of grand quality, but of the essence of pleasure.' But, for Ethel Wilson, the most valuable cultural commodity that had been brought to the edge of the forest was the small and excellent library of books which she read and reread until she almost knew them by heart.

Because no letters have survived from this period, it is almost impossible to date some of the things that happened when Ethel Wilson was in her twenties. For example, several members of the family (including Annie Malkin and Aunt Eliza) are shown in photographs to have been in England in the summer of 1910. This was the summer that Harold Malkin bought a MacLachlan automobile, put it on a boat to cross the Atlantic, and, once arrived, drove the family around England. Ethel may have taken the photos and put them in her album, but since she does not appear in any of the pictures it is impossible to say for sure that she was there too. It seems likely, however, that it was around 1912, when she was twenty-four, that she became engaged to John Pethybridge Nicolls.[30]

Nicolls's courtship of Ethel took place very publicly at church and family functions. He also owned property at Cowan Point and would take the Union Steamship ferry over on Saturdays to spend weekends on the island. Ethel, who was now twenty-four, was likely feeling the pressure of family and community to make a good marriage, but, if her fiction gives us a hint of what she was experiencing, she probably said 'yes' to Nicolls reluctantly. After all, he was forty-two, shorter in height than she was, a man wholly preoccupied with business and encumbered with a number of female relatives. Nonetheless, she accepted the large diamond ring he offered, and families on both sides were apparently very happy. Accordingly, a series of dinners and teas and luncheons were given by family and friends to mark the forthcoming event. Invitations to the wedding went out around the city and to Burslem and London and to wherever the Nicolls family had relatives and friends. And presents arrived – silver, crystal, and fine linens – much to the delight of the grandmother and aunts in the pepper-pot house on Barclay Street. But Ethel Bryant grew less joyful and less certain about her decision. She fought against her doubts but recognized that she did not want to marry this small, decent, middle-aged man. After a long struggle, she finally broke off the engagement; she was deeply ashamed of herself and desperately sorry for him, for it was a shocking turn of events in respectable Vancouver society. (Years later, however, this humiliating time would have its comic aspect. She told a friend that, as part of the Methodist community, she eventually attended Mr Nicolls's wedding – in 1923 at age fifty-three he was finally married – and was very embarrassed because there was her engagement ring on another woman's finger!)

The broad outlines of this phase of her life were saved for her last published novel, *Love and Salt Water*, whose protagonist, Ellen Cuppy, breaks off her engagement with a lawyer she finds she does not love. A more detailed reflection on entering marriage can be found in a very different, much more autobiographical first draft of *Love and Salt Water* titled 'Herself When Young,' in which Ellen is being pressed into marriage by a middle-aged musician. Franz ardently wishes to marry her, and she reasons to herself: 'He is musical. He seems honest. He is clean and has good manners. Here is a companion. He's a little short on sense of humour, or perhaps we have not the same kind.' But she asks, 'Do I want his company day in, day out?' She acknowledges eventually that it would be marrying out of compassion, and that it likely would not last: 'Where is [this feeling]? It has dissolved, or it has suffered a change into a relationship that you could never have thought up and would never welcome ... No, compassion is for every relation in life, public and private, divine and human, but it is not a reason for marriage.'[31] Was this the reasoning that Ethel Bryant followed the summer of her engagement to Mr Nicolls? Given the almost non-fiction nature of this manuscript, it seems likely.

I would date the engagement as 1912 because for the next year, according to the city directory, Ethel Bryant did not teach school, and there is clear evidence that she spent part of that time abroad. It would have been the most likely arrangement, if she was going to be married, that she would not return to teaching in the fall of 1912. Ethel Wilson never mentions the broken engagement in any of her memoirs, but she does refer to her ardent wish at one point to leave Vancouver and teach in the Cariboo country, 'where there were horses to ride,'[32] and perhaps this was the time. But the family vetoed her plans ('my Grandmother had extravagant fears of seduction and held a poor opinion of horses'), and she made a trip to England instead.

In this period, a voyage to Europe for any young North American with intellectual or artistic aspirations was a rite of passage in cultural apprenticeship. No one could pretend to be a genuine thinker or artist without having experienced the culture of the 'Old World.' For Ethel Wilson, it was different because she had come from that older culture and had returned to it for her schooling. Yet, there must have been something of the same experience of excitement and discovery in making that trip for the first time chiefly on her own. Unfortunately, it remains a dimly lit period in the story of her life. We know from a photo album that she travelled to England with Philip and Jo Malkin,[33] but other than that the facts are meagre and few. There is a picture of her on the *S.S. Minneapolis* dated 1913, and among her papers there is a program from London's Palace Theatre featuring a dance concert by Pavlova dated 30 April 1913.[34] We can assume that she spent part of that time with her Bryant half-aunts in London, and there is a photograph taken in Cornwall that shows her with her male cousins from Burslem, Harold and Alan Malkin (two of Sydney and Edith's sons). We know she likely made a visit to Burslem because in a letter many years later she mentions a return visit from Canada and the strange pleasure she had in going back to St Luke's Square, where she had lived for a year after her father died: 'looking at the advertisements of the Hanley Blood Tub ('Bind the maiden tightly and Thrust her in and Close the Iron Door Upon her,' the door had spikes in), at the pubs which were un-refined as yet, and reeking, at the closely packed small houses, at the dirt, the fumes, the pottery kilns, the strong tough smutty people.'[35] The only other reference Wilson made to the trip appears in an interview with Ronald Hambleton, in which she describes herself as a young teacher visiting a primary school in a sooty industrial section of one of the pottery towns. The contrast between the cheerless town with not a tree or flower, only the slag heaps from the kilns, and the airy classrooms of Vancouver with its trees and mountains, made her feel sad. She asked herself, '[H]ow can a teacher, with the best will in the world, give [the children] any beauty, or any curiosity?' And she thought of Principal

Burns, who said a teacher must take her pupils from the known to the unknown. But then a tangled-haired, grimy little girl of about seven stood up and recited in a soft Midlands voice Wordsworth's 'I wandered lonely as a cloud,' and she was humbled, recognizing that the English teacher had taken her pupils into the unknown with that poem and they saw daffodils, the yellow host beside the lake, whereas she was only teaching her children in Vancouver jingly, empty rhymes.[36] Staying with her aunt and uncle would have removed her physically from the grimier aspect of the Midlands, for they had sold 'Penrhyn' and built a new home, which they called 'The Limes,' not on the Waterloo Road but on an adjacent arboreal hilltop chiefly inhabited by successful pottery manufacturers. The amenities of this Georgian-style home were perfect in the young woman's eyes, the garden wooded and unspoiled, few smuts rising up from the smoking valley. But still she remembered many years later most vividly a grimy, tangle-haired girl who could recite Wordsworth's poem about a host of yellow daffodils.

There is evidence in her photograph albums that back in Canada she and Marion Martin made a trip at some point in 1913 to visit the Woods family in Edmonton, where she rode horseback, something that had become one of her favourite recreations. Mrs Woods feared that Ethel, who was twenty-five, was going to be an 'old maid' like so many of her aunts. Marion in the meantime was engaged to marry Robert Ward. Certainly the atmosphere was very different in Alberta – there were lots of single young men and very few English formalities were observed in the ranch country. Marjorie Woods Crookston remembered vividly the visit of the two young women from Vancouver: how beautiful Marion was, how alluringly feminine; while Ethel, after brushing her long coppery hair, would pile it in a tight bun on the top of her head in a way that matched her aloof, almost academic manner. She felt Ethel was too reserved and clever to attract young men.[37] Ethel, for her part, remembered Marjorie Woods 'as a most extraordinary young female who shook me with terror in youth, & said & did extraordinary bumptious things (a great success among the boys in Edmonton)' and used to say with grandeur, 'Au revoir pro tem, you peeps.'[38] Marjorie was 'story material' in Ethel's opinion, but there is no evidence that this intimidating acquaintance was the prototype for any of her creations.

We are told by McAlpine that when war broke out in 1914, Ethel Bryant wanted to go overseas and serve as other young women were doing, though McAlpine's evidence is a passage from *The Innocent Traveller*, because Wilson herself does not mention this in her memoirs. But it seems clear from the hiatus in her teaching career that this was an unsettled period in her life; 'a few years' is the title she gives this part of the heroine's life in *Love and Salt Water* to indicate a time that was without direction, forgettable. Before the war, she would have seen other young women from Vancouver going abroad – to study and travel. The three Wilson sisters, whom she knew from the Methodist Church and from summers on Bowen Island, had been spending time in England and on the Continent.[39] Kathleen, who would soon marry Colin Graham and eventually become one of Ethel Wilson's closest friends, went to a finishing school in Dresden, Germany, and then studied music in London for two years. Isabel was enrolled at the London School of Economics. Dr and Mrs Wilson took all three of their daughters and their cousin, Amy Wilson, on a grand tour of the Continent while Kathleen and Isabel were still studying abroad. After they returned, the girls all married into some of Vancouver's most prominent families. Alix Wilson became the wife of Blythe Rogers, another son of B.T. Rogers, the sugar refiner. Isabel married Reginald Tupper (a son of Charles Tupper), and Kathleen married Colin Graham, who was a doctor. McAlpine reports that this was a period of great boredom in Ethel Wilson's life. I suggest, rather, that it was a period of anxious uncertainty, because Ethel Wilson, as I know her, was too earnest and too sensitive to the perils and excitements of living to be simply bored. Why she remained single until age thirty-three when most women at that time were married in their early twenties can only be a matter of speculation. There is no question, as photographs and friends testify, that she was a strikingly beautiful woman, naturally poised and dignified. Perhaps in height and carriage she was a little intimidating to most young men. But perhaps, more likely, her shyness and a high-pitched voice, rapid speech, and nervous laugh were seen to mar her attractiveness. One admirer from that time remembered her as being 'lovely, but almost too ethereal.'[40]

Ethel returned to teaching in the fall of 1914, and life went on as usual at Barclay Street. There continue to be only a few brief glimpses of this time in her life. One is a set of photographs that were taken when she made a trip to Alaska in the summer of 1916 – first by train through the Yukon and then by boat to Skagway. She remembered this trip in a letter many years later, how 'the coast mountains, spanning from north to south, lay white and peculiar in shape, & [how] we stopped at a lovely beach and & sat in the sun & dreamed.'[41] Another glimpse is in a diary kept by her friend Kathleen Graham. Kathleen's husband, Colin, was overseas in the war at this point (Reginald Tupper and Blythe Rogers had also enlisted), and Kathleen was keeping an anxious vigil and trying to distract herself with a busy social calendar: she records simply for 28 December 1915 that she went 'to town in afternoon and then tea at Ethel Bryant's.'[42] Through marriage, the Wilson sisters had left the ostrich egg of their Methodist upbringing behind them, but Ethel Bryant still lived within its confines. Probably the most revealing comment she made on this period in her life is in a letter to Margaret Laurence, in which she states how well she understands the life of Rachel Cameron in *A Jest of God* for she had been an unmarried teacher once too.[43] Like many teachers, she looked forward to vacation time and a trip to the country. In her photo album there are pictures of her taken in 1918 in the Nicola Valley, a part of the country that would serve as a setting for her first published novel, *Hetty Dorval.* One photo is of a group of 'Indians' in the sagebrush hills near Merritt; another is of Ethel herself on horseback.

While the war in Europe went on for four years, the chief disruption on the home front was the outbreak of Spanish influenza, which hit Vancouver in three waves, the worst coming at the very close of the war in October 1918. From 18 October to 19 November schools were closed, public meetings in the city banned, and everyone coming into Vancouver was checked over and watched carefully. Dawson Elementary at Helmcken and Burrard, where Ethel was now teaching, had been turned into a temporary hospital with the desks removed and cots brought in for the sick. There was a severe shortage of doctors and nurses because of the war and because many of the medical personnel were ill, so that a call went out for volunteers, and Ethel Bryant offered her services. She continued to come to school, but instead of teaching her classes, she wore a long white gown with a mask that just left an opening for her eyes. She worked with others to keep the hospital school disinfected and the patients comfortable, but before long she was also stricken and sent to bed. During this time, more than eight hundred in the city died. Ethel was on her feet again when the soldiers started coming home, but she was left with a lifelong propensity for anaemia.

One of her greatest pleasures in those years was entertaining her small cousins, her uncles' children, not only at Barclay Street but at their homes. She would sometimes go to their houses after teaching and stay for supper, telling her young cousins 'marvellous stories that went on from week to week.'[44] But she was losing her immediate family audience as the years passed because the uncles were selling their homes in the West End and building grander homes in Shaughnessy, a new residential area to the south that was quickly becoming (and would remain) the most prestigious area of the city in which to live. The exclusive character of the West End began to erode around 1912 as apartment buildings were put up and small shopkeepers and clerks and various kinds of wage-earning employees took up residence there.[45] That year, Harold Malkin was the first of the Malkin brothers to relocate, building a spacious home he called 'Southlands' at 3266 South West Marine Drive. Fred and his family relocated to 1950 South West Marine Drive a few years later and called his new home 'Trentham.' Philip joined his brothers on Marine Drive across from the Point Grey Golf and Country Club, naming his home 'Dogwoods.' It would now take the families more than half an hour to drive into town. But they continued coming in turns to Barclay Street on Sundays, taking the ladies for a drive, and staying for tea; and sometimes Ethel would spend the weekend with one of the families in Shaughnessy, where she would inevitably tell the children stories.

There is no record of how it came about (perhaps Ethel's gift of amusing children suggested it to the uncles, or perhaps it was suggested by a narrative about South African diamond mines in an adjacent advertisement for Birks jewellers), but in 1919 the Malkin Company ran a serialized story written by Ethel as part of its regular advertising in the *Vancouver Daily Province*. It was titled 'The Surprising Adventures of Peter,' and the author was identified simply as E.D.B. The stories have the traditional elements of adventure – pirates and robbers, a jewelled treasure box, travel in exotic lands, and a faithful dog named Chum – and each instalment included a line-drawing illustration signed by 'F —.'[46] But the commercial purpose behind these stories is fairly transparent: Peter learns about the wonderful properties of vanilla, custard powder, and especially of a 'rare and fragrant herb' called tea. Each little story has a title, and one of these is 'On the Value and Comfort of Tea,' in which the reader is told that tea not only warms and comforts the body but promotes solidity in friendships among those who partake of it together. One can't help but hear the voice of the teetotalling Methodists as well as the city's premier tea salesmen in this didactic passage, as the audience for these stories was just as much the parents reading aloud as the children listening. As Ethel Wilson's first published writings, are these brief narratives distinguished in any way? Not by style certainly, though they are smoothly written, but perhaps in one feature of the content. Peter's first series of adventures takes place after he has gone to bed, fallen asleep, then wakened to find a fatherly figure, Sir

Richard Fenn from another era, at his bedside. Perhaps part of the innocent but curious pleasure of these tales is connected to Freud's idea of the *revenant* (in this case, the return of the dead parent so intimately associated with reading and storytelling), but that is to speculate in ways that the author herself would disparage. Doubtless, she would remind us that she was simply entertaining small children and her uncles were selling tea. The series ran from 3 March to 13 June 1919.

In 'Peter's Farewell,' there is a promise of more stories after the summer holidays, but they did not resume – perhaps because Ethel Bryant's life changed dramatically that year. On 17 March Annie Malkin died at home in bed, her white cap on her head, her Bible at her side. She was eighty-six, and, though she had grown frail, she had not lost her memory nor the strength of her convictions. Her death was natural and peaceful, but it as came as a shock to her granddaughter, who realized how much she loved the tiny little woman who had given her whatever happiness and security she had enjoyed. To express that love, she decided to 'lay her out' on her own, rather than call the undertaker.[47] She knew what had to be done because she had watched and taken part in such preparations at the makeshift hospital the previous fall. After the funeral and a time of grieving had passed, the family decided that the Barclay Street house was too large and should be sold. Belle and Aunt Eliza, who was now seventy-four, took an apartment at Englesea Lodge, a large brick building 'down' at English Bay near Stanley Park, the only building on the water side of Beach Avenue. From here Eliza could more easily extend her pleasure in promenading along the waterfront and engaging in conversation with passers-by, while Belle could enjoy the full unimpeded views of ocean and mountains that surrounded their residence. Yow was no longer needed to prepare their meals and was dismissed. Ethel said good-bye to the 'pepper-pot' and took a room at the Langham Hotel because the family also agreed that at age thirty-one the time had come for her to live independently.

The Langham was a respectable residential hotel on Nelson Street near Burrard, within easy walking distance of Dawson School, though a long walk to the aunts at Englesea Lodge. The occupants had private rooms but took their meals in a common dining room downstairs. The only direct reference Wilson ever made to this period of her life (and it is still an oblique one) was in a television interview when she discussed briefly the lives of some of her humble characters such as Vicky Tritt in 'Tuesday and Wednesday.' She told the interviewer that she had herself once lived in a boarding house, or private hotel, and had observed there women with no flowering in their lives, who had to earn their living, and knew a great deal of loneliness. 'I feel terrific sympathy for anyone who must stand alone and work out their salvation,' she added.[48] In 'Herself When Young,' the orphaned Ellen Cuppy, now in her early thirties, thinks to herself: 'I am one of many many women who are growing older. Many of us work; some 'live at home.' A large number are sublimated in work and interests and friends and are complete as persons and are happy. Some are lonely and unwilling to admit to themselves that they are unhappy. Their days and nights are arid. There is tinned food, but nothing fresh. The late afternoon finds them in a desert country ... [without] companionship, hardly a tent in sight. Shall I come to that country I ask myself?'[49] And in an article, one of her last to be published, Wilson writes that 'of all the sorrows that afflict men and women, loneliness is one of the most common to all, most secret, and most deadly.'[50] From these sober observations, I think we can conclude that this was another of those periods in her life when she was struggling to hold in check that originary experience of abandonment.

Mary McAlpine, nevertheless, creates quite a different picture (and probably both are true). She sees Ethel Bryant exhilarated by her new freedom and enjoying a good deal of popularity among people her own age. If the phone rang in the hall during the evening meal, the diners could be sure it was for Miss Bryant.[51] Certainly Ethel Bryant's sensitivity to the Miss Tritts in such places would have been overshadowed by the attention she was receiving from one of those callers. He was a young doctor, returned from the war, who was going to make a great difference in her life. His name was Wallace Wilson.

CHAPTER FIVE

Wife

1921–1930

No one can write about perfect love because it cannot be committed to words
even by those who know about it. – *Swamp Angel*

Wallace Wilson / The perfect marriage / Mother-in-law / Lac
Le Jeune / Children / Aunt Eliza's apotheosis / President of the
Medical Association / Europe

Few writers have celebrated the happiness of marriage to the degree
that Ethel Wilson did. It was the great fact of her life, far more important than her writing. Once Ethel and Wallace Wilson were married,
their friends and family could never think of them apart, indeed marvelled at the perfection of their union. As a writer, Wilson was sometimes puzzled that there was 'no literature of perfect and lasting
fulfillment of happy love'[1] and concluded that 'no one can write about
perfect love because it cannot be committed to words even by those who
know about it.'[2] Late in life, she would write to a friend that 'it has been
wonderful for us ... beyond imagination.'[3] No rumours or evidence of
mischief and heartbreak would ever mar this picture of perfect accord,
but a critical biography must try to assess what elements constituted
such a union and how they are of significance to the writer's art.

When exactly Ethel and Wallace Wilson first met is difficult to determine. They do not seem to have been linked romantically until after the
war, but it is almost certain they would have known of each other quite a
while before, because Wallace was a first cousin to the Wilson sisters
(Kathleen, Isabel, and Alix), whom Ethel knew from the Methodist
Church and from summers on Bowen Island. They were going out in

the evenings together by the time Ethel was living at the Langham Hotel in 1919, but in a letter to Desmond Pacey, she writes that she first met Wallace in London 'before the war,'[4] and since he was indeed living there and she was also in London in the spring of 1913, this is possibly the case. She would have been twenty-five.

Wallace Algernon Wilson was born the same year as his future wife, but nine months later – on 10 October 1888. His parents, originally from Ontario, were living then in Manitoba, where his father, Robert Wilson, shared a medical practice in Morden with his brother, David. When Wallace was four years of age and his younger sister, Amy, was two, the doctors moved further west with their young families to set up a practice together in Vancouver. But just a few months later, on 24 May 1893, Robert Wilson died at the age of forty-one.[5] Shortly thereafter, his widow moved her small family back to Ontario, where she was dependent on her parents, who farmed at Bell's Corners, near Ottawa. Their subsequent deaths left Bella Wilson enough money to live in Ottawa and eventually to send her son to the University of Toronto. From boyhood, 'Algie' (as his mother and sister called him) had determined to be a doctor like his father, but his impetuous, often clownish, behaviour as a boy left his relatives more than a little anxious about his future.[6] On one occasion, his Uncle David and cousin Alix came from Vancouver to visit his brother's family. A teenaged Wallace was late in meeting them at the train station, but when he saw their horse-drawn cab moving along the street, he pulled open the door and threw himself at their feet, welcoming them to Ottawa with a grin. In 1909, after completing his bachelor of arts at University of Toronto, he entered the university's medical school. He was a first-class student, but his love of pranks had not diminished. One evening he persuaded his friends at the laboratory to help him dress up the classroom skeleton – trousers, shirt and tie, coat, scarf, and hat – and they carried it out into the street with its arms across their shoulders. They got into a cab and drove off to their favourite pub. There, they set the skeleton up in a dignified position in the window of the cab, where it was partially illuminated by the street light. They paid the driver to wait, and from inside the pub, over their pints, they laughed at the reactions of people passing by.

In 1911, at his uncle's encouragement, Wallace applied to intern at Vancouver General Hospital. It is possible, of course, that he may have known Ethel Bryant during that year, although there is no record of their meeting. Wallace had been raised a Baptist, and so he and Ethel were not likely to meet through church activities. Certainly there was no very involved relationship because in 1912 Wallace left to do a post-graduate specialization in England. His mother also travelled abroad that year, wintering in Florence. He aspired to work with the famous Canadian physician William Osler, who was by then a professor of medicine at Oxford, and McAlpine reproduces an invitation Wilson received from Osler setting up a visit to the ward and laboratories at Oxford for 21 November 1912.[7] Whether he made that visit is now impossible to determine, but one can say with certainty that he did not work with Osler. Rather, he took a course in operative surgery that winter at Dreadnaught Hospital and decided, after gruelling hours of training on corpses in cold hospital laboratories, that he would not be a surgeon. According to McAlpine, he also pursued for one sweltering summer in New York City the possibility of a specialty in obstetrics. But these ambitions were set aside in favour of a general practice in Vancouver, which he set up under his uncle's guidance. That too, however, was short-lived because in July 1915 he joined the Royal Canadian Medical Corps and shipped out that fall to serve at Thessaloniki, a base for Allied operations in northern Greece. Serving in the same unit was Colin Graham, who was now married to his cousin Kathleen, one of Ethel Bryant's friends. Wallace did not come back to Vancouver until the war was over in November 1918.

If a little story McAlpine reports is accurate, then Wallace and Ethel were beginning to spend time in each other's company shortly after the close of the war. She writes that one day Ethel came into the parlour to tell her grandmother she was going out and that when she stooped to kiss her, the old lady asked where she was going. 'To the tea dance at the Vancouver Hotel,' was Ethel's reply, 'with Dr. Wilson.' 'But how kind of Dr. Wilson,' said her grandmother looking pleased. 'I didn't tell her,' said Ethel years later, 'that it was Wallace and not his uncle who was escorting me.'[8] Annie Malkin died just four months after the war ended, and this provides a date for the beginning of the courtship. Wallace's cousin, Alix, would remember that they began to see each other more frequently after Ethel moved to the Langham Hotel. Ethel discovered that this tall man with the attractive round face, large eyes, and big smile was not only a good dancer but that he had a number of interests in common with hers. They both enjoyed tennis and swimming, and they both liked to read. From an early point in their courtship, they started giving each other books and would spend long hours reading out loud in each other's company. And now that Annie Malkin was gone and Ethel could openly cultivate her love for the theatre, Wallace took her to plays and concerts. But perhaps what they enjoyed together most was the world of nature, long walks in Stanley Park and drives out in the country.

In early summer of 1920, Wallace proposed marriage, and Ethel sent her resignation to the Vancouver School Board on July 26. The engagement lasted through the fall, but there was no busy preparation for the wedding because they had decided on a small, simple ceremony. Ethel's deeply ingrained shyness dictated against any kind of showy social event with bridesmaids and a reception; moreover, at nearly thirty-three, she could no longer be the blushing young bride and so was even more determined not to be part of a spectacle. The marriage took place on the evening of 4 January 1921, a night of heavy rain. Uncle Harold was chosen to give the bride away, and he picked her up at the hotel and escorted her under his black umbrella to the car. In a letter years later, she wrote: 'When I was getting into Uncle Harold's car on this streaming wet wedding night, a handsome young English schoolboy who was staying with him said solemnly, "Miss Bryant, the Nuptial Hour Approaches!" I was shaking with fright.'[9] There were notices of the wedding in all of the Vancouver papers; the one carried by the *Vancouver Daily World* contains the most detail:

> The wedding was solemnized quietly on Tuesday evening in Wesley Methodist Church, Rev. R.J. McIntyre officiating, of Miss Ethel Davis Bryant, daughter of the late Rev. and Mrs Robert William Bryant, to Mr Wallace Wilson, son of the late Dr. Robert Wilson and Mrs Wilson, Nicola St. The church had been beautifully decorated for the occasion with palms and the season's flowers. The bride, who was given away by her uncle, Mr W.H. Malkin, wore a becoming suit of dark blue gabardine set off by Russian sable furs, and a small hat with a crown of silver lace and a brim of navy ostrich feathers, trimmed with French flowers. Her corsage bouquet was of Ophelia roses. During the signing of the register, Mrs Clelland sang Foster's 'Psalm of Love.' Both the bride and groom were unattended and after the ceremony left for Penticton. On their return they will take up residence in Vancouver.[10]

Whether they actually spent a honeymoon in the Okanagan Valley is unclear. A trip of this kind is not mentioned in the other newspaper accounts, and McAlpine, who conceivably discussed this with the author, says they did not take a trip directly after their winter wedding.[11] One reason may have been that Wallace, though professionally still very young, had just been given a senior appointment at Vancouver General Hospital and did not feel he could leave his post for very long. But another likely reason was they wished to make a somewhat rigorous trip up-country that was not really practical until better weather. The destination Wallace had in mind was a little lake high in the wooded hills south of Kamloops, known then simply as Fish Lake.

In the meantime, Ethel Wilson had to accustom herself to a new life which, in one respect unfortunately, was not so very different from the old. At the time of getting married, Wallace was living in the West End in a rented stone-and-timber bungalow at the north corner of Nicola and Beach Avenue with his mother. The small house at 1409 Nicola was perhaps the oldest home in Vancouver's West End.[12] It had no modern facilities: it was heated by a series of fireplaces, and had no refrigerator – food was kept cool in a wooden meat safe standing outside on the kitchen stoop. Wallace's sister, Amy, had married Ernest Buckerfield, and they were living in a small apartment where there was no room for Mrs Wilson, senior. Nor apparently would there be room for her when the Buckerfields moved to a house in Shaughnessy. So she remained at Beach Avenue with her son, which was not easy for his nervous new wife. Alix Wilson would say to Mary McAlpine: 'At the age of thirty-three, and after living with her grandmother and her aunts, [Ethel] felt, I think, that she had done her duty and now life was to be enjoyed and she should be free to enjoy it.'[13] Alix remembered Mrs Wilson, her aunt, as a dour woman without a sense of humour, though some remembered her for her laugh. Whatever the case, she was known to be difficult in her relations with others. When her parents died near Ottawa, for example, she engaged in a bitter quarrel with her brother over the disposition of the family property and never visited him again.[14] She had been widowed when she was young and her life had not been easy, and though Wallace was now thirty-two, it was hard for her to share her home and her son with his new wife. Wallace had always lived with his mother, except when he was at university or serving in the war. She was extremely close to him, and when they were apart she wrote him long, coquettish letters.[15] For Ethel it was a classic mother-in-law situation.[16] Wallace was busy with a growing practice and was away all day, leaving his mother and wife to share the running of the house. Ethel's sole duty was to answer the telephone and make a list of the patients who called for Wallace. There were inevitable tensions (Mrs Wilson called her son 'Algie,' while Ethel pointedly called him Wallace), but Ethel was too well brought up to rebel or create scenes, and when she found herself overimed by Bella Wilson's demands or her presence at the piano, her smile became a little stiff and she withdrew to her room, where she read and sometimes just took to her bed.

The postponed honeymoon, when she and Wallace were finally able to make the trip up-country in the summer of 1921, was a respite from domestic tensions and a time when Ethel Wilson could at last experience the full joy of her marriage. Their route by automobile would have been the narrow, often precarious road along the Fraser River, and they would have most likely stopped the first night at a hotel in the town of Lytton. This is where the two great rivers, the Thompson and the Fraser, converge, and where the blue and white Thompson is swallowed up and disappears into the swollen and muddy Fraser. For Ethel Wilson it was a powerful, perhaps frightening, sight and would occupy her imagination for years until it finally emerged in her fiction, most notably in *Hetty Dorval.*

The next day, they would likely have continued on through the sagebrush country, which is sometimes wooded but often barren, until they reached Kamloops, the cowboy town where cattle were collected for shipment to the slaughterhouses in Vancouver. From there a deeply rutted dirt road would have taken them high up into the hills forested with firs and lodge-pole pines, to an elevation over 4,000 feet, where they would come suddenly to Fish Lake. There is only one way to describe the effect of that discovery on the author, and that is to quote a passage from one of her short stories written almost forty years later:

> [A]nd when I got there, I tell you my heart rose up the way it does when you see your favourite lake away up in the hills all shining and saying Come on, Come on, and the sky all blue and the reflections of the forest upside down in the water and everything as innocent as a kitten. That lake is nearly forty-five hundred feet up and even in summer after hot days it can be cold and you can have storms like winter but there's a smell of the pines there and especially when the sun's on them and even when the rain's been on them, and all the way up there's the smell of the sage too. And right away when you see the fish jumping and hear the loons crying ... you know – well, it's heart's desire, that's what it is.[17]

Wallace had come to this particular lake because it was internationally renowned for its fly-fishing, especially for the abundant but elusive Kamloops trout. The first hotel had been established at this location in 1885, but accommodations in the 1920s were still modest.[18] When the Wilsons went in 1921 there was a two-storey lodge with a porch on the front, and among the trees on each side there were small log cabins. Meals and much discussion of weather took place in the lodge's dining room. One could take walks through the pine woods or along the lake, but the Wilsons would have spent the best part of their time in a clinker-built rowboat casting for the trout that sometimes swirl to the surface and other times rise up and hit the water with a plop. What fly to use and where to fish – in the centre of the lake or among the tule reeds nearer the shore – these were the kinds of questions discussed with the other guests and the owners of the lodge, who were a comfortable English couple when the Wilsons first went there. Ethel soon learned to be an avid fisher.

They returned each year, often in the crisp blue and gold days of September, taking a cabin on the hill overlooking the lake, and they followed a routine that they probably established during their honeymoon summer. After a day on the lake, they would row back to the lodge in the late afternoon, bathe, change out of their fishing clothes, and have drinks either on the porch or inside by the heater if the day was cold. At dinner, they traded anecdotes with other guests about the flies they used and the ever popular fish that got away. If it rained, they were content to stay inside and read because they brought a suitcase full of books and periodicals with them. Ethel thrilled to think how wild the country was outside the human sphere of the lodge – 'to think of loons on the lake, bears hidden in the woods, timber wolves nearby, otters, skunk, beaver.'[19]

Ethel Wilson is remembered at the lake as being self-assured, confident, almost extroverted, taking part in the dining-room conversation and amusing everyone with her witty remarks. At the lake, she emerged from her shyness and basked in the security that Wallace's love provided for her. Without question, a powerful component in that 'perfect love' the Wilsons enjoyed was the tremendous sense of safety and well-being that Ethel enjoyed within Wallace's protective sphere. In turn, her intelligence, humour, and beauty, always pervaded by a yielding gratitude to this man who had rescued her from loneliness, made Ethel a perfect wife and companion. As Muriel Whitaker, one of the lodge owners, has observed, the Wilsons certainly felt 'the inner rapture' of playing and landing a lively Kamloops trout, but clearly more important to them was the peculiar intimacy of being confined for several hours in a twelve-foot boat. In the 1930s, Fish Lake was renamed Lac Le Jeune in honour of a pioneer Catholic missionary in the area. In her fiction, Ethel Wilson would return to the lake several times, where it would be called Nimpish

Lake, Blue Lake, and, in *Swamp Angel,* her best-known work, Three
Loon Lake. Whatever its name, it remained for the author, and for her
husband, 'heart's desire.'

It was probably not easy for Ethel Wilson to return to Vancouver and a
life of compromise in what she felt was her mother-in-law's house. Her
sister-in-law, Amy, came to see her mother almost every day, and the two
liked to play the piano and sing. The human voice, Wilson complained
more than once, was her least favourite instrument.[20] She couldn't help
being irritated by Amy's frequent presence: the latter made no room for
her mother in her own house, yet came by every day to check on her
and stay for tea. Bella Wilson liked to entertain, and Ethel was required
to play the equable hostess to her mother-in-law's circle of friends. The
Wilsons employed a servant, so that she could not excuse herself to the
kitchen; rather, she was expected to take an eager part in the conversation. Years later, she described to writer friends those painfully difficult
social occasions, which frequently 'terrified' her: '"*teas*" they chiefly
were, of all abominations – 1 a day 2 a day 3 a day & everyone talking
more & louder & faster. As a young doctor's wife I did my best.'[21] But
she felt her best was woefully inadequate, and her early years of married
life were not the happiest ones.

Bella Wilson felt the tension and sought opportunities to travel and
visit friends. She was in Los Angeles in the fall and winter of 1921–2, and
in a letter she received from her daughter, Amy, we get a glimpse of
Ethel the first Christmas she was married. Amy had stopped for a visit at
the Nicola Avenue bungalow, and Ethel had shown her Wallace's
present to her – a beaver coat that had been in the family for many years
but had been refurbished. It had come out beautifully and was very
smart looking in Amy's opinion. 'Why were we so slow!' she exclaimed
with a tinge of envy.[22] She reported to her mother that Ethel wanted to
buy new chintz coverings for the chesterfield and chairs, but reminded
her mother that they in fact belonged to her and that when the time
came for her to live with her and Ernest, she would want them for her
own sitting room. Amy was aware of the tensions between Ethel and her
mother, but while promising her mother that some day she would be
invited to come and live at her home, she also had to negotiate a
mother-in-law situation with her husband, Ernest. In the same letter, to
curry her mother's favour, she complained that Ethel was being anti-
social. Amy had put together a group of friends for badminton and supper, but Ethel complained that so many at the party meant less time on
the courts. Ethel had refused to join the picnic-style supper; she and

Wallace had played a little longer and then gone home. In 1922, Ethel, Wallace, and Bella Wilson all moved out to a larger house at 1238 Connaught Avenue in Shaughnessy, but the domestic situation had not really changed. Ethel's response increasingly was withdrawal, and one of Wallace's cousins remembered a period in the 1920s when Ethel was thought to have suffered 'a little nervous breakdown.'[23]

Perhaps the social tension and inadequacy she felt was exacerbated by the failure to have children. The Wilsons never discussed their childless state with family or friends, and whether they actually wanted a family or not has been debated. Most people who knew them assumed their childlessness was not by choice.[24] Ethel Wilson had a special rapport with children, an ability to create a direct line of communication. She played a game with them: while touching parts of her body and keeping her mouth closed, she made a trilling sound. She would then invite the child to touch her, and if it was the right spot, she would let out another mysterious trill. They would both laugh and now be friends. If she felt the game had been played long enough, there would be no more trill and she would say the little bell must be broken, and the child would accept that.[25] Her photograph albums are filled with pictures of friends' children and the generations of little cousins that were born in the Malkin family. (Nancy Malkin Rowell, the last-born of the first cousins, was nearly thirty years younger than Ethel was.) Eventually, during the Second World War, the Wilsons took into their home a girl evacuated from England, whom they would refer to as their daughter and whom they remained close to, and anxious about, as if she were their own. One of Wallace's friends rudely inquired why they didn't have children, and he is reported to have answered in his jocular fashion that he didn't want to spoil Ethel's figure.[26] Two people who had known the Wilsons suggested to me that Ethel could never have shared Wallace with anyone, not even with a child.[27] I doubt if this was the case exactly. Women, especially in Ethel Wilson's social circumstances, were expected to have children, and perhaps not giving Wallace a child made her feel anxious and appear possessive in her relationship with her husband.

But there was no absence of family in their lives, and one of the liveliest family events that Ethel Wilson would save up for her writing took place in the fall of 1924. Since the royal visit in 1901 and Queen Mary's subsequent patronage of the Vancouver branch of the London Needlework Guild, Aunt Eliza had been in correspondence with the Queen every Christmas. In her 1923 letter, Eliza announced that she would soon be eighty, but that she was planning to visit England in the coming

year. To everyone's surprise (though perhaps not to Aunt Eliza), her
Majesty's secretary wrote to Miss Edge requesting that she come to tea,
specifying the day and hour. Just Miss Edge and Her Majesty! The meeting with the Queen comprises the chapter 'Apotheosis' in *The Innocent
Traveller* and focuses on how Great-Uncle John, who accompanied his
sister to Buckingham Palace in 1924, was made to stay behind in the
waiting room and how 'Aunty Topaz' told the Queen all the family news
from Vancouver. McAlpine, presumably from discussing the event with
the author, adds some contextual detail.[28] Belle Malkin accompanied
her aunt on the long trip to London, but by the time they had stepped
off the boat in Southampton and made the trip into the city, Eliza had
become overwrought by the crowds and the excitement of the forthcoming audience with the Queen. So she sent her regrets to the Palace,
but her Majesty, apparently sorry the appointment had to be cancelled,
arranged for another day and hour when she hoped Miss Edge would be
feeling better. And when that day arrived, she was indeed better and the
meeting took place, with a crestfallen brother John waiting for half an
hour in an antechamber.

It had been arranged that after the event in London, John would
accompany his sister and niece on a trip to Italy. They were joined by
cousin Edna Edge Dean, who had been the bridesmaid at the marraige
of Ethel's parents and was still known as the great beauty in the family.
The elderly foursome set off for Rome in November, but by the time
they reached Florence, it was clear that Belle was ill. A doctor was con-
sulted, who concluded her condition was serious, and so they turned
back for England. From there Belle made arrangements for them to
return home to Vancouver. She was in severe pain, and in Vancouver
her doctor diagnosed cancer. It was a long illness and an agonizingly
slow death – taking nearly two years. In *The Innocent Traveller* it is elided
to part of a sentence: 'the dreadful event – too tragical to contemplate –
occurred which took the life of Rachel with great suffering ...'[29] Belle
had spent her life (she was sixty-six when she died) serving others, and
there was an aura of personal unfulfilment about this severe, slightly
mannish single woman. Children did not warm to her; she was remembered instead as 'a rather terrifying lady.'[30] But Ethel Wilson was
haunted by the story of Aunt Belle's life, one which she knew might
have been hers if she had not met Wallace, and years later she told her
evacuee daughter about her last visit at the deathbed.[31] She was sitting
in a chair, watching and thinking what a good dutiful person her aunt
had been, when something compelled her to lean forward over the ema-

ciated figure and look into her eyes, now dull from exhaustion, and to say, 'Aunty Belle, you do know that you are the best friend I ever had and am likely to have.' Belle's eyes cleared and she sighed, and the niece felt certain at that moment that she was thinking, 'My life has been worthwhile after all.' Wilson said she didn't know what made her say that, but it seemed inspired by God.

There was an important change in Ethel Wilson's life in 1927. After more than six years of living in the same house with her mother-in-law, Ethel was at last to have the house alone with her husband. Probably the domestic tensions had been discussed at length between Wallace and his sister, because in 1927 the Buckerfields built a large home on fashionable South West Marine Drive, overlooking the Fraser River, and arranged for Bella to have a room built for herself in the new house. From a distance, Ethel was now able to express the loyalty and affection for Wallace's family that she genuinely felt, and she and her sister-in-law carried on a clever and friendly correspondence about their mutual friends and acquaintances, though Ethel would always feel uneasy about her difficult relation with her mother-in-law. This is strikingly evident in a little incident that arose when she was publishing her first novel, *Hetty Dorval*. She had unwittingly given her mother-in-law's first name to a small-town woman of easy virtue, a character of little worth. By then Bella had been dead for several years (she died in 1933), but when Ethel realized what she had done she flew into a panic and contacted her publisher, and although the novel was already in galleys, Macmillan changed Bella to Nella.[32]

But just when married life was at last comfortable and easy, it became difficult again. Wallace, who was a genial, generous, and popular man, was becoming known professionally for his dedication as a doctor and humanitarian, and also for his excellence as an administrator, and he was, accordingly, elected president of the British Columbia Medical Association in 1928. (His uncle, Dr David Wilson, had been the first president of the Vancouver Medical Association in 1898.) He accepted the post and Ethel was proud and pleased for him, but terrified for herself. Her role was to play either hostess or honoured guest at endless teas, cocktail parties, and dinners, sometimes mixing with two and three hundred people at once. This would be the case for much of her married life, during which time she would meet internationally famous and influential men such as Baron Rothschild, Sir Robert Ouvry, and Baron von Heydebreck, a German financier. Her lack of self-confidence and her sensitivity to all the frightening degrees of snobbery implicated in dress

codes, manners, and behaviour made this social life a continuously terrifying prospect. Wallace was distanced by his long hours at work and by
his untiring pleasure in his role as host and association president. Further, Ethel's Uncle Harold Malkin was the newly elected mayor of Vancouver, which put her in an even brighter spotlight. Few suspected that
Ethel Wilson was agonized by the part she had to play. She had been
taught when growing up that it was unkind to make others feel ill at ease,
so that instead of behaving with the reserve that was natural to her, she
forced herself to be outgoing at social functions, talking and laughing
with people as they enjoyed canapés and cocktails, even though, as
McAlpine writes, her smile felt as if it was set in concrete and could crack
at any minute into a thousand pieces and clatter to the floor.[33] Ethel
seemed to be in high spirits on these occasions, and this prompted some
women to make fun of her, to imitate her gushiness and shrill laughter
behind her back. They had no notion that beneath this unassailably
beautiful social creature there was a woman who felt a great deal of fear
and contempt for these occasions and wanted to run away.

The reward for this year in the spotlight was to be able to leave Vancouver and live in Europe for several months while Wallace did post-
graduate work in internal medicine in Vienna. They were not alone:
Kathleen and Colin Graham (their Wilson-family cousins) travelled with
them, as Colin, whose specialization was ears, nose, and throat, had also
arranged to do post-graduate work in Vienna. The two couples enjoyed
an easy camaraderie abroad and a close friendship that lasted the rest of
their lives.[34] Kathleen, born in 1889, was the oldest of the Wilson sisters
and had been a pupil at Miss Gordon's school when it opened. Ethel
had also known Kathleen and her sisters from the Methodist Church
and from those youthful summers on Bowen Island, although she had
been a little in awe of all three girls, who were socially accomplished and
made early, distinguished marriages into the Tupper and Rogers families. Wallace and Colin not only shared the interests of the medical profession, but they were both enthusiastic fly-fishermen, and in the 1920s
the Wilsons and Grahams went on fishing trips together to Lac Le Jeune
and Paul Lake in the Kamloops area. The Grahams had two children, a
son, Colin (nicknamed 'Budge'), and a daughter, Joan, whom the Wilsons regarded not with jealousy but with great interest and deep affection. Kathleen (known in the family as 'Kitty') was the shyest of the
Wilson sisters, and Ethel found herself, during their year together in
Europe, the leader in their activities.

The trip began with a stop in England, which gave Ethel the longed-for opportunity at last to introduce Wallace to her English families, especially the Bryant half-aunts in London. There are no letters or diaries that have survived from that year abroad, but there is a reference in the unpublished essay 'Private Happiness' to one of Hannah Atkinson's sons that makes it clear she and Wallace were in England in 1929. Her Aunt Hannah's sons were now grown men, one at least six foot four. Most of the Malkins were short, and so Ethel liked to think of her own height as being a Bryant trait. This tall, dark half-cousin, she writes, had a passion for archaeology, and when they met that year he had been 'tramping France with a few francs in his pocket, walking to wherever diggings of Roman remains could be found.'[35] She recognized a kindred spirit in this love for antiquity. As she had hoped, Wallace found this branch of the family especially interesting and would return with her to visit them at least twice more.

For a glimpse of the time spent in Vienna, we have only a brief reference to that year in an interview she gave many years later and in the short story 'We Have to Sit Opposite,' which records some of the experiences that Ethel and Kathleen had in the shops and art galleries of Vienna while their husbands were occupied with study and work. In the interview, we learn that the two couples would sometimes travel to Budapest and dine to the accompaniment of gypsy musicians. Both women collected antiques and were especially drawn to old silver, but their pleasure in shopping was undercut by the depressed state of the city, a foretaste of what they would encounter on their return to North America. Ethel remembered the poverty-stricken Viennese people forming long queues to obtain two or three slices of brown bread, or a few cigarettes.[36] The greater part of 'We Have to Sit Opposite,' however, tells of the two women travelling on their own by train to Munich and the outrageous fun they had telling tall tales about Canada to some rudely inquisitive German passengers. '"In Canada I have a bear. I have two bears," said Mrs Forrester conceitedly,' while her friend Mrs Montrose (the name alluding to one of Kathleen Graham's family names) informs the amazed travellers sitting opposite, '"I myself have five bears. My father has seven bears. That is nothing. It is the custom."' Years later, Wilson explained in a letter that she had hesitated to publish the story because she feared 'being "branded" with racial feeling,' but that the episode on the train 'was something that really happened.'[37] What is evident here is the conspiratorial fun the two women had together, Ethel in the lead, and, from letters written many years later, it is clear that the fun in this relationship never diminished.

The year abroad culminated in a cruise of the Mediterranean in the early spring of 1930. Wilson's photo albums give evidence of an itinerary that stretched from Gibraltar to the Middle East, including Palestine. At least four places left an indelible impression on the future writer. In a letter to her seven-year-old niece, Mary Buckerfield, on hotel paper from the Luxor Winter Palace, Ethel describes the heat and the colour and clamour of present-day Egyptian life.[38] But in one of her most powerful short stories, 'Haply the Soul of My Grandmother,' she tells of a couple visiting the Valley of the Kings and of being offered the purchase of a mummified human hand. The husband and wife feel suffocated by the airless tombs and by the hand wrapped in tattered grave-clothes, but most of all by the anonymous ancientness of the place and their own temporal insignificance as human creatures. The Wilsons felt more comfortable in the Arabian city of Acre, anchored reassuringly to the historical drama of Saladin and Richard the Lion Heart.[39] A piece of unpublished travel writing preserves Wilson's impressions of visiting the back streets of Algiers and of being taken one night to view a belly dancer perform.[40] The street down which they follow the guide is narrow and foul-smelling, and the dancer, while skilled, is old and obese: 'She danced standing still and her arms hung limp by her sides like the arms of a dreadful doll. Her stomach and breasts revolved under creased and dingy veils.' An old man listlessly beat a drum and a sinister-looking youth played a pipe. The visitors want to fly from the room, yet they are mesmerized by 'the skill of the shameless dancer who looked arrogantly upon them and stood rotating her stomach as an owl wrings its own neck.' Another disturbing place was the city of Istanbul, where she saw starving cats devouring dead cats – 'with all its implications,' she wrote more than twenty-five years later.[41]

Their experience of Greece, by contrast, left no sinister imprint on Wilson's writing, aside perhaps from an increased awareness once again of life's brevity and transience. Visiting the Athenian acropolis, she writes that 'we perishable ones look up at the [handmaidens] still supporting with modest dignity the southern portico of the small temple ... The wind blows freely through the warmly pale pillars and through the sublime ruins of the greater temple.' The narrator of 'Herself When Young' reflects that 'perhaps the unforeseen destiny of the Parthenon was that it should be the most glorious sight in ruins (but not ruined) that the spirit and mind and hand of man could achieve. Its beauty and the sense, not of the past but, of the flowing of all Time, make one silent upon the Acropolis.'[42] Likely she remembered Miss Mould's Greek history classes when she wrote of Pericles walking and talking in that place and when she wrote in conclusion that 'nearly everything that is significant in thought and form, nearly everything that is beautiful in principle and in prospect is in the air that blows through these ruins on the Acropolis.' Years later, she remembered most of all a quality of light in Greece and 'how it shone from rock & wall, like no other light.'[43]

In the summer of 1930, the Wilsons and Grahams returned, perhaps reluctantly, to Vancouver to resume their work and social responsibilities, but their subsequent lives suggest they were energized and valuably educated by that year abroad.

CHAPTER SIX

Apprentice
1930–1939

Apprenticeship / 'Aunty Spends the Day' / The Depression /
The politics of medicine / *New Statesman and Nation* / Trip to England /
The Lynds / Uncle Herbert

When did Ethel Wilson begin to think of herself as a writer? Her own story of how she came to her craft is a simple but somewhat disingenuous one. In interviews and talks she gave, she repeatedly described herself with great modesty as a doctor's wife with a very full social calendar who, late in life, had a notion to write. She said that she had written a few stories in the late 1930s, working in the car while her husband attended meetings and called on the sick. She had no ambitions to be published, she said, but was pressed by a friend to send one of her stories to the *New Statesman and Nation* in England, where, to her surprise, it was accepted. She said that during the Second World War, because of her husband's military service and her own Red Cross work, she forgot her writing and that it was not until 1946, while her husband was away and she was involved in arranging a medical convention in Banff, that she turned to writing again, completing in three weeks her first novel, *Hetty Dorval*. Accordingly, we have a colourful story associated with Ethel Wilson – that of the natural, untutored writer, the wife of a prominent Vancouver doctor, who turned whimsically to writing fiction and published her first book when she was nearly sixty years old.[1]

The Wilson Papers at the University of British Columbia Library, however, tell quite a different story. Among her papers there is a notebook that reveals she was working on *The Innocent Traveller* as early as 1930, nearly twenty years before it was actually published. We learn from her correspondence that in the 1930s she was trying to place her work in book form with major publishing houses in the United States.[2] Further, we learn that during the war she made contact with the Macmillan Company in Toronto and began the long process of turning her stories of Aunt Eliza into a publishable book. The idea of writing, moreover, was not taken lightly. Years later, she wrote that when she was young 'there was only a subsoil of consciousness of the arts in the west ... and I was frightened to take up a pencil & "write"; it seemed an absurd thing to do, bumptious.'[3] Ethel Wilson, then, was not exactly the untutored or unambitious writer she portrayed herself to be in public but, on the contrary, served a particularly long and earnest apprenticeship.

We can trace its outlines back to her natural gift for storytelling, which her young cousins remembered so vividly, and which had its first published expression in 'The Surprising Adventures of Peter' in 1919. Then, in the late 1920s, after the Buckerfields had moved with Bella Wilson out to South West Marine Drive, Ethel and her sister-in-law, Amy, began writing letters to each other, which, despite the telephone, was still regarded as the civilized way to communicate. Amy Buckerfield kept some of these among her memorabilia, and they include six fictional letters exchanged between sisters-in-law in 'Dumpshire' England in the early nineteenth century.[4] Here we get our first glimpse of Ethel Wilson's sense of humour, her delight particularly in mocking through misspellings, punctuation, and grammar the pretensions of people of all ranks and classes. The full set of letters describes a world of domineering but kindly husbands, friends, servants, and an unwanted relative. They focus on the elopement of Sir H. Stukely's daughter, Dora, with a riding master, and a go-between is suspected. The sixth letter from Eliza begins: 'O my dear Sister-in-law prepare yr. Self for this Shocking News. The Gilty Person on whom Sir H. Stukely's vengence is set is none other than yr. Willful Niece Camilla. O my dr. S.i.l. could I ever describe to you the Sene in our Hall yesterday when I innacently descending the Stares was confronted by the Angry Man.' The plot of the letters has fun with Ethel's personal experience of the horse-riding set, and one suspects there are veiled allusions here to Ethel and Amy's mutual acquaintances. In a *P.S.*, Eliza writes: 'I am Upp but Distrakted. Camilla rode away on her pony this p.m. & has not Yett returned. Estella Wormley who dropt in for a moment to Commiserate with me says she gest this all along but Dursent Breathe a word.' At the top of one of these letters to Amy, Wilson wrote: 'I think for pastime and amusement I'll write a series of letters called "My Dear Sister-in-Law" & send them to a maga-

zine. I'll probably peter out when it comes to doing it.' There is no indication that she went any further with the idea.

But a notebook dated 17 September 1930 gives evidence that she was
beginning to think seriously about a series of stories concerning the
Malkin family, that would stretch back to the mid-nineteenth century.[5]
One might wonder at first, looking at the notebook, if the opening date
was perhaps the title for a story episode, but after a break in the notes
comes the date September 18, followed by more notes and then another
interruption, which is marked 'later,' suggesting pretty clearly that this
was a work journal from that year. The notes, twenty handwritten pages
in all, are untitled, but they use the actual names of Edge and Malkin
family members, leaving no doubt about their origin or connection to
The Innocent Traveller. Whether she saw herself at first as writing fiction
or a family history is impossible to determine at this point; but the use of
actual names seemed necessary in order for her to start writing.

Her inspiration for the book remained close at hand and a continuing lively presence in the Wilsons' lives. After Belle Malkin died in 1926,
Aunt Eliza Edge, who was by then eighty-one, took rooms at Douglas
Lodge, an apartment building on Granville Street at Twelfth Avenue.
There she lived for another seventeen years, eventually employing a
nurse-companion, remembered by the family as simply Miss Bridges.
Her world had shrunk, as most of her contemporaries were gone; but
she continued to find life immensely interesting and still talked non-
stop to anyone she encountered and wrote lengthy letters back to
England to family members, friends, and distant acquaintances. Her
enthusiasm for England remained so strong that she even sent a box of
Okanagan apples to Labour leader Ramsay MacDonald every fall while
he was prime minister.[6] But the highlights of her week were a regular
Friday visit with Ethel 'to spend the day' and a Sunday drive out to one
of the nephews' houses. The nephews took turns. James Malkin remembered that for several years in the 1930s it was his duty every third Sunday afternoon to fetch Aunt Eliza from the Lodge and take her to his
parents' home in Kerrisdale 'for a cup of tea and a doze.' To a young
man in his late teens and early twenties, she seemed 'a terrible old bore,
talking and never listening,' but he remembered how kind Ethel was to
her.[7] In her novel, Wilson describes the commotion of her Aunt Eliza's
arrival Friday morning, burdened down with parasol, walking stick, and
several handbags stuffed with slippers, shawl, hats, books, and letters,
the taxi driver bringing up the rear with a rug and an umbrella. She
would stay and talk the whole day – through lunch, afternoon tea

(sometimes Kathleen Graham joined them), and dinner after Wallace had arrived home from work. He was fond of Aunt Eliza and enjoyed teasing her, and she in turn was flattered and, according to *The Innocent Traveller*, would become intoxicated by her success with this genial important man. In turn, she would become slightly critical of her niece, puzzled that this shy great-niece sitting 'mum as a mouse' was running her own house and had such a fine husband. Again according to the novel, she would criticize the way Ethel had taken up smoking, the way she dressed in a short skirt to play tennis, and how she seemed lackadaisical: '"You must be doing *something*. You should be more lively, Rose, more interested in everything."'

Perhaps through Aunt Topaz's words, Ethel Wilson was making a critical estimate of herself and her way of life at that time. She was now part of the leisured class in Vancouver, whose women managed servants and spent most of the day enjoying the privilges of their wealth and status. Ethel and Wallace Wilson were not exactly wealthy, but they were not affected financially by the Depression. In 1931 Wallace had been admitted to the Royal College of Physicians and Surgeons, and he set up a flourishing practice in the Medical-Dental Building on fashionable West Georgia Street. The Wilsons owned their own home in Shaughnessy, could afford to employ a cook and a gardener, and were able to spend time travelling, which included the annual fishing trip to Lac Le Jeune. But the presence in Vancouver of so many destitute people, victims of the economic depression, eroded Ethel's sense of well-being. She was always sensitive to and affected by the hardships and humiliations suffered by humble people. In her letter from Egypt to her little niece, Mary Buckerfield, she explained that flies covered the faces of the poor children, but that rich children were provided with protective veils.[8] She remembered years later how she and Wallace lived in the 1930s and viewed life from a physically comfortable but anxious angle, always distressed at things as they were but 'not knowing the answer.'[9] She remembered the terrible contrast between no work for hundreds of thousands of men and women, while Wallace was continually overworked. As a housewife, she would answer the door and be a bit friendly and say 'yes' the cellar needed cleaning or the grass cutting, even though the grass was short and the cellar was very small. It was easier to offer a bite of lunch 'daily & daily & daily, and wondering What will they do? What will their children be like?' She knew that other housewives down the street would also offer lunch, but what the men needed wasn't a meal but work in order to feed their families. She was all too aware that compassion didn't solve the terrible plight the world was in, 'neither did words nor violence nor conspiracy & no one had a corner on wisdom.'

Her life seemed out of step with what the world was going through. She had no children, but two dogs instead, wire-haired terriers. Walking them in the park directly across the street from the house was part of the daily routine (the activity of dogs, in fact, would be the occasion of her first two pieces of published fiction – 'I Just Love Dogs' and 'Hurry, Hurry'). For several years, she also had a cat named George whose character and behaviour were of great interest. Although she took a special delight in knitting, she had no particular interest in other manual activities such as gardening, and the kitchen was always looked after by a maid or cook. Instead, generous portions of her time were spent playing tennis in her short skirt ('"What your Grandmother would have said!"'),[10] swimming at the Club, and horseback riding at Southlands and along the bridle trails in Point Grey near the university. In 'Herself When Young,' she describes something of the exhilaration she felt on horseback: 'I took riding lessons that fall and winter ... There is nothing like it. The unity of horse with rider, the fine fresh air; you ride with busy or with vacant mind; you choose your trail, your pace; you ride alone or together.'[11] Her life thus was circumscribed by privilege and comfort; nonetheless, she was often without comfort, knowing how most of the world suffered. Although she and Wallace now attended services at the Anglican church, she was still imbued with that Methodist sense of duty and responsibility that made her feel personally guilty if rain fell on Dominion Day.

Because they had no children, the Wilsons took an unusually keen and sympathetic interest in the lives of their employees. One of the first of these was a Japanese schoolboy by the name of Tom Tokunaga, who lived in their house and worked for them after school hours. He did housework, but he was especially valuable as someone who would be at home to answer the telephone if Wallace's patients called when they were out. Ethel Wilson described Tom in an essay as 'distinguished in appearance, strong, quick, graceful, with classical features.'[12] The Wilsons grew very fond of Tom, and, because he loved Shakespeare, the three of them would read plays aloud together after dinner. When he became an engineer and returned to Japan, the Wilsons corresponded with him for several years, but during the Second World War they stopped hearing from him and feared he might have died or been killed. For several years, they continued to hire Japanese schoolboys who lived at the house and did work after school, and Ethel Wilson, who so much enjoyed their 'happy company,' wrote in effusive praise that they 'would be the flower of any nation.'

The Wilsons also employed a cook. The most memorable of these came to work for them in the early 1930s and stayed for about ten years. His name was Chow Lung, and, like Yow at the Barclay Street household, he came to dominate their lives for a time. Ethel Wilson told Audrey Butler that he came to them by default.[13] She had placed an advertisement in the newspaper for a cook, and, because there were so few jobs available, nearly a hundred white women and Chinese men answered. Before Chow Lung appeared for his interview, a large woman presented herself for the job with some excellent references in hand. Ethel knew she was not being fair, but the woman's extraordinary girth and grating voice made her unsuitable. She was not sure how to tell her, but then suddenly thought, and said, 'My husband is terribly fussy about his meals. I am afraid that I can only hire a Cordon Bleu cook.' Ethel was confident that in a roast beef and suet pudding city like Vancouver the woman would have to admit she was not a Cordon Bleu cook. But the woman took a different tack: 'I sure agree with him, Madame,' she said. 'Poor cooking puts my stomach right on the bum.' This became a great joke with the Wilsons and one of their favourite lines. When Mr Lung appeared next, he was quickly hired, but his ill-temper and strict rule over the little household sometimes made the Wilsons pause. Ethel, many years later, told her friends the Crawleys about this servant, focusing her anecdote, as so often, on language:

> Our Chinese cook, Chow-Lung (for many years) had his own word for perhaps. It wasn't for years that I knew that 'hopsum' was 'perhaps.' In conversation with patients per telephone, which Chow-Lung loved to answer:
> 'Is Dr Wilson in?'
> 'NO' (bellowed)
> 'Is he coming in for dinner?'
> 'Hopsum'
> 'Will he be in after dinner?'
> 'Hopsum.
> 'Hopsum he in, hopsum he out.'
> It was a sort of race between Chow-Lung & me to the telephone – I tried to save the patients from him.
> The poor bewildered patient would say 'Er – did you say he *would* be in after dinner – or not?'

The exasperated Chow-Lung would tell this stupid patient in a roar 'I tel-
lum you – *hopsum!*' & hang up.[14]

Like Yow, Chow Lung led a lonely existence and, according to Ethel Wilson's account, spent his free afternoons and evenings gambling and
smoking in Chinatown.

The Wilsons were not materially affected by the Depression, but the
majority of people were suffering in different ways, not the least of
which was in terms of medical services. In 1934 the B.C. minister of
health, George Weir, told the province's doctors at the annual B.C.
Medical Association meeting that the injustices perpetrated on the poor
were coming to an end, that he intended to see a bill for compulsory
medical insurance put through the legislature. Wallace, whose prestige
among his peers was very high, was drafted to head a team of doctors
who were concerned that the government come up with a good health
insurance scheme. Wallace, who was known as 'the calm voice in the
midst of turmoil,'[15] chaired this committee for eight years. In what was
known as the annual Wilson Report, he explained to the BCMA meeting
in 1935 that 'no attempt is being made to argue against pre-payment
plans for the provision of medical care, but it must be pointed out that
such plans in no way guarantee an elevation of the standard of the
health of the people.' The scheme, he argued, must include preventa-
tive medicine. His committee's position was that the profession should
only support a bill for compulsory medical insurance if members of the
BCMA were included as advisors. This position was ignored by the Liberal government of Duff Pattullo, and a plan was drawn up in 1936 without participation from the medical profession. Some two thousand
doctors met, and only two voted in favour of supporting the bill. When
it was passed in the legislature in 1937, Wallace sent a wire to the premier to say B.C. doctors refused to work under the Act, calling it 'ill-
conceived and unworkable.' The bill was shelved *sine die* and never promulgated. In the February 10 issue of the Vancouver *Daily Province* there
was a harsh cartoon of Wallace made to look like Hitler with accompanying text that identified him as 'responsible for the serious decline in
health of the current health bill.' It went on to say that 'Dr. Wallace Wilson who gave such a concise, convincing and conclusive argument
against this legislation should be given an additional degree of "D.T.,"
"Doctor of the Tongue."'

Wallace, who had been so visible in this struggle, paid a political
price. In 1937 a new chief was to be appointed at Vancouver General

Hospital. Wallace, nearing fifty, was seen by his peers to be in every way the ideal candidate for the post. He was a senior member of the staff at VGH, had been president of the BCMA, and was a founder of the B.C. Cancer Foundation. He was regarded as 'authoritative and efficient ... but always friendly and genial,' an excellent administrator in every way. But the minister of health was ill-disposed towards Wallace as the spokesman for the medical establishment, and the post went to another man. Wallace left VGH after an association of fifteen years. He was soon afterwards named chief of medicine at Shaughnessy Hospital, but felt despite the strong support of his colleagues that it was nonetheless a defeat. What his wife thought about the doctors' decision not to support the medical insurance plan, we cannot know for certain. We know from a letter written several years later that she thought the bill was flawed because it did not include those who were truly indigent (without homes and employment); it only covered those who could pay into the health insurance scheme.[16] She may have had reservations about the position taken by the medical profession, because it blocked a social program that in principle she supported, but she would never have been disloyal in her support for her husband.

Wallace's prominence in his field meant a heavy social calendar for his wife, but it seems clear that in the 1930s she had begun to apportion some of her time for writing. In a few letters to her sister-in-law that have survived from this period, she still looked for excuses not to attend large parties and teas,[17] but by other accounts she was growing a little more self-confident socially, less likely to be effusive and to overreact at gatherings. People were universally fond of Wallace, finding him warm and charming. They were likely to find his wife a little cool and reserved, her wit sometimes too sharp for comfort.[18] Her elegance and poise, moreover, were intimidating to those who did not understand that they were protective covering for someone who was, and would always remain, shy and insecure. Part of her armour was her impeccable dress sense; everyone who remembered her would observe that she was one of the most handsomely tailored and elegantly coifed women in Vancouver. But more important to her sense of self-worth was the craft she was secretly attempting to master, staying in bed until late in the morning – writing and rewriting.

To her friends and acquaintances in Vancouver, Ethel Wilson seemed to break suddenly onto the literary scene with the publication of her story 'I Just Love Dogs' in 1937. Moreover, she was being published in one of Britain's leading journals, the fashionably left-leaning *New States-*

man and Nation. When the Wilsons were married, 'an impecunious cousin' in England gave them a subscription to the *New Statesman,* and they had become loyal and deeply interested readers.[19] It is not surprising that when the journal accepted three of her stories, Wilson became uncharacteristically communicative about her success. She apparently told her Uncle Philip Malkin almost at once that the stories had been accepted,[20] and a family friend, Justice Bruce Robertson, remembered her unusual excitement when 'I Just Love Dogs' arrived in print.[21] The family also shared that excitement when Philip Malkin returned from a business trip to London and told everyone that one day when he stepped out of the Savoy Hotel, he saw a double-decker bus with a banner advertising the latest issue of the *New Statesman and Nation* and listing Ethel Wilson as one of the authors one must read.[22] She had turned forty-nine that January, and so it was a late start for a literary career, but no less exhilarating for the author.

There are different stories explaining Wilson's debut in the *New Statesman and Nation.* One is that Reginald Tupper (the husband of Wallace's cousin Isabel) read a few of Ethel's stories in 1936, recognized their quality, and urged her to send them to the *New Statesman,* which he considered the best periodical in print.[23] Wilson gave two somewhat different accounts of getting started. In one, she says she 'tried her hand at "a few little stories" and on reading them over said to herself "that's not bad."' She secretly sent the stories off on her own: 'I had no standard of measuring whether it was impertinent to expect to be printed, and I didn't like to ask anyone.'[24] Her other account is that she was pressed by Sylvia Lynd, an English literary friend, to try writing short fiction and to make a submission to the journal. I rather think that Wilson decided on her own to send the stories to England but credited Lynd as a way of modestly presenting herself as a reluctant amateur. But certainly Sylvia Lynd – and her husband – were connected to Wilson's emergence as a writer, and their importance as mentors must be acknowledged.

Sylvia Lynd, born the same year as Ethel, had established herself early as a fine lyric poet. Her 1917 collection of poems and short stories titled *The Thrush and the Jay* exhibits a delicate perception, particularly of children. Her husband, Robert Lynd, was literary editor for the London *News Chronicle* and an essayist, who wrote topical and satirical pieces under the pseudonym of 'Y.Y.' for the *New Statesman and Nation.* According to Audrey Butler, the Wilsons first met them in Vancouver:

... the Lynds visited Vancouver sometime pre-War (in the Thirties) and were 'feted' by Vancouver intellectuals. The Wilsons wrote to them at their hotel and said that they did not want to gush over them, but that they were admirers of his contributions to *NS&N* and if they both felt they would like a quiet Canadian week-end of a non-intellectual sort (the Wilsons were always humble about their own intellectuality) they would be more than welcome at 1238 Connaught Dr. The couple from England accepted and a very happy, satisfying relationship sprang up.[25]

From two letters written by sister-in-law Amy Buckerfield to Ethel in 1936, we learn that the date of that meeting was sometime in the first half of 1936 and that one of Ethel's half-aunts, Margaret Bryant, was a friend of Sylvia Lynd,[26] which explains perhaps why the Wilsons would have presumed to contact them when they were in Vancouver. Although Ethel said that Sylvia encouraged her to make a first submission to *New Statesman and Nation*, it may well have been that her first piece (or pieces) had been accepted before she introduced herself to the visiting writers. The Lynds were published by the Macmillan Company in England, and perhaps it was the Topaz stories that Lynd encouraged Wilson to submit to an English publisher.

It might seem strange that a writer from British Columbia would turn to English publishers, but that would be forgetting the close tie that persisted over the years between the Malkin family and their 'home' in England. Letters went back and forth every week, and a year seldom went by without a member of the extended family travelling to England or someone from 'home' visiting the Malkins in Vancouver. One of Ethel's youngest cousins, James Malkin, always remembered vividly a visit from Aunt Edith and Uncle Sydney in 1932. James was a teenager who had taken up smoking, and at dinner Sydney, with his withering sarcasm, said to the boy, 'Do you mind if I eat while you smoke?' But when James went to England in 1935 with his friend Colin Graham (Kathleen and Colin's son), Aunt Edith met them at Liverpool in her new, brightly polished Daimler, and a few weeks later as the boys were setting off on their grand tour of the Continent (they were just twenty), Uncle Sydney gave them each five pounds, roughly the equivalent of $500 apiece today.[27] These anecdotes illustrate how intimate the connection with England remained for the family fifty years after the Malkin brothers first arrived in Grenfell, Saskatchewan. England persisted as a cultural centre: the sons of the Canadian Malkin brothers were educated there during the 1920s and 1930s, Philip Malkin Jr attending The Leys, the Methodist public school in Cambridge, at the same time as the future writer Malcolm

Lowry. But Ethel Wilson, trying to get published, may also have preferred the distance and anonymity of London as well. In Vancouver, she lived to some extent in the public eye: Wallace's career, especially the role he played in the politics of local medicine in the 1930s, meant that she had little privacy, and 'Malkin's Best' was the brightest advertisement in the harbour. If her writing had no worth, it would be easier to hear this from editors abroad than from magazine publishers in Canada who might be acquaintances of the family.

'I Just Love Dogs' appeared in the 4 December 1937 issue of the *New Statesman and Nation* and was reprinted shortly after in E. O'Brien's *Best British Short Stories of 1938*. The following summer, the Wilsons spent two months abroad, mostly in England, and it turned out to be an exhilarating experience for the fledgling author. This was not the first time that Ethel had accompanied her husband to a medical convention. In 1936 she had driven with him to California, where there was a meeting to attend in San Diego. Almost certainly this trip provided the subject matter for her famous story 'Mrs Golightly and the First Convention' written several years later. Wallace had arranged the English trip so that he could attend the Royal Medical Association meetings that were being held in Plymouth in July 1938. Ethel kept a travel diary; it is the only writing of that kind that has survived with her papers, and we have, accordingly, an exceptionally detailed record of her thoughts and activities during that curiously formative summer.[28] Although she was already fifty, when most writers have reached and often passed their peak of productivity, Wilson was still in the process of finding her subject material and her identity as a writer. This trip would focus on visiting the different branches of her family but, perhaps more importantly, on situating herself, ever so tentatively, within the literary establishment in London.

It began in pure pleasure with a trip to Boston, which gave her a chance to see Harvard University in Cambridge while Wallace was preoccupied with business. From there they boarded the *Scythia* on June 26 for the crossing to Southampton. Ethel's physical, perhaps we can say sexual, pleasure in being alone with her husband on this long sea voyage emerges in her jottings: 'Very contented and happy. Such a good night. Oh my dear Wallace.' Heavy fog wrapped round the ship, but in their plain cabin she writes we are 'both completely happy ... Boohoo goes the foghorn. Algie and I rest so comfy.' Interestingly, it is the one time in all her writings that she uses his mother's pet name for her husband. Her usual intimate short form is 'Waas.'

When they reached London on July 5 there was the excitement of a pile of notes and invitations waiting for them in their hotel on Ryder Street. Ethel was eager especially to see her half-aunts again. The last report she had of them was from her sister-in-law, Amy Buckerfield, who with Ernest and their daughter Mary spent several months in England in 1936. The Buckerfields met with the Bryant sisters at least twice during their stay. The first meeting was with Margaret at their hotel, and they liked her very much, though they were a little distanced by her socialist politics and her rapid manner of speaking. Their second meeting was at Margaret Bryant's small flat in St Pancras, where they were also introduced to Hannah Atkinson. Ethel must have felt warmed by her sister-in-law's response to Hannah. Amy wrote: 'I fell in love with Mrs Atkinson with her Madonna face, bright colouring, soft brown hair parted in the middle, and the sweetest smile.'[29] Hannah was in the company of Russian friends and there was talk of the translation Hannah had done of Pushkin's *The Golden Cockerel*, which was to be published that year for Christmas. There was also talk of a play that Hannah and Margaret had written for children that was to be produced at the Winter Garden during the Christmas season. Amy and Mary read out some of the parts to the great amusement and delight of the authors, who had not heard it read aloud before. The vividness of Margaret Bryant, especially her intellectual acuity, emerges in another long letter Amy wrote to Ethel. This is an important letter because here we glimpse something of the struggle that took place over Ethel when Robert Bryant suddenly died. Amy Buckerfield quotes Margaret Bryant as saying, '"I would have worked to the bone to have given Ethel a good education. But I was not religious and so they feared for that ..."'[30] Margaret, unmarried and with no responsibilities outside her job, believed she should have been the one to raise Ethel. She felt Ethel deserved a better education than the one she got at Trinity School, which in her opinion was limited by its religious affiliation. In her opinion, Ethel had a brilliant mind, like her father, and deserved all the opportunities a good education can provide, but the Malkins had vetoed her intervention. Ethel was keenly aware of this continuing interest and pride taken in her by her father's family.

At once Ethel made contact with her half-aunts by telephone, and a series of visits was quickly arranged. On the 7th, gentle, musical Aunt Hannah and Aunt Elizabeth came to the hotel for sherry and a long talk. Although Elizabeth was profoundly boring, Ethel was thrilled to be with them again. Later that same day, she and Wallace went to watch the debate over the Coal Bill in the House of Commons. She quickly found her sympathies were for the miners and described in her diary the secretary to the Ministry of the Mines as 'thoroughly detestable in his grey morning suit, bald head, and superficial, ineffectual, yet on account of superior numbers, effectual.'

On the 9th the Wilsons spent the day in upper-class surroundings attending the Eton and Harrow cricket match at Lords with James and Ella Fell, wealthy friends from Vancouver, but in the evening they went out to a party at Aunt Margaret's little flat 'in a colossal & dark & ancient pile in St Pancras.' The contrast to the earlier part of the day was a stark one. Aunt Margaret's friends were hard-working intellectuals and professionals who had spent their lives working and living in dark flats, which saddened Ethel when she thought about the waistcoats at Lords. Yet, these people were very interesting to know and included a young man from Balliol College studying history, a little tired woman doctor, one of Hannah's sons, whom she described as 'a bounding springy enthusiastic welfare worker and a very nice youth,' and an expatriate Russian couple, one of whom (Raissa Lomonossova) had written an introduction to Hannah's Pushkin translation. Talk of history and the arts filled the apartment, but there was also talk of Hitler and the growing fear of Germany. The hospitality included sherry and refreshments, and Ethel was aware how much the gathering meant for her busy little aunt, and in her own mind she felt the lovely lunch at the Lords hosted by Vancouver friends was nothing compared to the humble sandwiches and lemonades. But the difference quickened her social conscience, as so often happened in England. She recognized that although her aunt's small flat was furnished in good taste, it was cold nonetheless, restrained and grim: '& I got very depressed as I thought how much more of London lives at the St Pancras level. Hundreds live at Lords level, thousands perhaps, but thousands or millions below that level.' Then follows an aside which in its equivocal manner anticipates the future novelist: 'Well, nobody's happy all the time, & nobody's unhappy all the time, & that's what it amounts to.'

There were more visits with the Bryants: the next day she went out to Aunt Hannah's by subway to meet her cousin Kitty and husband and once again 'terrible boring little old aunt Elizabeth ... whom I embrace and avoid.' Kitty was a happy, sensible, very nice woman, but Ethel was drawn by her special affection for Aunt Hannah, who, she felt, was a woman especially endowed with kindness and wisdom. Hannah's gentleness was in contrast to Margaret's intensity and need to live for a cause, whether the betterment of the human race or the well-being of her sister's family. To Hannah and her scapegrace sons, as she made clear to Amy Buckerfield, Margaret had given 'nearly every blanket off her bed.'[31] In the meantime, Ethel had an experience which gave her something of a shock. A man by the name of Sir Arthur Newsholme came to lunch at the hotel on July 8. Except that he was a healthy, genial man of eighty-one, his identity is not explained in the diary. However, he was presumably a friend or associate of Robert Bryant, because he told Ethel a secret history pertaining to her father – namely, that at one point he had contemplated marrying again. Ethel wrote in her diary: 'Thank god Lady Newsholme advised Father as she did, or I'd have had a stepmother, a wild stepbrother, no Wallace, and I wouldn't be where I am now having the best time in the world.'

Part of that 'best time in the world' was anticipation of a dinner party at Robert and Sylvia Lynd's where she had been promised some of London's fashionable literary company. The party was arranged for Friday evening, July 15. There was a slight disappointment when they arrived at Keats Grove, Hampstead, because Rose Macauley, one of the country's most distinguished novelists and literary critics during the 1930s, had not been able to come at the last minute. But J.B. Priestley, London's popular satirical playwright, was there with his wife, as were Mr and Mrs Joyce Cary, Mr Cary being introduced to Ethel as a good writer of novels about Nigeria. An elegant dinner of lobster in mayonnaise, mushroom soup, roast duckling, and strawberries was served by a housekeeper and butler, and conversation flowed easily and wittily among the four couples. Priestley dominated the table with his opinions and clever repartee ('a fine resonant talker ... who knows what he thinks, & says so'),[32] and Ethel felt afraid of him, though found his wife 'completely natural and charming.' Joyce Cary, by contrast, whose works were then unknown to her but would have a considerable influence in the future, impressed her as uncommonly natural, a man 'unimpressed by *himself* and much more interested in other people and in *ideas*.'[33] She sat directly opposite from him at the dinner table and would often think afterwards that she would have liked to have known him better, but Priestley's presence had made her shy. Later, when they had moved to the living room, Priestley talked to Ethel 'a little severely' about indigenous culture and the importance of repertory theatre in Canada, though, she wrote in her diary that night, 'it came down to this partly – I want you to see *my* plays in Canada – so you should support Repertory.' Two other guests joined the party after dinner, a tall young man by the name of Campbell, a

peer's son Ethel concluded from the conversation, and a very smart and
soignée young woman, a public speaker whose name Ethel concluded was
Lady Rooke (though Wallace had heard Lady Butler). The conversation
was 'snappy and witty' and never touched on '*The Situation*' (Hitler and
Germany) except briefly when the women were alone in the livingroom.
Nor was there a discussion of books, though everyone was assumed to
have written some. The Priestleys and Carys left for their train at mid-
night, and Ethel felt freer once Priestley was gone. The remaining company had whiskies and Robert Lynd became 'funny and Irish' and they
enjoyed themselves immensely until finally the Wilsons felt they should
leave. 'Lady Rooke' drove them 'wittily into town' from whence they taxied back to the hotel.

But before they got into the car to leave, the Lynds walked them down
the lane to the house where Keats had lived. In *Swamp Angel* Ethel Wilson writes that a meeting partakes its essence not only of the persons but
of the place of meeting.[34] In her diary entry that night, she described
the Lynds' small home as beautifully decorated in 'soft beigy green
misty warm colours,' with large windows and warmly polished wide-
board floors. And she described the dining room with its long narrow
table, pale blue cloth, candles, and a low dish of pink roses in the centre. But many years later when recalling that evening, she would refer to
the presence of Keats's house next door, 'where in an upper room he
lay ill, and wrote those words to Fanny Brawne: "I shall see you pass. I
shall follow you with my eyes over the Heath ... Come round to my window for a moment when you have read this."'[35] Certainly the connection with Keats, one of the great poets of the English language, was part
of the literary magic of that summer evening in London in 1938.

After a few more days of shopping and visiting London's art galleries,
Wallace rented a car and left to attend the meeting in Plymouth. Ethel
took a train by herself to Burslem, where she was met by her cousin Alan
Malkin, now an orthopaedic surgeon. She stayed at her Aunt Edith's
summer house and drove 'through old haunts,' and for the next few
days took a meal and spent an evening with each of her male cousins
and their families. But she was anxious all the time about Wallace's
whereabouts in 'trafficky' England, and was greatly relieved when he at
last could join her again.

From Burslem they drove east to visit those Bryants still living in Lincolnshire, the county with 'the mild and milky name,' whose green
wolds and windswept fields seemed so far from the slagheaps of
Staffordshire. They visited and were greatly impressed by the cathedral

at Lincoln and then continued eastward to Alford, where they stopped at her father's grave ('All very good,' she wrote in her diary), and they took a room for the next couple of days at the 'Park House' inn. Near Alford they found 'Aunt' Lucy Bryant, who was really Robert Bryant's first cousin and a niece to Maria Riggall, the housekeeper when Ethel was a small child. This stirring up of old memories and associations increased when they went to visit Uncle Herbert and his wife, Aunt Lena. Although he was a half-brother, Herbert resembled her father in that he was tall, had the nose of an eagle, a beautiful speaking voice, and the Bryant sense of humour.[36] He had been headmaster of a very old grammar school and was now, at seventy-two, retired. Perhaps it was the startling story she heard in London – that her father had contemplated remarriage – that awakened in her a desire to know more facts about her father's family. Although Wallace was securely by her side, Ethel would always be haunted by her absent father, and tried to make him more real by asking her relatives for stories. She would set a few of these down in short essay form.

During their visits with Uncle Herbert, he told them a strange story about her father's oldest brother, Tom,[37] a spirited youth who had gone to South Africa for adventure and had never returned home – just 'a few letters, fewer, no letters, no word of Tom, and at last the parents' buried sorrow.' One day when Robert as a young missionary was riding one of the interminable dusty roads of the veldt, he came upon a ragged man plodding towards him. He gave him a cursory glance, thinking of something else, but when the shabby man looked up, Robert was stopped by something familiar in his appearance. It was his brother Tom. Robert was overjoyed and led him back to his bungalow and prepared him a meal, but the older brother, humiliated perhaps to be discovered in this condition, just wolfed down his food and hardly spoke a word. After Tom had thrown down his knife and fork, Robert asked him if he would like to sit outside and have a talk or go to bed. 'Bed sounds alright to me,' said the brother. Robert offered him the one bed in the bungalow, a bowl and jug of water, and went to the other room to get him a nightshirt, but when he returned Tom had already gotten under the sheet without undressing, dusty boots and all. He was turned away with his eyes shut. Robert looked down at the tramp in his bed and thought how he must have suffered, that he was no longer Tom, but a stranger. Robert slept on a mat in the next room and when he woke up in the morning his brother was gone. He never saw him again, but the family heard later that Tom died alone in South Africa of enteric fever. This haunting little story, as Wilson retells it, has almost a biblical cast, accentuated by her capitalization of the word 'Father,' and has echoes in the parable of the sleeper in *Swamp Angel.*

From her own memories of her father, Ethel recalled another strange story, that the famous French poet Paul Verlaine had been his teacher in the little Lincolnshire village of Stickney.[38] It seemed incredible that this accomplished and notorious man should have lived in such an unlikely part of England, but Uncle Herbert said it was true. He lived there, as everyone recalled, in quiet dignity with his mother; he was then a man of thirty. It was, as Wilson had learned from reading about the poet, an uncharacteristic interlude in his turbulent life, which was better known for his drunkenness, the abandonment of his wife and child, his love affair with (and violence towards) the poet Arthur Rimbaud, and his imprisonment for beating his mother. For a couple of years, he returned to Catholicism and a pious life, and it was then that he lived in Stickney far from temptations. The villagers especially loved Mme Verlaine, Uncle Herbert said. Ethel then asked her uncle if he remembered anything very special about Verlaine, and he was embarrassed to admit that only one trite incident stayed in his mind. ' "There was," said Uncle Herbert, "a little boy in the class who had a running nose and no pocket handkerchief and Paul Verlaine roared to this little boy in an awful voice "SIR! SWEEP YOUR NOSE!"'' and that was practically every word that Uncle Herbert remembered spoken by the famous French poet Paul Verlaine.' It was a small anecdote, but in Uncle Herbert's sunny garden it was told in a beautiful voice, wrote Wilson, 'that was also the voice of my Father.'[39]

During this visit, Ethel probably asked to hear about her parents' wedding, because Herbert Bryant had served his brother as best man. He would have told her what a large event it was in the life of the town, the Burslem chapel crowded in every part and a large throng unable to gain admittance standing in the chapel-yard and outside the gates. Lila Malkin was not only the oldest daughter of the town's principal employer, but a teacher in the Methodist Sunday school, who enjoyed 'the earnest esteem of her scholars and fellow teachers.'[40] Emotions were mixed to see her departing for a 'distant home.' If Uncle Herbert described the wedding in detail, perhaps he related that the service (according to a newspaper account at least) was performed by Reverend Owen Watkyns, 'a colleague of the bridegroom in the mission fields of the Transvaal,' rather than by Reverend Fred Macdonald, though Mrs Macdonald is listed as one of the wedding guests and Ethel preferred to believe Macdonald's account that he had performed the ceremony. Uncle Herbert would no doubt have told her that her parents had spent a honeymoon in Stratford-on-Avon, where, judging by the calendar, Ethel would have been conceived.

The Wilsons returned to London for more shopping (what to buy Aunt Eliza?) and visits with the half-aunts. On July 30 they drove out to Nottingham with Aunt Margaret to see the ancient castle on the rock and the oldest inn in England, where the Crusaders stopped en route. There was a little incident Ethel would remember and relate.[41] On the smoke-stained walls, she saw three Victorian-era photographs of a frightening-looking man. She turned to the landlady and asked, 'Who is that terrible man?' The landlady answered quite affectionately, 'Oh, that was just Charley Peace the murderer. 'E lived around the corner and 'e used to 'ide from the police up that there big chimney.' Shuddering, Ethel said, 'What an awful man!' But the landlady replied, 'Oh Charley wasn't that awful. 'E never murdered the Poor, 'e only murdered the Rich, them as could afford it.' It gave Ethel, as she said, another way of thinking about the rich! – a comic view of the class struggle in England.

Wallace's business then took them to Scandinavia and the Netherlands for the first two weeks of August. In her diary, Wilson describes the flight from Copenhagen to Stockholm as 'a scene of unearthly beauty – the marvelous Sweden of waterways and forests and crystal air.' The vast stretches of unspoiled landscape in the Nordic countries made her think of British Columbia, though the cities she conceded were superior – Stockholm with its fine architecture, each apartment with its spacious, canopied balcony overhanging a waterway, sensible Helsinki with its clean, brightly tented beaches, and Copenhagen with its sophisticated *joie de vivre*, its beer gardens, the Tivoli – all so far removed from Methodist Vancouver.[42] Amsterdam, however, brought home again how cramped it was in most of Europe ('the quite terrible neatness and economy of Holland'), and how everyone was living in the shadow of fear generated by Hitler and his armies. She was told while she was in Holland that Jews made up 10 per cent of the Dutch population and that more refugees from central Europe were coming into the country every day. She had been oppressively aware while flying to Stockholm that they were on the same plane as Hitler's film director, Leni Riefenstahl. On August 16 she wrote: 'German manoeuvres began yesterday and one million men are under arms today. Everyone is saying that everyone is tense but calm – and that's about it. Those in the know – but what is "the know."'

Back in England, as they neared the end of their trip, Wallace finally persuaded Ethel to pay a call at the office of the *New Statesman and Nation*, something he would have found easy and pleasant to do himself, but which caused her great anxiety. He argued that if they were publishing her stories, they would be curious to meet the author. She wrote in her diary: 'I was *terrified* & felt a *perfect* fool, and I was quite sure I'd not know how to begin & they'd say "Oh yes, really." For stimulus I wore my new green Finnegan suit & hat, & for placebo I took a grain of phenobarbinol.' Her nervousness and confusion were perfectly matched by the taxi driver's inability to locate 10 Great Turnstile (for four pages in her diary, she describes all the false turns the taxi takes); then finally she arrived and 'palpitated into the N.S. Office & [assumed] the Lit. Ed. was too busy for words. But he saw me ... and he was one of the nicest people I've ever met.' Others came into Raymond Mortimer's office to chat with her 'and asked heaps of questions, & I do hope I wasn't too frivolous & I told them about the phenobarb & they laughed a lot.' 'Well I had a grand time' was how she concluded her description of the visit to the offices of the *New Statesman and Nation*. Then she met Wallace for lunch, and they went shopping for a silver teapot. The trip concluded with their ship's return to New York and arrival home by train on September 8.

'Hurry, Hurry' was published in the *New Statesman and Nation* 25 November 1939.[43] It has been one of Wilson's most frequently anthologized stories. Its power lies in the modernist way of making a small personal moment reverberate with universal application. A woman walking alone with her dogs on Sea Island encounters first a wounded hawk with bright knowing eyes, then a man hurrying towards her who tells her to turn back because he has seen a hungry cougar up ahead. The beautiful walk along the dyke, with the spectacular mountain backdrop, has suddenly turned into something frightening – as in a nightmare, the woman can't run fast enough. And the narrator reveals that it was not a cougar that lay ahead on the path, but the body of a woman whom the hurrying man has just murdered. Many forms of fear – of being alone, of natural cruelty, of human violence, and the spectre of death – emerge from this slight but powerful story, which is hardly a story, but more accurately a vignette. It is written with Wilson's unsentimental precision of language, which is often used to describe what is seemingly most sentimental – the beauties of nature or romantic love. Here, for example, the blackbird's song begins on a clear flute's note, then 'grate[s] like a rusty lock ... sweet and very ugly.' The slightest descriptions can be suddenly all-encompassing in their reach. The story was published just as the world had slipped into the Second World War and seems in this light an irrelevant piece of writing, but in its own way it describes exactly what has happened when a beautiful world has turned into a nightmare. This, of course, is a judgment in retrospect, and one which credits writers with a portentous sensitivity to the times in which they live. If this is too large a claim, I think nonetheless that this little story of suddenly being 'on a brink' can be credited as Wilson's first important publication, one which anticipates her best books and stories to come.

The story's origin and composition also anticipate Wilson's methods as a writer. She explained twelve years later to anthologist Robert Weaver that the events of the story actually happened to a friend 'decades' before, not on the dykes but in Stanley Park, and that the man had warned the woman with her dog that she should turn back because there was a bear up ahead, not a cougar. The man was eventually convicted of murder and was hanged. Wilson said simply that she translated the story to the dyke because she was 'only moderately fond of forests.'[44] Two aspects of composition stand out here: first, that she used someone else's experience and transposed it to another setting, so that one can say only the 'setting' is autobiographical; secondly, that the story had been at work in her imagination for many years, that it was material that had been saved up. This happens repeatedly during her career as a writer, and we will find in her last novel some of the events from her life when she was in her twenties, but dressed in the garments of another character and another place and time.

CHAPTER SEVEN

The Innocent Traveller

1930–1949

A notebook / Secret life / War / Audrey Butler /
Little Rock / Death of Aunt Eliza / Macmillan /
The Innocent Traveller

Part of the colourful story of Ethel Wilson's literary career is that during
the Second World War she set aside her writing for volunteer work with
the Red Cross. She said later that, with the world in crisis and her husband once again in military service, the writing and publishing of stories
was forgotten. But, in fact, she did publish two stories during the war –
'On Nimpish Lake' in *Canadian Forum*, July 1942, and 'We Have to Sit
Opposite' in *Chatelaine*, May 1945 – and a correspondence she initiated
with the Macmillan Company in 1944 gives evidence that she had been
working on her 'Topaz' stories and was in negotiation with American
publishers and agents for several years. Unquestionably there were dis-
tractions: her husband's welfare and that of her extended family always
came first; the demands of society life remained pressing; and during
the war, another person came to live with the Wilsons in their home.
But in the background, in what was her secret life, she continued to
hone her craft and look for publishers. In a candid moment, she once
admitted it was 'imperative'[1] for her to write, something like a compulsion, and the nineteen-year history of *The Innocent Traveller* before publication is a striking instance of art viewed in this light.

The first evidence for an extended piece of writing that would eventually be known as *The Innocent Traveller* is the small workbook dated 1930
with several pages of notes describing something like chapters for a family history.[2] The list of contents ranges from events in England in the
early nineteenth century to notes on an Italian grocer in Kelowna in the

summer of 1930. Some of the entries are familiar to anyone who has read the novel and refer to sequences to be written about Eliza's endless talking, the Edge sisters at school, and their friendship with Miss Pocock and Miss Pinder. More interesting from a biographical point of view are the entries which were not developed as part of the novel, some of which give tantalizing glimpses of family history that has otherwise disappeared. They are often worded (like the letters Wilson wrote her sister-in-law, Amy Buckerfield) as parodies of Victorian fiction. These are some sample entries:

Saintly behaviour of gt grandfather Elijah Malkin and ultimate confinement to bedchair

The totally indefensible behaviour of great grandmother Edge with reference to Hannah and strong drink [probably related to an actual story Wilson wrote titled 'Lay Your Commands upon Her, Joseph'][3]

The thwarted desires of the Rev F.W. Macdonald with regards to Jane [Macdonald was the Methodist clergyman who, Wilson believed, married her parents.]

Curious behaviour of a gentleman under cover of a tea table causing offence and dismay to lady involved (aunty herself)

Brother John goes to bed with a fork with which to impale rats in wainscotting

Spencer, his art, marriage, and teeth [perhaps Spencer Edge, who married Emily Bennett]

The secret history of the unjustifiable dislike of Sydney for the brothers William and John [Perhaps there is a reason suggested here for the departure of the younger Malkin brothers, William Harold and John Philip, for Canada, though Wilson's antipathy towards Uncle Sydney may have exaggerated certain feelings in the family.]

After several entries of this nature there is a break and what Wilson titles an 'Editor's Note.' It reads: 'The above, with other collateral family histories, provides rich and unhappy material for the Eugenic Society.' Some entries refer to the life of the Malkin family in Vancouver:

Sniffy attitude of 'Vancouver Society' towards Local Council of Women

Mrs. Dougall and her daughter [This is presumably a reference to Harold Malkin's mother-in-law and wife, Marion.]

The Nicolls family, their history and characteristics [This probably refers to the man to whom Wilson was for a time engaged.]

Mrs. Jonathan Rogers – her prowess and progress.

An Italian grocer in Kelowna

Unfavorable allusions in minor key to other persons in Kelowna

It is impossible now to determine what these Kelowna sequences might have been based on. We know that the Wilsons occasionally stopped in Kamloops and Kelowna when they travelled up-country, though Lac Le Jeune was usually their destination. Then the entries return to Burslem:

Life & times of Josiah Wedgwood

Methodism and the Malkins

Swooning of pretty widow and subsequent removal from chapel

A Methodist vamp, or, she had lovers in the conference

Re-enter Sam Skadding, an orphan of 70 (Editor's note – at what age does one cease to be an orphan?) [Sam Skadding is a character referred to in *The Innocent Traveller* who continues to write letters to Aunt Topaz in old age.]

The Robert Martin family (excessively uninteresting) from Genesis to Revelation during soup.

What these notes suggest, and there are several pages of them, is the scope of history that Wilson was initially contemplating as her subject and her satirical approach to the material. But when the first of the family stories appeared in print – 'I Have a Father in the Promised Land' was published 4 February 1939 in the *New Statesman and Nation* – the comedy was tempered by an element of gentle pathos, and Ethel Wilson's characteristic irony informed by compassion emerges as her fully developed signature trademark. In a tribute to Ethel Wilson near the end of her career, her publisher John Gray compared her to someone who sits down at the piano for the first time and can play, but he knew that this was not the case, that the apprenticeship – the practising – was just not visible.[4]

Traces of Wilson's professional apprenticeship are evident in her early correspondence with the Macmillan Company.[5] We find in those letters that in 1937 she was writing to Maria Leiper, an editor at Simon and Schuster in New York, presumably showing Leiper her stories, certainly discussing the possibility of publishing a book with her company. These letters also reveal that she was in correspondence with Houghton Mifflin in Boston, as well.[6] According to Wilson, Maria Leiper had for a long time been enthusiastic about the 'Topaz' stories, but other readers at Simon and Schuster wanted to see them made into a novel. The matter was stalled there, although Leiper was still hopeful that a book of some kind would emerge under her editorship. This was not information that Wilson was eager to divulge, but as she was entering into the possibility of publication with Macmillan, she found it necessary to set the record straight as regards previous and ongoing commitments. She felt indebted to Leiper for her several years of interest and encouragement, but could see by 1944 that the Topaz stories were never going to find an audience in the United States. During the 1930s and early '40s, family and friends had little notion of how seriously Ethel Wilson was taking her writing. It was a very private activity. She said that even Wallace, whom she often accompanied on his doctor's rounds, knew better than to ask what she was doing: 'I no more told my husband that I was "writing a story" than he told me of the human tragedy or comedy that held him so long in the small dark house on Capitol Hill, while I sat writing by a very dim light, outside.'[7]

Ethel Wilson's secretiveness was probably rooted in lack of self-confidence. If one wants to probe its origins, it perhaps began with the death of her father and became part of her character as she was moved about among four different homes within a year of his death.[8] It bred habits of secrecy. She became dependent on her own company because relations with others were repeatedly severed, could not be relied on to last despite all the kindness she was shown. She sometimes thought of her self-reliance as a form of pride but found it necessary for survival.

Secrecy and insecurity would lie close to the heart of her imagination, which drew much of its power and insight from knowing the world to be an unsafe and potentially lonely place where suddenly someone you love can disappear forever. But the secret life was not all bleak – it had its pleasures. Mary McAlpine tells how Ethel Wilson, in a curiously unseemly way for someone her age (she was in her forties) and in her social position, liked to go to the movies in the afternoon by herself. She especially enjoyed the vulgar, slapstick comedies of the English music-hall entertainer George Formby, who appealed mainly to lower-class audiences. McAlpine writes, presumably on the basis of interviews she conducted, that Ethel Wilson's high, trilling laugh could be heard all over the theatre. She also tells us that Wilson used to meet a mysterious woman for lunch every Thursday in the dining room of the Hudson's Bay store downtown. She did not tell anyone who she was, but called her simply Miss Cosychat, because when they parted the lady would always say 'Goodbye Mrs. Wilson. I'm so looking forward to our next cosy chat.'[9] Perhaps this woman was the inspiration for one of the characters in her fiction, someone like Aunty Emblem in 'Tuesday and Wednesday,' because her characters were sometimes, by her own account, drawn from strangers, people she observed on the streets, on a bus, or in a store.

Ethel Wilson said the war made her forget her writing and, while that was not entirely true, certainly there was much to preoccupy her during that anxious time. Encouraged by friends like Phyllis Rochfort and Babe Taylor, she volunteered for the Red Cross, at first rolling bandages and packing boxes to be shipped overseas; and subsequently she edited a bi-monthly mimeographed bulletin for the Red Cross which was titled 'Vancouver Calling.'[10] Its purpose was to keep the workers in touch with what was going on, and for that her prose is crystal clear, businesslike, and unsentimental. But in the bulletin there are other snippets of her writing, sandwiched among the reports, that are designed to entertain the volunteers. One of these features is titled 'Excerpts from the Diary of Samuel Pepys Junior of Vancouver, B.C.,' wherein Samuel swings between such patriotic ideas as keeping a pig in the backyard during the war (because he loves pork) to whining about a dinner of cold scraps because his wife has worked too late at the Red Cross. His wife and her half-aunt argue whether or not the Red Cross is efficiently run. Another feature turns on 'My Aunt Flo' and her three friends, Mrs Mink, Mrs Mole, and Mrs Masterman, characters that are not so very distant from the presentation of Aunt Topaz and such cartoon-like characters as Maybelle Slazenger and Mrs Spink in books to come. There was more sober effort involved for her in writing a handbook for the Red Cross and in arranging a bureau of speakers for its meetings.[11]

When in 1940 the Germans started bombing the industrial Midlands, the Wilsons wrote to the relatives in Burslem and offered to take two of the cousins' small children for the duration of the war. But the Malkins in England were afraid of the boats being torpedoed on the Atlantic, and so the children were not sent. Then Robert and Sylvia Lynd wrote asking if the Wilsons could give refuge to part of their family. Both of their daughters had become Communists at Oxford, and one had married a Jew; they were terrified that he would be hunted down if the Germans landed in Britain. So they asked if Ethel would write to say her brother was in England and to invite him to Canada. However, as the Wilsons were socially acquainted with Baron von Heydebreck, a pro-Nazi organizer in the West, and he knew that Ethel had no brother, so she wrote back to Sylvia Lynd saying she had cousins not a brother in England. In the event, the Lynds' pregnant daughter and her husband were not willing to leave the country, so that the complicated and anxious arrangements came to nothing.[12] Later, Ethel heard of a sixteen-year-old girl from England who was in need of a temporary home, and after she and Wallace met her at Christmas dinner at the Buckerfields, they invited her to come and live with them. It was early 1941 when Audrey Butler moved to their house on Connaught Drive, and she stayed until 1943.

The relationship with Audrey Butler, whom the Wilsons came to refer to as their daughter, was overall an intensely happy and satisfying one.[13] Audrey's father had business connections with friends of the Buckerfields, and Audrey saw her removal to Canada at sixteen as an adventure, rather than a dash for safety. Audrey's earliest impressions of Ethel Wilson were twofold. From the outset, they enjoyed an easy rapport: they went swimming and played tennis together, and Ethel, with her love of silliness and caricature, nicknamed Audrey 'Miss Bomb' to suggest her style on the courts. But at the same time, Audrey was very much aware of Ethel Wilson as a grande dame in her social milieu, where silliness and fun were exchanged for genteel reserve and an ironic manner. Wallace, in Audrey's eyes, was the ideal man – open, bluff, good-hearted, without contrivance. She saw the Wilsons as perfect companions to each other, never a harsh word or critical glance exchanged between them. Ethel doted on him, but he exerted no power over her; they were equals in every respect.

The Wilsons enjoyed sharing their favourite walks with the young girl
– in Stanley Park, out on the dykes in Richmond – and in the summer of
1941, they took her to the Okanagan Valley with them on vacation. (The
following year, the girl would spend part of the summer on her own
horseback riding at Paradise Ranch in Penticton.) But a special pleasure
to share with the girl was the acquisition of a property on Bowen Island.
The Wilsons and the Grahams heard that a log cabin with 145 acres of
land was for sale on the northwest end of the island, and they arranged
to buy the place jointly. Much of the land was still forested, and trees
came right up to the cabin, but there was an open stretch that provided
room for a vegetable garden and a breath-taking perspective over ocean
and forest-covered islands. The Wilsons called the property 'Little
Rock,' with reference to a small rock jutting up out of the sea in the
cove directly below the cabin. The Wilsons and Grahams added a room
for a housekeeper, whitewashed the log walls and stone fireplace, and
used primary colours – bright yellow, green, and burnt-orange – on the
floors and furniture to give the cottage rustic warmth. They made apple-
box book shelves and lit the place with candles and kerosene lamps.
Irene Howard points out that everything was done as cheaply as possible
because of wartime restrictions, but the effect as you arrived through
the woods was beautiful and harmonious.[14] With Audrey to share the
cottage, it was for Ethel Wilson like reliving the pleasures of her own
young days at Point Cowan on the southern tip of the island.

With her love of the wilderness and her prowess at all kinds of physical activities, Audrey was the perfect young woman with whom to share
the island. But (and this is what made Audrey so special to Ethel Wilson) she also shared her evacuee parents' great love for Shakespeare,
and, as they had done with Tom Tokunaga twenty years before, the Wilsons would read Shakespeare out loud together with Audrey, in parts,
after dinner. The love of Shakespeare remained with the Wilsons as
long as they lived. Audrey finished high school in 1942 (she was by then
eighteen) and that fall enrolled in the agriculture program at UBC. The
Wilsons delighted in their role as surrogate parents, watching this
adventurous, uninhibited young woman develop and seeing her
through the stages of her schooling. She was popular at school, and they
enjoyed the company of the young friends she brought to the house.
But in 1943 Audrey decided to join the Canadian Navy as a WREN. Suddenly she was gone from their midst, sent for training to eastern Canada, then overseas. She did not come back to Vancouver for four long
years.

Audrey's departure was just one in a series of ruptures that Ethel experienced in 1943. The year before, Wallace had joined the army again. He had been made commanding medical officer for the Pacific Northwest and was now poised to leave and serve in any way that was expected of him. Indeed, trips ensued to eastern Canada and to England, where Audrey had gone and where bombs were still falling. Ethel did not do well living on her own when Wallace was away; it reawakened that childhood fear of being abandoned. This was compounded by a change in living quarters. Before Wallace began travelling with the army, they decided to sell the house on Connaught Drive with its garden and upkeep and take an apartment in the West End for the duration of the war. They had lived at the Connaught address for twenty years, and Chow Lung, who had been with them for ten of those years, left with the break-up of the household, and Ethel had to find a new cook and housekeeper for the apartment.

At year's end, there was yet another change: Aunt Eliza, who appeared likely to celebrate her centenary, died at Fred and Julia Malkin's home on 31 December 1943 in her ninety-ninth year. It was during the hardest part of the war, when news of casualties visited so many families in the city. Aunt Eliza's death seemed of little importance at that point in time. The funeral was on a day of heavy rain; Ethel had the 'flu and could barely make her way to the service. But Aunt Eliza did not depart without leaving the makings of a good story, which was eventually published in 1986 as an 'author's epilogue' to *The Innocent Traveller*.[15] Written as part of Wilson's essay on family history titled 'Reflections in a Pool,' but subsequently removed by the editors at *Canadian Literature*, the story of Aunt Eliza's funeral began with an account of Eliza's long-time friendship with Dolly Tibbetts, a meek little woman whom she easily dominated and teased mercilessly. The family always felt sorry for Miss Tibbetts. Strangely Miss Tibbetts died just the day before Aunt Eliza. Everyone, of course, had found the irrepressible Eliza overwhelming, and Wilson tells us that she even started writing a story wherein Aunt Eliza, lying in her coffin and surrounded by many floral tributes, found the occasion too exciting, sat bolt upright, thanked everyone for coming, and commented on what they were wearing. Eliza's funeral was not quite like that, but it was funny nonetheless. The obituary notice had requested no flowers should be sent; amidst the privations of war and the tragic deaths of young soldiers, an amassing of flowers for such an old lady seemed inappropriate, and a canopy from the family had been ordered instead. But when people arrived for the service, the coffin was naked. The Malkin relatives started blaming each other ('No one ordered the canopy?'), and an old woman sitting behind Ethel wheezed to her daughter, 'Not a flower! Shameful I call it! And them so rich and stingy.' But Miss Tibbetts had been buried that morning, and by mistake the canopy had gone on her coffin and was out at the cemetery at that very moment. Wilson concludes her narrative: 'What a treat for Miss Dolly Tibbetts, what an incredible ironic postponed delight! Her little smile wafted over us in the chapel air. Not a flower, not a leaf.' Aunty's death was the end of an era for the Malkin family, but the ancient lady herself was not mourned. In fact, Ethel subsequently wrote to a friend: 'Thank God her disturbing presence is removed. But I question whether even the angels can quite cope – I couldn't. It is really a blessing we don't all live forever.'[16]

Apparently Ethel said to Wallace's cousin, Alix, before she and Wallace were married, that one day she would write down her stories, 'but not until Granny, Aunt Eliza and Aunty Belle are dead.'[17] Perhaps it was Aunt Eliza's death that pushed Ethel along with her plan for a book about the family's history, because it was the following year that she entered into negotiations with the Macmillan Company to have her 'Topaz' stories published. On 18 November 1944 she found the courage to mail a bundle of stories 'To the Literary Editor' at Macmillan in Toronto. She explained by way of credentials that three of the stories had appeared in the *New Statesman and Nation* and that her friend Sylvia Lynd had encouraged her to pursue book publication. She also explained that her stories had attracted an American publisher, but that she wanted her work to be published at home in Canada, adding with characteristic modesty, 'I send these, not with expectations of acceptance, but with plain humility, as I am not sure whether they are good, a little good, or no good, or whether they would interest a public at all.'[18] Then, only two days later, she wrote again and asked that the stories be returned to her. Distance, she said, has put them into perspective – they are 'so trifling, old fashioned, and of personal interest only.' She added that in the enormous events which agitate the country, the public requires 'social awareness' in its reading or 'something truly funny and entertaining.'[19] For a month, she heard nothing; then came a letter from Anne Blochin at the Macmillan Company, which she must have opened with trepidation, saying: 'We have been delighted to read your manuscript of short stories, and as book publishers, think you certainly have a novel half cooked in the first and third sections. If you cannot make something out of that Topaz saga you're not the writer I think you are.'[20]

'A novel half cooked': this would be a judgment hanging over *The Innocent Traveller* for the next four years of revision and publishing negotiations, and would extend into some of the reviews that subsequently tried to determine the book's genre. On 17 January 1945 Ethel wrote to Anne Blochin that she had put all she had into it for a few days, writing a couple of new chapters to frame the whole, and had mailed the manuscript off again, now calling it 'The Painted Curtain.'[21] (The manuscript went through so many drafts and revisions – there is a bewildering collection of these with Wilson's papers at UBC – that it is impossible to tell from her correspondence which sections of the book she is referring to.) The two reader reports on the revised manuscript were diametrically opposed. Anne Blochin pressed for a more coherent, connected narrative: 'the author must submit herself to the novel form and the discipline of plot if she is going to pull this book together.' Blochin foresaw the possibility of a second 'Jalna' series, the commercially successful novels Macmillan was publishing by Mazo de la Roche. Margaret Blackstock, however, with more prescience as it turned out, wrote in her report: 'I would say that this would never make a straight novel. It seems to me it would be much better if this were not attempted, but that the author rather take the character, Topaz, as the central figure in a series of dramatic episodes.'[22] Wilson's subsequent silence clearly reflects the confusion and discouragement she apparently felt in getting such conflicting advice.

Then Ellen Elliott at Macmillan took over Wilson's file and wrote on 15 May 1945, encouraging her to continue with 'Topaz.' There was another month's silence in Vancouver, and then Wilson wrote to explain that her husband had been ill with an infection and that 'making a novel is at the moment something that I would have a great antipathy to.'[23] In retrospect, this reference to her husband's health carries an ominous implication, because this infection would recur and become one of the most traumatic events of Ethel Wilson's life, and some might argue the inspiration for some of the most powerful aspects of her writing. Mary McAlpine dates the original accident as taking place in 1942, but one of Wilson's letters makes it clear that it happened in the late fall of 1944, for she says Wallace has had a pioneer accident and has had to be hospitalized.[24] They were at Little Rock and one evening Wallace had been chopping wood for the fireplace when Ethel heard him call from outside. When she opened the kitchen door to the cabin, she found him holding onto his leg, which was spurting blood. The axe had slipped, and he had cut an artery. He told her how to apply a tourniquet and then instructed her to get a needle, boil it, and while she held the kerosene lamp, he sutured his leg with six stitches. Ethel panicked and ran three miles through the darkness of the forest to reach a telephone at Snug Cove to notify their doctor. There was heavy fog, and he could not come over until late the next morning. The cut led to an infection, and Wallace was hospitalized for a few days. He got better, but the infection in the wounded area was slow to disappear; it broke out again in the spring, and when it recurred in the same area of his leg a few years later, it would have devastating effects.

Ellen Elliott tactfully prodded Wilson, nonetheless, to continue her writing, and Wilson finally wrote back and said that she was thinking of publishing the Topaz stories herself, '*pour la famille*, for otherwise [Topaz] and her circle will never see the light. And she should not be entirely passed out of sight and memory.'[25] Elliott in reply pointed out that private publishing was an expensive business, and she mentioned that an American agent by the name of David Lloyd was impressed by 'We Have to Sit Opposite,' which by now had appeared in *Chatelaine*.[26] Wilson remained silent, until suddenly on 10 October 1945 a new manuscript arrived on Ellen Elliott's desk. It was for a short novel titled 'Hetty Dorval.' The history of *Hetty Dorval* and the events in Ethel Wilson's life during its composition and publication will be followed in the next chapter.

In the meantime, *The Innocent Traveller* had four more years of writing and negotiations before it would see the light of publication. With a contract signed for *Hetty Dorval*, Wilson in the fall of 1946 wrote to Miss Elliott about her Topaz stories once again, saying she would see what might be done about the flow of narrative in the book. But she points out that Clarence Day's *Life with Father*, a series of family sketches published in 1935, was not marketed as a novel and was nonetheless immensely successful. She adds in a postscript that she feels 'Topaz' is 'good enough in writing to overcome aberration in form – whereas in Hetty [she can] only rejoice in one very good sentence.'[27] In March of 1947 she resubmitted the Topaz stories to Macmillan in Toronto with the title 'The Dancer' and sent a copy as well to Maria Leiper at Simon and Schuster. Leiper, who had been urging the project forward now for ten years, wrote back to say the manuscript was making the rounds at the office. She added: 'I have read it, every word of it (a rare thing in a publisher's office), and all with great delight. It seems to me much improved, and a joy in every way. Whether or not the sales experts will agree with me remains to be seen.'[28] Wilson, reporting on this letter to Ellen Elliott, observes wryly, 'This is like sending a hospital bulletin on a patient's progress.' In spite of Leiper's enthusiasm, the final report at Simon and Schuster was not positive. The readers viewed the book as 'fluttery and pallid' with 'no solid skeleton,' and felt the writer was wasting her talent on this particular project. They saw no sales for a book of this kind in the United States. Wilson was discouraged to get this news, as much for Leiper as for herself, and although this brought her relationship with the Simon and Schuster editor to a close, she would never forget her encouragement and loyalty in the early years of trying to get published.

In the meantime, the editors at Macmillan in Toronto hardly knew what to do with the manuscript and busied themselves with the final production and early reviews of *Hetty Dorval* in their correspondence with Ethel Wilson. At the end of June, Ellen Elliott left her job at Macmillan, and John Gray took over the Wilson file. He decided they should send it to their counterparts in the London and New York offices of the company, because in Toronto they were too close to the manuscript and needed another opinion. In the meantime, a reader in Toronto did file a report August 13, which took no clear position on whether the manuscript was publishable or not. The reviewer, identified only by the initials F.W., liked very much the Jane Austen-ish aspect of Wilson's writing, the delicate and sympathetic ironies, the small observations on life, but pointed out that the book is presented as a chronicle, and that Wilson is not really able to manage the larger movements of history and change and people en masse that the chronicle or saga requires; the Great War, laments the reader, is presented vaguely, and important years of history are skipped.[29] The report that came from London that same month, however, was positive and assured in its opinion and was not spooked by the question of genre: 'This is not a novel, nor biography, nor autobiography, though something, probably, of each. That does not matter at all ... it is witty, delicious,' and so forth.[30] By September, Macmillan of London had offered Wilson a contract.

Hearing the news from London, John Gray wrote to Wilson to say that Macmillan Canada would want to do its own production of the Topaz book, and by 18 January 1948 he had another reader's report on file. Likely influenced by the positive news from London, this reader, signed E.J., while finding the manuscript episodic, was wholly persuaded by the author's ability to create the atmosphere of a time and place and described it as 'charming, amusing, the work of a vivid imagination ... altogether a refreshing and enjoyable tale.'[31] Gray wrote to Harold Latham, his counterpart in New York, and persuaded him to take 1,000 copies of the Canadian edition, saying that while the Topaz stories might not do well commercially, he wants to do the book 'because of the good stuff that is there, and also for the future.'[32] He and Latham both felt the book was still too episodic. Later that year, however, Gray was told by Daniel Macmillan at the head office in London that all the production of the book would be done in England, though 1,500 copies would carry the Canadian imprint.

In the meantime, in her anxious way, Wilson was sending both offices a seemingly endless series of last-minute edits and revisions; and to the London office, photographs of Eliza and Great-Uncle John in case the press might want to use them in some way. But in this last stretch, she also wrote three new chapters – 'Recurring Pleasures,' 'Down at English Bay,' and 'Family Prayer' – which are among the best pieces in the book. The big problem which she kept turning over in her mind was the question of a title. 'Portrait of Topaz' and 'The Dancer' had been two of the working titles she had used for a long time, but neither was entirely satisfactory. Some of her other suggestions to Gray, such as 'Told in Vancouver' and 'Vancouver Aunt,' were even less satisfactory. She wondered at one point if 'Down at English Bay' might serve as a title, since it was where so many of her happy memories of childhood in Vancouver were centered, and was turning out to be one of her favourite sequences in the book. Other titles she played with were 'Prophane Dust,' 'The Water Glider,' 'Unimportant Journey,' 'The Youngest Daughter,' and 'Journey to Vancouver of a Small Bird.'[33] Titles, in fact, would bedevil Wilson throughout her career; they seemed to narrow a work's focus and be at odds with what was expansive in the writing itself. Audrey Butler feels she probably unwittingly helped Wilson arrive at her final choice. Audrey made a long-anticipated return to Vancouver and to UBC in the late summer of 1947, and Ethel showed her the stories. They had often talked about Ethel's grandmother and aunts coming to Canada before the turn of the century, and Audrey, who had in fact known Aunt Eliza in extreme old age, had always referred to them as 'innocents abroad.' Now she referred to Aunt Ethel's stories of innocent travellers, and on 12 December 1947 Wilson wrote to John Gray announcing her new title.[34] Both Gray and Daniel Macmillan in London wrote back to say it was a fine choice. Although she does not say this in her correspondence or essays, Wilson probably felt both words in this title retained the spirit of youthful adventure that, ironically, characterized the relocation of three aging English ladies to Vancouver, though in fact it was her own youth that constituted the seeing eye of the book.

After nineteen years of planning and writing, *The Innocent Traveller* was finally published in the summer of 1949, six copies arriving at the Wilsons' apartment on August 16. The biggest pleasure, so long anticipated, was sharing them with the members of the family, all of whom were delighted to have their history preserved in this sophisticated and entertaining form.

That pleasure was reinforced by the local reviews of the book, which were brief but positive. The Vancouver *Province* described the book as 'engrossing,' while the *Sun* drew attention to a 'polish and lustre' in the writing just barely glimpsed in her work before. Both newspapers were interested in the author's local identity, and under her picture in the *Province* there was a caption stating that the author 'is known to most Vancouverites as the wife of Dr Wallace Wilson, well-known Vancouver doctor.'[35] Being in the spotlight this way with her husband's name attached made it especially important that the reviews be encouraging. There were enthusiastic notices from other parts of the country. The reviewer for *Saturday Night* delighted in Topaz and said that with *The Innocent Traveller* Wilson's literary reputation was established beyond a shadow of a doubt.[36] Claude Bissell in the *University of Toronto Quarterly* identified the special ingredients of Wilson's writing as humour, gentle satire, and 'a good deal of sense and sensibility,' suggesting the Jane Austen aspect of Wilson's art that subsequent critics would also point to.[37] Surprisingly, the American reviews were quite positive, given the reluctance of American publishers. The *New York Herald Tribune, Saturday Review of Books,* and *San Francisco Chronicle* were all exuberant in their praise, as was the *Christian Science Monitor*, which praised the book, knowingly, as a labour of love and called it a delight.[38]

One of the finest reviews appeared in the *Toronto Star*, saying that the writing was so good that one can open the book at almost any page and read with appreciation and reward.[39] But in Toronto's other major newspaper, the *Globe and Mail*, William Arthur Deacon, regarded as Canada's most influential book reviewer, was very critical. He found the book structurally weak, the first half dull and pointless. Although he regarded the second half set in Canada to be more interesting, he viewed the book generally as a 'life-with-father theme turned feminine and ... a weak attempt at nostalgia for historic backgrounds.' But in this lengthy review, the chief focus of his attack was the character of Topaz. 'A novel,' he argued, 'should involve some working out of human destiny,' but Topaz's life 'never came near the dignity of tragedy ... she made no impress on anything or anybody ... she maintained her own integrity at zero.'[40] He also dismissed Wilson's presentation of second-ary characters in her story. In a letter to Frank Upjohn, vice-president and manager of the trade department at Macmillan in Toronto, Wilson put on a brave face, saying not without irony that, as a review of the kind of 'novel' Mr Deacon wishes to see written in Canada, it was quite fair. What she felt unjust was Deacon's attack on her subjects, 'his taking poor Topaz's butterfly wings between his strong fingers and reducing their sparkle to ugly dust.' Deacon referred to the man Topaz once loved as a 'dim fop,' and Wilson tells Frank Upjohn how he in fact intro-duced valuable bills into the House of Commons, particularly in con-nection with the betterment of conditions for children in Victorian England. In dismissing Rachel (Aunty Belle) as a 'colourless soul,' Dea-con, she says, has missed Rachel's secret love of the beautiful and her devotion to '"ordinary" duty,' which is for most people the mainspring, and '"ordinary" people are life.' Wilson points out that the characters appear this way in their relation to Topaz, who is the focal centre of the narrative, but she deeply regrets that she has exposed these people, who were so precious in her own life, to the hostile public gaze of a critic like Deacon. 'I am, you see, defending my "characters," not myself,' she con-cludes.[41] The Wilsons had friends in Toronto, including the distin-guished physician Duncan Graham and his wife, Enid, and Ethel felt embarrassed by what she felt was the public ridicule of her book and family in the *Globe and Mail.*

Two other national publications, both of which had printed her fic-tion, ran negative reviews of *The Innocent Traveller.* The reviewer for *Canadian Forum* wrote that Topaz Edgeworth lived a placid life that is 'as tiresome to the reader as it must have been to her.' Topaz, he insists, is a 'great bore.' This reviewer also laments that Wilson missed an opportu-nity to present something of the vivid life that characterized Vancouver from the 1890s forward. He concludes bluntly: 'If you are interested in knowing how much can be written about negative personalities, then read *The Innocent Traveller.*'[42] *Echoes,* which had published 'The Cigar and the Poor Young Girl' in the fall of 1945, also ran a short negative notice, suggesting it must have been with tongue in cheek that Wilson would write a family history focusing on a woman 'almost incredibly stu-pid from youth to extreme old age.'[43] Equally disappointing was the brief notice in the *Times Literary Supplement* back in England. The description of the train journey across Canada is identified as 'an agree-able feature of the book,' but Topaz, who is meant to appear as a charm-ing scatterbrain, doesn't really charm, and 'few of the minor characters come to life.'[44] This dismissive review was again an embarrassment, and she could only hope that it went unnoticed by relatives and old friends 'at home.'

What are we to make now of this somewhat eccentric book? Is it only of antiquarian interest, a family history executed with literary skill, or does it have features that give it an abiding interest? Late in life, looking over the books she had written, Wilson wrote to her close friend (and husband's cousin) Kathleen Graham saying, 'I particularly love *The Innocent Traveller* because it shows a true picture of home and my Grannie, & my Aunt [Eliza] and Auntie Belle.'[45] Clearly, family history remained for the author the essential motive behind her narrative. But when she was writing the book, Wilson was also aware that *The Innocent Traveller* had value as social history, particularly the story of English culture being transplanted to Canada. She alludes to this in the novel itself when she says that 'the history of families like the Hastings family is to some extent the history of the city of Vancouver,'[46] and she wrote to one of her editors at Macmillan several years later that the book's value was in depicting 'a middleclass English family arriving [in Canada], ideas, prejudgments & all' and 'the terrific contribution' such families as her uncles have made.[47] Certainly, the story of the family in all its branches, their life in the Methodist Church, their persisting ties with England, the descriptions of West End respectability and Gastown's disrepute, the story of Joe Fortes and of the Chinese servants, Yow and Fooey, all comprise a rich portrait of Vancouver's social history that reaches beyond what Deacon called mere nostalgia for historical backgrounds.

But readers continue to founder, as they did when the book was first published, over the fact that the central character in the book is someone of so little value to society. Topaz does no work, never marries, and remains a rather foolish, self-absorbed individual in what would today seem a privileged parasitical relationship to the Hastings family, though in Victorian times her status in the family would never have been questioned. Wilson herself argued that this was part of the book's uniqueness, that it celebrated the life of someone who enjoyed life immensely, amused herself and others, departed, and left no trace – the record, in other words, of a useless person, who made no more lasting impact on the world than wind on water, or the warbling of an unimportant bird. She recognized, of course, that Topaz's story was very different from stories of valuable lives or unhappy lives, but it was a record nonetheless of someone who enjoyed life with great zest, and that, she said, should be part of the human story too.

Wilson's defence, of course, does not identify two of the book's outstanding features – its remarkable achievement in terms of style and its
sophisticated ironies. If we are shown how much Topaz Edgeworth
enjoys her life, we are presented with this 'commotion of living' from an
ironic point of view that both satirizes Victorian social conventions and
views all human existence finally as a commotion in time. Some of the
ironies are purely comic ones, as when we witness nonagenarian Grandfather Edgeworth proposing marriage to two sisters in their eighties in
order to secure himself a wife and provide Topaz, nearly fifty, with a
mother. Others, like the upset at the Minerva Club over one of its potential members taking swimming lessons from a black man, have a direct
satirical dimension. But W.H. New, one of Wilson's first serious critics,
delves deeper for significant irony. He points out that the novel reveals
the sweep of history over one hundred years, portraying a world that
changes quickly. 'Its effect,' he writes, 'is to make any social order or
"absolute" code of morality that people establish seem ... ironic, for the
only constant in such a life is change.' Topaz, however, does not change;
her happy attachment to the past and her obliviousness to her dependency on the family in the present make her an increasingly comic figure. Her lack of depth as a character (she is compared in a telling
metaphor to a water-glider skimming along the surface), and especially
her increasing anachronism, make us aware of how temporary and con-
tingent the social order always is. The narrator's view of Topaz as insignificant, 'just small bright dots of colour,' creates an ironic perspective
on a society that constructs and sustains the priviliged world in which
Topaz finds contentment and protection.[48]
    In a study of the novel's structure, Mary-Ann Stouck illuminates a
design within each chapter of the book wherein the opening establishes
a conventional setting and evokes forms of behaviour that are required
or expected. Then someone, often Topaz, acts in a way that is seen to be
inappropriate in terms of the setting, that disrupts conventional expectations, but finally and most importantly the situation is resolved so as to
restore the status quo, for as Stouck observes 'no matter how much it
shocks her relations, Topaz's behaviour is never allowed to challenge
seriously the essential foundations of her world.' Even when the family
domain is not the setting, this pattern prevails. 'I Have a Father in the
Promised Land' is set in the rituals of church-going: here ordinary
restrained Methodist demeanour is disrupted by a new evangelical
preacher and young Rose's over-earnest emotional response, but order
is restored by young Aunt Miranda's preoccupation with her engage-

ment ring and, comically, by Aunt Topaz's belated realization that she had all sorts of relatives in the Promised Land and, by not standing up to acknowledge them, had missed an opportunity. The novel abounds in images of containment and social harmony, though Wilson fully recognizes the constraints and stifling conformity necessary in this social structure if someone like Topaz is going to survive emotionally and economically.[49]

Postcolonial readings of the novel have been less sanguine about this structure and its political implications. The most rigorous of these can be found in *The Invention of Canada* by Arnold H. Itwaru, who reads Wilson's work as affirming one racial group's supremacy at the expense of all others. Topaz, he argues, was raised in a Victorian social order that insulated her from the world outside its boundaries. Infantilized by her society's definitions of propriety and coherence, she carries to Vancouver a romanticized idea of history and nature. Meeting a black porter in Montreal, her reaction is '"Ah! Negroes!"' like a child's first exclamation upon seeing an exotic animal in a city zoo. She sees him as a curiosity, writes Itwaru, but quickly invents him within her notions of normality by assuming he has a wife and family (without waiting for his response to her questions). This, Itwaru argues, brings 'the negro' into a behavioural world approved of by Topaz. More disturbing to Itwaru is the voice of the narrator describing the porter according to racist stereotypes – a man with 'unusually wide swelling nostrils and a proposterously fine set of dazzling white teeth.' Topaz wonders how such splendid teeth are acquired – is it a matter of diet, or perhaps cleaning with a stick? Itwaru points out that critics make much of Ethel Wilson's Christian humanism, but he argues this cannot be used 'to exonerate the sedimentation of racial patronization (the other side of racism) in her work.' He argues further that Wilson does not allow us to see non-white characters as having other histories and cultures. The Chinese servants in the novel are stereotyped as suspicious figures, wily and sullen. When Fooey is praying, we are told he is 'thinking in Chinese of God knows what.' Joe Fortes, by contrast, is patronized by being grossly romanticized in terms of his majestic physical stature and beautiful brown body compared to that of a seal. Non-white men, writes Itwaru, are emasculated, defined exclusively in terms of their service to the dominant race. Topaz's English order, like the tide and her self-mythologizing, finally run out and are replaced by a new social and economic order, but it is one which has its roots in the racist order that preceded it.[50]

Also writing from a Third World perspective, but reading Wilson in terms of Indian philosophy, Anjali Bhelande brings into focus, in the most comprehensive study of Wilson to date, something of the author's intention with regards to self and history.[51] Bhelande argues that what concerns Wilson is the plane of consciousness beyond dualistic logic where there is no conflict between self and other, where the individual has transcended separate consciousness and become one with the community and the world at large. She identifies various characters in Wilson's fiction as aspiring to, or reaching, this state of 'being the other,' and Rachel and her mother, Annie Hastings, in *The Innocent Traveller* are among these. Rachel transcends self through duty to the family, while the grandmother's selfless involvement with others, argues Bhelande, is an instance of a character experiencing joy and peace by serving God. For Rachel and her mother, the fulfilment they experience does not spring from a negative fear of being found selfish, or from guilt, but from transcending self and becoming 'the other' through service.

The advent of the Second World War in the novel coincides with the ending of Aunt Topaz's life, and the text, observes Bhelande, becomes haunted with images and reflections on time's passage and the dissolution of all things in it. Topaz does not mourn the past – she is eager for her next adventure – but for the reader the passing of her lifetime compounded by the tragedy of youth cut down in war is emotionally very powerful at the novel's close. Wilson feared sentimentality in her writing, and Bhelande reveals accordingly how a passage in the novel, echoing directly the Bhagavad Gita, puts history and time on another plane. The Bhagavad Gita describes a great battle pending between two related families. The poem takes place on a battlefield in the form of a dialogue between the warrior Arjuna and Krishna, the supreme Deity. Arjuna is urged to fight without fear or guilt because in terms of the Divine scheme, the battle is already over and he is merely God's instrument. Bhelande draws our attention to the following passage near the end of *The Innocent Traveller.*

> The voice speaking from the field of battle had always, in the nature of things, been prepared to speak. The battle had always been, and was completed before it had begun. The mother sat with the bit of paper not an hour old, and her heart which failed within her told her, 'I have always known this, it has always been; when he was so high, this was approved in Time and I sat here with this paper.'[52]

The mourning mother in Wilson's passage, writes Bhelande, is bitterly aware that the death of her son was ordained long before the battle began, but her attachment to her son blinds her to his immortality, just as Arjuna was blinded by his attachment to the kinsmen he must do battle with. In the paragraph following the description of the grieving mother, Wilson describes the paradoxical nature of that immortality as the impersonal revealed by the personal and the timeless 'disclosed in the world of Time':

> The permanence of the fleeting and prodigal joy of this timeless world was without responsibility or question. The unearthly light of morning on the flank of the hill departs and is eternal and no one can prevail against it. The permanence of the impermanent frail flower is for ever. So is the sunshine on clover and the humming bees. The teasing whisper of the little wave on the shingle turns and always creeps in again. The beauty of structure of a tree or of a mountain changes but will never change.[53]

Bhelande's analysis of these passages illuminates a series of references to Time throughout the book and in works to follow. Sometimes those references are the expected nostalgic ones, longing for a simpler and seemingly happier life in the past or in a forest setting; at other times, we leap forward in an unsettling way to the future, as when the family is travelling to Canada in the late 1800s and the narrator tells us of an unborn grandson who will see the same landscapes in eastern Canada one day. Time is both an emotional and a philosophical dimension in *The Innocent Traveller,* a layering of artistic elements that would characterize most of Wilson's work. Bhelande is correct in observing that critics have not paid full attention to this more demanding aspect of Ethel Wilson's art. But they have demonstrated, nonetheless, that Wilson's writing is philosophically sophisticated and artistically complex, and *The Innocent Traveller* is in every way significant in this respect.

The Innocent Traveller was reprinted in both London and Toronto in paperback in 1960 and sold well until it went out of print in 1970. It became part of McClelland and Stewart's New Canadian Library 'Classic' series in 1982 and was reissued in 1990 in the NCL's new format with an afterword by P.K. Page and a cover that featured E.J. Hughes's painting *Lighthouse at Prospect Point.* In apt phrasings that connect with Bhelande's reading, Page writes that Wilson, as 'master of implication, mistress of delicate balances ... carries us lightly, as though bearing no weight at all, through a myriad of interweaving mini-stories, deftly skirting the real pain, burning us only a little, but burning us just the same.'

Given the superficiality of Topaz, why is she so memorable, Page asks. The answer, she suggests, must lie in the fact that 'Wilson's inscribing eye – her incising, incisive eye – is sufficiently infused with a loving spirit that we catch her love.'[54] There is perhaps no better estimate of Ethel Wilson's art.

CHAPTER EIGHT

Hetty Dorval
1945–1947

... directly the war was over, a sort of hoarded up feeling came to write again,   ✗
& I did. – Wilson to Desmond Pacey (1964)[1]

Three weeks of rain / Quiet machinery / Matters of style /
A pseudonym / A dust jacket / The first convention / John Gray /
Publicity / *Hetty Dorval*

In the middle of reworking her manuscripts for *The Innocent Traveller*, Ethel Wilson paused at some point in 1945 and wrote the short novel *Hetty Dorval*, which was her first book to be published. The details of its composition and sources are obscured by Wilson's wish to present herself as a writer purely by chance, with no particular ambition to be published. In a talk she gave at the UBC Library in 1957, titled 'Somewhere near the Truth,' Wilson says that in 1946, in connection with her husband's work as the president-elect of the Canadian Medical Association, she had assumed the role of organizing the women's functions for the annual convention. She was terrified by the responsibility and 'sweated with apprehension.' To remain sane and functioning, she says, she wrote a book to occupy her thoughts and sublimate her unprofitable fright.[2] In her 'Preface' to the Alcuin Society edition of the novel, however, she says it happened this way: that at the end of the war, faced with a hiatus of emptiness and rain while her husband was still away, she had a dream which took her to the bridge where the Fraser and Thompson Rivers meet. For three weeks of rain, she sat at her desk and wrote, and before her husband had returned she had produced a small work named *Hetty Dorval*. Mary McAlpine appears to have interpreted the dream literally and describes Wilson taking a train to Lytton, staying in a room at the Brody House hotel, and working at a desk from which she could see the two rivers coming together.[3] There is no evidence, however, in letters or family recollections that she did this, and it is unlikely that she would have travelled there on her own. Finally, in a letter to Ellen Elliott at Macmillan dated 2 November 1945, Wilson says that about two nights after VJ Day (September 2), she was feeling frustrated that she could not seem to write except from actual and personal experiences, and then woke up the next morning with a completely imagined short novel in her head. She wrote for two weeks and by then was in sight of the end.[4] The common thread in these four versions is that the author was alone for a period of time and wrote the story quickly, unlike her other books, which took her years to write. Whatever the circumstances of its composition, she would always refer to *Hetty Dorval* in disparaging terms, such as 'amateur,' 'slight,' 'hokum,' even 'illegitimate' – a book with only one very good sentence in it.[5]

While Wilson was no doubt overwrought by her husband's absence, the bad weather, and the spectre of a convention to be organized, there was a more practical reason for her sitting down to write a short novel. From the time she started sending out her Topaz stories in the late 1930s, publishers were urging her to turn her family materials into novel form. Anne Blochin's first response to the Topaz stories was that 'the author must submit herself to the novel form and the discipline of plot if she is going to pull this book together.'[6] I think Wilson wrote *Hetty Dorval*, and wrote it quickly, to see if in fact she could write something with a plot of at least novella length, much the way Edith Wharton began her short novel *Ethan Frome* as a way of disciplining herself to write in French. The plot of *Hetty Dorval* is a very simple one: the narrator, a country girl named Frankie Burnaby, for a time falls under the spell of Hetty Dorval, a beautiful older woman with a mysterious past who moves to the little ranching community of Lytton, B.C. But gradually Frankie begins to have doubts about Hetty's character. Wherever she goes – to school in Vancouver, across the Atlantic on a ship, in London – Frankie keeps encountering Hetty and is both attracted to her and repelled. Eventually she learns of Hetty's unsavoury affairs with rich and powerful men, observes her predations on her own young friends, and angrily casts her out of her life. There is nothing extraneous in plot, character, or setting, just the bare bones of an initiation story, but Wilson decided to call it a short novel when she wrote to Ellen Elliott in October 1945, and the latter was very excited to hear that Wilson had taken the company's advice. She explained that if this short novel brought Wilson some recognition in the market, then they might be able to publish 'Topaz' as stories.

The editing and publishing of *Hetty Dorval* went fairly smoothly. A complete manuscript arrived on Elliott's desk November 22, and by January she was able to send Wilson some of the praise set down in the readers' reports. Anne Blochin described the manuscript as 'a *very* strong piece of quiet machinery' that outlines 'the psychological triumph of inherent good over attractive evil.' Peggy Blackstock, the other in-house reader, was even more exuberant in her praise, calling it 'a grand story – the real thing,' asserting that the style never falters and that 'the character of Hetty is developed brilliantly, as is the growth of the girl Frankie.'[7] In summarizing the reports, Elliott points out that 'without exception we all like your descriptions of British Columbia.'[8] In reply, Wilson admits that 'the thing I have a rooted passion for is the scenery in that (Hetty) country which, if writing about ... one could not forebear to dwell on.'[9] The readers had only two major suggestions for revision: they wanted Wilson to drop the short paragraph at the end of chapter 1 which tells in advance of the drowning of Frankie's friend, Ernestine; and they absolutely insisted that she drop an epilogue titled 'At the Bungalow,' in which Hetty returns again to Lytton after the Second World War. It was an anti-climax, they argued, spoiling the powerful effect of what they saw as the real end of the story, Hetty's move to Vienna just before the war begins. Wilson was persuaded that the epilogue should go but argued that the drowning of Ernestine should stay near the beginning because 'it is the regretful and striking thing a child could not help telling' right away. 'Children,' she added, 'are very proud of knowing people who have accidents, especially if fatal.'[10] Nonetheless, in the first round of negotiations, she was willing to defer to the readers' opinion and delete the drowning of Ernestine.

She was not, however, so cooperative about matters of style, whether word choice, spelling, or punctuation. An editor, it was said, felt more freedom to remove a character from Ethel Wilson's work than a comma.[11] This was such an important matter for Wilson and so central to her understanding of art that it is important to look at a few examples that occurred in preparing *Hetty Dorval* for publication. The editors wanted her to drop the word 'fastidious' because they felt it was too sophisticated for twelve-year-old Frankie to use, but Wilson wrote back '"fastidious" remains please!' asserting that an only child living a rather lonely life in a house with a library uses such words with great satisfaction: 'I know because I was and did.' She argued for the somewhat archaic spelling of 'waggon' because in her opinion the Anglo-Saxon variant has a 'solid, double, labouring, almost creaking look and sound, [w]hereas "wagon" (like the French "wagon-lit") is Continental.' She also protested vigorously against 'cannot,' even though the formidable Winifred Eayrs, custodian of house style at Macmillan and sister of the former company president, argued that the only time two words are used are in such cases as 'I can not only read French, I can talk it as well.'[12] But punctuation was the most ticklish issue. In passages of conversation, Wilson wanted to leave out some of the commas because conversation 'is a headlong affair, and people do not always speak in comma'd phrases as in a well arranged paragraph.'[13] But, in other parts of the text, she relied heavily on 'the workmanlike comma and full stop,' concerned to avoid as much as possible the use of dots, dashes, question marks, and exclamation marks, which she felt have a feminine, popular magazine look.[14] On most of these points, Wilson eventually had her way, as she suggested to Elliott should be the case: 'How kind of you to realize that I mean what I write. The charming woman who types for me used to correct my punctuation. But as I always intend it for purposes of phrasing and significance, she kindly blindly copies it now.'[15]

The author had two special requests to make concerning the publishing of this short novel. In a letter of 19 January 1946 to Ellen Elliott, she asks if it would be possible to publish the book using something akin to her maiden name – 'leaving the dull Ethel out and being Davida Bryan' (as in Ethel Davis Bryant).[16] Before Elliott could answer, Wilson wrote again the next day suggesting Mary Millett Davis, Millett being a distinguished family name in the Edge family.[17] Elliott was not very receptive to the idea of a *nom de plume*, pointing out that she had already established something of a reputation with the name 'Ethel Wilson,' especially with her popular short story 'We Have to Sit Opposite' published in *Chatelaine*. Since, by the author's account, there were no 'real-life' characters in *Hetty Dorval*, Elliott could not see why she wouldn't continue to use her real name.[18] But Wilson wrote back saying, 'I don't mind Millett Davis getting remarks like "This is a terrible novel ... Miss Davis must learn to etc" because I feel detached about it, but my husband and friends would feel more awful than they need if E.W. got it in the neck, poor woman.'[19] More letters were exchanged on this question, and Wilson suggested a compromise: 'By Frankie Burnaby as told to Ethel Wilson.'[20] But the editors at Macmillan held out, convinced that 'Ethel Wilson' was already a bankable name, and she finally conceded.

In a letter of 3 July 1946, she wrote to Ellen Elliott from Bowen Island: 'I discussed with myself and with my husband the name of the author, and decided to throw inhibitions to the winds, and be Ethel Wilson. I wired accordingly to you yesterday.'[21] Her 'inhibitions' were both artistic and social. She was not confident that *Hetty Dorval* had much worth as writing. She had told Elliott that she was not quite at home with *Hetty*, that she preferred a light touch in her work and that *Hetty* was all very serious.[22] It would be easy for critics to dismiss an earnest little book of this kind. Her social standing, especially as the wife of the president of the Canadian Medical Association, made her acutely sensitive to being ridiculed in the press as a second-rate writer. There may also have been some anxiety about 'real-life' associations, because in the first letter to Ellen Elliott mentioning the story she did say that, drawing from her own experience, Hetty was 'a very pure profile of a thoroughly bad creature,'[23] and Vancouver friends speculated on the model for Hetty, even suggesting one of Wilson's cousins.

Her other request was that the book have a very simple dust jacket. She was particularly opposed to what she called 'Beautiful Woman on Cover,' which would be banal in her opinion and add to any lushness in the book.[24] Instead she urged that a map of the Lytton country appear on the front, and she arranged that an artist friend, Nan Cheney, prepare a cover illustration. The appearance of the book became an anxiety almost as urgent as the question of a pseudonym. Macmillan appears to have ignored the idea of a map, perhaps judging it would be too regional in its appeal, but were persuaded to prepare a very simple jacket, with just the book's title in white lettering on a clear green background. Wilson's one last anxious request was 'I hope my name on the book will be *small* print. It would not look well, large.'[25] That request was also ignored. But she was allowed to prepare copy for the inside back flap, two short paragraphs which give yet another version of how she came to write the novel. She says in the first paragraph that many of us who live in British Columbia find that its mountains, forests, and water become 'incorporated into our fabric of memory, and perhaps into our being,' and she asks if place or what we sometimes call scenery bears any relation to personal or national character. In the second paragraph, she tells of an abandoned log cabin that she and her husband used to drive past in the sagebrush country every year and how it eventually collapsed in on itself. But in this story, she says she rehabilitated it, brought it back into civilization 'and some characters moved in.' This description on the back flap pleased her, but her publishers' insistence that her photo also appear on the jacket did not. They wanted a studio portrait. She eventually conceded but sent a 'snap' that her niece, Mary Buckerfield, had taken of her and Wallace in the country that was anything but flattering. The author, standing in a field in a tweed jacket, is squinting impatiently into the camera; her hair is windblown, and the photo is slightly blurred, defying all the conventions of dust-jacket glamour pursued by someone like Gabrielle Roy. When the book was printed, however, Wilson was more than pleased with the chaste simplicity of the binding and cover. It is 'a *lovely* looking little book,' she wrote honestly to Elliott, and she could 'now take what comes much better.'[26] The surface attractivenes of her books remained important to Ethel Wilson, much the same way being well dressed was always of paramount concern, a form of security and protective covering.

In the meantime there was the terrifying conference at Banff. Ethel had to play the wife of the president-elect of the CMA and move to centre stage with her husband, organizing activities for the doctors' wives who were accompanying their husbands to the convention. Since Vancouver did not have the facilities to handle such a large meeting at one venue, it was decided to hold the conference at the Banff Springs Hotel. She went with Wallace to Banff in January 1946 to work out the logistics of the meeting on site and reported to Ellen Elliott April 3 that they had reached the acutely detailed part of the convention planning. The meeting took place in June, and perhaps something of Wilson's experience of the event has been preserved in her story 'Mrs Golightly and the First Convention,' for she apparently told Audrey Butler that several times at the meeting she kept forgetting the name of one of the wives – a Mrs Fuchs – and how much better it would have been right after the war if the name had been Polish or Norwegian rather than German. McAlpine tells us that Ethel probably did her job well, and that she added her own thoughtful and imaginative touch to the execution of her duties. She apparently asked the wives of the CMA officers if they would go shopping with her because she had presents to buy for home and would like their advice. On the last day of the convention, these women found that the items they admired in the shops had been wrapped and delivered to their rooms with a note of thanks from Ethel Wilson.[27] Kindnesses of this sort were often done anonymously. A nurse at one of Vancouver's hospitals, who recognized Ethel Wilson, observed that she left a gift for a patient at the receptionist's desk with the anonymous instruction that it was 'from a friend.'[28]

That summer, Ethel reported to Ellen Elliott from Bowen Island that she was in rather poor health. Perhaps it was fatigue after the stress of the convention, but she was more likely complaining about the anaemia that had plagued her since the flu epidemic of 1918. In many of her letters, she refers to the 'deep injections' she must have every four days to stay healthy, and in the letter to Elliott she writes that Wallace is coming up to Little Rock 'with a harpoon and a quart of liver extract.'[29] When Ethel Wilson was said to have 'taken to her bed' or was 'resting' like a nineteenth-century neurasthenic, the reason was most likely tiredness caused by her blood condition. She was also subject to sudden nosebleeds that were very hard to stop. They would happen under stress at public functions (she was especially appalled when her nose bled copiously at Rideau Hall on one occasion), but they sometimes happened in the night while she slept.[30] Unsympathetic acquaintances, not knowing of her medical condition, would say, 'Oh, she was forever going to bed,'[31] reflecting their dislike of Ethel's reserved manner and their distaste for hypochondriacs.

But by early fall of 1946, she was energized sufficiently to set out on a three-month trip across Canada, accompanying Wallace on his duties as the president of the Canadian Medical Association. She sent Winifred Eayrs, her copy editor, a list of addresses where she could be reached during the first part of the trip – places like the Hotel Bessborough in Saskatoon, the Royal Alexandra in Winnipeg, and, in Ottawa, the Chateau Laurier. What she was especially looking forward to was meeting the staff at Macmillan in Toronto. On October 17 they gave a little luncheon for her at the office at 70 Bond Street, where, after two years of correspondence, she finally met in person Anne Blochin, Ellen Elliott, Peggy Blackstock, and Winifred Eayrs. But most important for her that day, she met for the first time John Gray, recently returned editor-in-chief of the company, who would become her editor, confidant, literary executor, and beloved friend.

John Gray, descended from an affluent and well-educated Ontario family, had started to work at Macmillan before the war. On his return to the company in 1946, he brought a great deal of energy and enthusiasm not only to building up the Canadian branch of the Macmillan publishing company, but to promoting serious literature by Canadian authors. He had taken over the editing and promotion of established writers like Mazo de la Roche and Morley Callaghan, and was encouraging the talents of first-time novelists like W.O. Mitchell. A pipe-smoker and raconteur, Gray had something of the bluff, genial manner of Wallace, and Ethel felt entirely comfortable with him from the start. Gray felt a similar rapport with the Wilsons, and when business brought him to Vancouver, as it frequently did, he would always make time for a visit at the Kensington. Wilson had worked cordially with Ellen Elliott, but it was working subsequently with Gray that made her association with the Macmillan Company such a happy and profitable one. Elliott had recognized Wilson's talent, but Gray entered into a personal friendship with the author which constituted one of the creative conditions for her writing.

That fall the Wilsons travelled the length of the country, including the Maritime provinces, Ethel being especially interested to see Charlottetown. From Ottawa she wrote to both Ellen Elliott and John Gray to thank them for the luncheon, and she mentioned attending the espionage trial in which Igor Gouzenko, the Russian clerk who had defected and wore a hood through the trials, gave testimony about an extensive spy ring operating in Canada. She admitted to being spellbound watching Gouzenko grilled: 'Such a sturdy boy – or man – he compelled my admiration,' she wrote.[32] (Curiously, he would be linked to her a few years later when his novel, *The Fall of a Titan*, would be the jury's pick for the Governor General's Award for 1954 instead of *Swamp Angel*.) While still in Ottawa, she wrote to Winifred Eayrs November 6 to say she had dined the night before at Government House: 'It was beautiful – beyond compare. I enjoyed it so much.' She did not take these privileges lightly. She recognized humbly how very fortunate she was, how marriage to Wallace was the fulfilment of her dreams in so many ways.

Hetty Dorval had been advertised as part of Macmillan's fall list, but a paper shortage and other delays at the printer meant a spring 1947 publication instead. Ethel Wilson might well have wished for further delays because she was not quite prepared for the next stage in becoming the author of a book – doing publicity. On March 6 she wrote to Miss Elliott: 'HELP HELP HELP – and as fast as you can. I thought all there was to a book was (a) I write it (b) you publish it (c) "they" read it.' She went on to explain that two women from newspapers had approached her about interviews, and she had put them off. 'The fact is I am *terribly* publicity-shy, and would rather not write a book at all than suffer with publicity.'[33] By April she had calmed down enough to entertain three women journalists in her apartment, though she made them promise there would be no mention of her family in the papers and no photographs, and that she would see in advance and give approval to anything they wrote for publication. Even with these assurances and a rather pleasant hour spent with the young women, she would write to Ellen Elliott: 'the "publicity" part does wake me up with terrors in the night.'[34] Wilson received her author's copies of *Hetty Dorval* on May 5th, and that weekend, May 9th, the publicity articles appeared in all three Vancouver newspapers.[35] Because she placed such restrictions on the young journalists, the articles are not very interesting and would not have stimulated much interest in buying the book. They all record the author's account of the story coming to her in a dream and pretty much writing itself, and they record her opinion that the time for the great Canadian novel probably won't come until the country is more unified and has grown older in knowledge and traditions. The writer for the *Vancouver Province*, whose article is superior in conception and style to the others, includes Wilson's observation that Canadian settings in all their unique variety are there to be caught in words as a backdrop to the endless stories of human relations. Wilson seems to be suggesting, in other words, that setting more than anything else is what will distinguish a novel as being Canadian.

Because she was going to be in eastern Canada with Wallace on CMA business, the Macmillan Company decided to hold a launch for the book at the company office on Friday afternoon, May 16th. The guest list was made up of distinguished media and business personalities, and included Roy Britnell, among a number of other Toronto booksellers, Helen James and James R. Scott from the CBC, several prominent newspaper and magazine reviewers, and some of the company's authors. Among the latter was the influential *Globe and Mail* critic William Arthur Deacon, who would become Ethel Wilson's arch foe in the Canadian literary community.

The reviews of *Hetty Dorval* were divided. Most reviewers saw the plot as a moral allegory, one putting it very enthusiastically in a class of psychological fiction with the stories of Henry James.[36] There was praise for her handling of the B.C. setting, and several reviewers drew a comparison with the early Willa Cather, particularly 'the singing quality' of *A Lost Lady*.[37] 'Rarely in recent reading,' wrote the reviewer for the *Chicago Sunday Tribune*, 'have I encountered an author who has transferred her love and understanding of a remote and beautiful countryside to paper with such skill.'[38] But moral allegory and landscape description were not enough for the reviewer of the *Halifax Daily Star*, who wrote that 'the characters are just pencil sketches, not very clear, and there seems no apparent reason for their story having been published.'[39] William Arthur Deacon, in the first of his negative reviews of Wilson's books, wrote in the *Globe and Mail* that Frankie is so normal and wholesome

that the first half of the story fails to produce much excitement and that
the story concludes just when it is gathering force dramatically. Hetty,
he argued, was a 'far more vital centre of reader-interest than the gap-
ing child.'[40] Deacon's disparaging review appeared in the Toronto
paper the day after he met Wilson at the Macmillan reception. The
reviewer for the *New York Times* was even harsher, dismissing the book as
a poorly written morality play and a dull story.[41]

Although Wilson had not enjoyed the publicizing of her work in Vancouver, she did enjoy reading the reviews as they came in. However, in
July, John Gray had something quite different to propose: he had been
approached by a Hollywood agent who wanted motion picture rights for
Hetty Dorval, and he reminded Wilson that she, according to their contract, would have to give approval. He hoped, of course, that she would.
A film version of the novel would help sell many copies of the novel and
would bring the Macmillan Company a substantial bit of money as the
author's agent. Wilson's immediate response was that if the book were
ever to be filmed, she would much prefer an English production. Within
a week, Gray wrote back to say that in fact a public relations man from J.
Arthur Rank, a British film company, was also showing an interest in
Hetty. All of this confirmed the Toronto company's faith in Wilson as a
valuable writer. It had not been this way with the other branches of Macmillan. Gray had tried to persuade the parent company in London to do
an English imprint of *Hetty Dorval*, but in February, Daniel Macmillan
had written disparagingly of the proposal: 'We have examined the
proofs of Miss Ethel Wilson's novel *Hetty Dorval*. I am afraid that this is
not a book which we could import – in fact it is not the sort of book
which in our opinion should be published at all. However, of course,
you will have to publish it as you are already committed to it. It is quite
harmless, but it seems to have very little merit.'[42] But hearing of film
interest, he wrote in August to John Gray to say: 'We have reconsidered
this book. If no other English publisher has offered to manufacture it
we should like to publish it here ... We should also like an option on her
next book.'[43] This was all very exciting to Wilson because nothing
pleased her more than the idea of being published 'at home.' An agree-
ment for an English edition was in fact signed in early September, and
the following year, with a strong note of recommendation from Sylvia
Lynd as advertisement, the book was published to consistently positive
reviews in England. The reviewer for *Punch* called it a first novel of
unusual promise, pointing to the book's sureness of language and
vision, and commending the author for saying a great deal in a short

space.[44] Especially gratifying for Wilson was praise in the *Tatler* from the distinguished novelist Elizabeth Bowen, who wrote that while the book was short it was 'so remarkable as to convince me that its author should go a long way.'[45] She praised especially Wilson's ability to evoke intense atmosphere. But Wilson would always be cautious: 'A "good" review,' she wrote, 'brings guarded pleasure, a sober joy. One rejoices carefully but does not become intoxicated. It is possible that the critic may, on that day, be in love.'[46]

John Gray's patience with Ethel Wilson was sorely tested early in their relationship. The Hollywood agent persisted all fall in trying to get the rights to *Hetty Dorval*, and Gray kept encouraging both parties to work out a deal, but Wilson was dragging her heels hoping for an English production instead.[47] In November, Rank finally turned *Hetty* down, and Gray wrote to Wilson eager to proceed with the Hollywood negotiations. Wilson answered his letter this way: 'My feeling is so strong against it, I cannot argue it away ... My responsibilities are many, but I do wish to continue writing, with as clear and fresh a mind as possible. Cluttered up with Hollywood in this connection ... I would be defeated.'[48] Gray wrote back graciously: 'Please don't worry any more about it on our behalf or for any other reason. We shall say "No" and will not ourselves waste any energy in regretting the decision.'[49] He received three more inquiries about film rights to *Hetty Dorval*, including a CBC production, and the answer remained the same, although a CBC radio dramatization, 'Stage 48,' produced by Andrew Allan, went ahead for 15 February 1948. The only other use of *Hetty Dorval* was a condensed version in *Woman*, an American magazine, which featured the story in its November 1947 issue. John Gray was no doubt disappointed by Wilson's recalcitrance on all matters concerning the publicizing of her work, because actual book sales in Canada were proving somewhat meagre. In six months, *Hetty Dorval* had sold less than a thousand copies, and he wrote to Daniel Macmillan in London that he accordingly did not anticipate printing the next Wilson book in Canada. At the same time, he had enormous confidence in Wilson as a writer. He was willing therefore to take the long view, indulge her personal eccentricities regarding the public, and nurture her talent for the future.

Although sales of *Hetty Dorval* were not strong the first year, it would prove during the author's lifetime to be her best-selling book.[50] Many readers, thinking for a moment about Wilson's oeuvre, are likely to remember before anything else a beautiful woman and a girl watching a skein of wild geese flying south over the sagebrush country.[51] Wilson said the book was entirely fiction, only linked to real life by seeing a log cabin near Lytton fall into disrepair, but when we know something of the author's life, we can also see how the book was shaped by and grounded in some of the transforming experiences of her youth and middle years. She knew the ranch country around Merritt and Lytton from the many times she travelled east by train and from a holiday she spent in the Nicola Valley as a young woman; and we know that after breaking her engagement with John Nicolls, she wanted to move to the interior, ride horses, and make her living there as a teacher. She and Wallace stopped regularly at Lytton on their trips to Lac Le Jeune, and in 1940 she published in the *Vancouver Province* an account of a night spent there during a fair which featured Howard the Lobster Boy on its midway.[52] While she insisted *Hetty Dorval* was fiction, she nonetheless wrote to her editor that there was an association with actual experience, that Hetty was 'a very pure profile of a thoroughly bad creature'[53] she had known, though the prototype and the fictional character were also very different. There is no way of learning now about the woman who sat for the portrait of Hetty, nor is there any need to know of this woman, but the impact of such a person on the author when she was young and impressionable was obviously strong. Several other phases of Wilson's life can be glimpsed in this story: Frankie Burnaby's time spent at Miss Richards's private school for a few girls near Stanley Park echoes directly Wilson's early days at Miss Gordon's school on West Georgia Street; Frankie's friendship there with Marcella Martin parallels Wilson's with Marion Martin. The novel follows Wilson's ocean voyage to England to attend school as a teenager; and her experience of England's windy Atlantic coast, an English 'uncle,' a father's death, and a trip to France while still in England all have some basis in Wilson's life. Finally there is knowledge of Vienna before the Second World War. In spite of her protests to the contrary, it is possible to read *Hetty Dorval* on certain lines as one of Wilson's most autobiographical narratives, like *The Innocent Traveller* the distillation of life saved up.

There has been considerable discussion of *Hetty Dorval* in the critical literature that has grown up around Ethel Wilson. Attention has focused especially on two aspects of the book: the significance of landscape or setting, and the psychology of the title character. W.H. New notes generally that Ethel Wilson's characters are always observed in relation to environment, that the connection to place is central to her way of exploring human relationships and the philosophies people construct to deal with life's exigencies.[54] In *Hetty Dorval* Wilson herself refers to the 'genius of place'[55] as a powerful, shaping influence, and in *Love and Salt Water* she asserts that 'the formidable power of geography determines the character and performance of a people.'[56] Perhaps Wilson believed the argument that a Tartar relocated to France would after a generation or two become the most rational and civilized of men. Certainly, in a letter to academic friends who were staying at Little Rock on Bowen Island, she stated her belief that a landscape can produce happiness in people. 'That funny little place,' she wrote, 'has almost, I think, a human quality of its own, not perfect, but very strong. A sort of daemon, or genius loci, or something that has in places given rise to those terms. It can like people, or dislike people, & is most engaging to those who love it.'[57] Several critics have traced Frankie Burnaby's ability to break free from Hetty Dorval's selfish influence to her childhood in an open, sparsely populated country, where human decency and community values are essential to survival. More specifically, details in Wilson's description of the sagebrush country around Lytton have been read as symbolic of the book's human drama: the flight of the wild geese as an emblem of freedom desired by both Hetty and her young admirer; the clear Thompson River being overwhelmed by the muddy Fraser as reflecting Frankie's transition from innocence to experience under the sullying influence of Hetty.[58] Wilson resisted such readings, or at least she would disclaim any such intentions on her part as the author; for her, a river was a river, she would say, not a symbol. But she also recognized that readers trained to read in this way might very well see different levels of meaning in her descriptions of nature and setting.[59]

The bulk of the criticism surrounding this text, however, focuses on the nature of the title character. She is viewed almost unanimously as a negative presence in something like an allegory of good and evil, wherein an adolescent child is being tempted away from the values of her family and community by a mysterious woman's glamorous representation of beauty, freedom, and sexual power.[60] In the eyes of young Frankie, the various images of Hetty (on horseback, watching a flight of wild geese, in the cottage surrounded by her elegant furnishings and library of 'yellow books') all fall together to create a forbidden, romantic picture of sophistication and freedom, enhanced by an unwillingness to become involved in the mundane affairs of a small town. 'I will *not* have my life complicated,' she says to Frankie; but this becomes a problem for the girl, who is very aware of her mother's favourite line of poetry, 'No man is an Iland, intire of it selfe.' Hetty Dorval is eventually revealed as a destructive force in people's lives, breaking up marriages, using people to her own ends, and abandoning them when she is no longer in need of them. She has no scruples and is concerned only with her own security and immediate comforts. Barrie Davies has argued most cogently for the allegorical nature of this character by linking her with a series of beautiful but destructive seductresses from literature, including the sirens and Circe from classical mythology, La Belle Dame sans Merci, and especially Lamia, the serpent who took the form of a beautiful woman. Davies convinces us that allegory is part of Wilson's intent by looking at suggestive details in the language: Hetty's siren-like singing, for example, and her 'charm,' which leaves Frankie under a 'spell' and a 'trance'; the naming of Hetty's dog, Sailor, which might recall for the reader Circe's turning of Ulysses' crew into animals; or the snake imagery of Hetty curled up on her couch and, in the final scene, assuming an 'S' shape in Frankie's bed.[61] In his archetypal reading of the novel as an adolescent's rite of passage, Northrop Frye also draws attention to the S-curve in the bed, one compounded perhaps of secrecy, perfidy, and sexual knowledge.[62]

But reading the story as an allegory of good and evil detracts from its impact as a drama of flesh and blood characters and also from its power as a cautionary tale. Is there a way instead of thinking about Hetty Dorval as someone we might encounter in our everyday lives? Is there a political dimension to this novel, which ends so deliberately with rumours of coming war? In an article about Ethel Wilson as an elegist, P.M. Hinchcliffe refers briefly to Hetty Dorval as a psychopath, whose moral monstrosity resides in her ability to forget anyone or any event that would burden her with responsibility.[63] In a similar vein, Jeannette Urbas refers to Hetty as 'a freak of some kind, an anomaly of nature.'[64] The research and literature on psychopaths render Hetty Dorval almost a textbook study of this psychological phenomenon.[65] Most disturbing in their character is the lack of emotions and feelings that are normally identified with being fully human. As someone semi-human, Hetty is linked in surreptitious association with Torquil the Lobster Boy, whom Frankie and her friend Ernestine pay money to view at the Lytton fairgrounds. Frankie wonders: 'Was Torquil the subject of some affliction that separated him tragically from his fellows ...?' (45). Much later she asks 'what' is Hetty? 'Could she really have a friend?' (85). As social predators who charm and manipulate, psychopaths make their way through life leaving a trail of broken hearts, shattered expectations, and empty wallets. They make a very good impression at first and generate a state of excitement in their victims' lives; and, indeed, Frankie Burnaby's first impression of Hetty watching the geese in flight is of a very pure profile, almost spiritual, and life for the twelve-year-old girl in the dusty little B.C. town is suddenly exciting in a way that it never had been before. Frankie becomes enthralled by Hetty, and when the latter sings of the beautiful lady who inspires undying love, she thinks, 'Why, that's Mrs Dorval her very own self' (30). Frankie describes herself as 'bedazzled' by Hetty, 'under a very fancy kind of spell, near to infatuation' (30). But beneath the psychopath's charming façade there is someone dishonest and manipulative, which Frankie glimpses near the beginning of their acquaintanceship when she sees Hetty's false behaviour with the minister and when she is urged by Hetty to keep their relationship a secret. She is also presented early with the most fundamental aspect of the psychopath's nature – the inability to connect with other people on a basis of empathy or responsibility. '"I will not have my life complicated by others"' (29) is Hetty's constant refrain, as she moves without conscience through a series of marriages and scandalous affairs that bring tragedy ('"... in the end the wife ... took her own life, she was so unhappy. And then of course the husband was distracted but [Hetty] calmly left him and went away ... with a rich oil man"' [83]). Nor is she moved when she faces, finally, the fact that the housekeeper she has always treated so shabbily is actually her mother. Mrs Broom denounces her daughter: '... you've brought me nothing but trouble from the minute you could speak and you've never given me any real love ... you're rotten bad and selfish' (93–4).

The psychopath rarely keeps any connections to family, but it is Frankie's connections to her parents, particularly her mother, which rescue her ultimately from Hetty's spell over her. Mrs Burnaby is guided by John Donne's famous line 'No man is an Iland, intire of it selfe,' which serves as an epigraph for the story and is repeated several times in the text. This understanding of responsibility for others moves Frankie as a nineteen-year-old to protect her English friends from the destructive influence of this woman she now sees as wholly false in all her dealings with people. Frankie writes, 'I was sure that if Hetty in an idle or lonely moment entered the integrity of Cliff House, she would later as idly depart and leave a wreckage behind' (86). The Donne epigraph also becomes the basis for the novel's political vision. As she hurries through a London night to rescue the Tretheways, Frankie has a prevision of the coming war, of the city turned 'craters, rubble and death' (86). As R.D. MacDonald observes, the large demonic forces at work leading to the air raids of the Second World War are here closely associated with Hetty Dorval, and this kind of evil is ubiquitous for Hetty is constantly on the move: Shanghai, Vancouver, London, and other parts of Europe.[66] The small drama of Frankie doing battle with Hetty is framed by this vision of global disaster and the psychopathology of powerful dictators who for a time brought civilization to the brink. The two sentences at the end of the book reinforce this vision. Hetty, always on the prowl for rich and powerful men, has gone to Vienna in 1939 with a man with a German name, Jules Stern. We are told: 'Six weeks later the German Army occupied Vienna. There arose a wall of silence around the city, through which only faint confused sounds were sometimes heard' (104). Whether Hetty and Stern are involved in political intrigue that paved the way for the invasion, or whether Stern, whose name might also suggest that he is a Jew, will be a victim of the coming holocaust, is left deliberately ambiguous, just as Hetty's apparent love for the things of nature remains a redeeming feature in the portrait of this otherwise 'thoroughly bad creature.' In this story, a psychopath's powerful impact on an impressionable girl becomes a catalyst for self-examination, but it also becomes a vehicle for some of Wilson's enduring preoccupations, particularly the difficulty of seeing through appearances, and the impossibility of knowing 'truth.'

Hetty Dorval has been reissued in three different editions since 1947. It was reprinted in a run of 5,000 copies in Macmillan's Laurentian Library in 1967, which made it available for student purchase in paperback for the first time. That same year, it was selected for a special limited edition printing of 375 copies by the Alcuin Society of Vancouver. For this handsome cloth edition, the typographic design was done by Charles Morriss, Gus Reuter preparing lino-block engravings. Printing and binding were done by the Morriss Printing Company of Victoria, a press distinguished for its fine quality of production, and Ethel Wilson wrote an introduction telling how she came to write the book. In the 1980s the novel was no longer available in paperback, but it reappeared once again in 1990 when all of Wilson's work was reprinted in the New Canadian Library. In an 'Afterword,' Northrop Frye calls *Hetty Dorval* a 'first novel of a writer of great ability and a sure sense of direction' (108). Wilson would have been delighted that Frye paid her this compliment. In 1952 she had requested that Northrop Frye write a review of *The Equations of Love* for *Northern Review*. He was someone she admired for his urbanity, learning, and wit, but, in her words, he was 'too big and too busy and too important,'[67] beyond her, and he did not do the review. However, over the years she caught up with him.

CHAPTER NINE

The Equations of Love
1947–1953

'Now, my young friends,' [said Mr Chadband,] 'what is this Terewth ... firstly (in a spirit of love) what is the common sort of Terewth ...' – *Bleak House*

Truth ... is opinion, of course. – Ethel Wilson to John Gray[1]

'Private Happiness' / Wallace's illness / Cut Off / 'A Wilderness of Monkeys' / 'The Journey of a White Lady Friend' / Reviews / *The Equations of Love*

In August of 1947 the Wilsons left New York on the luxury liner *Queen Mary* for their first trip to England together since 1938. Though Wallace's duties as the president of the Canadian Medical Association concluded that summer, he had been selected to represent Canada at the first meeting of the World Health Organization, so that he and Ethel were bound for Paris, where the meeting was scheduled for mid-September. Meanwhile they had time to visit relations and friends in England. Ethel does not appear to have kept a diary while on this trip, but on the journey home (via ocean liner, then train across Canada), she wrote a lengthy essay titled 'Private Happiness,'[2] which preserves the essence of many of her experiences abroad. The essay was never published, but revisions to a typescript suggest that it had been composed for a public audience. How do people who have suffered through six years of war and have lost so much find happiness in their lives again? This is the question the essay poses, balancing the claims of private versus public happiness, the status of the rich versus the plight of the poor. Wilson does not claim to be a politician or a philosopher, just 'a woman observing "people"' in the course of their daily lives, but the essay is imbued with the author's social conscience, which was always made keener when she returned to the places of her childhood.

The luminous and luxurious days at sea on the *Queen Mary* bound for Southampton – the cabin walls quilted with green satin, the beds superlatively soft, the food superlatively good, sport, music, dancing, every physical and social want supplied with spontaneous skill and courtesy – these days for Wilson were unsettling because she knew them to be 'a flight from reality, and a flight that could only be taken by highly favoured persons.' Reality on arrival was the devastation of war and its effect on thousands of Londoners who, like her father's half-sisters and their families, barely managed to live above the poverty line. One of the first visits they made was to Aunt Hannah, now in her eighties and still living in the Spartan little apartment in a block of flats that reminded Ethel of a prison. Across the road, she noted, was an emptiness where a bomb had landed, and further up the street she could see where another area had been laid waste, which included a large Nonconformist chapel destroyed while ministers and laymen were in a meeting. Aunt Hannah, the German scholar and last pupil of Clara Schumann, had lived through all these terrifying events. Margaret Bryant, her youngest sister and close companion, had died in 1943. Hannah's life was now closely circumscribed. Too frail to climb up and down the steep stairs, she was dependent on kind friends and tradesmen for her shopping; a roof-top balcony was her only place for a walk and fresh air. In spite of all she had suffered through and the infirmities of old age, she was in her niece's eyes still the charming and fun-loving person she had always been, still reading, still listening to educational programs on the BBC, still uninterested in the material luxuries of this world.

When the Wilsons visited, one of Aunt Hannah's tall sons, still in uniform, was staying with her. An archaeologist and linguist, this cousin had always fascinated Ethel because he embodied for her the imagination and spirit of adventure that she felt characterized her father's side of the family. In his twenties, he had been tramping Europe with only a few francs in his pocket, making his way to wherever Roman diggings could be found. In his thirties, he was running medical supplies into Spain to the Nationalist Army. Now in his forties, he had served through the war and had spent the last two years in the British Zone in Vienna, where his five languages were an important asset to his work. He took the Wilsons for a drive in his car, 'scarcely bigger than a bathtub,' to show them a heavily blitzed area of the city around Cripplegate. Wilson writes: '... we thought we had seen devastation, but nothing like this. It is a silencing scene, as empty and arid as the moon. Here great city buildings became instant rubble in a few hellish hours ... [I]n a dreadful exposed nakedness lie an infinity of cellars, outlined and laid cleanly bare, sunk beneath the levels of existing bits of streets. All the values and activities which once filled the now empty air have vanished.' But her cousin was able to find something good in what had happened, pointing to a low wall exposed by the bombing and explaining that it was a bastion of Roman London never suspected in that area of the city before. The ever-enthusiastic archaeologist had made a find. Ethel was glad to know that Aunt Hannah's sons still made her life rich in this way, even though they had little money to help her with. She was also gratified to know that the parcels she had sent from Canada, with food and sometimes money and always with love, had made an important difference to her aunts' lives as they struggled through the war years. She intuited correctly that this would be the last time she would see her father's family, and in her essay she dwells for a paragraph on 'Time,' on how the present moment is always slipping away, and only has significance if connected to the past and also to the future, 'which is being prepared for us by unmeasurable forces.'

This haunted quality to post-war London, as Wilson experienced it, is preserved in a sketch she first wrote as part of 'Private Happiness,' and which she later polished and published as 'The Corner of X and Y Streets' in *Mrs Golightly and Other Stories*. One night the Wilsons stepped out of Kettner's, their favourite Soho restaurant, into an ill-lit street, at the end of which was the theatrical-looking façade of a bombed and gutted church. Seemingly from nowhere, a large, pale young man appeared under a high street lamp playing an accordion. With his intelligent face raised to the light, he looked to Wilson like a disillusioned Oscar Wilde. 'Where does he live,' she thought to herself, 'what does he do, and why does he have to play the accordion in Soho with a tin for coins hanging from his shoulder?' Others gathered to hear the music and 'stood like shadows' on the street corners. Then a tall, graceful young woman 'lifted her voice' and began to sing with the accordion player, and a grotesque man in black began to dance slowly like a marionette, calling out, 'I'm a seaman, I am ... I bin in strange ports ... I seen terrible things.' Then, while all eyes were on the strange dancer, the music stopped and the accordion player was gone, and the girl standing in the shadows who had been singing was gone, and when the Wilsons looked back to the street, the dancer was gone too. And there were no 'shadows' left, but just ordinary people walking up and down Romilly and Frith Streets. The music and the sinister dancing were like a dream, leaving no trace, but Wilson learned subsequently that Oscar Wilde used to frequent Kettner's. In her published version of this incident, she changed Romilly and Frith to X and Y Streets to convey something of the abstract and eerie nature of what she had experienced. For Wilson, who as a child had once glimpsed old Queen Victoria out in a barouche, the streets of London were heavily burdened with both cultural and personal history.

But London was also alive to Ethel Wilson in terms of the future of her literary career. She visited the Macmillan offices, met briefly with the company president, Daniel Macmillan, and signed a contract for *The Innocent Traveller* and for an English publication of *Hetty Dorval.* She came away with genuine admiration for the president, for his intelligence in literary matters and for his business acumen. Macmillan, in turn, was impressed by the meeting and wrote to John Gray on September 8 that he had just seen Mrs Wilson, that 'she seems to be a very intelligent person and will, I hope, write more and even better books.'[3] The Wilsons were fêted once again by the Lynds and their literary friends. Ethel had confided to John Gray that while she was eager to see Sylvia and Robert, she had asked them not to include the Priestleys, because she found him too forceful. She would prefer instead to meet Rose Macauley and Desmond McCarthy, whose books and reviews she had read and admired for years.[4] But a reference to Mrs Priestley in 'Private Happiness' makes it clear that they were part of the gathering. Several years later, she would recall that she met J.B. Priestley twice and that both times he drove her into her shell. With his dramatic (but pompous) voice and his stage cigar, 'he has the art of making one feel very dull,' she lamented.[5] She also regretted that, once again, Rose Macauley was unable to attend the party. Nonetheless, there was the excitement of literary and political gossip and there was again the special ambiance of an evening spent near Keats's house. London also meant pleasant hours browsing in rare bookshops and shopping for old silver.

There were two less pleasant aspects to the trip. For reasons she found hard to articulate precisely, Ethel was ill at ease in France, sensing 'something unfamiliar and alarming below the surface of living.' The marks of war's violence were less apparent in Paris than in London, but with the enemy inside their towns and houses, resistance, confusion, and mistrust of each other, she felt, had become imbedded among the French population. People on the Continent, Wilson observed, have perfected the art of living well, but in England they have learned the art of living together. Coming back to England after the Paris meeting was 'like a hitherto unexperienced freedom.'

Wallace had been in England during the war, and on that visit he had not only spent time with their evacuee daughter, but had met Audrey's parents as well. A steady correspondence had flowed back and forth between Audrey and the Wilsons while she was serving in the WRENs, and it was arranged that on this trip Ethel would also meet the Butlers.[6] It was probably a mistake, because actual parents intruded on Ethel's fantasy of Audrey as her daughter. Here, after all, Audrey was involved in her own parents' lives again. At their meeting, the Butlers and Ethel held themselves in polite reserve, and the bluff, good nature of both Audrey and Wallace could do little to thaw the cool atmosphere of the encounter, especially between Ethel and Audrey's Belgian-born mother. The discussion focused on the possibility of Audrey returning to UBC in the coming year and whether she would take up residence with the Wilsons again. It was agreed that she had a place to stay if she returned to Canada, and the Butlers, whose means were reduced by the war, had to acknowledge the generosity and kindness of their daughter's Canadian benefactors. The Wilsons took the *Queen Elizabeth* back across the ocean, arriving in New York on October 1st. Wallace went to Ottawa on business, while Ethel returned alone to Vancouver by train, putting down on paper her thoughts on private and public happiness.

Shortly after their return, they learned that Audrey had decided to resume her studies at UBC, and by November 10 Ethel was writing to John Gray to say that their evacuee ex-WREN had arrived and she would have less time now for her writing. Audrey Butler remembered being welcomed back with great warmth by both the Wilsons, but she soon became aware that something had changed in her relations with Ethel. Instead of accepting her the way she was and giving her space in which to develop as she had done before, Ethel now seemed to demand Audrey's full attention and loyalty. There was a tension which seemed to be rooted in Ethel's jealousy of Audrey's parents in England, and it manifested itself in small things such as Ethel's annoyance that they must serve fish on Fridays because of Audrey's Catholic faith. The three-bedroom apartment in the West End had a bedroom and a separate bath for Audrey's use, but it was a smaller accommodation than the house on Connaught Avenue, where, in addition, Audrey had her own sitting room and study. When she was unhappy, Ethel would become silent, and Audrey was aware of the frequently strained atmosphere around the apartment. Then, after Christmas, Ethel without warning arranged for Audrey to live at a boarding house nearby. It had the antique and slightly demeaning name of 'Queen Mary's Coronation Hostel for Gentlewomen Born in the United Kingdom and Seeking Employment in British Columbia.' It seemed a bleak place to the young woman, who had been treated more than royally herself before; moreover, room and board used up nearly all of her monthly allowance. She stayed in Vancouver less than a year.

But Ethel Wilson was about to encounter much greater unhappiness, which would change her life forever. In a letter to John Gray dated 4 April 1948, she tells of Wallace being in hospital with an infection. When he returned from a series of business trips feeling very tired, they had arranged to spend a few days at Little Rock; but while they were at the cottage, he developed an infection which seemed to spread rapidly throughout his body. With great difficulty, they got back to the city, and within hours Wallace checked himself into hospital with several areas of his body now broken out in a violent rash. He was very ill, and in her letter Wilson writes, 'It is a *nightmare* – and other things seem immaterial.'[7] When she wrote again to Gray two months later, she was even more distraught because Wallace was still in hospital, his illness having become further complicated by a mysterious secondary infection. She asked that 'To W,' the dedication for *The Innocent Traveller*, be expanded to read 'To Wallace, my dear husband,' and went on to say to Gray: 'The point of my whole life has always been in him. We await the turning point upwards of this ferocious illness, which continues with relapse after relapse, borne [by Wallace] with the utmost courage.'[8]

Wallace's illness began as a common form of dermatitis, with the skin on certain areas of his body becoming red and extremely itchy. But what started as an inflammation of the skin was unwittingly protracted by a violent, undiagnosed reaction to a course of antibiotics used to treat the original infection. For nearly twenty months, Wallace was very ill and might have died.[9] His whole body became inflamed, his glands were swollen, and his hair fell out. Anything touching his body was torture, so that a sheet had to be draped in a tent formation over the hospital bed, without touching his naked body. Wilson wrote to John Gray in September of 1948: 'My husband's illness continues almost unabated. He is still in hospital, 3 nurses daily for 5 months ... the savagery and cruelty of the skin continues day and night, attack following attack.'[10] Those who knew the Wilsons remember how courageous and uncomplaining Wallace was, but how Ethel was in a state of near hysteria for most of that time.[11] She spent a long portion of each day at his bedside, dissecting the doctors' reports and analysing his progress, and bringing to the hospital his main meal prepared at home each day. Her high-strung, intense nature seemed constantly to be at the breaking point. Audrey Butler spent the evenings with her, because she did not manage well alone in that long stretch between leaving the hospital and Wallace's phone call at ten-thirty every night. There was talk of sending Wallace to the Mayo clinic in Rochester, Minnesota, but he was too weak to make the trip. Still thinking they were treating an acute form of dermatitis, possibly caused by stress, a couple of Wallace's doctors decided that Ethel was perhaps part of the problem and should not be allowed to visit the hospital for a month. It was arranged that she would stay with Alix Wilson and her second husband, Massey Goolden, who were living in a comfortable house by the sea on Vancouver Island. Alix recalled later how they would be sitting in the living room talking and Ethel would suddenly flee the room, weeping. Wallace's illness roused in the author the primal fear going back to her childhood of being abandoned by the man she loved who protected and cared for her.[12] Friends glimpsed something almost pathological in her love for and dependency on Wallace.

Because there was little improvement in his condition and nothing that doctors could do for him at the hospital, Wallace was permitted to go home at the beginning of November 1948, but by mid-December he was still no better. Ethel wrote to John Gray: 'He has been home nearly 6 weeks, and has continued to suffer day and night. He had a serious relapse a few days after return, and for four weeks we have been fighting a 3rd dreadful infection, including large erosions suddenly appearing on the exhausted skin, the hands broken down for the 6th time, also the feet, with an average of 1 hour's sleep a night.'[13] Wilson herself was exhausted for she had a household of six to plan for and oversee – two nurses daily, the housekeeper and her husband, and Wallace and herself. At the end of March 1949, she wrote to Gray that they have 'entered the second year of this hellish and mysterious thing,' with no steady improvement to report.[14] During the winter of 1949, Wallace returned to hospital for two operations to remove centres of infection, but after some temporary relief there was another relapse. His whole body – bones, joints, and glands – was now affected by this prolonged trauma to his system, and his hands and feet had become misshapen. 'I have borne the unbearable,' she wrote to Gray in despair, 'and we don't yet see the way out.'[15] For nearly a year there is no mention in her correspondence of her writing except for a few queries about permissions to reprint her work.

Then, when things could not have seemed worse, there was a change, and Wallace began to improve slightly. He was able to get up and move around the apartment in bandages and silk pyjamas, and by late April, Ethel could tell John Gray that they were able to do without the night nurse; for the first time in thirteen months, Wallace had been able to dress, and they had been out for a short drive. Probably the antibiotics had been reduced or changed, and this had brought some relief. But his condition was still not understood medically, and further treatment brought about another major relapse in August 1949. It was only when the doctors stopped prescribing antibiotics altogether that Wallace began to get better. On October 29 of that year, Ethel could finally report to John Gray that he was getting better, that they no longer had a nurse at the apartment, and that they could go for walks along English Bay, possibly to part of a symphony concert that evening. Ethel admitted to another correspondent that she was very tired, but happy and thankful that their ordeal seemed to be over. She had no spare faculties yet, however, for any other kind of work.

Wallace's protracted illness had an enormous impact on Ethel Wilson the writer. She had started writing fiction in the shelter of Wallace's love – marriage came first, her writing a distant second. Deaths naturally occurred in the fiction she had written (family deaths over time in *The Innocent Traveller* and, in the background, the death of Frankie Burnaby's father in *Hetty Dorval*), but after Wallace's illness the spectre of separation, accidents, and sudden death moved to the foreground in her writing. The most direct and dramatic instance is a story titled 'A Visit to the Frontier,' which she wrote when Wallace was recovering but which she did not publish until 1964, when her career was over.[16] She explained to friends in a letter that the story had its genesis when Wallace was in hospital, with nurses around the clock. 'Life was terrible. One night, unaware, standing in the middle of the bedroom, I said loudly: "We are Cut Off!"' That, she wrote, was followed later by a dream in which she and Wallace were travelling by train across the prairie: '[S]omething happened. There was mental confusion ... We were at a station called Cut Off ... there were irrelevant happenings. The other passenger was [Boris] Pasternak. When I woke up I wasn't exactly frightened, but I felt I had all but died.'[17] From childhood, Ethel had known how uncertain security and happiness were, but now she would regard life as even more fragile and provisional.

'A Visit to the Frontier' describes in a powerful and eerie fashion the boundary crossed by the author during Wallace's illness. Some readers have found the story terrifying. The first part, following Ethel's dream, describes the Forresters on a train crossing the prairie, as the Wilsons had so often done while Wallace was president of the CMA. Lucy Forrester, regarding her husband Marcus reading the paper across from her, reflects on the happiness of her marriage: 'How heavenly fortunate I am ... that ever since we first loved each other, every day has renewed our love. Never have we taken it for granted but have always known, without saying, that it is our greatest thing.' She reflects, too, on the fact that there is no literature that describes perfect and lasting love, and acknowledges that it is impossible to put such fulfilment into words. Then for a moment there is something like a crash, some sort of physical impact, a large boulder perhaps hitting the train, which slows down, and the conductor announces they will be stopping for an hour and a half at Cut Off. Lucy and a porter agree that there are some strange names in this part of the country – The Leavings, Dog Pound, Ghost River. (Wilson was in fact using actual names, although The Leavings had by the 1940s been changed to Granum, Alberta.) When Lucy and Marcus step onto the platform, he startles her by referring to the fact that en route they had changed trains (she cannot remember this), but she forgets this almost at once because she is so taken by the freshness of this place – the brilliant air, the sweet smell of the evergreens, and a dazzling and powerful river that rises up into fountains. She becomes separated from Marcus, but for a time she is so invigorated by the landscape, the friendly people, and the sight of Indian girls racing their horses through the hills that she does not worry. Then she hears the station bell and reboards the train, but she discovers as it is pulling out that Marcus is not on board. The conductor says they must have changed trains, and so she jumps off before her train gathers speed and lands on a polar bear. She runs for the other train and finds the compartment she and her husband had shared, but again he is not there. As this train begins to pull away, she jumps once again, falling on the prairie, at which point the speaker of the story tells us that perhaps those like Lucy who had died in the train wreck would meet again in transfigured delight in that beautiful and happy country, though 'we do not know.' Wilson held this story back from publication, feeling perhaps it would draw bad luck. She gave a copy to their cousin, Reg Tupper, who acted as their lawyer and her literary executor, and she instructed him to put it in a safety deposit box, only publishing it after their deaths.[18] Audrey

Butler understood its power in terms of the author's experience. She also recognized how much Wilson was changed by the experience of Wallace's prolonged, life-threatening illness. There was no tension now between the two women; their open and loving relationship was fully restored. Ethel looked at life from a longer perspective and was grateful and humble every day that she and Wallace had come through the greatest trial of their lives. This joy was not only something they shared, but radiated to all who knew them.

On 21 March 1948, just ten days before her husband became ill, Wilson wrote to John Gray, sending him part of a new manuscript. It is the first mention in their correspondence of the novella that would eventually be known as 'Tuesday and Wednesday,' although Wilson at the outset was calling it 'Wilderness of Monkeys,' Shylock's phrase in *The Merchant of Venice* (III, i, 124). She said the story had been brewing for some time and was now 'pouring itself out with great ease and pleasure.' She was especially interested in the character of Victoria May Tritt because 'nebulous though she is ... she is the linch-pin of the story.'[19] Until near the end, 'Tuesday and Wednesday' is a story with almost no plot. It records two days in the life of Mort Johnson, a feckless, easy-going odd-job man, and his slatternly, shrewish wife, Myrtle, and describes a number of other working-class East Vancouver characters who move within their sphere, characters like Myrtle's radiant Auntie Emblem, her neurotically withdrawn cousin Vicky Tritt, Mort's friend Pork, who works at a funeral parlour, his logger friend Eddie Hansen, old Wolfenden, who lives in Stanley Park's hollow tree, and several others. The narrator is superior, and through the comic effects of language, she reveals the sentimental, pretentious, and self-deceiving nature of the characters whose lives would appear to follow no pattern or purpose until the end, when suddenly Mort and Eddie Hansen drown and Vicky Tritt invents a story of Mort's heroism in attempting to save his friend. Wilson was all too aware that the story was short on conventional plot, but she felt strongly that it was one of the best pieces she had written.

When she heard nothing back from Gray for two months, she asked if he would return the manuscript. In the meantime, he had passed it around the office collecting readers' reports.[20] The two on file are both fairly negative, but for very different reasons. The first one, signed F. Webb, saw an increasing problem in Wilson's stylistic 'mannerisms,' arguing that the combination of authorial asides with stream-of-consciousness was totally confusing for the reader. This reader was also distressed by what he called the author's arrogance towards her characters in these asides, especially irritating 'for its guise of supreme tolerance.' He went on to say that 'in all this I detect a fundamental fear of character, a determined shying away from problems' and no savage grappling with God or the Devil. This is an interesting judgment, rooted very much in notions of fictional realism and the poetics of the emergent New Criticism, by which Wilson's style would be judged somewhat harshly for the next thirty years. She would be viewed as an old-fashioned writer for speaking directly to her readers in this way, until the 1980s when a postmodern poetics would prevail, foregrounding the constructed or 'made-up' aspect of writing and the self-reflexive nature of the speaker in a text. In a postmodern light, character would also come to be seen as something constructed in language rather than a transparent reflection of life. Curiously the second reader, signed 'E J,' felt that Wilson was sympathetic to her characters, but that her style and structure were too wandering and leisurely to sustain interest. John Gray tried to summarize these criticisms in as gentle and constructive a fashion as possible, but admitted his readers felt she was 'dominating the characters a little too much' and that the 'author asides ... make one too conscious of your manipulation of the scene.'[21] By the time she had heard from Gray, Wallace's crisis had deepened and Wilson set her writing aside from more than a year.

In fact, it was two years before she wrote to John Gray again about new work; in a letter dated 14 April 1950, she stated that during intervals of leisure she was working at 'something called, perhaps, *The Journey of a White Lady Friend.*'[22] This is her first reference to 'Lilly's Story.' Three months later, she decided to send Gray a parcel of new material which included a completed version of 'Tuesday and Wednesday,' the first two parts of what she still called 'The White Lady Friend,' and two stories, 'Mr. Sleepwalker' and 'The Cut Off.' The latter, which she also referred to as 'A Visit to the Frontier,' was sent just for Gray's perusal, to share with him something of the 'death in life' feeling that she had experienced during the last two years.[23] 'Tuesday and Wednesday' (which she also referred to sometimes as 'Monday and Tuesday') was in her opinion the only piece ready for a reading, but company files reveal that John Gray sent all four pieces out for assessment. Only one reader's report is in the file,[24] and while this anonymous assessor found little of interest in the short stories, he or she thought 'The White Lady Friend' had a lot of promise and that 'Tuesday and Wednesday' was now publishable. 'Some excellent humour and truth to life' as well as 'a valid

criticism of life today' was the judgment. Gray wrote to Wilson in September saying the company was pleased with the manuscripts but was
perplexed by their length.[25] Wilson had suggested that 'Tuesday and
Wednesday' be published on its own as a very small book (it is the same
length as *Hetty Dorval*), and she cited critical successes in this genre by
Evelyn Waugh (*Scott King's Map of Europe*) and Philip Toynbee (*Tea with
Mrs Goodman*),[26] but Gray thought her two novellas would do best published together.

Although Gray was ready to accept the two stories for publication, he
tried to persuade Wilson to tone down what were considered to be her
unfortunate stylistic mannerisms. He said that reading about Lilly he
found the tone patronizing in places, and, like the others who had read
the manuscript at Macmillan, he was anxious that she remove the authorial intrusions.[27] Wilson defended herself by citing the practice of other
writers like Fielding, Trollope, and E.M. Forster,[28] but Gray, very much
influenced by contemporary thinking, replied that the 'big guns' who
sin in this respect 'don't gain anything by doing so, but succeed in spite
of it.' Such intrusions, he added, create detachment from rather than
sympathy for the characters.[29] Wilson wrote back submissively saying
that she was trying to revise the manuscript so as to eliminate the personality and opinions of the writer, but confessed it was 'counter to
[her] natural inclination.' She was not imitating the big shots, she says;
it was simply natural for her to write that way, because she herself has
always enjoyed the companionship of a writer who expresses himself in
this talkative fashion.[30] In March of 1951, Gray wrote to say that he was
very pleased with the revisions she had made and was sending the manuscripts off to Daniel Macmillan in London.[31] By June he was able to send
her a wire of congratulations saying that the London company would
publish the novellas and that all she needed now was to arrive at a title
for the book as a whole.[32]

Wilson was jubilant to get the news from London, because she began
to feel increasingly that her real audience was in England, where an
appreciation of language and style was so much stronger than in North
America. But again she was bedevilled over the matter of a title, which
for her was always one of the hardest parts of any writing project. 'Tuesday and Wednesday' had begun as 'Wilderness of Monkeys,' but had
changed to the more prosaic but serviceable days of the week. 'Lilly's
Story' had been written with 'The Journey of a White Lady Friend' as
the working title ('Journey' was changed at one point to 'Pilgrimage'
and then both were dropped in favour of simply 'The White Lady

Friend'), but during the revision process, 'The Equations of Love' emerged as the title for the story of Lilly Waller, and she submitted that title to the publishers in England. But then came the struggle to find a title for the two pieces together. A number of possibilities were discussed: 'A Lie for the Defence' seemed to have application to both stories, wherein, as Wilson pointed out to Gray, lies are in fact closer to the truth; 'The Gulls' and 'Gulls and Angels' were also suggested for, as she observed, 'if a symbol *does* fly through my mind' (though she deplored what she called the cooked-up use of Symbols), 'it is birds, and probably, gulls, – always.'[33] A variant on this was 'The Laugh of the Sea Gull,' but she eventually rejected that title as sounding too cynical. Since all her readers had responded positively to 'The Equations of Love,' finally she affixed that title to the volume as a whole and gave 'Lilly's Story' to the second of the novellas inside.

Wilson's correspondence with Gray about 'Lilly's Story' is the author's most extensive discussion of any of her books. In July 1950 she sent him the first two chapters and an outline of the rest.[34] 'Lilly's Story,' in fact, began with Yow from *The Innocent Traveller*, who had a white lady friend, and when Yow went to jail for stealing from the Hastings family, she 'made other connections.' 'What connections?' the author asked herself; why was she so unfastidious and what was her childhood? What happened to her? Did she ever achieve respectability? These questions were the germ of the new story.[35] The plot of the published version remains much the same as her outline in the letter to Gray, except in one significant detail. After leaving Yow, Lilly lives temporarily with a miner in Nanaimo, leaves him, has a child, invents a deceased husband, and over time, working as a housekeeper on Vancouver Island, achieves respectability for herself and her beautiful daughter, Eleanor. But when the latter marries into Vancouver society (and here the original version differs significantly), she gives birth to a Chinese baby; Lilly's world of deceptions is shattered, and Eleanor dies, incredulous, shamed, and heartbroken. When John Gray was in Vancouver in the autumn of 1950, he visited the Wilsons at their English Bay apartment, and they all discussed the credibility of Eleanor as Yow's child and her Chinese characteristics being wholly recessive.[36] Wallace agreed to consult his medical friends on this question of genetics, but when no hard and fast answers were forthcoming, Ethel decided to play it safe and change the ending of her story, creating not a tragedy but a comedy out of Eleanor's happy life and Lilly's late marriage to a Mr Sprockett. She also told Gray what she thought was at the heart of both of the novellas: '*Tues. and Wed.* and the

W.L.F. are, really, studies in self-deception and lies. I became much interested in this, having observed how influential deceptions (self and otherwise) are in personal, group, and national relations ... Truth is sometimes absolute, but very often a relative matter, as we know, yet frighteningly unethical (because the lies win) but so is life, very often.'[37] In another letter, however, she defends Lilly, of whom she has grown very fond: 'Lilly can only survive by lies – which are sometimes truer in essence than the "truth."'[38]

The Equations of Love was published in March 1952. (Ethel had declined Gray's playful suggestion that she do publicity by riding a bicycle on a tightrope over the Fraser River.) 'Tuesday and Wednesday' was dedicated once again to Wallace, but also to their cousin Reginald Tupper, who was married to Isabel Wilson; 'Lilly's Story' was dedicated to her aunt, Jo Malkin, and 'those never-failing friends' who had helped Ethel through the long period of Wallace's illness, especially for driving her faithfully to and from the hospital. In spite of her publisher's hesitations over the style of these stories and their marketability, Wilson felt unusual confidence and pleasure in the work she had completed, and when the reviews started to appear in the spring of 1952 her faith in the two stories seemed to be justified. The Canadian reviews were entirely positive, including at last a very favourable notice in the *Globe and Mail* (though not written by William Arthur Deacon).[39] Typically, the Canadian reviewers, conscious of high praise for Wilson in the English press, were now ready to agree that she was a writer of the first order, 'one of the most powerful forces,' wrote Stuart Keate, 'to come out of Canada since uranium.'[40] They found everything to praise in *The Equations of Love* – the author's ironic yet sympathetic presentation of the poorer social classes, the economy of her style, her use of setting and carefully selected detail. There was a preference expressed for the humble realism of 'Lilly's Story' over what some reviewers described as the 'rather arty' experimentalism of 'Tuesday and Wednesday,'[41] but none of the Canadian reviewers dismissed either story as uninteresting or of little consequence. Gael Turnbull's article in *Northern Review* is especially interesting for its focus on the characterization of Vicky Tritt, which, he argues, contains an intensity of feeling not found elsewhere in the book and is of far greater significance than the antics of Mort and Myrtle, or the dogged faithfulness of Lilly. With Vicky Tritt, he suggests, Wilson lets us 'look into an enormous cavern, the darkness of some bottomless pit' compounded of loneliness and the insupportable sorrow of humanity, and he hopes that some day Wilson will write on such themes on a larger scale.[42] Claude Bissell's notice for 'Letters in Canada' is perhaps the best overview of Wilson's achievement in *The Equations of Love*. He points out that she changes her subject matter from relatively sophisticated middle-class life to probing the lonely and frustrating realm of the poor, but does not sacrifice her grace, her wit, or her fluency. Her adroit handling of point of view, he points out, preserves a nice balance between sympathetic identification and ironic objectivity. She takes her Canadian setting for granted: 'there is nothing self-conscious and assertive about [her] use of the local scene.'[43]

The American reviews were equally enthusiastic, although they came nearly a year later and for a different book. John Gray had tried to persuade H.S. Latham, his counterpart in the New York office of Macmillan, to bring out an American edition of the two stories. But Latham wrote back regretfully in October 1951 to say that at an editorial board meeting the staff rejected the proposal on the grounds that it would be even harder to market two novellas than a collection of short stories.[44] A couple of weeks later, however, he reported that he had turned the manuscript over to a literary agent by the name of Ruth May, who worked for Macmillan in acquisitions but who also worked to place manuscripts the company could not use.[45] An older and emotionally volatile woman, May would prove to be one of Wilson's most devoted admirers, and after reading the manuscript for *The Equations of Love*, she set about on a tireless quest to find a publisher in the United States.[46] She sent the manuscript to most of the major publishers, including Harcourt Brace, Putnam, Random House, McGraw-Hill, Norton, Holt, Crown, World Publishing, Knopf, and Doubleday (she was certain her friend Kenneth McCormick would see the quality of the writing), and she also tried leading magazines such as *Good Housekeeping, Ladies' Home Journal, Redbook*, and *McCall's* for serialization of one or both of the stories, but came up empty. (In Canada in the meantime, novelist W.O. Mitchell, who was fiction editor for *Maclean's*, turned the novellas down for serialization, just as he had previously rejected Wilson's short stories for the magazine.) Then, after eight months of circulating the manuscript, May received a phone call from John Fischer at Harper's to say they wanted to publish 'Lilly's Story' as a short novel on its own.

Lilly's Story was issued in the United States in April 1953,[47] and on the dust jacket there was strong praise from two leading American fiction writers. Eudora Welty was restrained calling it 'a moving story, told with wisdom, quietness and power.' But Jean Stafford, author of *The Mountain Lion*, was quoted at length: '*Lilly's Story* charmed me altogether. It is made up of so many pleasing and substantial virtues that I hardly know which I savor most, whether the comedy – sometimes clownish and sometimes sweet – or Lilly's winning, bald, unique integrity or the grace and certainty of the writing itself. I was so involved in the story that I could not have borne it if the ending had not been happy.' The book was greeted by a number of similar very positive reviews bearing such titles and phrases as 'Up from Skid Road,' 'Humane Novel of Woman's Rise in the World' and 'uplifting story of the triumph of human character,' all signalling the rags to riches theme so resonant for American readers.[48] Some focused on the motif of motherly sacrifice and compared the book to Olive Higgins Prouty's *Stella Dallas*,[49] which had been made into a popular movie and was enjoying continued success as a radio serial in the United States. Only a few of the American reviews commented on the writer's technique and art of expression. Most memorable perhaps in this regard was the reviewer for the *New York Herald Tribune*, who wrote 'this fairy-tale for grown-ups' achieves its magic by the author's sure light touch 'that makes most other novels seem as though they had been written with battering-rams.'[50] The one exception to the general chorus of praise was a few jaded lines in the *New Yorker* which described Lilly as an 'uninteresting waif' whose tale is an 'inertly written lesson on how to creep through life.'[51]

Although Wilson was delighted that her novella was otherwise so well received in the United States, delighted especially for Macmillan that she should be regarded as a valuable property given the mediocre sales of her work in Canada, her chief pleasure nonetheless was in the English reviews and the sometimes vigorous debates that attended them. Especially thrilling was the review in the *Listener* by the eminent man of letters Séan O'Faoláin, who, after castigating the majority of contemporary writers for their cliché-ridden styles, talks about his 'immense joy' in reading Ethel Wilson's *The Equations of Love*, which, he states, is a rare example 'of how English ought to be written, and of an original and unspoiled mind.' He admits he knows nothing about Wilson except that she is a Canadian and that she is said to have published two other books. But if they are as good as *The Equations of Love*, he argues, and if she continues to write books of this quality, then he would say that 'within her gamut, Ethel Wilson is one of the most charming and accomplished writers of fiction in English now living.'[52] This was heady praise for someone whose self-esteem was rather fragile, and she couldn't help feeling a second rush of excitement when the *Vancouver News-Herald* reprinted the review a few weeks later making it available for her family and friends to read. To one friend she wrote that she was 'intoxicated' by a piece in the *Observer* by Marghanita Laski which compared 'Tuesday and Wednesday' to the best *nouvelles* of Rebecca West.[53] What Wilson enjoyed in these reviews was the fact that discussion of her work was framed within larger discussions about literature and culture and sometimes about the craft of writing itself. She grew weary of reading the Canadian reviews because they were mostly plot summaries: 'how much more stimulating, and really enjoyable,' she wrote Gray, 'is a vigorous anti-review compared with the dead fish one meets lying about – I mean, just a re-tale of story.'[54]

One expects Wilson enjoyed most of all reading through the six-page transcript for a broadcast on BBC's *The Critics*, in which *The Equations of Love* was discussed by a panel of distinguished commentators on the arts. Novelist Elspeth Huxley began by observing how beautifully Wilson used words, her style fresh, spirited, and sensitive. She also singled out Wilson's gift of sympathy – her ability to be analytical but also affectionate to her characters. But another critic, Arnot Robertson, countered that she found the style intolerable, characterized by extreme coyness and intrusive asides: 'I loathe being nudged in the ribs by the author.' Another critic defended the style as a way of speaking through the characters, while another went on to discuss whether Wilson should attempt something on a larger canvas or not. Finally the discussion turned to whether style is as important as subject matter. This exchange of ideas with a focus on 'Tuesday and Wednesday' and 'Lilly's Story' was enormously exciting for Wilson, and she was thrilled to know that her Aunt Hannah, eighty-eight years old, was reading the reviews and still listening to book discussions in her little flat in London. Hannah Atkinson wrote her niece two letters in March 1952 conveying her excitement at hearing her niece's work discussed on two radio programs, *The Critics* and *Writers on Sunday*. 'I'm so proud of my aunt-ship,' she wrote. 'I'm simply bowled over by the two stories myself. I've read and re-read them & I do so rejoice in your success'; and on receiving an autographed copy of *Equations*, she added 'I shall treasure it more than I can say.' Ethel, in turn, treasured these letters, which she kept and which form part of her small personal archive.[55]

While *The Equations of Love* created a great deal of interest with reviewers when it was first published, it has not subsequently attracted the same kind of interest from literary critics as Wilson's other works have done. Books and articles that examine all of Wilson's writing give some account of the two novellas in passing, but there have been no articles to

date written exclusively on 'Lilly's Story' and only one that is focused on
'Tuesday and Wednesday.' The latter, by Beverley Mitchell, suggests that
we might see Mort's adventures and death as a parody of Homer's *Odys-
sey*, a Vancouver variant on James Joyce's *Ulysses*.[56] While such an elaborate literary joke seems an unlikely intention on the part of the author,
and the examples linking the characters and incidents in 'Tuesday and
Wednesday' with the earlier epics are strained and sometimes far-
fetched, Mitchell does draw our attention to the idea of an urban Every-
man following his daily routine about the city unaware of a larger design
in which his movements are enmeshed, for certainly there are elements
of literary design in the story, though not exactly classical or parodic
ones. Perhaps the most obvious of these is the pattern that portends the
hero's death. It begins with his name, Mort, the French word for 'dead,'
and follows him until his fatal accident. He spends Tuesday unwittingly
playing with death: he tells his employer that his wife might have 'a
slight touch of cancer'; he accompanies his friend Pork to his workplace
at a mortuary, where he imagines Myrtle lying in one of the plush cas-
kets; and he finds her a bouquet from one of the arrangements that
arrived too late for a funeral. Wednesday he tells his prospective
employer that his wife is suffering from a fatal malady, but it is Mort who
dies suddenly that evening in a confused scene in which he becomes
entangled with his friend Eddie, who is drowning. Even before he
drowns, Vicky Tritt sees Mort's death in preview, as it were, when on her
way to church she glimpses Mort trying to keep drunken Eddie upright,
'wrestling,' as they make their uncertain course along the street. Mort
dies while Vicky is at the service, but she tells her story of Mort supporting Eddie and trying to save him in the water, creating a heroic, mythic
version of the final minutes of his life.

One of the best essays about Ethel Wilson is by the distinguished
American critic Blanche Gelfant, who examines towards the end of her
lengthy and comprehensive study the creative acts of storytelling that
occur in Wilson's fiction.[57] The characters in *The Equations of Love*,
observes Gelfant, tell lies without hesitation. This is how Mort and Myrtle subdue and prevail over one another, and it is how Vicky Tritt temporarily releases herself from the prison of her shyness and insecurity
and from her powerlessness. Vicky creates a hero out of Mort Johnson,
gives Myrtle a dignified role to play as the hero's widow, and for a few
moments she becomes herself the centre of rapt attention. In a different
vein, Lilly tells lies as a strategy for survival; they are the means by which
she creates a meaningful life for herself and provides a happy and valu-

able identity for her daughter. Identity has always been situational and shifting for Lilly in her search for security and respectability: born Lilly Waller, she assumes different names in the course of her life, including Maudie Watkins, May Bates, Mrs Walter Hughes, and finally Lilian Sprockett (Lily without the third *l*). Our tacit endorsement of Lilly's self-inventions that lead to her success as a mother and eventually as a wife makes us ask what is the nature of truth, or in the words of the book's epigraph from Dickens, 'what is the common sort of Terewth?' The confusion of lies with truth, suggests Gelfant, points to the reality of fiction, which becomes an important and clearly articulated theme in Wilson's writing from this point forward. As Wilson wrote Gray, 'truth ... is often a relative matter ... sometimes truer in essence than the "truth."' As postmodern readers, we recognize something familiar in this episte-mological stance that Wilson's contemporaries would have questioned and perhaps felt uncomfortable with. Hetty Dorval's re-inventions do make us uncomfortable because their intent is purely selfish and the results destructive. Nonetheless, Topaz's failure to change with time leaves her stranded in the mid-nineteenth century, her zest for life not quite blinding us to the fact that she is a bore and contributes almost nothing to society.

Reviewers of *The Equations of Love* were surprised by Ethel Wilson's shift in subject matter. By this time, she was known as the wife of one of the country's leading doctors and a member of a socially prominent Vancouver family. Her creation of characters from the city's east end seemed incongruous with her personal background and the subjects of her earlier fictions, and to some of her readers she appeared to be 'slumming,' writing for fun about a world of which she knew little. But biographical knowledge reveals some close connections between author and subject in these short novels and helps the reader to appreciate the complexity of some of the themes in her writing. Gael Turnbull astutely observed, for example, something dark and compelling in the charac-terization of Vicky Tritt, a glimpse into an abyss of loneliness vast and frightening, usually 'concealed' but always there like 'the sorrow of humanity.' Living in a boarding house when she was in her early thir-ties, Wilson experienced herself something of the meagre existence of unmarried women who, as she phrased it, had no flowering in their lives.[58] It reconnected her to phases in her childhood and young wom-anhood when she felt herself to be painfully alone in the world, when books provided sustenance the way discarded newspapers and movie magazines do for Vicky Tritt.

But there is a stronger biographical connection evident between the author and her fiction in 'Lilly's Story,' which was written after Wallace's illness. As an elderly woman, she said that when her father died 'the bottom dropped out of everything' and that she never felt safe again until she married Wallace. After his long illness, she would write increasingly of human vulnerability: '... you are walking along through the grass on the cliff top, admiring the pretty view, when – crack crack.'[59] The search for a safe place emerges in this novella as a motif that persists through the rest of Wilson's writing. Lilly Waller, hounded by the police and disrepute, finds a refuge at Comox on Vancouver Island, where she works as a servant for the Butlers and can raise her child to be 'like folks.' Despite Butler's amorous advances, which Lilly quickly rebuffs, there is peace and security in this well-ordered, tasteful home and its environs by the seashore. Two ancient figures of a horse and a hound in Chinese pottery on the mantelpiece speak, like Keats's Grecian urn, of a world that does not change with time: the hound held his head lifted 'as if listening for centuries for a master who did not come,' and the horse 'grazed peacefully forever where no grass grew' (167). Lilly's pastoral retreat at Comox (where we know Wilson herself once summered as a girl) has its centre on a sand spit where she takes Eleanor to play, where 'the fresh loveliness of the place with a light breeze blowing brought Lilly to one of those perfect moments of time that seem to last forever' (178). But the narrator warns that they 'do not last forever, and are so fleeting that they make some people afraid.' Lilly witnesses on the spit a kitten stalking a robin that is trying to kill a snake, while overhead flies an eagle ready to pounce on the kitten.[60] Lilly is made aware again that life consists of hunters and the hunted, just as the pottery figures, the horse and hound, are emblems of that life. 'Everything after something,' reflects Lilly, and her illusion of perfect security is broken. Further, the sand spit turns out to be a cemetery for animals who had been ship's mascots and had died at sea, and we are reminded of another enemy – the passage of time and the dissolution of all things in it.

'Lilly's Story' is replete with such sober reflections and with genuine sympathy for the central character. 'Tuesday and Wednesday,' by contrast, is a comic fiction, and the author remains detached and superior throughout. Both novellas, however, are about servants, a subject that Wilson had given much thought to, for never during her life did she live without people hired to do menial work for her – housekeepers, cooks, gardeners, typists, seamstresses, and, in old age, nursing staff. As observed before, because the Wilsons did not have family, they took an extraordinary amount of interest in servants, whether lonely, irascible Chinese cooks like Yow and Chow Lung, a Finnish maid who was an ardent Communist, or white Canadians from working-class backgrounds. Ethel Wilson's involvement with and observations of such people are at the heart of the two novellas, especially her more than twenty-year connection with Mrs Tufts, who, recommended to Ethel by both Babe Taylor and Amy Buckerfield, did occasional housekeeping for the Wilsons while they lived at Connaught Drive, but who became their sole cook and housekeeper for ten years in the West End.

Marion Tufts was a middle-aged woman with two grown sons who had come with her family to British Columbia from New Brunswick in the 1920s. Her husband, after working at a local sawmill for some years, was employed as a night watchman at Woodward's department store during the years that Marion worked full-time for the Wilsons. Mrs Tufts was a great storyteller, and Ethel enjoyed both her garrulous self-assurance and the wry sense of humour with which she flavoured her stories. Wilson praised her in a letter to John Gray as 'a remarkable woman, the wittiest person I have ever known.'[61] She delighted not only in her shrewd observations on human nature but her 'incorrect' way of speaking. Wilson at times found herself overwhelmed in this respect: she wrote to Gray that 'Mrs T. still speaks incorrectly, and when W. was away so long and I was immured with her – I caught it and had to check "I been" and "I seen" and "I gotta" in my own speech.'[62] (But, in fact, Wilson sought opportunities to practise this kind of vernacular talk. When Wallace was recovering from his long illness, Mrs Tufts's son Theo was hired to drive their car, and he remembered how Ethel would try out different phrases and 'common' ways of speaking as they made their way around the city.)[63] One also catches a glimpse of someone like Mort Johnson in Wilson's account to Ellen Elliott of their gardener and caretaker at the cottage on Bowen Island: 'Our hired man that we fired this weekend [was] the most likeable fellow (an "alcoholic," proudly so called) – "Say, doc, I never touched one drop of your hard liquor! No *Sir*, I wouldn't touch a man's hard liquor. I drank up your sherry and native wine, but not a drop of your whiskey. No *Sir!*" (This statement untrue). His halo grew and grew, it was terribly funny, he got nobler every minute.'[64]

In a couple of talks she gave about her writing in the late 1950s,[65] Wilson said one of the elements in the writing of 'Tuesday and Wednesday' was her increasing awareness of the irrationality of cause and effect in ordinary human relations. She gave as an example a man growing increasingly annoyed as he waits for a woman. She is late and all her attractive qualities disappear as he becomes more angry. Then suddenly a man he knows stops and tells him his investments have gone up in the stock market. The prospect changes; he no longer dislikes anyone, and when the woman comes along he once again finds her charming and becomes deeply involved with her. In Wilson's view, circumstantial contingencies were so often at the root of unstable human emotions and behaviours. Such shifts in mood and self-awareness occur throughout the story and create the conditions for satirical social analysis.

'Tuesday and Wednesday' is a vivid satire of working-class people viewed as lazy, deceitful, self-indulgent, and self-vindicating. In the Dickensian mode of the epigraph, Wilson gives the characters names like Pork, Uren, Mottle, Flask, and Tritt, and in their actions reveals them, in turn, as egocentric, sentimental, and vain. But the satiric, seemingly judgmental stance of the narrator is undercut by something like a self-portrait within the text and her comic presentation of Vancouver's affluent class. Both Myrtle and Mort Johnson are employed by the wives of wealthy businessmen, but Mrs H.X. Lemoyne and Mrs H.Y. Dunkerley are shown to be pathetically dependent on their employees. The portrait of Mrs H.X. Lemoyne, 'anxious to please' and terrified of Myrtle's superior airs, is especially marked by Wilson's sense of the ridiculous, ineffectual figure she sometimes cut when trying to 'manage' servants. As Mrs Lemoyne apologizes to Myrtle for the unexpected luncheon to be arranged that day, she is aware of herself becoming voluble and undignified, and, as she runs about the kitchen, she becomes angry with herself for being so weak. Mrs Dunkerley is similarly presented as a foolish woman in relation to her servants, 'twittering' and 'flying across the grass' to bring Mort a cold beer and to offer him a ride down the hill. Her husband, Horace Dunkerley, lumber magnate and self-made man from Nova Scotia, comes very close to being a cartoon version of the Wilsons' friend, West Coast lumber giant H.R. Macmillan. (Dunkerley, in fact, is called H. Macdonald in an early manuscript version.) In the instinctive antagonism felt between Mort and H.Y. Dunkerley, Wilson brings together both points of view, that of the 'working man' and that of the 'self-made man.' She does not take sides but shows us the deep-seated hostility the two men instinctively feel for each other. Snubbed by his employer, Mort 'felt outraged that Dunkerley to whom life had evidently been kind should act in this snobbish way to Mort just because Mort was a working man' (40), while Dunkerley 'nearly explode[d] when he heard the simple word "working man" uttered, unless it was applied to anyone who knew what "work" was in the sense that he, Horace Dunkerley, knew ...' (38).

In a letter to Professor Desmond Pacey, Wilson describes her reservations about Virginia Woolf's writing as related to the English novelist's patrician view of life and her failure to understand working people. It seemed to her that Woolf, for example, 'mis-read entirely Arnold Bennett ... and his view of poor persons, poor houses, poor places, mean streets, and their relative beauty and importance to those concerned – both dwellers and observers. She was surprisingly blind to all that.'[66] At times, Wilson expressed an open distaste for the English novelist and evoked her name to disparage hothouse 'drawingroom' people: 'Virginia Wolves sitting about *feeling* sound, scent, colour, line ... over-civilized, over-sensitive.'[67] Wilson's own sympathies for working people with little education and few opportunities because of circumstances of birth are set out clearly in 'Lilly's Story.' Like some of the servants Wilson once observed in her Uncle Sydney's home, Lilly brings order to everything she touches: '... order flowed from her fingertips, and sheets, pillowslips, blankets, bedcover fell obediently into place' (241). At the same time, Lilly is content to live herself in minimal circumstances, in just one small room at the Butlers' and at the Valley Hospital, where she feels safe. At both places, she works long hours and is fulfilled by the work she does; at both places, her employers become wholly dependent on her service. Wilson's reflections on the nature of work and the relations of master and servant are an important centre to this novella. Just as Lilly is about to announce to Mrs Butler that she and Eleanor will be leaving, the narrator observes: 'Performance of a duty well and constantly and with what appears to be affection over a long period of time generates a responsibility and obligation on the part of the server to the served one, and on the part of the served one to the server' (185). She goes on to observe how close the bond can be and what painful dependencies can accrue. But while Wilson understands the sharp loss felt by Mrs Butler and by the Matron at the hospital when Lilly leaves them, her sympathy nonetheless remains with Lilly, who, because of her passion for her child, is immune to the emotional claims of her employers.

The complexity and pleasure of both novellas derive in part from aspects of style that Wilson's editors tried to discourage, especially the intrusive narrator and the mimicry of speech. Wilson had always insisted that 'story is nothing much. All depends on the "way of telling."'[68] And for her the 'way' was rooted in the voice of the narrator. In a preface she wrote for 'Tuesday and Wednesday,' Wilson playfully established her authorial credentials as a woman lacking a university education and a driver's licence, but who is widely read (the Bible, Shakespeare, *Alice in*

Wonderland) and not afraid of the implications of morality. She titled this preface 'The Theory of Angels,' and speaking to the book's dedicatees, Wallace Wilson and Reginald Tupper, she proposed that every person has an angel, a being who lives within that person's ambiance or aura unless crowded out. An angel, she explains, is different from conscience, which is a faculty or principle, unlike an angel, which is a being, although an angel is often confused with conscience because its duty is 'to keep alive and active the principle of good within a man.' She gives Annie Malkin, her grandmother, as an example for whom an angel's work was never impeded, whereas Adolf Hitler was a case in which an angel was forced out, suffocated, leaving the host to inflict on the world the most cruel and contagious wrongs.[69] Wilson was persuaded to drop this preface, but, of course, angels for Mort and Myrtle were left to play their part in the story. They are the occasion for the most extreme instances of authorial asides in Wilson's writing, because their existence is entirely dependent on the author's perception, not the character's and certainly not the reader's. When introducing Mort, the author explains to the reader that 'a man's angel, after a long residence within or around a man, knows its host (or charge) very well indeed; far better than you or I, who, looking, see perhaps only a stocky middle-aged man ...' (12). One of the most important functions of the authorial asides, as becomes clear in this introduction to Mort through his angel, is to make clear to the reader that authorial omniscience is impossible, that all perceptions derive from the personality and assumptions of the speaker ('I ... see ... perhaps only a stocky middle-aged man').

Wilson distributes the story's point of view among all her characters, so that within one paragraph we sometimes have as many as four points of view converging. Equally important is the voice of the author-narrator, who, to give another example, tells us how much she likes Mrs Emblem. 'I think,' says the author, that 'in order to be perfectly happy, she still needs to look after someone. You cannot help liking Mrs Emblem. She is so nice ... she is ... to me – alluring' (54–5). The way other characters see the world is often embedded in the texts by their stigmatized speech. 'They was a man,' bursts out Vicky Tritt as she begins her story of Mort's heroism. 'He seen a man and it was Morty,' she continues, 'and he took and dove right in after Eddie Hansen' (117–18). Other characters are allowed to speak in an unpunctuated flow of words that conveys their garrulousness. This frequently rough texture to the prose again draws the reader's attention to the contrived, fictional aspect of the writing, qualities that a later generation of readers came to appreciate. In a prescient article published in 1965, Helen Sonthoff identifies Ethel Wilson as one of those writers who make the reader experience the writing, who could write a sentence 'that made you know yourself knowing it.'[70] Wilson always said that 'Tuesday and Wednesday' was her favourite piece of writing, and perhaps that is the aspect of the book that pleased her most.

For several years, *The Equations of Love*, chiefly 'Lilly's Story,' attracted more popular attention than any of Wilson's other writings. Even before the American edition appeared in April 1953, 'Lilly's Story' was translated into German as simply *Lilly* and published in Switzerland in 1952. Two more translations appeared: 'Lilly's Story,' again titled *Lilly*, came out in Danish in 1954, and both novellas were published together in Italian as *Equazioni d'amore* in 1958, with 'La Storia di Lili' appearing first in the volume. It would be the only book by Wilson to be translated into another language. 'Lilly's Story' was also translated into French, but the prospective publisher judged the translation to be of poor quality and did not proceed with the publication. There was also interest expressed in doing Dutch, Swedish, and Finnish translations, but these were never followed through.

In her assiduous efforts to place Wilson's work in the United States,[71] Ruth May made a deal with Omnibook, and in the fall of 1953 *Lilly's Story* was syndicated in several American and Canadian newspapers, including the *Vancouver Province* and *Montreal Standard*. The story accordingly became widely known, and because the novel sold steadily in the United States, Harper's reprinted it in 1955. Then Avon bought the publication rights from Harper's and brought out a new edition in 1956. This interest was generated in part by the possibility of a film version of 'Lilly's Story.' From the outset, Ruth May tried to sell 'Lilly' to the movies, sending the story while still in manuscript form to Paramount, Twentieth-Century Fox, and Columbia Pictures. In 1953, Twentieth-Century Fox made a tentative offer of $5,000 for film rights, but then backed out before finalizing the deal. The other film companies showed no interest. Then an offer came from dramatist and screenplay writer John Patrick, whose play *The Hasty Heart* had been immensely popular on Broadway and who was currently adapting Vern Sneider's novel *The Teahouse of the August Moon* for what would be an equally successful Broadway production. Patrick's agent offered $1,000 for a year's exclusive option and then $6,500 more if the option was exercised. There was talk of Shirley Booth's interest in playing Lilly. Booth had just won an Oscar for her role in the 1952 film *Come Back, Little Sheba*. Patrick was slow to make any progress, but just when it appeared he had dropped the project, he took up the option and in January 1955 paid the $6,500 agreed upon. Patrick did fashion a screenplay titled 'Feather in Her Hat' from Wilson's novella and in 1963 sold it to MGM, but a film was never made. The only dramatic version of 'Lilly's Story' was a CBC radio production for *Stage 53* broadcast on 12 January 1953.

The *Equations of Love* was published by Macmillan in 1974 in their Laurentian Library paperback series, and then was out of print for a number of years. In 1987, 'Tuesday and Wednesday' was published with six other novellas in an anthology edited by Douglas Daymond and Leslie Monkman titled *On Middle Ground*. The *Equations of Love* was reissued in 1990 as part of Wilson's complete works in the New Canadian Library. There is an aptly chosen painting of Vancouver Island by E.J. Hughes on the cover titled *An Arbutus Tree at Crofton Beach* and a personal afterword by Alice Munro, who first read the novellas when she moved to Vancouver in the early 1950s and came to near worship of the author's prose style, the 'hard clear prose, the glaze of perfect sentences.' They carry a lot of associations for Munro, tied intimately to her own discovery of place in British Columbia, but she focuses her afterword on three aspects of the writing that we continue to think about and question, and she wonders if the author loses such debates over time. First, there is the way that in 'Lilly's Story' Wilson takes conventional morality and stands it on its head. Lilly after all succeeds in the world by telling lies, but in our contemporary world, where truth is fiction, we applaud. There is the charge of racism in Wilson's presentation of Yow, and Munro exonerates the writer by reminding us that we are all to some extent prisoners of our time, that Wilson was recreating the feel of an earlier era when a term like 'Chinaman' was current, but most importantly she points out that Wilson was the first to recognize in fiction the Chinese presence in British Columbia and created in Yow a complex, independent, and intelligent character, perhaps the most interesting man in the story. Munro also reflects on the tone of Wilson's prose, anxious that the patrician author not be condescending to the poorer, serving class, and that the sentences retain their perfect ease and economy, their ability to deliver whole worlds. On all these debated aspects of the writing, she is confident the author wins.

CHAPTER TEN

Doyenne

1950–1954

Authors Anonymous / Writing in Canada / Friendships / Disabled /
Palm Springs / Portugal

The American novelist Willa Cather once wrote to a friend stating that, if lucky, a writer will experience in a lifetime a year or two in which artistic achievement and personal happiness come together.[1] For Ethel Wilson that time was the early 1950s. Her writing, especially after the publication of 'Lilly's Story,' was attended by both critical and popular success, and novels and stories continued to flow from her pen. The conditions were right. In John Gray, she had an editor who assisted with personal interest in the shaping of her longer works, and there were magazine publishers and radio broadcasters who were eager to have her next story.[2] Although they were now in their mid-sixties, she and Wallace enjoyed relatively good health, and they could afford to travel for several months at a stretch. They were surrounded by family and friends who gave them a strong sense of well-being and a connection to the community. Creativity, achievement, and security all came together for Ethel Wilson in the early 1950s, and 'private happiness,' though it would prove fleeting, was for a time something solid and real. In a letter to Dorothy Livesay, she gave an account of her good fortune: 'By all the rules I should have conflicts (I had them in youth – plenty) ... and [with reference to Wallace's protracted illness] I had enough trouble a few years ago to last a thousand years ... But at present! oh golly, it's too good. Hardly fair. And the writing, just enough gift to set the thing nicely ablaze.'[3] As always, she identifies Wallace as the source of her happiness: 'Living with the person I live with is my chief pleasure and at last, by some osmosis, I've acquired not his selflessness and lack of egotism but a certain amount of common sense and realism, a working philosophy that has no grand name, and an inability to take oneself too seriously.' She concludes with the observation that 'possibly a bit of current personal frustration would make me write better but I'll gratefully take things as they are.'

Her letter was written the day after a meeting of what Wilson referred to as the writers' group or, as they were sometimes called, 'Authors Anonymous.'[4] From the time she started to publish, she had refused to join literary organizations; as a result, she was certain she had made a permanent enemy of the *Globe and Mail* critic, William Arthur Deacon, when she declined his invitation in 1947 to be a member of the Canadian Authors Association. ('From the first time Mr Deacon looked grimly at me in Toronto, and became aware of my holding backness re joining associations, I knew he liked neither me nor my work.')[5] Wilson's refusal to join was, as so often, a matter of self-confidence and not wanting to appear pretentious. Deacon, in fact, had first sent an application her way in 1938 after the publication of 'I Just Love Dogs' in O'Brien's *Best British Short Stories*, and she had simply ignored it, refusing to take seriously yet the idea of herself as a published author. With only one short novel and a handful of stories to her name in 1947, she still did not feel she had produced enough work to assume, in her opinion, the rather grand title of 'author.'[6] She made an exception in 1949 when the poet Dorothy Livesay pressed her to join a 'writer's' committee charged to make a report to a royal commission on the state of the arts in Canada, although she would not actively participate in preparing the report. ('Beyond [my] name and dollar ... I can't go.')[7] Her instinct for privacy combined with her ironic view of the self-importance many writers assumed made her reluctant to be part of any collective. She wrote to Earle Birney that 'a room-full of "authors" is a thing to flee from ... What is there that is so grim and humourless about "authors" en masse?'[8] Nonetheless, when Birney around 1950 asked her to meet with a small group of local 'authors,' most of whom had published little at that point, she was persuaded to join them, and their monthly sessions became a regular and stimulating part of her life for the next five years. The group began as a result of Earle Birney's first attempts to teach creative writing at UBC. Ex-students wanted to continue discussing their work with each other and to get advice from their former teacher. They met in each other's homes and invited published writers in both prose and verse to join them. During the time when Wilson attended, besides

Earle Birney the group included on a regular basis Robert Harlow, Dorothy Livesay, William and Alice McConnell, Eric Nicol, Robert Patchell, Ernest Perrault, and Mario Prizek. On a few occasions, the blind poet Alan Crawley was also present. They read for each other and criticized work in progress, making editorial suggestions and discussing strategies for getting published. The group was friendly and mutually supportive, but it had a serious mission – to help create a literature for Canada. It was fired by Earle Birney's passion for his craft.

The group frequently met at the Wilsons' elegant West End apartment. Bob Patchell remembered his hostess in this way:

> She could strike terror ... into the hearts of people who were 'not properly brought up.' When we walked in the door we were trying to be Edwardian gentlemen and trying at least to keep the language of our criticism to polite English rather than the usual Anglo-Saxonisms that most of the time we hurled at each other about our literary efforts.
>
> The apartment was impeccable. I have never seen so much silver. She was the most gracious person I have ever met. It's funny, she was very modest about her writing, yet she wanted you to know what she had done. I remember she gave me her short story 'Hurry, Hurry,' which she'd written about fifteen years before, and later she asked me what I thought of it.[9]

William McConnell also recalled how tastefully appointed the high-ceilinged apartment was with mahogany antiques and oriental carpets, and how redolent of the love and respect of the two occupants for each other. 'In Ethel's conversation all the furnishings and art objects were connected to some pleasurable experience in their lives together – travel, family, friendships.'[10] McConnell was especially interested in what hung on the walls – a photograph of Winston Churchill, a good print of Holbein's *Wet Nurse*, the Burne-Jones drawing given to Ethel's parents, and a whimsical drawing of three hens and a chick, all pecking the ground, which Ethel would tell friends represented her Barclay Street childhood. The walls were lined with books and there were English periodicals scattered everywhere. Before the meetings began, Wallace would welcome the guests warmly, mingle and engage with them in hearty, animated conversation, and then when Ethel gave him the signal, he would leave the group to their discussion, joining them again at the end for a cup of tea or a nightcap. Ethel Wilson could not imagine an evening in her home that was not framed by Wallace's presence in some way. In their third-floor apartment overlooking English

Bay, Ethel Wilson was becoming the doyenne of British Columbia writers, visited by editors and publishers from other parts of the country, advising and supporting local writers in their work.

Wilson shared that stage with Earle Birney, whom she first met when he came west to teach in the English Department at UBC. They had corresponded in 1942, when Birney was collecting stories for a Canadian edition of the American literary journal *Story*. At his invitation, she had sent him three stories, including 'On Nimpish Lake,' an enigmatic sketch describing two men fishing at Lac Le Jeune. Characteristically, she wrote that it was very possible he would not care for these stories 'with their so very feminine thumb print,'[11] but Birney in reply insisted that '"Nimpish" was the best piece of prose he had been sent for *Story*.'[12] However, the *Story* project fell through, and 'On Nimpish Lake' was published that year, at Birney's suggestion, in *Canadian Forum* instead. When they met, she liked both Birney and his wife, Esther, and although she always demurred when it came to giving an opinion on poetry, she affirmed to others that his was a major talent. Esther Birney recalled their early friendship with much warmth, but was at the same time puzzled that this elegant society woman should extend so much kindness and hospitality to a young Jewish girl from London's east end.[13] Wilson was no doubt attracted to Esther's witty and ebullient personality, but she was also sympathetic to working-class people, especially those with some education and a lively interest in the arts, like her father's half-sisters.

Earle Birney's ideas – his sometimes fierce socialism, his mixing of art and polemics, his belief that creative writing can be taught – engaged Wilson more than the ideas of any of her other Canadian contemporaries. At a meeting of the authors group on 13 May 1952, Birney read his long verse play 'Damnation of Vancouver,' which takes the form of a public hearing on the future of the city – whether it should be destroyed or not. Witnesses for the prosecution include the explorer Captain Vancouver, who says that on the whole he preferred 'the sweep of fir and cedar,' a Salish chief who eulogizes the simplicity and abundance of native life, and Gassy Jack Deighton, pioneer saloon-keeper, who believes that only the roisterers and pretty girls, those who really enjoy life, are worth saving. The counsel for the defence is Mr Legion, a slick entrepreneur who speaks in the language of the Chamber of Commerce admen; his praise for the city and its hucksterish future is another form of damnation. The next morning, Wilson wrote Birney a long letter praising many things in the poem,[14] such things as the caring for a place where one has lived and worked and the fear that it is following the wrong course into the future, and the inclusion of the medieval poet Long Will of Langland, who sums up the case for the prosecution by describing the harried, browbeaten working people and the frenzied scramble of the middle class for money, the worship of Lady Meed. But she especially liked the inclusion of Mrs Anyone late in the play, whose defence of the city is based solely on the simple joys of living – pleasure in the mountains and ocean, concern for her garden, and her love for her husband. 'I woke today with my husband,' says Mrs Anyone, 'To the bronze clashing of peaks, / To the long shout of the ocean, / And the blood alive in my cheeks.'

But Wilson's praise for the poem was qualified by her articulation of ideas quite different from Birney's, ideas worth considering because they are central to her thinking on a number of issues. Her chief reservation over 'Damnation of Vancouver' was that Will Langland, in his attack on the predatory rich living off the working people and slum dwellers, did not acknowledge those in between – humble, middle-class people with small homes and gardens. His social vision, she implied, was flawed. 'You've got to see those [small homes],' she wrote, 'as well as the expensive glass palaces and the mean streets.' Moreover, Langland in Birney's poem sees only what is deplorable in the city, does not see 'the invisible tide of good' performed by both rich and poor. She gives as an example her Uncle Harold, who had donated in his wife's memory the Malkin Bowl theatre to the city. He was a man, she wrote, who loved Vancouver, like a woman or a friend, and he did countless other good things for the city that people don't know about because they do not bear his name. There are many such 'good ... and selfless persons' in Vancouver and she mentions her husband too. Her point here is that not only is Birney's social vision flawed but his artistic vision is limited too, the tones of the poem being black and white, the intent polemical. For her this does not work as art, and she says so rather bluntly: '... an indictment becomes dull and loses its force, and as a piece of art or a piece of moral indignation, it fails. This is a real difficulty to me.' For Wilson, human behaviour was never so simple, never black and white, but compounded of a whole range of impulses and motives, and determined by conditions and situations. Even the 'thoroughly bad' Hetty Dorval, her most black and white creation, is softened (complicated) by her love of nature. One further criticism Wilson makes of Birney's poem is again directed at the characterization of Will Langland, who, she feels, is conveying a sense that life was better in the medieval weald of

Kent. 'But was it?' she asks. 'And how noble was the Indian?' she wonders, suggesting that Birney is evoking a false nostalgia for a simpler
period. Wilson could succumb to such sentimental illusions easily herself and guarded constantly against them.

Wilson wrote at length to Birney about his poem, but at the meeting
she characteristically said very little. In a letter to Dorothy Livesay, she
explained her reticence this way: 'I'm quick in [emotional] response
but too slow in reasoning, so I dare not express myself at once, even
when I feel my objection to be valid – and then the argument has moved
on.' In the same letter, she put forth one of her strongest beliefs about
art: '... it is a fact worth mentioning about the technique of any literary
art, that you either possess it in a considerable measure from the start,
or you never acquire it. It is a thing to be improved, perfected, modi-
fied, individualized, but it is never to be got at by a process of laborious
learning.'[15] This was a view diametrically opposed to Earle Birney's and
his program for the teaching of creative writing. Eventually it would
divide them in a hurtful and public fashion.

Wilson, of course, recognized how very generous Earle Birney was to
his students and other local writers. To John Gray, she wrote that Birney
'helps young or older writers to the nth degree. He gives spare time,
strength, consideration, very explicit criticism to these, but is kind.'[16] In
her own way, Wilson was also kind to fledgling writers, not only in host-
ing the writers' meetings at her apartment and giving picnics at Little
Rock in the summers, but in her generous aspirations for most members of the group. In a letter to Gray of 10 January 1952, she describes
some of the members in detail.[17] 'Mario Prizek,' she explains, 'writes
strange verse, plays, and stories. He paints strange explosive pictures.
He likes strange music. He makes excellent theatre decor. He is, to my
mind, still under the spell of symbol, too much. But he is absolutely sincere, there is nothing phony about him; I think he has something near
genius ... and he's an awfully nice person.' The Wilsons gave Prizek the
use of Little Rock in the summer of 1951, but he only spent two weekends there, having taken a job at Woodward's department store. She was
similarly positive about Ernest Perrault, whom she regarded as 'completely natural' and his stories 'masterly.' 'He would scorn to try to
impress,' she continues. 'I should like to think that he would be one of
the best of short story writers. He's good.' She was less enthusiastic
about Bill McConnell: 'He and his little wife are very *earnest*,' she wrote,
and she found McConnell's writing in places 'pretentious and self-
conscious.' She admired one of his pieces in *Northern Review*, but even

there found the bits of dialogue 'lofty and self-conscious,' adding that if that was the way artistic young people talk, she would eat her felt hat. 'No, I think McConnell has few marks of promise unless he stops posturing.' It should be mentioned in fairness to McConnell that she was prejudiced against him because she found him socially presumptuous. To a woman nearly thirty years his senior, he overstepped the bounds of politeness by calling her 'Ethel' from the first day they met. From her point of view, it implied a casual intimacy which had not been established, and to her surprise and dismay the others followed. She got used to it and came to enjoy the easy company of these younger writers, but was puzzled by the curious combination of seriousness and casual off-handedness exhibited by the McConnells. To John Gray, she made fun of their talk about writing a 'nahvl,' saying they were 'too darn serious, the dear things.'[18] She never made an assessment of Bob Patchell in her letters and only occasionally mentioned Bob Harlow as writing a good story. She did, however, enjoy Eric Nicol: 'I chortle in joy over [his] masterpieces re. CBC. He *is* funny and has two advantages over his opponents – he has a true love of form, literature, whatever it may be, fortified by an excellent education, and can be just as tough and much funnier than they, and is much cleverer.'[19]

Although she felt warmly towards most of her young writer friends, she took a cautious view of Canadian literature and its accomplishments, and was not alone in this view. Robert Weaver, who was producing the program *Canadian Short Stories* for CBC radio, wrote to Wilson in January 1953 to say the literary scene in Canada was pretty discouraging. He had bought fifteen stories the previous fall, but without re-airing these stories he could not keep the program going.[20] Alan Crawley, who edited *Contemporary Verse*, and John Sutherland, the editor of *Northern Review*, reported to Weaver the same dearth of good material. In her letter to John Gray in which she assessed some of the members of the writers group, Wilson set down an overview on the subject: 'We have, after a war, an uprush of writing, or perhaps more truly, of aspirations to write. A sudden access of university education applied to a necessarily material generation, and in both cases, relatively little tremendous talent ... I cannot help this unpleasant thought that at the present time ... our talents are fairly mediocre, while our aspirations are considerable, and still tinged with self-consciousness. Well. *you can't rush it.*'[21] She saw her generation as watering the ground and her own two novellas about to be published as 'just curiosities.'[22] (It should be reported here nonetheless that the 'Authors Anonymous' did water the ground in significant ways.

Birney, Livesay, and Wilson unquestionably made lasting contributions to Canadian literature, and Eric Nicol became a humorist with wide appeal. Most of the younger members of the group also left their mark. Robert Harlow published several well-received novels, the best known of which is *Scann* [1972]. Ernest Perrault, while making his living in advertising and public relations, wrote and produced film documentaries, short stories, radio and television plays, and three novels. The first and best-known of these, *The Kingdom Carver* [1968], is a saga of the opening of the Pacific Northwest timberland and the coming of age of a young woodsman. Bill and Alice McConnell established Klanak Press, a fine art press for publishing high quality editions of chiefly B.C. poetry and prose; and later in his life, McConnell published a collection of his own stories with the title *Raise No Memorial* [1989]. Mario Prizek left his mark as the CBC producer of video recordings of Glenn Gould playing Bach [1982].) Nonetheless, throughout the 1950s, Ethel Wilson was plagued with the sense that Canadian writers had thus far accomplished very little and that creative writing classes and a self-conscious program of 'writing for Canadians' would not be effective in changing this.

In Canadian literary history, Ethel Wilson can be seen as taking a vigorous part in two debates on the nature and prospects of Canadian culture, specifically literary culture. As early as 1947, responding to the reviews of *Hetty Dorval*, she was writing to John Gray on this subject: 'It seems to me that what Canadians have to aim at is not to write something *Canadian* (they'll do that anyway) but to write *well*.'[23] For the next ten years, she would make known in both letters and public forums her view that deliberately writing on Canadian subjects for a Canadian audience was a false approach to both literature and culture. Her position was simply that if something was written in Canada, then it was automatically Canadian; the more important task, she asserted, was to write well. Wilson's position was diametrically opposed to that of William Arthur Deacon, the *Globe and Mail* critic whom she viewed as her detractor and adversary. Deacon was an ardent proponent of the new literary nationalism that had emerged in the 1930s and that had been given a powerful stimulus by Canada's participation in the Second World War. In two publications, *My Vision of Canada* (1933) and *A Literary Map of Canada* (1936), he called for an 'authentically Canadian' literature that would describe for the world the realities of Canada and its cultural values. Hugh MacLennan's *Two Solitudes* and Gabrielle Roy's *The Tin Flute*, both published in 1945 and dealing with tensions between English and French Canada, met that agenda perfectly. Wilson's first two novels, with large portions of each story set in England, did not. In fact, Deacon advised readers of *The Innocent Traveller* to skim quickly over the first part of the novel until the trio of female adventurers set off for Canada.

Wilson's attitude prefigures that of the twenty-first century, when a novel may be written and published in Canada but its characters come from everywhere. Anne Michaels in *Fugitive Pieces* and Dennis Bock in *The Ash Garden* bring characters to Ontario who try to make sense of the enormous losses they have inflicted and suffered in the Second World War. Michael Ondaatje's *The English Patient* is set in a ruined nunnery in Italy at the end of the war, and only one of its four principal characters, wanderers, comes from Canada, the others coming from Hungary, India, and Italy. Two of Ondaatje's other books are set in Sri Lanka, while from a Toronto suburb, Rohinton Mistry painstakingly recreates the Bombay he left in the 1970s. All these writers have won a huge readership worldwide because their books are well written. Two of Wilson's most frequently anthologized stories, "We Have to Sit Opposite," set perhaps in Austria, and "Haply the Soul of My Grandmother," set in Egypt, could be seen to anticipate this direction in Canadian writing.

But, in 1949, Deacon's ambition to define and foster a 'specifically Canadian culture' was given further impetus by the establishment of a Royal Commission on National Development in the Arts, Letters and Sciences.[24] (This was the public agency to which Wilson reluctantly gave her name and a dollar at Dorothy Livesay's insistence.) For two years, under the chairmanship of Vincent Massey, the commission held hearings throughout the country, promoting legal recognition of the necessity of a Canadian culture. The order in council for the commission had stated that it was 'desirable that the Canadian people should know as much as possible about their country, its history and traditions, and about their national life and common achievements.' It also stated that 'it is in the national interest to give encouragement to institutions which express national feeling.' While the report of the commission made recommendations that led to the establishment of the National Library and the Canada Council, both of which Wilson highly approved, it also fostered a self-conscious attitude about Canadianness in the arts which she felt led to phony posturing and the frequent subsidizing and encouragement of second-rate talents.

On several occasions, she gave clear statements of her views, summing them up at one point in a letter to Dr Malcolm Ross, then professor at Queen's University and editor of the *Queen's Quarterly*.[25] In 1953 they were in correspondence over a piece of writing that Ross had solicited for a forthcoming issue of the quarterly (an untitled excerpt from *Swamp Angel* appeared in 1954), and, as frequently happened, Wilson's letter of 8 July 1953 digressed to include a number of topics. But central to the letter is Wilson's statement '... how much I disagree with "writing for Canadians."' In a lengthy passage, she writes in an uncharacteristically firm and outspoken way, without the qualifiers that usually circumscribed her statements: 'I feel very strongly that the writing of Canadians should and must be Canadian in aspect, but not deliberately so, with a dreadful conscious eye on the potential reader, Canadian or otherwise. A writer should write, and if he be neither phony nor self conscious, he will hit a true mark.' She develops her argument by distinguishing between national and regional writing, only the latter, in her opinion, being capable of achieving universality. Taking herself as an example, she says that although she knows many countries well and Canada from coast to coast, she could only write about British Columbia and its people. In her view, good writing is 'rooted in association, affection, and apprehension of place and people.' Writing about Canada as a whole would risk abstraction. As examples, she gives Proust writing about Combray, Balbec, and a small section of Paris, and Mark Twain writing about the people of the Mississippi. To these she adds Hardy's creation of Wessex and Emily Brontë being bounded by the Yorkshire moors. 'All these universal and strongly regional writers simply wrote,' she points out, 'not *for* anyone, and they became part of the literature of their own countries and beyond.'

One can read these strong opinions as a veiled retort to Deacon's exclusion of Wilson from his canon of important Canadian authors. To her there was something 'menacing' in his nationalist program of 'writing *for* Canadians' and his ability to shape single-handedly the literary taste and opinions of the whole country. Her first two books, treated roughly in the pages of the *Globe and Mail*, had not sold very well in Canada, and she was painfully aware of Deacon's powerful influence on the marketplace. What disturbed her was the lack of good debate on the subject, and at one point she even let herself be persuaded to take part in Vancouver in a panel on the subject of Canadian writing.[26] Naturalist Roderick Haig-Brown, historian Bruce Hutchison, and John Gray were the other members, with Haig-Brown and Wilson promoting the cause of regionalism. By this point in her career, Wilson was in correspondence with a number of influential men and women of letters in Canada – anthologist Robert Weaver, professor and critic Desmond Pacey, novelist Mazo de la Roche – and she never lost the opportunity to argue against the nationalist position, which she and other Western writers came to view as an idea and bias bred in Central Canada. Looking at Ross's *Queen's Quarterly* review of the Willa Cather biography by E.K. Brown, Wilson referred with approval to Brown's observation that 'Cather had always understood that a person's relation to a place might be as valuable to him ... as any relation he might have with other persons. What happens in one place could not happen in just the same way in any other.'[27] In 1955, Wilson would take her argument onto the national stage in the CBC television program *Profile*, in which she was interviewed by Professor Roy Daniells, rehearsing again her argument that writers must first write *well*, and then a literature of high quality would emerge in a country. Wilson was developing a distinct public persona – that of a gracious and unassuming writer, but a writer nonetheless with strong opinions on matters of region and literary culture. She would be asked to write articles putting forth her views, but most of these requests she turned down. Closely linked to the issue of developing a national literature was the matter of teaching creative writing, and on this subject Wilson also had very strong beliefs, but we will leave that until later when we return to an account of her relations with Earle Birney at the end of the decade.

Ethel Wilson's public profile was also raised by the unexpected response to a broadcast on the CBC of 'Lilly's Story.' In 1950, Robert Weaver, producer of the CBC program *Canadian Short Stories*, arranged for a reading of 'Mrs Golightly and the First Convention,' which proved popular with the radio audience. Subsequently, with the enthusiastic support of one of his readers, Joyce Marshall, he commissioned several of her fictions to be read on the CBC, including a story titled 'Statistics,' which was apparently returned to the author as requested but later destroyed, for no manuscript remains with the author's papers at UBC.[28] 'Lilly's Story' received an hour-long dramatization on Sunday evening, 23 January 1953. It was deemed a critical success and pleased the author and her friends. But some members of the public were deeply offended by what was regarded as the story's sordid subject matter – it was described in a couple of Montreal newspapers as an immoral story involving sexual relations between a Chinese and a white girl. According to a gossip columnist, protests were being sent to the office of Prime Minister St Laurent.[29] In this era of careful scrutiny of the media (the McCarthy investigations were in full swing in the United States) the broadcast of 'Lilly's Story' became a case in point for a special committee of the Canadian Senate that had been struck to investigate 'the sale

and distribution of salacious and indecent literature.'[30] R.W. Keyser-
lingk, a member of the committee, rose to his feet in the Senate on February 12th and reported to his fellow members that 'Lilly's Story' was a
sordid tale told graphically and in extremely poor taste. He summarized
the story this way: 'Lilly, described by the CBC narrator as "a pale slut," is
in her middle teens when a Chinese cook (speaking dreadful "pidgin"
English) tries to seduce her by offering her gifts. He gives her silk stock-
ings for instance in a public restaurant, makes her take off her old stock-
ings and put on the new ones while he watches her legs. She agrees to
go to his room to spend the night in exchange for a bicycle. Police, looking for a stolen bike, intervene.' He continued by pointing out that the
time of the broadcast was 9 to 10 P.M. on Sunday evening when children
were still listening to radios. He also suggested that the portrait of a
lecherous Chinese seducing a pale white girl would do little to improve
relations with the peoples of Asia. In the House of Commons, a Reverend Hansell spoke to the same issue, asserting the book was obscene.

Wilson made no public statement in response to these accusations, but
Toronto novelist Morley Callaghan took up the issue on her behalf when
The Equations of Love was passed over for a Governor General's Award. In
an irate piece published in *Saturday Night*,[31] he questioned whether the
members of the awards selection committee had not in fact been intimidated by the inanities of the Senate committee. Did they, too, consider
the story obscene? Did they really consider David Walker's *The Pillar* (the
winner for 1952) a piece of writing superior to Wilson's *The Equations of
Love*? (Ethel Wilson's books, in fact, would never be considered the right
choice for the Governor General's Award. Committees with little taste or
foresight would choose Philip Child's *Mr Ames against Time* over *The Innocent Traveller* in 1949 and Igor Gouzenko's *The Fall of the Titan* rather than
Swamp Angel in 1954. Like so many titles in the list of Governor General's
Award winners – *Three Came to Ville Marie* instead of *As for Me and My
House* in 1941, *The Deserter* instead of *The Stone Angel* in 1964, *New Ancestors*
instead of *Fifth Business* in 1970 – these are books that have long been forgotten, while Wilson's novels continue to be read and reprinted.) When
Wilson did not win the national literary award, she wrote to Gray: 'I do
feel I let you down a bit. However I am convinced that Mr Walker's book
has far greater stature – & you do know, don't you, that I am constitu-
tionally unable to feel badly personally about a thing like that. I have so
much luck & fun it is almost frightening.'[32] She would express her fear
over and over again that too much success might put her off her guard,
that her happiness was always in danger of being shattered.

Wilson's little bit of infamy over the CBC production of 'Lilly's Story'[33] did not intimidate her or dampen her spirits, but rather amused her and Wallace, and was a lively topic of discussion for their friends. During this high tide of creativity and public recognition, one of the chief pleasures in Ethel Wilson's life was the number of friendships she and Wallace enjoyed. Until she became a published writer, her social life had focused chiefly on family (abiding connections to the Malkins and the lively and interesting company of Wallace's cousins, especially the Grahams and Tuppers). There were acquaintances made through Wallace's profession, though shyness and lack of self-possession made Ethel a retiring figure on Vancouver's social scene. But the boost in self-esteem through her writing career and her public involvement in the arts community regionally and nationally drew her into a number of friendships that were both enormously stimulating and pleasurable. Some of these were exclusively literary, although all her friendships were shared with Wallace. She knew Alan Crawley, the blind editor of *Contemporary Verse*, well before her own reputation as a writer was firmly established. There is no record of how they met, but Wilson mentions him in 1946 letters to Ellen Elliott at Macmillan. It was not poetry that drew them together because Wilson, with only a few exceptions such as Donne and T.S. Eliot, had no great feeling for verse and confessed to Elliott that she subscribed to Alan's magazine 'on the whole without enthusiasm, though with appreciation.'[34] Rather, it was something like a meeting of minds, a shared sensibility about both literature and life, that united them, and also the pleasure Ethel experienced in the company of Alan's loyal wife, Jean, who by reading to him made it possible for Alan to do his work. The Wilsons and Crawleys spent many happy hours together socially, and the letters Ethel Wilson wrote to these friends are among the most personal and delightful of any that have survived.

She seems to have connected first with Dorothy Livesay when the latter was soliciting respondents for the Massey Report in 1949, and continued to know her in the 1950s as part of the writers' group that frequently met at the Wilsons' apartment. A widow making her living at that time as a freelance journalist, Livesay decided in 1952 to write a piece on Wilson for *Saturday Night*. It was designed to promote interest in both the author and her new book, *The Equations of Love*, parts of which Livesay had heard Wilson read out loud to the writers' group. This would turn out to be the most informative article about Wilson published in the 1950s, but Wilson wasn't entirely pleased with its execution. After conducting interviews and writing the article, Livesay sent a copy for Wilson to look over. There were some errors, and Wilson marked these on the copy she returned to Livesay, but only one was corrected in the printed version.[35] More irritating to Wilson were certain phrasings that made her sound a little superior in attitude. Livesay wrote, for example, that a strict, conventional upbringing had given the author self-assurance. She asked that 'assurance' be changed to 'a sense of proportion,' but Livesay chose not to make the changes or simply didn't bother. And though her enthusiasm for Wilson's writing remained intact in the article, she wrote a surprisingly cool, critical letter to Wilson after reading the two published novellas, faulting what she regarded as a contrived ending to 'Lilly's Story,' the use of the omniscient narrator ('a creature who I feel simply does not belong to this age'), and the author's disregard for the background characters in 'Lilly's Story.'[36] Without putting it into words, Livesay was implying perhaps that Wilson's social status did not fit her to describe and judge working-class characters in fiction. Wilson probably sensed that she could be difficult, aside from politics. Thereafter she was always a little cautious and reticent in her relations with Livesay, though she recognized and admired her for her generosity of spirit and her passion for the arts. (Just before Livesay's article appeared in late July of 1952 there was a shorter but similar biographical piece in the *Vancouver Sun* by reporter Cy Young. Making reference to the quick acceptance and reprinting of 'I Just Love Dogs,' it was titled 'Shortcut to Success,' and its greater accuracy probably pleased Wilson considerably.)

Further afield, Wilson had come to know members of the literary community in other parts of Canada. She met Morley Callaghan at parties hosted by the Macmillan Company and at the home of John Gray and his wife, Toni, and though she was not especially impressed by Callaghan's reputation as a friend of Hemingway, she did think his early novel *Such Is My Beloved* a distinguished work of fiction for its balanced portrayal of goodness and evil in human affairs,[37] and she was flattered, of course, by his public enthusiasm for her own writing. A more complicated friendship developed between Ethel Wilson and Mazo de la Roche, the best-selling author of the Jalna series. They met in Toronto in the early 1950s when Enid Graham, the wife of one of Wallace's doctor friends, took Ethel to the famous author's house for tea. The friendship progressed through visits (de la Roche had an adopted son living in Vancouver) and through letters which at first were addressed to 'Dear Miss de la Roche' and eventually to 'My Darling Mazo.' They had mutual friends in Robert and Sylvia Lynd, who had entertained de la

Marriage of Eliza ('Lila') Davis Malkin and Robert William William Bryant in Burslem, Staffordshire, 14 April, 1887. Far left, second row, is John Wilcox Edge. Behind the bride is Eliza Edge. In the front row from the left are Philip Malkin, Annie and James Malkin, Robert and Lila Malkin, Edna Edge, Joseph Edge and second wife, Jane. All are figured in *The Inno- cent Traveller*.

At either end, Robert and Lila Bryant aboard a Union Castle steamship en route to South Africa, May 1887.

The Methodist parsonage and Ethel Wilson's birthplace in Port Elizabeth, South Africa.

Lila and Ethel Bryant, 1888.

Robert and Ethel Bryant, ca. 1890.

Ethel Bryant, ca. 1894.

English Bay, Vancouver, 1890s.

Ethel Bryant in her early teens in England, ca. 1902.

The Malkin family in Vancouver, 1907. Standing at back and along wall: Fred Malkin, unidentified servant, Philip Malkin, Julia Eldridge Malkin, Edith Stormer Malkin. Middle group seated on steps: Eliza Edge, Belle Malkin, Marion Malkin holding Richard Malkin, Joseph Malkin, Georgina Grundy Malkin, Ethel Bryant holding Lucile Malkin. Front row from left: William Harold Malkin, Sydney Malkin, unidentified servant holding Lila Malkin, Annie Malkin, unidentified servant.

Ethel Bryant with eight of eleven Malkin cousins in Vancouver, 1912. From left: Richard, Lucile, Joseph, Lila, Marjorie, Ursula, Locke, Ethel, and Robert.

Wallace Wilson in First World War uniform, ca. 1916.

Ethel Wilson, ca. 1921.

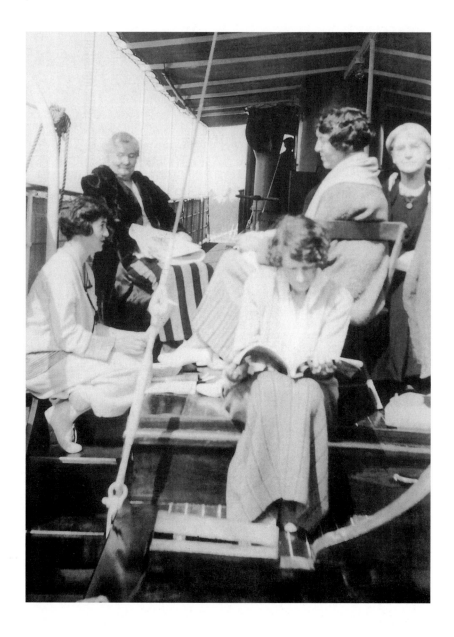

1930s photo of Ethel reading on a boat with Wilson and Buckerfield in-laws behind her.

Ethel and Wallace Wilson fly-fishing in the B.C. interior, ca. 1930.

The Malkin family, 1935. At back from left: Harold Molson, Richard Malkin and his wife Muriel, Joseph Malkin, Lucile Malkin, Wallace and Ethel Wilson, Robert Malkin, Georginia Malkin, Locke Malkin. Front from left: Ursula Malkin, William Harold Malkin, Julia Malkin, Philip Malkin holding Richard's daughter Suzanne, Eliza Edge, Rick Malkin, Fred Malkin, Lila Malkin Molson and son. Seated on rug: Richard Malkin's son, Wyatt, Joseph's wife Jean and their son Toby. In this photograph Eliza Edge is ninety years of age.

Ethel Wilson and her 'evacuee' daughter, Audrey Butler, at 1238 Connaught Drive, 1941.

Ethel Wilson, 1940s.

Wallace Wilson in uniform during the Second World War.

'Kensington Place' at the corner of Nicola Street and Beach Avenue in Vancouver, where the Wilsons lived in a third floor apartment from 1943 to 1965 and where Ethel wrote her books.

Ethel Wilson's first publicity photo, 1947.

John Gray, Ethel Wilson's editor and close friend at the Macmillan Company of
Canada.

Dust jacket for Macmillan edition of *Swamp Angel* (1954).

Recipients of first Canada Council Medals, February 1962. Back from left: E.J. Pratt, Healey Willan, Vincent Massey, A.Y. Jackson. In middle: Marius Barbeau and Lionel-Adolphe Groulx. Seated in front: Bess Harris, Ethel Wilson, and unidentified woman.

Wallace Wilson (left) presents totem sculpture by Bill Reid (right) to Neal
Harlow in 1961.

Photo of Wallace and Ethel taken by Nan Cheney, ca. 1962.

Roche several times when she lived in England. Joan Givner, de la
Roche's biographer, rightly observes, however, that the friendship was
not based on literary admiration. As late as 1955, de la Roche was asking
John Gray to send her a copy of Wilson's *Swamp Angel* because 'I am
ashamed to say I have read nothing of hers,'[38] and Wilson suggested in a
television interview that Canada had yet to wait for a notable novelist to
appear. Wilson, in fact, was always skirting around the fact of de la
Roche's fame in her discussions of Canadian literature, acknowledging
her wide reputation but being reluctant to comment on the quality of
her work. An example of this hedging and its awkwardness occurs in the
script for a talk she gave on the novel at the Vancouver Institute. In
selecting three outstanding Canadian writers for discussion (Morley Callaghan, Sinclair Ross, and Robertson Davies), she pauses for a moment:
'Someone will say, "But Mazo de la Roche is our most widely read novelist."' That is true, Wilson replies, 'Miss de la Roche is a case by herself.
She needs no defence from me,' and goes on to call her a 'remarkable
woman' rather than a remarkable writer.[39] Wilson assumed a position of
deference in her relation to Mazo de la Roche and praised her for a
writer's vision of life in Ontario that was unknown to Western Canada.
We can assume that she felt Mazo de la Roche's work was not distinguished in terms of style.

What Wilson thought of de la Roche's lifelong companionship with
her cousin, Carolyn Clement, we cannot know. In fact, in all her correspondence and other writings, Wilson only refers once to homosexuality
and this in a neutral, rather disinterested way. After meeting the English
novelist Angus Wilson, she wrote to the Crawleys: 'He's a funny looking
little man aged 49 but looks older. I have always understood that he has
a characteristic common to many bachelor artists & writers, but of
course I do not know. Even if so, that does not prevent him from being a
very interesting person to talk to.'[40] In the 1960s, she entertained novelist Jane Rule and her companion, Helen Sonthoff, in her apartment,
and though *Desert of the Heart*, Rule's ground-breaking novel about les-
bian love, had been published, Wilson does not mention this in a letter
recording the visit, but simply says how extraordinarily nice and interesting the two women are.[41] In *The Innocent Traveller*, Wilson describes Mr
Sandbach, Aunt Topaz's great love, in such a way as to suggest what we
would now call a gay identity, but homosexuality for the most part
appears to have been outside her sphere of experience or interest.

In the 1950s, writers and editors who were privileged to travel made it
a habit to visit at Kensington Place, where they were elegantly enter-

tained, sometimes for tea, often for drinks and dinner served by Mrs
Marshall, the housekeeper who replaced Mrs Tufts in 1951. John Gray
stopped there whenever he was in Vancouver, and the poet A.J.M. Smith
was another welcome guest. Wilson had special affection and admiration for Robert Weaver, who worked tirelessly in the cause of bringing
good Canadian writing to the attention of the general public; his presence in Vancouver was always a happy social occasion for the Wilsons.
Desmond Pacey, the first academic to write with serious enthusiasm
about Ethel Wilson, was also welcomed to Kensington Place when he
was in Vancouver.

The Wilsons' very active social life, sometimes four dinners out a
week, included a number of artist and academic friends in the city,
many of whom they came to know through Nan Cheney. In 1937, while
the Wilsons were still living on Connaught Drive, Nan and Hill Cheney
moved to Vancouver from Eastern Canada. He was a radiologist, and
she was a medical illustrator, both pioneers in their fields. They bought
a house three doors down from the Wilsons and soon came to know
them through medical connections. Ethel compared Nan's beauty to
that of the *Winged Victory* that had so stirred her as a teenager travelling
in France.[42] Nan and Ethel shared a sense of humour compounded of
the ironies in human behaviour and the delights of language in assess-
ing that behaviour. Bewailing people with no sense of humour, she was
once wrote: 'Wouldn't it be *awful* to live in such solemnity.'[43] But one of
Cheney's first memories of Ethel Wilson, according to Mary McAlpine,
was only funny from Nan's point of view. Marius Barbeau, the famous
ethnologist, was staying with the Cheneys for a few days in the summer
of 1939, and Ethel expressed a wish to meet him. When she came to tea
at the Cheneys' house, she arrived, as always when feeling diffident,
dressed very smartly – a hat, white gloves, 'as if she had just stepped out
of a dress shop.' Barbeau, by contrast, was an untidy little man, wearing
a pink and beige striped suit that looked as if he had slept in it all across
Canada. His white hair was unfashionably long for those times, curling
below his collar. The contrast in attire, acutely striking in an age of still
rigid dress conventions, provoked a sense of the absurd in Barbeau, who
spent the hour being anecdotal and funny. Ethel had come with serious
questions and left the meeting feeling flat.[44] Although she was over fifty
at that point, she had little self-confidence when introduced to people
with distinguished reputations. How different that was by the 1950s,
when Nan Cheney, now a widow and working as a medical artist at UBC,
drew Ethel into her circle of artist and academic friends, which included

Group of Seven painter Lawren Harris and his wife, Bess. Now it was Ethel who was more likely to be intimidating, and humorous anecdotes were certainly very central to civilized discourse at Kensington Place. When Dylan Thomas visited Vancouver, Wilson met him socially at a reception at the Buckerfields and subsequently entertained friends by describing him as a dissolute cherub.[45]

The sense of play that Wilson was capable of in her friendships is well illustrated in a letter she wrote to Nan when there were negotiations afoot for the filming of 'Lilly's Story.' Nan was having a difficult time financially, and Ethel wanted to help her out with a gift of money but had to find some way to make this act of charity palatable. Disguising her handwriting, she wrote to her in Lilly's voice:

Dear Madam

There is a nice gentleman in N.Y. has ast me if he can try to get me a job on the Movies. He hassent got the job yet but he sent me some money today in Case he gets it Bless his kind Hart.

I am getting my dear Husband a nise hat and maybe a case of wisky tho I don't use licker myself.

I have ast my sekerterry name of Wilson to make me a check to send you with love to sellerbate same and maybe you will buy a hat or some wisky or put by for your holiday wichever you prefer.

Humbly remaining with love and oblidge and plese to share the Fun – Lilly.[46]

Nan Cheney loved Ethel very much, but she knew that most people preferred Wallace's company. She told Mary McAlpine that 'everyone was crazy about Wallace. He was a wonderful man. I think a lot of women were in love with Wallace. Ethel was, oh, a little cold.' But she added: 'I'm sure there was nobody else in his life but Ethel. He seemed absolutely devoted to her.'[47] I had the same conversation with Nan Cheney by telephone, in which she elaborated on the fact that Ethel was very aware that people preferred Wallace's company to hers. 'That didn't matter,' said Cheney, 'because Ethel felt so secure in his love for her.'[48] Certainly there is no evidence to suggest that she was deceived in feeling secure in Wallace's faithfulness. Dorothy Livesay was the only person who ever suggested to me that Wallace had a roving eye. 'He pinched my bottom once, and he shouldn't have,' she asserted, but I have concluded that the anecdote was likely fictional, telling us more about Livesay perhaps than about Wallace Wilson.[49]

Through Nan, Ethel met Dr Garnett Sedgewick, head of the English
Department at UBC, who had read her early stories and pressed her to
continue writing. 'You're damn lazy,' he said to her from his privileged
position before *Hetty Dorval* and *The Innocent Traveller* were published.[50]
His successor, Dr Roy Daniells, became one of Wilson's great admirers
and eventually persuaded her to appear with him in a television interview in 1955. In this period, the Wilsons came to know Audrey and
Harry Hawthorn of the Anthropology Department, and Margaret and
Larry Mackenzie, the latter serving as the president of UBC from 1948 to
1962. But the professor and his wife who became the Wilsons' closest
academic friends were Geoffrey and Margaret Andrew, with whom they
frequently dined at the UBC Faculty Club and enjoyed long conversations about literature and politics. Margaret was a social worker and
librarian, and a granddaughter of George Grant, the distinguished president of Queen's University; Geoffrey taught in UBC's English Department and later was appointed a member of the Canada Council, moving
his family to Ottawa. The Wilsons took great pleasure in the Andrews'
four children and let the family have Little Rock for part of two summers. Wilson wrote to Mazo de la Roche: '... it is a joy to us to think
of them there ... When a child's letter begins "Dear Mrs Wilson,
the weather is lovely here, thank you so much ..." one's cup of joy
sparkles.'[51]

In 1953, Wallace retired from his practice, but he remained almost as
active as when he had been going to the office five days a week. He
belonged to a number of national and community organizations, and
his gregariousness and strong sense of civic duty resulted in his frequently holding offices. He chaired the Ethics Committee of the Canadian Medical Association and simultaneously lectured on medical ethics
at UBC. He was also president of UBC's Friends of the Library Association. He was a founding member of both the B.C. Cancer Foundation
and the Narcotics Association of Vancouver, and worked long and hard
for the city's Housing Council, starting something called the Second
Mile Club, for lonely, single men living in bleak rooms in the city's east
side. He was president of the Community Chest and Council and also
served as a consultant at Shaughnessy and at Vancouver General hospitals. He was also a member of the Vancouver Club. Through the Malkins
and through Wallace's high profile in so many charitable as well as medical organizations, the Wilsons knew several people in Vancouver's business community. They counted among their friends the lumber
magnate H.R. Macmillan (who also happened to be Mazo de la Roche's

second cousin), Austin Taylor, chairman of the Home Oil Company in the 1950s, and Leon Koerner, another giant in the forest industry. With their wives, these leaders in the province's business world were part of the social circle that Ethel Wilson now moved in easily. They paid her court as one of Canada's increasingly celebrated writers – 'What are you writing now?' they would ask, for they loved her books, they said, and perhaps best of all they loved knowing an author with a reputation beyond the province. Among this group, the Wilsons were especially friendly with Thea and Leon Koerner, a childless couple who had fled Nazi-invaded Austria in 1939 because Leon Koerner had a Jewish grandmother (Thea was Swedish). Leon, with his brothers Walter and Otto, had made a fortune through a special process of curing hemlock and marketing it with the name of Alaska pine. The Koerners spent part of the winter in Palm Springs and urged the Wilsons to join them there. In March 1953, Ethel and Wallace arranged to drive to southern California and take a cottage at Indio, a not very fashionable but quiet spot twenty-three miles from Palm Springs.

In a letter to Mazo de la Roche, Wilson describes herself to be truly a northerner, always ill at ease among the strange smells and places of the south. Even Palm Springs and the great desert of southern California is 'almost repellent to me,' she writes. She would 'rather sit out the winter [at home] and enjoy the rest of the year there or, if fortunate enough, go to England.'[52] The Wilsons were persuaded, however, to go south in the winter of 1953 on the basis of medical advice, for Ethel had developed an acute form of arthritis in the hip and it was generally held that the heat and dry air of the desert would bring relief for this kind of suffering. In the late 1940s, Wilson had slipped on a wet rock at the cottage on Bowen Island; in later years, she was convinced she had cracked or broken her hip bone in the fall. But doctors diagnosed the persistent and exhausting pain as osteoarthritis, and in February of 1951 she went to Vancouver General Hospital for three weeks to try cortisone treatments, which were then experimental and very costly. At first, they seemed to bring relief, and she was able to write John Gray that the time in hospital was 'a lovely island of almost painlessness & flowers, and kindness, & spoiling,'[53] but the pain and lameness soon returned and she had to resign herself henceforth to taking pain-killers and being in a wheelchair for the purposes of moving around. In public, she would almost always appear in her wheelchair, giving Wallace a graceful, almost regal gesture of her hand to indicate when she was ready to move along. Although the pain was sometimes excruciating, her self-discipline and 'sense of proportion' held self-pity in check. She could write, 'I hate the fatigue & pain of this arthritis which is so *preventing*, so limiting & exacting,' but then she would remember how she last saw her Aunt Hannah and would say to herself: '"Fathead, shut up, how dare you with so many blessings & friends." You've only got to think of yourself as living alone in a top room, *with* joints, & crawling down & back daily for your bottle of milk, to fall on your knobby knees in gratitude.'[54] And reading the exciting reviews of *The Equations of Love*, she writes to John Gray: 'What's an aching bone, nothing to this interesting life.'[55]

But the prospect of relief from pain, however temporary, tempted the Wilsons to try southern California. They drove first to San Francisco, which had become one of their favourite cities, and then, at the Koerners' invitation, to Palm Springs and the nearby resort town of Indio, where they took a cottage at Hayes Desert Palms Guest Ranch, simulating their arrangements at Lac Le Jeune. Part of the therapy suggested by the doctors was to use the pool several times a day, a pleasure for someone who had always enjoyed swimming for both exercise and recreation. But, sitting under a date palm tree, she wrote to John Gray to report that while her hip had been feeling better that winter, in the dry heat and soaking pool it had become more painful again. She concluded reluctantly that the undue activity probably made it worse.[56] She also wrote to Earle Birney, who was an ardent traveller, and described the pleasures of their environs – the palm trees and songbirds and the sweet yet sharp scent of the grapefruit grove – but she also deplored the commercial development of the area, especially the billboards defacing the desert and the extraordinarily beautiful mountains. In this letter, she tells Birney an anecdote about having lunch with the Koerners one day (to Earle, whose communist past she was aware of, she says simply 'rich foreign friends') and being approached in her wheelchair by a man wearing very small bathing trunks and a gold medal around his neck and being asked by this man if she thought God was good. Looking at the blue sky and landscape, she assented happily, although her thoughts filled with places like Russia, where the proof would not be so easy. The man in the bathing trunks then asked what she had been eating, and when she could only wiggle her hands in front of her mouth, he said 'spare ribs, mouth organs' and went on his way. Afterwards Ethel learned that he was head of Twentieth Century Fox, the film company her New York agent was in negotiations with about 'Lilly's Story.'[57] In the end, the trip, confirmed for her how much she did not care for American culture, an attitude that was becoming increasingly pronounced in her writings. Before leaving on the trip, she had written to John Gray, 'I shall not be able to *think* down in U.S.A.; it will all be so enraging.'[58] She viewed the McCarthy hearings with alarm and deplored the American escalations in the Cold War. While they were in California, they witnessed after a series of test explosions in the desert 'a massive arrangement in the sky, filling nearly all one side, a great souptureen like mass with steel-like bands – all quite symmetrical and unnatural. It remained stationary for 6 hours ... it was colossal, and alarming.'[59] She also regarded contemporary American writers as lacking in style and moral sensitivity. Finally, it was the northernness of Canada that exerted its appeal. In May she and Wallace drove up to Lac Le Jeune, and she wrote to Earle Birney that 'all the Californias cannot compare for us. The drive here was heavenly.'[60] And to Frank Upjohn at Macmillan: 'I like Lac Le Jeune 1000 times better than California, all smiles.'[61]

Although the trip to southern California had been physically taxing, the Wilsons began planning a long trip for the following winter, one that would take them on a Holland-America Line freighter from Vancouver through the Panama Canal to Europe. They set out in late November after a lively farewell party in the ship's saloon with Vancouver friends; according to Mary McAlpine there were flowers and presents and Wallace kept the drinks flowing.[62] Ethel wrote to Margaret Andrew from San Francisco describing a rough passage along the west coast, but also describing her delight in the whales (blackfish) and porpoises playing in the ocean: 'Their life is one long game.'[63] The food on board was rich, delicious, and too plentiful, and being immobile she found herself a sitting duck for endless talkers; but there was a comfortable cabin where she could rest her facial muscles, and she admits she wouldn't have missed the experience for anything. They had expected to be in London for Christmas, but rough seas on the Atlantic delayed the vessel's progress, and then on entering the Scheldt River for Antwerp, the freighter became stuck on a sandbar for two days. In a letter to Earle Birney dated 31 December, thinking about her age and the great stretches of untravelled rivers from the Low Countries all the way to the Black Sea, Wilson reflects '... oh what opportunities missed – and taken!'[64] That little exclamation characterizes the voice of the writer who feels the evocative power of place and time, but is grateful for and fulfilled by what she has experienced within her finite human reach. A more romantic writer, like Gabrielle Roy, concerned with haunting effects in her prose, would have stopped after 'what opportunities missed.'

It was the new year of 1954 before the Wilsons reached London, where they had a host of friends and relatives to visit before leaving for two months in Portugal. One of her half-cousins drove them about the London environs, including Acton and the street where Ethel had lived with her father when he died. On that same drive, to Ethel's delight, they came to Petersham and stopped to visit the little church and grave-yard where Captain George Vancouver was buried.[65] When they set out on January 19, they took with them Marion Martin Ward, Ethel's girl-hood friend, who was a widow living in London and having a hard time financially. In letters that Ethel wrote to the Buckerfields and to Earle Birney, we get an account of some aspects of the Portugal stay.[66] While in Lisbon, they paid 'an affectionate visit' to Henry Fielding's grave, Wallace wheeling Ethel out to see the resting place of one of her favou-rite authors. On the coast, they rented a cottage at the picturesque fish-ing village of Estoril. Here, with Marion Ward, they established a routine of reading and sightseeing, with drinks in the late afternoon and a fine restaurant meal in the evening. The one occasion she would never for-get was being taken by their Portuguese driver Antonio to hear an evening of poetry and fado, the national music, which Ethel described as 'a strange melancholy lament [that] carries with it an age-old sort of tragedy, or slavery – indeed Portugal over-run by Phoenecians, Romans, Celts, Moors.' She knew Portugal was regarded as 'a simple and "back-ward" country,' but felt it had some things to which a country like Can-ada might aspire. She was especially taken by the presence in the parks of bookcases with glass doors, which an attendant would unlock for a few cents and rent a book for a couple of hours. Altogether it was a happy, restful holiday, and they vowed to return. It also proved condu-cive to work, and Ethel did the final revisions here for her next book.

The Wilsons returned to Vancouver in April via Ottawa and Toronto. There was a special reason to visit the capital: Vincent Massey, the gover-nor general, had invited them to lunch at Rideau Hall, and they had accepted. His Excellency was an avid patron of the arts (he had been in charge of the commission that eventually led to the formation of the Canada Council), and he was an admirer of Ethel's books, especially *The Equations of Love*. She told John Gray about the luncheon in confidence because she did not want Vancouver gossips to bruit it about, but at the same time she was glad her Uncle Harold had heard of the invitation through his son in Ottawa, because she knew it would mean something special to him.[67] The luncheon was unfortunately marred by one of Ethel's massive nosebleeds, and she had to excuse herself from the table in order to stop the bleeding. The last few days of the trip were spent in Toronto, where they visited the Grahams and her friends at 70 Bond Street. The critical and popular success of her last book gave Ethel a glow of self-confidence and enormous pleasure as she visited the offices which had made it all happen. What were the aches and pains, indeed; her life was very good.

CHAPTER ELEVEN

Swamp Angel
1951–1954

Somewhere, I think, the person in a story must touch not only the constructive imagination, but also the earth ... and receive life and strength from that earth.
– 'The Bridge or the Stokehold?'

'Country Matters' / A revolver / Genius of place / 'Hunt the Symbol' / Critical reception

Swamp Angel was the new book that Ethel Wilson was putting the finishing touches to in Portugal. 'Lilly's Story' was bringing her popularity and a bit of money, but this new book written at the height of her creativity and personal happiness would become the novel for which she would eventually be best known. There is no question that it is her masterwork.

The composition of *Swamp Angel* was leisurely, spanning more than two years, but it was anything but straightforward. There is a bewildering array of pencilled notes, manuscripts, and typescripts at UBC Library on all kinds of paper (including blue airmail paper), which would require painstaking collation to establish an order of drafts and revisions.[1] However, what does seem clear is that the novel developed from several different sources – from at least three separate stories that were eventually incorporated into the larger work. The first mention of material that would become part of the novel is in a letter to John Gray in December of 1951, after work on *The Equations of Love* was completed. She says simply that she is working on a story called 'Country Matters,' which she will develop further when she and Wallace go up-country in the spring.[2] Although the Wilsons did make a trip to the interior of the province in

July of 1952, the manuscript titled 'Country Matters' describes life in the Fraser delta region – the Chinese market gardens, the fishing boats on the river, the sawmills on shore. It would form part of Wilson's manuscript for *Swamp Angel*, but would eventually be almost wholly excised by her editors in Toronto. Another story that would become part of the novel is titled 'Sweet Influence Doth Impart,' which describes the journey of a woman up the Fraser Canyon. Here it is easy to recognize the hero of *Swamp Angel*, Maggie Vardoe, except that her name in this story is Christina. 'Sweet Influence Doth Impart' seems to refer to the impact of landscape on human affairs, a strong theme in all of Wilson's writing, while Christina suggests perhaps a female pilgrim's progress, a not unlikely association for someone of Maggie's character and principles. A third discrete manuscript that forms part of *Swamp Angel* is titled 'The Swimmer,' but in the short story the swimming is purely an abstract activity unconnected to any human drama and the swimmer is male.

Wilson was mostly silent about this new work of fiction during 1952, though that would be the year in which the largest part of the writing was done. There is an undated letter, which may be from 1952, in which she says she is working slowly at something but that she has 'too many interests ... liking to do everything that time and place allow with Wallace (that illness of his made marks on me – nothing else is as important as being with him).'[3] She also reports a full calendar of visitors at Little Rock. Instead of reporting on her new work, her letters to John Gray that year were full of the excitement surrounding 'Lilly's Story' and Ruth May's efforts to sell it to the movies. She states in a letter at the beginning of November 1952 that she is 'getting perilously near to the end of a small opus'[4] and refers again to her 'new bit of work'[5] in a letter to Gray in January 1953, where it becomes clear that a first draft has been completed and she is waiting for her typist, Mrs Bell of the Hotel Vancouver, to finish preparing a clean typescript to send off. She calls her new work 'The Swamp Angel' and makes a brief reference to a gun of that name that she and Wallace once owned. (Perhaps this is a good place to mention some of the other associations around the book's title. The term 'swamp angel' in the United States is, like the better known 'hill billy,' used to designate a member of a group of Americans who remained in rural isolation in the twentieth century while most of the country became increasingly urban. A 1920s novel by Dorothy Langley, set in the swamplands of southeastern Missouri, was originally published as *Mr Bramble's Buttons*, but was reprinted as *Swamp Angel*. A more popular use of that name in fiction occurs in *Freckles,* a 1904 novel by Gene

Stratton Porter, who was especially well known for titles such as *A Girl of the Limberlost* and *Laddie*. The hero of this story, who has come to live in a swampy region of Indiana, falls in love with a beautiful young girl who is known locally as the Swamp Angel. Closer to home, Wilson, with her interest in local history, might have heard that nineteenth-century settler George Gibson, of Gibson's Landing, built himself a sloop he named *Swamp Angel* with which to explore Howe Sound.)[6] Whether Wilson knew of these books, or of the epithet for swamp dwellers (she wasn't very interested in American culture), or of George Gibson's boat, it is impossible to say.[7]

Her reticence about the new manuscript, however, had little to do with the title. She explained her uneasiness this way: 'Directly a writer owns a reputation, great or very small, the question of submitting a new manuscript becomes quite a different story, however small the ms.'[8] She did not want to fall below the level she had set for irony in *Equations*, but the new story unfortunately did not call for that kind of writing. For what it was worth, Mrs Bell, who had typed the earlier works, was very enthusiastic and appended a note to the typescript when she had finished: 'I do hope John Gray will like "Swamp Angel" – shouldn't be surprised if he'd like it even better than its predecessors.' She was especially enthusiastic about its local features: 'You'll be giving people new glasses through which to see their province – it was all beautiful, and Maggie was perfect as the presiding spirit of Three Loon Lake. I'm glad "Swamp Angel" will be there to correct Mr Woodcock's version. B.C. turns squalid in his hands.'[9] Ethel sent 'The Swamp Angel' [*sic*] to the Macmillan office in mid-February, and by March, when she and Wallace were in California, she had John Gray's reply, in which he summarized the opinion of two readers and his own views.

The exchange of letters between John Gray and Ethel Wilson over the composition and editing of *Swamp Angel* is a rare and wonderful instance of a writer and editor working together both creatively and harmoniously. What is interesting is that Gray was not especially astute when it came to the formal aspects of Wilson's work that distinguish it today from the work of her contemporaries – he did not like her use of omniscient narration, saw her writing as too spare and fragmented – yet the goodwill and deep affection that he felt for her created exactly the right conditions in which Wilson could work and flourish. Gray's first report on *Swamp Angel* was not entirely encouraging.[10] He began by saying that 'we believe this is in the way of being the best book you have done, but none of us has the feeling of it being satisfactory yet. At its present length one has the impression of two stories which don't really fuse together.' He identified what he and his readers saw as two major problems – the many digressions in the text which distracted the reader, and the incompleteness of Maggie's story. He did not like the ending whereby Maggie throws a gun into the lake. This did not constitute a rounding out of her story, in his opinion, but suggested more to come. He also advised that she cut back on the descriptions of the British Columbia landscape, especially accounts of certain roads which Maggie did not take when she was making her escape. While praising the writing, his view was that the manuscript needed a lot more work yet. Wilson wrote back: 'Long on style and short on story. How true.' But she went on to say she was delighted with his letter because it held up a mirror in which she could see the work more clearly. She hoped he 'didn't feel the least twinge in writing,' and then added: 'Of course you didn't, the way is always open between us.'[11] In his end of March reply, Gray said to Wilson that she must have found his letter disappointing, perhaps bitterly so, but that her letter does not show it. 'Working with you is a great privilege – and a constant delight,' he added.[12] Of course, this was mutually true.

Gray had shielded Wilson, in fact, from some quite harsh commentary in one of the reader's reports. 'L.H.' thought that the story was 'slight,' that Mrs Severance was 'boring' and irrelevant, and that both Joey Quong and the gun were unbelievable. This reader felt the author took few pains to make her story 'real' – two men named Albert and Alberto, an unnamed swimmer with no connection to the main plot: 'Mrs Wilson wanders and daydreams in her writing ... she doesn't seem to be a finisher.' 'L.H.' did not like the talk about essences near the end of the novel or the passage about a sleeper. Instead of philosophical meditations, 'L.H.' wanted more action to develop character and in a follow-up report suggested Wilson create a relationship between Maggie and Haldar Gunnarsen, one that would make the three-way connection between Maggie and the Gunnarsens more substantial. 'L.H.' keeps asking, 'What happens to [Maggie]? What happens to the Gunnarsens and Three Loon Lake? How do Vera and Maggie resolve their differences if they do?' This reader, desperate for more action, even suggests that Vera could run off with another man, abandoning husband and child, 'as some women do.'[13]

The concern at Macmillan that *Swamp Angel* was short on story is one that many readers are still likely to make, because most of the novel's action does indeed take place in the first two chapters. These are sus-

penseful chapters because Maggie Vardoe is executing her secret plan
to leave her abusive husband, Eddie, and we are immediately caught up
in the danger of her situation. But after she has left Vancouver for the
interior and successfully started over as a cook at a fishing lodge, her life
is the more mundane one of work and relaxation at the lake, marred
only by the jealousy of Vera Gunnarsen, the lodge owner's wife. The
other main thread to the narrative follows the lives of Maggie's friends,
the Severances, who live in the city. Hilda in middle age marries and has
a child; her mother, Nell Severance, once a circus performer, has an
accident and eventually dies. Nell's brilliance as a performer turned on
her ability to juggle and fire a type of revolver known as a swamp angel.
Before her death, she sends the revolver to Maggie for safekeeping and
disposal, and the novel ends with Maggie, after a showdown with Vera,
throwing the gun into Three Loon Lake. Rather than on plot, the novel
depends on the juxtaposition of scenes and characters and the artful
deployment of symbolic actions.

After hearing from Gray, Wilson seems to have set the manuscript
aside for a while, and then taken up the task of revisions. What seems to
be a second draft suggests that she did not make a great number of
changes: the description of an alternative route leaving Vancouver
through the Fraser delta – the stuff of 'Country Matters' – was ex-
punged, and Maggie's throwing of the gun into the lake was moved to
the middle of the book. What Wilson did revise and polish were the
philosophical meditations that 'L.H.' found both distracting and irrelevant. Whether she chose to revise some of these passages because the
Macmillan readers saw them as problematic or because she was striving
for something more artful according to her own taste is impossible now
to say. But it is worth looking for a moment at one example because it
illustrates dramatically how much she did prune her work. In the final
chapter of the novel, Maggie, before she throws the gun into the lake, is
wondering to herself what happens to all the physical things that have
mattered in one's life. Do they finally just disappear, leaving no trace? In
what is certainly an early draft, Wilson approaches the matter this way:

> Objects and animals which have been loved by people acquire a virtue of
> their own – houses, dogs, jewels, weapons, a mirror, little tools. Maggie now
> possesses only a yellow bowl and a fishing rod and a plain gold ring, but
> they have their own virtue. The yellow bowl might be crushed to dust, the
> fishing rod might not survive a fire, it might be possible for her plain gold
> ring to slip and be lost; but all would remain, each with its own properties

and its small immortality, because each has, for Maggie, its proper life. To Mrs Severance, nothing is now left except some memory and love, and these she will retain, if only in their essence. So, now, she has arrived at that place where she is able to lose, and yet to retain, the essence and virtue of the Swamp Angel, too.[14]

In the published version of the novel, this homily with its certainties, becomes a question that haunts the reader long after the story is over: 'Yet does the essence of all custom and virtue perish?' (208).

Otherwise it would appear that small adjustments in phrasing, a few additional sentences here and there, constitute the greater part of the work done. Ethel Wilson was never in any way demanding or difficult with her publishers though, given the remarkable success of 'Lilly's Story' in Britain and the United States, she might very well have taken a superior stance in negotiating the publication of her next work. Rather, she remained deferential and 'uncertain,' while holding out nonetheless for her version of her work. She was an 'uncertain writer,'[15] to use her own words, because she recognized that her work fell somewhere between two clearly defined readerships: on the one hand, it lacked popular appeal in plot and characterization, which was the stuff of best-selling authors and their readers; on the other hand, because she did not have a university education, she was not sure her writing had the kind of intellectual substance that appealed to sophisticated readers.

In one of the most important letters she wrote to John Gray, she says at the end of July 1953 that in a despondent frame of mind she is returning *Swamp Angel* '(or Up Country or what you will)' for further examination and criticism. Then she describes succinctly what she thinks constitutes her writing:

My genre is very limited. It seems to be uneasy human relations and 'Nature' and 'things' with relation to People. Not exactly animism but tinged with.

As for the writing – that is the only way I can write – of beauty and emotion, and then with a horrid fear of sentimentality, tipping it back on the other side with a flat statement. The thing is to get the balance.[16]

Referring to *Swamp Angel*, she says she is sorry that it is still so short. She had written earlier to Gray that she could not do 'what Walter Scott called "The Big Bow Wow,"' that she felt she would be a fool to try, that she could only do her own things in her own way. 'My small output of writing,' she added, 'is the outcome of meditation, and discarding – and there's not much to show.'[17] The same day that she returned the *Swamp Angel* manuscript to Gray, she also wrote to Professor Desmond Pacey explaining that the new novel she was brooding over was again going to be short. 'I cannot help it. These people's lives are not epic and if they were, I have not the kind of ability to expand them to anyone's profit or pleasure.'[18]

John Gray's return letter of August 4th was very sensitive to Wilson's anxieties, and he reassured her that her work was the envy of many notable writers: 'How could you ever doubt again that your writing is good? ... [J]ust know that we are eager to read you always, certain that even when we have suggestions to make, the reading will have been an illuminating and stimulating experience.'[19] Gray seems to have overlooked the fact that Wilson did not revise *Swamp Angel* extensively and that it remained short. Perhaps he was satisfied to see she had removed the description of the Fraser delta and had relocated the throwing of the gun sequence, confirming his role as editor, or perhaps, to do him justice, he felt it would not work to push her any further. He did, however, in a subsequent letter, make one suggestion that Wilson accepted and that admirers of this novel can thank him for. In the first versions, while she and Mrs Severance are visiting in Kamloops, Maggie gets news that Vera Gunnarsen has died. Gray wrote on the 20th of August: 'The death of Vera, unexplained and unprepared for, yet solving everything, seem[s] a little too easy – almost pat. Couldn't she have pneumonia?'[20] Wilson agreed to revisit that aspect of the manuscript when she wrote back to Gray, but she said in turn that she wanted to put the throwing of the gun at the end. This compromise seems to have suited them both, and something truly creative emerged from the ideas they exchanged. Of course, as has been noted before, the life or death of a character was often of less importance to Wilson than the placement of a comma or the choosing of a word. With the revised ending, she sent a note to Gray saying here it is, 'very unambitious, a very very modest and humble tale ...with, I trust, a feeling of going on living and doing things.' There was no rounding out of Maggie's life, no resolution to the conflict with Vera, no rousing climax to the story, just the strange action of a woman throwing a gun into a lake; but John Gray made no further suggestions for changes.

Swamp Angel, like most of Wilson's writing, is composed of materials that she had known and thought about for many years. 'Country Matters,' the first title for the manuscript, draws attention to an original source of inspiration – the Lac Le Jeune region near Kamloops, where she and Wallace had spent their honeymoon in the summer of 1921, and to which they returned almost every year until the war. When she sent a copy of *Swamp Angel* to Audrey Butler, she wrote that 'all [the book] is to me is the transference of this beloved part of Br. Col. to paper, and certain odd things in human relations and outside them.'[21] While she was writing *Swamp Angel*, she referred a couple of times in letters to an actual gun of that name that she and Wallace had owned, and also to her own experience of once throwing a revolver into the sea, remarking, 'It is a wonderful experience on a bright day and if done with intention.'[22] She says no more about this event, and its circumstances and 'intention' remain a mystery. She did expand, however, more than once on the history of the gun they owned, describing it most fully in a letter to Desmond Pacey:

I hope you have time to listen to this little story. My husband's grandfather (who was old when Wallace knew him) had a little nickel and mother of pearl revolver, very old, and on this little gun were inscribed in a flowing script the words Swamp Angel. He gave it to my husband. I became very much attached to this object – very very interesting to me because there it lay, inert, incompetent, but with a story (perhaps danger, defense, death) implicit. We knew nothing of its origins. I had it always in sight.

When the last war came and my husband joined up again, at the time of his joining there appeared in the papers a very peremptory order from the police that the possessor of any kind of firearm whatever must turn it in on pain of penalty. Well, I never thought the police would keep a useless outdated weapon, and I asked my husband to take it in for registry.

He said, 'What nonsense! no one could fire that revolver!' And I said, 'Oh, please! If you're going away and for some reason I got into trouble over not having turned in our little gun, it'll be just one thing more – I couldn't bear it.' So he thought I was very silly but, to oblige me, took the gun in, and they kept it!

Well, there was too much to occupy me, but I did grieve for my little gun, and eventually it became more mine and more alive because I could make a book about it, and I didn't miss it any more. The gun continued to live again, in a sense.[23]

She explained in an epigraph for the novel itself that the name 'Swamp Angel' originally denoted 'an 8-inch, 200 pound ... gun, mounted in a swamp by the Federals, at the siege (1863) of Charleston, S.C.' and that 'subsequently, there was an issue of small revolvers, inscribed "Swamp Angel."'

The book was also made of some of her personal pleasures and interests – her passion for fly-fishing, her fascination with birds and animals, and her love of Staffordshire china, which plays a decisive role in Maggie's life at the lodge. But the characters in the novel, she insisted, were largely 'made up.' In a television interview, she said Maggie was based on a woman she saw in a West End flower shop, someone who made such a strong impression that, without ever talking to her, she knew what she was like, what she would think, and what she was likely to do. She was 'calm,' 'brave,' 'kind,' and had a lot of 'common sense.'[24] In an undated letter to John Gray, she says of her hero: 'She is a thoroughly nice person, & I have often seen her in a flowershop. Not very pretty but quite lovely (not illiterate, not over educated).'[25] Mrs Severance, however, just appeared 'name and all,' and she had no idea from where. She never saw her, she says in the interview, yet she knew what she looked like and what she would say. Her origins, however, were a mystery.

Wilson made final revisions and corrections to the proofs while they were in Portugal in February 1954, and the novel was published in August of that year. Still enjoying profits from the publication of *Lilly's Story*, Harper's arranged to bring out an edition of *Swamp Angel* for the U.S. market at the same time. When Ethel came to sending Audrey Butler a copy, she chose the American version because she felt it had more distinction than Macmillan's.[26] She liked the type and general finish of the Harper's book, and thought the running heads and binding had great charm. The Macmillan edition was smaller, with a dark blue dust jacket depicting a cartoon-like figure of a woman in a boat tossing a gun into the air. This edition carried a rather severe head and shoulders photo of the author on the back cover wearing a dark suit, pearls, and a hat crowned with veiling. She is not smiling and looks all of her sixty-six years. She may have winced when she read in the author's note that 'Lilly's Story' was being made into a film because, in fact, interest in the project by that time had pretty much dried up.

The readers for Harper's had felt like John Gray that the story was not long enough, the characters not fully developed. Negotiations resulted in Wilson writing two more chapters that would develop the character of Vera, her miserable childhood on a stump ranch, her meeting and marriage to Haldar Gunnarsen, and their purchase of the property at Three Loon Lake. Wilson also added a long paragraph at the close of the book describing Maggie's rowing back to the lodge. Wilson thought these additions improved the novel: 'Harper's chapter 12,' she wrote to Desmond Pacey, 'is to my way of thinking the best chapter in the book and how I wish it were in the Eng. & Can. editions.'[27] But the Harper's request came after the Macmillan edition had gone to press.

Reviews appeared in late August and continued through September. They were decidedly mixed and confirmed John Gray's marketplace hunch that readers were going to find the story incomplete. But one of the first notices to appear took Wilson by complete surprise. In a piece for the *Globe and Mail* of 21 August, William Arthur Deacon pronounced *Swamp Angel* a first-rate book and described what he called the 'remarkable' career of its author. He reminded his readers that the earlier books were in his opinion flawed – *Hetty Dorval* a melodramatic jumble and *The Innocent Traveller* weakened by so much space given to the central character's early life in England. In all three books, including *The Equations of Love*, effects were achieved by the too easy division of environments. He wrote that *Swamp Angel*, by contrast, had natural unity and developed logically out of the 'superbly presented' character of Maggie Lloyd. He praised the author for conveying wisdom about people and life, and commended her expertise in the 'sure selection of incidents and dialogues ... Would that more novelists could convey so much so briefly.'[28] Wilson, in her own words, was 'astonished' by Deacon's testimonial,[29] which not only reflected a radical change in its stance towards her writing, but praised those aspects of the novel that she had felt to be most vulnerable – its reliance on philosophy rather than plot and its studied spareness in technique. It was a confirmation of her personality and style from an unexpected quarter. There were good reviews in the *Vancouver Province*, *Winnipeg Tribune*, and *Toronto Daily Star*, all of which confirmed the maturity and accomplishments of the author.[30] In *Canadian Forum*, Hilda Kirkwood praised the book for the magic of its setting and emphasized the recognition of a style that was unmistakably Wilson's.[31]

But reviewers in the United States and Britain were less enthusiastic this time. American reviewers missed the emotional engagement with a central character that Lilly had provided and felt the story was too incomplete to be satisfying. Coleman Rosenberger wrote in the *New York Herald Tribune* that Wilson snares the reader's attention at the outset by describing Maggie's flight from her husband, but shifts quickly from a compactly plotted story to one which focuses on 'the miraculous interweaving of creation,' a story that contains many passages of descriptive beauty and 'a finely poetic examination of man's fellow creatures on the earth,' but which, on the whole, is inconclusive.[32] The writer for *Saturday Review* saw the book as technically weak, and the reviewer in the *New York Times* saw the sequences with the Severances as only tenuously connected to the main plot and as distracting interest from Maggie.[33] The novel did not sell especially well and was not reprinted when stock finally ran out. English critics may have missed the particular play of irony that was such a strong element in *The Equations of Love*, but like the American reviewers they faulted the book for its lack of strong structure. The notice in the *Times Literary Supplement* praised the vivid evocation of British Columbia, but said that it was not enough to compensate for the shortage of plot and the book's failure to bring characters together with a sense of inevitability.[34] The reviewer for the *Listener* (which had run the glowing review of *Equations* by Séan O'Faoláin) faulted the novel for 'trite scenes' that normally are found in 'glossy fiction' and likened Wilson's prose to a pastiche of William Faulkner.[35] She was naturally disappointed in the response from outside the country and wrote to Gray that it has left her feeling flat: 'I have never felt easy about the book ... Yes, it's pretty awful & thin, isn't it!'[36] She went on to compare *Swamp Angel* to a raisin loaf which has some good raisins, but the dough is no good. Yet, from Macmillan in London, came rumours that both J. Arthur Rank and Associated British Pictures were considering *Swamp Angel* for a film. She couldn't help but be buoyed up by that: '[It] would be lovely, don't you agree ... B.C. upper country would be a new field for their cameras, & I can see many situations, & a whole world of people presented.'[37]

Swamp Angel did not have as much immediate appeal to general readers as Wilson's earlier books, but academics found much of interest in this novel from the outset, particularly what was regarded as the novel's complex network of symbols. The discussion of symbolism started in the American reviews of her books. The sequence in 'Lilly's Story' describing the snake, robin, kitten, and eagle was read as symbolizing the world of the hunters and the hunted in which Lilly makes her way. In a 1955 interview, Wilson described her surprise that in the reviews of *Swamp Angel* the clash between an eagle and an osprey in the novel, should be regarded as a symbol for the conflict between Maggie and Vera Gunnarsen.[38] For Wilson, an avid bird-watcher, it was simply part of the environment of the upper country that she was recording – 'a battle of swift line and shape, of hunger, attack, defence, loss, but no symbol at all.'[39] In his initial review of the novel, Desmond Pacey described the revolver as a thematic motif, but eight years later in his introduction to the New

Canadian Library paperback, he rephrases the idea, arguing that in this novel 'simple objects become complex symbols.' He examines the eagle and osprey and the relation of kitten and fawn as symbolic renderings of cruelty and compassion in creation, but focuses especially on the gun, calling it an endlessly suggestive symbol for conveying the novel's themes: '... out of the swamp, an angel, out of the primitive slime, in due process of time, emerges the divine.'[40] Wilson felt strongly that something 'phoney' had developed in the 'new' critical discourse. Lawrence Olivier's film of *Hamlet* was for her a case in point: Olivier had introduced Freud's Oedipal complex as a way of interpreting the play. Wilson thought the film was well acted, but she resisted the incest symbolism because it drastically narrowed her experience of *Hamlet*, possibly her favourite Shakespeare play. For her there was no such symbolism there; Olivier 'just made it up.' She agreed that certain scenes and images in works of art have deep symbolic power, but argued that no artist could create such passages with their symbolic impact in mind. Rather, symbolism occurred because of the power of the passage and the rich imagining of the artist's mind.[41] Within *Swamp Angel* itself, Wilson refers to this debate when Mrs Severance has fallen on the street and the gun tumbles out of her grasp. The gun had come to represent her past life and power as a circus performer, but the people on the street just see a gun. As she is recovering, she thinks, '... all this nowadays of symbol, symbol, symbol ... destroying reality' (100). In fact, because it has become a symbol, she decides she must part with the gun, for it obscures something in the reality of her everyday relations with her daughter, Hilda. Wilson seems to be suggesting here that symbols are abstractions that can cut one off from actual living.

The popularity in the 1950s and 1960s of symbolism as a way of discussing the arts – and teaching literature specifically – puzzled and irritated Wilson to the point that she finally set down her thoughts in a little essay titled, with a jab, 'Hunt the Symbol.'[42] The main purpose of this short piece is to distinguish between a false and authentic understanding of the term 'Symbol.' What she rejected vigorously was the self-conscious attempt to write in step with a certain critical fashion promulgated in English and creative writing departments. She was baffled by a young student who told her that a story he had written was no good because he just couldn't get a symbol into it. In her view, it was simply a vogue spreading like chickenpox into the lower scholastic levels and would not last. At the same time, she agreed that in her novel *Swamp Angel* the symbol of the gun does occur, but with this significant difference – she did not plan it. The gun's occurrence was ingenuous and honest, not concocted. It arose out of the materials that inspired her story and gradually became 'a symbol of not clutching the loved physical or concrete object, but preserving its immortality in non-possession.'[43] To ridicule the practices of English departments, she imagines in her essay a professor-student exchange in which hair on a bathmat is a sex symbol and a thermos in a story is a sex symbol, and then rehearses William Golding's essay in the *Spectator*, 'Gradus ad Parnassum,' in which William Blake is described taking an English course and the professor reviewing his work says, 'I don't quite get the symbolism of the stars throwing down their spears.' The professor also pursues the confusing symbolism in 'what hand,' 'what eye,' 'skies,' 'wings,' 'what hand,' at which point the poet flees into the college garden followed closely by Beauty. To Wilson, as she said in a letter, it was all 'absurd didactic deadening ... talky-talk.'[44] She would not change her views on the subject, again anticipating a later generation with whom New Critical practices fell out of favour.

While she could not admire Desmond Pacey's determination to read symbolism into every aspect of her work, Wilson did endorse his attempts to explicate the philosophical aspects of her writings. He viewed Wilson as a Christian humanist, creating in her fiction a remarkable gallery of lonely, desperate, and bizarre characters who are offered salvation through moments of compassion informed by universal love. In his introduction to the first NCL paperback of *Swamp Angel*, Pacey presents Wilson's personal philosophy as identical with that of Mrs Severance, who says to her future son-in-law: "I believe in faith. I believe in God ... and in man, to some extent at least" (131). Pacey cites Wilson's recurrent fondness for the famous lines by John Donne: 'No man is an Iland, intire of it selfe; every man is a peece of the Continent, a part of the maine ... I am involved in Mankinde.' In this book, they are spoken by Mrs Severance, who, looking back over her life, sees a 'miraculous interweaving of creation' ... an 'everlasting web' (200). While Mrs Severance articulates the author's philosophy, observes Pacey, Maggie puts it into practice: she performs acts of compassion throughout the novel, especially when she aids an elderly businessman, Mr Cunningham, who was nearly lost on the lake during a storm, and when she comforts Vera Gunnarsen after her suicide attempt. Other critics have pointed out the Christ-like quality of that compassion, figured most dramatically in Maggie's kneeling and rubbing the feet of both Mr Cunningham and Vera when they come out of the cold waters of the lake. Her actions embody for Wilson the essential message of the Christian gospel: 'Bear ye one another's burdens, and so fulfill the laws of Christ.'[45] Paul Comeau has pointed to the Christian iconography in the novel's landscape: Maggie's journey into the wilderness takes her through the town of Hope, past three crosses planted on a hillside, to the waters of a remote lake. Her journey (and one might think of Maggie originally being named Christina) enacts a pilgrimage towards self-discovery through Christian humility.[46] This reading of the novel is perhaps most fully realized in a parable-like passage, and one of Wilson's most eloquent, where the narrator describes a selfless act of compassion, relating it to Maggie's situation with Vera:

> There is a beautiful action. It has an operative grace. It is when one, seeing some uneasy sleeper cold and without a cover, goes away, finds and brings a blanket, bends down, and covers the sleeper because the sleeper is a living being and is cold. He then returns to his work, forgetting that he has performed this small act of compassion. He will receive neither praise nor thanks. It does not matter who the sleeper may be. This is a beautiful action which is divine and human in posture and intention and self-forgetfulness. Maggie was compassionate and perhaps she would be able to serve Vera Gunnarsen in this way, forgetting that she did so, and expecting neither praise nor thanks – or perhaps she would not. (114–15)

With the new wave of feminism in the 1970s, critical interest in *Swamp Angel* shifted to the study of woman's power in the novel. Maggie's independent and courageous action of leaving a loveless marriage and reinventing herself through work was regarded as a remarkable fictional gambit for the 1950s. There were no comparable plots in Canadian fiction at that time. The novel, moreover, contained another strong female character – a fat, wilful old woman who made her living with great gusto as a circus performer and who spent her life with a man who fathered her child but whom she never married. Such original characters in the novel were celebrated in articles with titles like 'Strong Women in the Web,' 'The Hidden Mines in Ethel Wilson's Landscape,' and 'Maggie's Lake: The Vision of Female Power in *Swamp Angel*,' all of which speak to issues of power, even violence, in Wilson's fiction.[47] In the third article, 'Maggie's Lake,' Donna Smyth calls Maggie a Fisher Queen, armed with wand and grail (her fishing rod and yellow bowl) on a quest for self-knowledge and self-healing, a quest that ends in a restoration of harmony not only for herself but for her community.[48] Maggie becomes a centre of power, not a 'boss' in the traditional male sense of authority, but a leader through work, love, and trust.

There is a tension between these two ways of reading the novel – the Christian humanist and the feminist – which captures exactly Wilson's view of human experience as a series of unresolvable paradoxes. The gun is the leitmotif that illuminates that view best. It had its origin in a battle fought to end slavery; it is an image of power and mastery over others, and that is the direct clue. In the novel, it belongs to Nell Severance, for whom it had become in her lifetime a symbol of her triumphs as a circus performer and of her happy union with her partner, Philip. But for her daughter, Hilda, it is a constant reminder of a childhood made unhappy by her mother's frequent absence and by the shame she experienced in the schoolyard when forced to acknowledge that her mother was a vagabond with the circus. Strangely, Wilson presents a happy 'marriage' which has disadvantaged the child. Nell keeps the gun at her side, and when talking to Edward Vardoe, Maggie's husband, she twirls it menacingly, reminding Edward and the reader of its power. But when Mrs Severance falls while taking a walk on the street and the gun tumbles outside her grasp, she decides she is no longer strong enough to control its destiny and sends it to Maggie for safekeeping and disposal.

The transfer of the gun opens up the significance of Maggie's story. As Nell's spiritual heir, Maggie is a strong woman who wants to be free and to have control over her own life. The reader's first impression of her is wholly positive. She is calm and resourceful, and after the introduction of her husband, a truly unsavoury individual, the reader admires her courage in breaking away. Her strong, creative instincts are such that in one season she can rescue the fishing resort from bankruptcy, forget her tragic past in New Brunswick (her soldier husband, her child, and her father all died in quick succession), and before the second season is over save from death Mr Cunningham, who offers her an attractive and remunerative position in the East as a reward. But given Wilson's fascination with the meshing of contraries, I think we are meant to ask if there is a negative side to Maggie's character, as well. Maggie leaves Edward Vardoe, thinking of the 'nightly humiliation' she endured while living with him, but if Maggie does not enjoy the marriage bed, why did she marry him? The implied answer is that she was attracted to his weakness – the poor boy with 'spaniel eyes,' unfit for the army, working in her father's store. Perhaps Maggie instinctively felt she could have power over this man and that marriage would be no loss to her freedom, though she in fact comes to see her second marriage as a period of 'slavery.' Vardoe, as a member of a patriarchal society, insists on supremacy in their relationship, and so she leaves him. At Three Loon Lake, she fashions for herself a world in which she has power over all the males: her contact and adviser, Henry Corder, is old; the owner of the lodge, Haldar Gunnarsen, is crippled, his son Alan is still a boy, and the Chinese-Canadian brothers, Angus and Joey Quong, are ready at all times to do her bidding. Only the jealousy of Vera Gunnarsen spoils Maggie's haven, for it curbs her freedom (she must constantly watch herself so that Vera's suspicions are not aroused). The irony is that Maggie does not want Vera's husband or son; she prefers to live, as she swims, alone. In the water, she atavistically wishes she could become a simpler, more primitive form of life: 'Who would not be a seal or a porpoise? They have a nice life, lived in the cool water with fun and passion, without human relations, Courtesy Week ...' (126). At this point in the narrative, we are made to recognize that Maggie's flight to freedom is really a flight to greater responsibility, that paradoxically a virtue like compassion can constitute betrayal.

Mr Cunningham's offer of a position is the turning point in the story. Will Maggie 'run away' again from a difficult situation (she has run from New Brunswick and from Vancouver), or will she stay with the Gunnarsens and try to make their complicated relationship work? Nell Severance visits Maggie up country, and in their talk she urges her to recognize that all things are connected in 'the everlasting web' of creation and that 'no man is an island.' Earlier in the novel, Maggie had an intimation of this herself when she considered the Quong family living in intricate harmony in Chinatown, and later when she thought about how many people were involved in designing and creating the English crockery Mr Cunningham had sent as a gift. In this conversation, Mrs Severance admits that, preoccupied with her juggling and her mate, Philip, she had lived on an island herself and had unwittingly condemned her daughter to an unhappy childhood. In fact, only after the old woman has given up the gun (symbol now of selfhood and power) does Hilda begin to live a 'normal' life. She marries Albert Cousins, another of the novel's gentle men, and though Mrs Severance describes Albert as a 'lamb,' she also tells Maggie that 'he rules [Hilda] with a rod of silk' – perhaps Ethel Wilson's description of the ideal marriage relation.

The closing scene in the novel shows Maggie, after Nell's death, throwing the Swamp Angel into the lake. The act is coincident with her

decision to stay at the lodge and strive for a working relationship with
the Gunnarsens. 'These people were now her family,' she thinks to herself. 'She had no other. One can say, "To hell with the family," but the
family remains strong, dear, enraging, precious, maddening, indestruc-
tible ... If I cannot cope with Vera and her folly, thought Maggie, I've
failed. She challenged herself, and went on' (182–3). Her acts of compassion, which stem from her power to save others, paradoxically do as
much harm as good. Maggie's throwing away of the gun is perhaps Wilson's attempt to resolve that paradox. The gesture is an act of self-
denial, a symbolic relinquishment of both power and freedom, a submission in order to become fully part of the human community, the
everlasting web. But whether or not Maggie will succeed, we cannot
know. The ending of the novel brings no formal closure.

   Swamp Angel, then, is a novel which takes up certain philosophical
questions. Wilson long pondered the matter of compassion and charity.
It was important in her life because she and Wallace were financially
comfortable, and, not having children, they could make gifts to people
less fortunate. But how to help others without assuming a superior position? Wilson's answer in the novel is contained in the sleeper passage,
where the recipient of charity never learns who has given assistance,
where the donor remains anonymous. Wilson observed instances of this
in the charity practised by her Uncle Harold Malkin. When he gave his
money for the construction of the Malkin Bowl, he did so openly, in the
family name, to commemorate his first wife, Marion, a tireless worker
for the arts in Vancouver. But with other charities and individuals, he
was frequently an anonymous benefactor. Wilson herself, as mentioned
before, is remembered bringing a gift for a friend to the front desk of a
hospital, but refusing to give her name. The harder question she asked
is whether such acts of kindness have any lasting impact. Maggie Vardoe, about to throw the gun into the lake, stretches this question a little
further and asks, 'Does the essence of all custom and virtue perish?' Wilson believed there was an adding up, that over eons humankind evolved
as a potentially 'civilized' species because of all the acts of kindness and
love freely given. Yet, in the novel, Maggie has it hard (and so does the
reader): would serving Edward Vardoe or Vera Gunnarsen finally make
any difference?

   In other compelling ways, *Swamp Angel* has emerged as a significant
novel. In the mid-1980s there appeared two essays on the metafictional
aspects of the book which illuminated both its sophistication and complexity, and, unknowingly, spoke to the anxieties expressed by Wilson's

editors and publishers in the 1950s.[49] Heather Murray demonstrates convincingly that *Swamp Angel* is not a traditional realistic novel, though in the context of its publication and marketing, it was certainly assumed to be so. In a conventional realistic novel, Murray points out, the world of the characters is offered as an empirical reality which is interpreted for the reader by a sympathetic narrative voice, and these two levels – the narrated story and the narrating – remain clear and distinct. In *Swamp Angel* this convention is broken: point of view becomes a problem, and voices in some passages are hard to identify.

What follows is not Murray's example, but it is a succinct moment in the text when at least four voices merge, confusing and possibly discomfiting the reader. It allows us to speculate on the nature of Wilson's writing. In this passage, Hilda Severance, married and pregnant, is just concluding a brief conversation with her husband on the telephone:

> '[D]on't forget the chops darling.' At the word chops she lay down again. She would feel better later in the day. People said Really Hilda you look lovely. How enchanting, how devastating the future of humanity. She felt she had always known this, which was not the case. (197)

This free-flowing prose, which approximates stream-of-consciousness, dispenses with the lexical and grammatical markers distinguishing direct and indirect speech. Here Hilda speaks directly to her husband (in quotation marks); then the conventional sympathetic narrator tells us that she lies down, indicating that Hilda experiences morning sickness. But in the next sentence, where we are told Hilda will feel better, we begin to hear more than one voice. The sympathetic narrator may be speaking, or it may be Hilda reassuring herself on the basis of the experience of previous days, or we may be hearing the ghost of another speaker, the voice of a woman in the community (or a doctor) whose words 'You will feel better later in the day' have become unreported indirect speech. The community around Hilda is summoned as a voice in the next sentence, where one representative person, or perhaps several in turn ('People'), tell Hilda that pregnancy makes her look 'lovely.' But the next sentence – 'How enchanting, how devastating the future of humanity' – is spoken by a voice that can not be identified. It could be attributed to Hilda, reflecting something like the mood swings in her pregnant condition; it could be an amalgam of opinions at a social gathering in the Cold War era; or it could be the sympathetic narrator stretching herself to make a generalized statement that, typically in a Wilson text, brings together contraries that do not mesh together. In the final sentence, we return at first, seemingly, to the sympathetic narrator, who simply tells us what Hilda is thinking – 'She felt she had always known this' – but then suddenly another voice is heard, a narrator who is not sympathetic, but stands quite apart from her character and from a long perspective makes an ironic assessment of Hilda's limited self-knowledge. This break with the conventions of realistic story-telling – this intrusion of the author – is what repeatedly disturbed the readers of Wilson's manuscripts at Macmillan and made them press for revisions.

But this mixing of voices has its parallel on the levels of genre and theme, where Wilson's intentions become simultaneously clearer and harder to estimate. The genre of the realistic novel gives way to poetry in the novel's evocation of place, but more jarringly it shifts, as Anjali Bhelande has shown, to philosophical meditation (both Eastern and Christian) in passages like the description of the cold sleeper quoted above or the speculation in the swimmer passage on whether external reality exists outside of human perception. Similarly, the theme of a woman's self-recovery must make room for disquisitions on power, death, and the nature of reality, seemingly outside the circumference of Maggie's quest. In altering the boundaries of the realist novel, Wilson provided for her story greater linguistic and conceptual freedom, including freedom from a formal or ideological closure to the narrative. Rather, we are left, like the discomfited readers at Macmillan, with a set of opposing patterns – a realistic novel that refers itself for closure to unclear philosophical speculation, a story of human nature that seems diminished by Nature, a virtue like compassion that proves specious, a story of Christian progress that seems at times undercut by the Eastern wheel of birth and death.

The second important article about *Swamp Angel* published in the mid-1980s also draws attention to Wilson, occasionally throwing a spotlight on the artist pulling levers in the wings, but focuses particularly on her metafictional strategies as a mythologist. Brent Thompson argues that Wilson viewed the natural world very differently from her contemporary Canadian writers. Maggie Vardoe does not cringe in terror at a hostile or even indifferent wilderness, but instead submerges herself in her environment, as we witness in the opening scene, in which a fringe of her mind flies after the birds. The object of her quest, argues Thompson, though she does not consciously realize this, is to recover the presence of the mythic in her life. On another plane, he suggests, Wilson

can be seen as restoring the gods to a landscape that had been demy-
thologized by the Cartesian self imported from the Old World. In this
light, nature was viewed at best as a huge beast (a dragon in Pratt's
poetry) so indifferent to the human presence it is hard to know whether
it is alive or dead. On her journey into the wilderness, Maggie goes
through a rebirth, escapes the Cartesian world of reason and mathematical order, and embraces an anthropomorphic order revealed by the
language of her perception, in which, at Hope, the trees are 'noble,' the
mountains have 'rumps,' the waters at Hell's Gate Canyon are 'raging,'
and the wind 'sighs' in the pines. 'What a land,' thinks Maggie, as she
continues her journey. 'What power these rivers were already yielding ...
Even a map of this country, lines arranged in an arbitrary way ... stirs the
imagination beyond imagination' (73). In the swimming section, surrounded by water, forest, and hills, Maggie expands until she is a figure
nearly the proportion of Blake's Albion lying on his rock:

> Maggie stands on the dock and looks around her. She is contained by the
> sparkling surface of the lake and the pinetree shores and the low hills, and
> is covered by the sky. She dives off the dock, down into the lake. She rises,
> with bubbles, shakes her head vigorously, and strikes out ... She is a god
> floating there with the sun beating down on her face with fatal beneficient
> warmth, and the air is good. (126)

Thompson sees Mrs Severance as also created with mythic overtones.
Her name suggests Fate, and in her withdrawal and indifference towards
society, she is something like a fire-breathing dragon (smoke 'blew twin
spirals through her nostrils'); she is an aloof creature of uncanny size sitting on a mound of treasure – her swamp angel, but also her 'mound of
years.' Hilda calls her 'a wicked old woman.'

But with these mythic suggestions, Thompson argues, Wilson is not a
belated nineteenth-century romantic searching for a transcendental
spirit rolling through the universe. She is instead very much a twentieth-
century writer striving to reconcile that idealism with Einstein's relative
universe of isolated islands of humanity. Einstein's universe acquired a
new constant – light, or rather the speed of light – while the old con-
stants, absolute time and absolute space, became relatives. Wilson seems
to exploit this new theoretical understanding in the first chapter ('The
escarpment looked solid at times, but certain lights disclosed slope
behind slope, hill beyond hill, giving an impression of the mountains
which was fluid, not solid' [7]), and after Maggie is reborn at Hope and

she enters the forest, we are told, 'Time dissolved and space dissolved ...'
(39). In this relativist spirit, we are made to recognize by the plot that
both Maggie and Mrs Severance are fallible human beings and that
mythologizing is a figment of the human imagination: Maggie as the
god-swimmer transforms back into a woman who heads back to the
kitchen and has trouble serving Vera; Mrs Severance, who, according to
her daughter, 'liked playing God,' is shown to be very human in her
neglect of her daughter and her clinging to the past. Only when she recognizes her error, and sends away the gun, can the new generation be
born. Thinking about Mrs Severance's objection to symbols (and to this
we can add the author's repeated caution on this subject), Thompson
concludes that for Wilson symbols can only be approximations of what
humans and their environment are, approximations which can destroy
reality if relied on too much and for too long. Thompson calls Wilson a
'wary mythologist,' but in fact his study of *Swamp Angel* as myth and not
myth brings us back to her fascination with contraries, best revealed in
her favourite figure, the oxymoron. *Swamp Angel* is especially rich in
these wordings, which were also favoured by John Donne: for example,
Maggie is described with 'unrevealing grey eyes of candour' (8), Joey
Quong stands 'with awkward grace' (26), and we are told that 'all fly-
fishermen are bound closely together by the strong desire to be apart'
(174). These curious and often startling phrasings are further devices of
metafiction; they draw attention to the writing itself, and we become
aware of ourselves reading sentences, as Helen Sonthoff observed.
Through them, the author speaks, not to the story or characters, but
directly to the reader about a reality compounded of opposites and a
craft that is committed to illuminating that reality.

New readings of *Swamp Angel* are likely to emerge from ecofeminist
reasoning, which one might see anticipated in the author's reflections
on her novel and in some of the earlier criticisms of her work. When she
wrote to John Gray saying she feared the scenery might displace the
'lady' as the central figure of the story, she was clearly only half in jest.
She came closer to identifying something very important in the novel
when she said to Gray that her subject was '"Nature" and "things" with
relation to People. Not exactly animism but tinged with.'[50] The idea of a
living animate force in landscape is more clearly articulated when she
describes the Lac Le Jeune area for Frank Upjohn at Macmillan, saying,
'[This] landscape of lakes and mountains is almost anthropomorphic.'[51]
Critics have not been blind to this feature of Wilson's work, but writers
like W.H. New, who takes up the phrase 'genius of place,' and John

Moss, who writes about the geophysical imagination in *Swamp Angel*,[52] examine landscape solely in terms of its impact on the human world. Ecofeminism, by contrast, focuses on the interdependence of the human and non-human, on something like Wilson's 'everlasting web,' and in so doing collapses the binaries of culture/nature, human/animal, man/woman, white/non-white, which perpetuate hierarchical systems of difference and Other-ness. Ecofeminism not only examines the influence of nature on the human subject, but the human impact on the natural environment. Viewed as something like an animate force, nature in Wilson's writing, especially *Swamp Angel*, is a complex matter, and it is central to one of the novel's paradoxes when its wise old woman, Mrs Severance, expresses her contempt for scenery and says, 'Everything of any importance happens indoors ...' Yet she is the one who describes 'the miraculous interweaving of creation' and speaks to a central tenet of ecofeminist thought when she quotes Donne's 'No Man is an Island.'

Swamp Angel was the first of Ethel Wilson's novels to be reprinted in the New Canadian Library series. It was published in 1962 with a rather unattractive drawing of the author on the cover. On receiving a request to publish from Malcolm Ross, who initiated the series, she suggested *The Equations of Love* instead, since it contained 'Tuesday and Wednesday,' the work she thought was her best.[53] As noted before, she did not think very highly of the introduction by Desmond Pacey. I wrote an introduction for a 1982 reissue of the novel in McClelland and Stewart's New Canadian Library Classic series; she might not have liked that introduction either, but would almost certainly have approved of the cover art with a *V* of wild geese flying over a grassy landscape. In 1990 it was reprinted again in the NCL as part of Wilson's complete works, this time with a painting of a lake by E.J. Hughes on the cover. There was a significant difference in this reprinting in that David Staines, the series editor, chose to use the text of the American edition with its additional paragraphs and chapters. The excellent introduction by George Bowering touches all bases and is certainly one of the best places to start reading about this highly complex novel. Bowering admires Wilson above all as a stylist and marvels at how she 'used her great sentences to make brightly visible' the physicality of British Columbia. A large print edition was published in 1996 by Fitzhenry and Whiteside with an introduction by Elizabeth Thompson. To date, a film of *Swamp Angel* has not been made, although in the late 1980s the Toronto-based actress Frances

Flanagan made a serious and concerted effort to bring Maggie Vardoe to the screen. A script was prepared, and casting included the colourful and very popular American character actress Colleen Dewhurst to play Mrs Severance, while Paramount pictures indicated serious interest in distribution. But when Dewhurst suddenly died, Flanagan could no longer raise the financial support to carry on, and, as happens with many such projects, the film was finally abandoned. In the meantime there is a Vancouver area women's choir that sings under the name of 'Swamp Angels.'

CHAPTER TWELVE

Love and Salt Water
1954–1956

The real reason why I am writing this book is that ... I am enjoying the writing.
– 'Herself When Young'

... and perhaps our whole existence, one with another, is a trick of light.
– *Love and Salt Water*

Frightening changes / D. Litt. / CBC *Profile* / Victoria / 'The Writer and the Public' / Portugal again / 'Miss Cuppy' / *Love and Salt Water*

The Wilsons returned from Portugal in early March of 1954, and for a few more months they enjoyed the high tide of their popularity and personal happiness. The Empire Games (now called the Commonwealth Games) were held in Vancouver that summer, and though she was confined much of the time to a wheelchair, Ethel found her youthful enthusiasm for athletic competitions rekindled. She and Wallace attended a number of the events, 'going daily to fencing & boxing, attending & giving parties.'[1] In August they had a happy two weeks with the Andrews and their children at Little Rock, and in September made a trip to Lac Le Jeune. Ethel wrote to an acquaintance that 'those golden days [in the upper country] were heavenly – the aspens turning honey gold – the whole picture sumptuous.'[2] Coming and going, they visited Jean and Alan Crawley, who were now living in Penticton. In spite of misgivings about the 'childish treble' of her voice,[3] Ethel agreed to appear on CBC radio in the new year, and the taping was done on their return from the interior. Then, in mid-October, their lives underwent a sudden, frightening change. According to McAlpine, Wallace was attending a medical convention on his own at Harrison Lake, roughly 90 miles from Vancouver.[4] During one of the morning sessions, he felt a heavy pressure in his chest and a pain run down his left arm. He left the convention hall, went to his room, packed his suitcase, and, after checking out, made the two-hour drive home. Ethel was apparently at a luncheon, and so he phoned his doctor and then drove himself to hospital. There he would be in intensive care for several weeks. He had suffered a major heart attack.

Wallace was probably relieved that Ethel was out when he prepared himself for hospital, because her near-hysterical reactions whenever he was ill were hard for him to bear. His illnesses reawakened in her something like a state of terror, reviving all the fears and insecurities of her childhood. There are no letters until 8 November, when she writes to Earle Birney to say that Wallace is out of the oxygen tent but improvement is imperceptibly slow. She says of herself that she cannot function socially when her husband is ill: 'I have to retreat.'[5] A month later, Wallace was still in hospital, but she could say to John Gray, 'I'm coming alive John after such tension. We're not *on* Easy Street perhaps, but nearly, I'm sure.'[6] Wallace was home for Christmas, but Ethel refused all social engagements for the season, confining their activities to phone calls and the occasional visitor at the apartment. She now recognized more clearly the value of their reserved but efficient housekeeper, Mrs Marshall, who brought perfect order to their lives, keeping the mahogany and silver polished to brilliance and serving the kind of elegant and tasteful meals they had come to expect. She wrote to Mary McAlpine: 'During our manifold afflictions, Mrs M has been wonderful past belief, a support indeed. I am so grateful to her, & will never be inwardly cross again at her allergy to "entertaining." She has contributed very much to our weathering our gales.'[7] The winter was spent quietly as Wallace slowly gained his strength back; for the present, they were thankful for small pleasures. Ethel wrote to friends about the view from their apartment over English Bay and the enormous delight it afforded them: 'The view, day & night [is] almost hypnotic. The many many tugs, so elegant & lovely, little & big, are very endearing.'[8] Elsewhere she added that water traffic, which is so agreeable to watch, 'unfolds and spreads the imagination so much further than land traffic.'[9] All the same, they enjoyed watching the to and fro of people on the streets below, coming to recognize certain 'characters' among them, and speculating on what kind of lives they led.[10] Ethel spent the mornings in bed because she was working at another novel, which would be informed by the life they were now leading – with reflections on illness and mortality, on perception and truth, and with the presence, benign and threatening, of the sea.

It wasn't until April that they ventured forth on a small holiday to Victoria. Wallace was feeling himself to be fully recovered and was thinking about the possibility of attending a medical convention in Ontario in June. In the meantime, Ethel had become proactive in preparing for their return to a busier life. She was determined that Wallace stop smoking, for she had been told it made heart conditions more difficult, and gave up cigarettes herself. She would become overwrought when she learned that he still smoked the occasional cigarette with his friends. Before leaving for Victoria, they bought a new car with power-steering to make driving physically more manageable. While staying at the Empress Hotel for a week, she wrote to Mazo de la Roche: 'Why everyone doesn't live in Victoria, I can't think. Victoria in springtime is divine – fields of daffodils, innumerable rocky bays, no signs of urbanity outside the immediate town. I adore it.'[11] Thinking about the social life that she had curbed since Wallace's coronary, she said in her letter to de la Roche that she loved her friends, but did not like society in general. Nonetheless, in Victoria she and Wallace made a tentative re-entry into the social world that they had avoided all winter. A dinner was arranged with Canadian historian Bruce Hutchison and his wife, and they almost certainly visited with Wallace's cousin, Alix Goolden, and her family at Cordova Bay. Somewhat ruefully, Ethel reported to John Gray that at the hotel there were invariably 'packs of acquaintances' in the lobby and she was anxious that Wallace might overtax himself unaware, but she conceded in her letter that 'going in low gear, Wallace goes very well.' Best of all was a freak April snowstorm in Victoria, where 'with a lovely big room [we] hole up happily.'[12] A secure, safe place in a storm had much appeal to Ethel that spring because she had made, under pressure, some commitments which were now making her feel anxious. UBC had written to say she had been selected for an honorary doctorate. Persuaded by her friend Larry MacKenzie, the university president, she had agreed to accept the degree and attend the ceremonies, but now she was worrying about her lameness and her chronic shyness when in the spotlight. Just as worrying was a commitment she had made to Dr Roy Daniells to appear with him in a television interview for the CBC. Finally there was the trip to Ontario that Wallace was so eager to make. Perhaps they were taking unwise risks in becoming so active again.

The May convocation went smoothly, and Ethel was proud to report to John Gray that she was the first woman to receive an honorary degree from UBC.[13] During the ceremony, it struck her that 'in that very spot where the scarlet and black procession moved up to the platform ... bears killed the pigs of a boy I knew whose father had a stump farm in a clearing in the forests of Point Grey.'[14] There was indeed still that delight of being close to origins. She was not required to walk for the full length of the procession. She was fêted on campus by academic friends, including the anthropologists Audrey and Harry Hawthorn, Geoff and Margaret Andrew, and the MacKenzies, and that same evening Wallace arranged a dinner for her at the Vancouver Club, which, to her surprise, included thirty-four guests. The Wilsons had become increasingly involved in the affairs of the university and decided at this time to donate funds for the creation of a 'listening room' for music in the library. Ethel would eventually designate UBC Library as the recipient of all royalties and moneys earned by her books after her death.

More stressful than expected was the filming of the television interview. The producers of the CBC series *Profile* had envisioned using a variety of Vancouver settings for the film – to evoke the world of Ethel Wilson – but a cold, wet June kept frustrating their plans. Wilson wrote to Mazo de la Roche that what purported to be a half hour's conversation turned into two weeks' work. She describes sitting on a bench at English Bay with Roy Daniells 'with lights blazing at us and the wind blowing cold down the back of our necks for 5 hours and with someone saying "Cut" every minute and then readjusting mechanics.'[15] In fact, segments filmed at English Bay and Stanley Park were not used, and the film version of the interview takes place entirely in the Wilsons' apartment.

Wallace was eager to attend the CMA convention in Toronto, insisting he was well. They took the train, as a physically less stressful way of crossing the country, and Ethel again expressed her pleasure in being alone and cocooned with Wallace – 'no people (so to speak), no telephone, no responsibility, but too short.'[16] She made the trip expressly to protect Wallace from overextending himself, knowing his vulnerability as a gregarious and generous man. She wrote in advance to Mazo de la Roche that she was becoming hard-boiled about social commitments: 'Am in revolt, and from now on, *no* duties performed, *no* responsibilities assumed ... Dear W., life is too good to do such silly things as "duties" now.'[17] The Wilsons stayed at the Park Plaza Hotel on Bloor Street, as had become their custom, and they did keep a few engagements, including a visit with de la Roche and their mutual friends, Enid and Duncan Graham, and an evening at the Grays,' which included Morley Callaghan and Claude Bissell. In April the latter had written a letter to the *Globe and Mail* divorcing himself, as one of the three judges of the Governor General's Awards, from the decision to give the award to Igor Gouzenko ('a pot-pourri of journalism and politics ... by any standards not a good novel').[18] His choices were Davies' *Leaven of Malice*, Wilson's *Swamp Angel*, and Charles Bruce's *The Channel Shore*, so that Ethel spent an evening with the two men who had made her neglect by the awards committees something of a national matter.

On another evening, for half an hour, Ethel slipped away from a social gathering of doctors and had a drink in the roof cocktail lounge with John Sutherland and his wife, Audrey, whom she described in a letter as a shy and gentle young couple.[19] She felt enormous admiration for John's struggle to publish *Northern Review*, one of the two literary magazines in Canada in the early 1950s (the other was Alan Crawley's *Contemporary Verse*). She had met John a couple of years earlier in Montreal and would never forget the circumstances, which she described in the last essay she published:

> We had arranged to meet ... outside the Windsor Hotel in Montreal on a steamy summer day through which, strangely, a humid heavy breeze blew. My husband was at his medical meeting and I stood waiting, when a slender young man crossed the street and came towards me. He wore a crumpled white shirt, braces, no coat, and the humid breeze lifted his long tie as he came up. He looked very young indeed and his eyes, widely set, had an innocence that invited friendship. He said he was John Sutherland and was I Mrs Wilson and did I mind driving in his car because it was very dirty? It was. Of course I did not mind. We got in, and John fiddled with things and then said he had just bought this very old car and had learned to drive – a little – but had never driven it before into the city. Did I mind? I said No, but as we sped through the traffic lights and dodged people and all but grazed cars, I said in my heart to my husband at his meeting Oh goodbye goodbye, I am leaving you forever, I shall never see you again! ... [H]e asked me if I was a Christian. I was surprised at his question, which was most reasonable but unexpected, and answered that I am indeed a Christian and very grateful but not a good enough one, and not entirely conventionally a Christian – in formal belief and observance, I meant. Then I said 'But ...' and at my next statement the Chevrolet shied and jumped and I hung on to the door. John had the habit of turning to look at you if ques-

tion and answer became important and this made driving still more haz-
ardous.[20]

By the time they met again in Toronto, she knew that Sutherland had
put his heart and soul into the discovery and stimulation of what he felt
to be good and original writing in Canada, though not in any self-conscious chauvinistic sense. She especially admired his attempts to engage
Canadians in a critical dialogue about their literature and culture, and
she was shocked to learn of his death at thirty-six the following year.

Ethel had enjoyed the stay in Toronto, but she was aware that she may
have appeared rather cool and austere to friends. She explained it this
way to Mazo de la Roche:

> Having always been rather a softy, and trying to oblige one and all, Wal-
> lace's two illnesses (and perhaps particularly the last one) seem to have
> canalized everything into leading a life that will be to his physical advan-
> tage, to his happiness, and to the prolongation of our happy life together,
> and so other responsibilities and commitments have become sometimes
> negligible. The last two or three months have consisted so much in saying
> NO (I *won't* serve on a committee, I *won't* have certain people or groups to
> tea or dinner, I *won't* have small 'littery' engagements), so that his days and
> evenings won't be disturbed, and so that I shall never get so physically tired
> that I become a liability. This has never needed to happen before, and now
> it does happen – he tires so easily and must not tire.[21]

The CBC television interview was aired 28 July 1955, and she wrote to
John Gray to say that watching it was 'like the day of judgment when one
will suddenly be faced by one's most hideous self.' She thought the
sound and the photography were good, especially of Roy Daniells and
the tea service, and felt the content of the program was quite acceptable
(no phoney or self-conscious moments), but was thoroughly dismayed
by the close-ups of her aging face and concluded 'never & never & never
again.'[22] As her reputation grew, Wilson became increasingly conscious
of her age, because publicists would often show surprise to find that this
relatively new novelist was in fact a woman now approaching seventy.
From the beginning, she had claimed a birth date of 1890, shaving two
years off her actual age. Macmillan's publicity files reveal that she often
refused to give her age, claiming it was simply not relevant to the publication and discussion of her books, and that at one point she said she
was 'just over fifty' when in fact she was in her sixtieth year.[23] The best

part of the film experience in her opinion was working with Roy Daniells, who in her view was a man of 'honesty & directness & humour, at the same time reserving opinion when he thinks advisable, & he seems to me a scholar.'[24] She had enjoyed an acquaintance with Daniells for several years, writing to him in 1948 to say how much she appreciated his public lectures on the Baroque and his volume of verse titled *Deeper into the Forest*.[25] He was a department head at UBC, both respected and feared, but in the film he is little more than a mild foil for Wilson, who, in her own words, was quite 'spontaneous and gusty.'[26] Indeed, those who knew Ethel Wilson as a shy, self-effacing woman were surprised by her strongly opinionated and playful manner in the film. It was her moment on stage (the half-aunts once thought of her as an actress), and she did her part very well. But her own opinion of the film she summed up in a little German proverb she often quoted: 'Much cry but little wool, said the devil when he sheared a pig.'[27]

There was one bit of patching up to do. Mazo de la Roche wrote somewhat testily to say she had watched the television interview and understood Ethel to have said that it was a shame that Canada had not yet produced one novelist of note. 'Of course I did not say that,' Ethel shot back, adding: 'Wouldn't it be (and I bow to you) a silly remark.'[28] She went on, however, to restate her case against writing 'Canadian' novels. 'Region is universal and unifying,' she argued, but nationality is not. Feeling perhaps that her letter had been hasty, she wrote again two days later, not mentioning Canadian novels and reputations, but turning to matters of health.

Because Wallace had continued to gain strength over the summer, they decided in August to take a holiday in the B.C. interior, booking for three weeks at the Eldorado Arms Hotel in Kelowna. Ethel's increased lameness and Wallace's coronary ruled out fly-fishing and the rough little cabin at Lac Le Jeune. Also ruled out now was Little Rock on Bowen Island, located more than three miles from help should a crisis arise. Moreover, there Wallace could no longer do the physical work required to keep the property in good shape. They would have to dispose of it in some way, or at least make arrangements for its upkeep. In the meantime, they were enjoying the amenities of the Eldorado Arms and 'the scent of flowers in the air, & balm of Gilead, & sage.'[29] Aunt Eliza had stayed there once many years before and had disturbed everyone by discovering furniture from the Duke of Sutherland's Staffordshire estate that had come there via one Duchess Blair, of whom Eliza had disapproved. It amused Ethel and Wallace to think how Aunt Eliza held such a low opinion of the present owner's grandmother and how irrelevant such opinions had come to be. They spent their holiday time reading, especially histories of Europe and of Canadian exploration, Ethel often knitting, and at least twice drove to Penticton to visit the Crawleys. Ethel's hip was painful and they both missed Lac Le Jeune, but, as she wrote to de la Roche, she was counting her blessings nonetheless.[30]

Continuing to protect Wallace from the press of social obligations, Ethel persuaded him that they should spend Christmas 1955 on their own in Victoria. As a couple without children, the Wilsons always found themselves lonely and simultaneously overwhelmed by family and friends when the holidays came around. The strong sense of something missing in their lives and a period of unhappiness is revealed in a strikingly bitter observation she made to John Gray 19 December: '... our *awful* Christmases (carving turkeys & good cheering at hospital dinners, 2 family dinners, old patients sitting waiting, sick people, drinking parties) are over; [they] used to render Dec 23–28 hideous ... we are stealing away to Victoria the day after tomorrow to that same nice large bedroom at the Empress that overlooks the harbour, with the car & many books, & never a word to Victoria family and friends, till the Day is well over – for their sake even more than ours.'[31] Some of their friends and relations in Vancouver judged Ethel's protectiveness as unhealthy, almost eccentric.[32] Wallace seemed wholly recovered from his coronary and they missed his company at Christmas gatherings, but Ethel constantly pleaded health when turning down invitations. His illness unquestionably made Ethel more jealous of the time he spent with others. At this time of year with its focus on family life, Ethel would have been acutely aware of her failure to provide Wallace with children, and she preferred now that they amuse themselves with strangers. She entertained John Gray with a letter from the Empress in which she describes the lobby and dining-room scene at the hotel as an 'Ugly Contest' – five hundred elderly well-dressed Americans, some of the older ladies with very décolleté bones. One rushed up to her and said, '"You look like a million,"' and she heard Wallace murmur morosely, '"Yes, mine,"' referring to her expensive new dress from London. Another came up to her in her wheelchair: '"Oh say you precious thing! Was it an accident? What did you say your name was?"' As for the Christmas dinner, she added that 'the suckling pig must have been weaned in 1952, but the carols were magnificently sung.'[33]

When they returned to Vancouver, Ethel had to face the fact that she

was to undergo surgery. There was a lump in her breast, and her special-
ist felt certain it was cancer. He prepared her to have a mastectomy on
29 January 1956. In the meantime, she had agreed to make a presentation at a conference on British Columbia writing at UBC on the 28th,
which she was happy to do as a distraction from what lay ahead. The title
of her session was 'How Does a Writer Reach His Audience?'[34] and par-
ticipants on stage and in the audience included Roderick Haig-Brown,
George Woodcock, Floris McLaren, Anne Marriott, Roy Daniells, and
some of Ethel's friends from 'Authors Anonymous,' Earle Birney, Bill
McConnell, and Dorothy Livesay. Addressing the assigned topic, she
began by telling how she was published first in England by *New Statesman
and Nation*, and then, somewhat misleadingly, she reported, without
mention of the Topaz stories, that she wrote *Hetty Dorval* and went
searching on her own for a publisher in Canada, describing the happy,
intimate association with Macmillan that followed. She also mentioned
the importance of her American agent, Ruth May Bendukov. But then
she shifted the direction of her talk, going against the grain, and arguing that reaching an audience is 'only a little – if at all – aggravated by
the pleasant experience of living in British Columbia, on the outside
edge of the map of this continent.' Good writing, wherever it is done,
she stated, will eventually reach an audience. Here she rehearsed again
her anti-nationalist position when identifying writers, giving a fresh
example. 'I was much pleased by the words of a novelist from (I think)
Montreal, by the name of Mordecai Richler. He was asked, "Do you call
yourself a Canadian writer or a Jewish writer?" He said, "Neither. I call
myself a writer."' In a final segment to her talk, she turned to the importance of the audience, 'without which [writers] are only half alive.' Audiences, she urged, are created by the careful education of children and
by parents reading to them from the classics at bedtime. In the audience
at UBC was an aspiring young short story writer named Alice Munro,
who was in awe to have a glimpse of the Canadian writer who thrilled
her most. This was the first extended paper that Ethel read in public; in
typescript, it is twenty-one pages and presumably took at least forty minutes to deliver. Her letters give every indication that she enjoyed the
experience, which is corroborated by the fact that for the next nine
years, surprisingly, she gave several more such talks.

The day following her appearance at UBC, she underwent surgery at
the Vancouver General Hospital and emerged from the anaesthetic to
find a room full of roses. There was a vase from Wallace, several from
relations and friends, and a large arrangement from the Macmillan

Company. She wrote to Mary McAlpine 4 February 1956: 'I've been a lucky woman – reports all good. Post-operative pains in chest & throat quite hellish but nearly subsided, the amputation itself being the least of it – so how fortunate.'[35] Two weeks later, she was able to write John Gray and say that the tumour had proved to be benign and that she could now put any worries about herself behind her. Full recovery was slower than she expected, and she and Wallace continued to keep social engagements to a minimum. Since Wallace's heart attack, she had only attended one meeting of 'Authors Anonymous,' and after her surgery she stopped going altogether. This was consistent with her view of writers' groups that she had put forward at the UBC conference: 'I have an instinctive and increasing scepticism – perhaps wrong – of anything that might suggest or lead to local grouping, or coterie, in writing. I am aware that a working "group" may be exciting and beneficial in [the other arts] but not, to my thinking, in writing. [It] is a terrifically personal job.'[36] The only work she agreed to do that winter was a taping of the UBC talk for CBC Radio. Bob Patchell (whom she knew from the writers' group) did the taping for three fifteen-minute segments, which were aired on Sunday evenings in April. Continuing to mend fences with Mazo de la Roche, she paid tribute to her friend on air by pointing out that she had achieved a vast readership in many countries, a feat rare among Canadian writers. She also praised Alan Crawley and John Sutherland for their pioneer work with small literary magazines.

Ethel was spared listening to what she regarded as her 'repulsive voice,' because by 6 April 1956 she and Wallace were on their way to Europe for another holiday in Portugal. They stopped first in Amsterdam, where they had arranged to spend a few days with Audrey Butler. She had been employed with the British embassy in Brussels and was now in the Foreign Office in London, where the Wilsons would be spending the last part of their trip, but Ethel clearly preferred to have their visit at a distance from Audrey's family this time. They had sent her a ticket to join them in Amsterdam for a few days and booked her into a connecting room. The flight had been more exhausting for them than they had anticipated. Audrey, waking up the morning after their arrival to find the Wilsons both asleep, went for a walk around the city, but at mid-day found them still fast asleep. She recalled that she then 'ordered beer, coffee, & a variety of sandwiches for 3 and told "room service" to KNOCK HARD: they were surprised/delighted and we thoroughly enjoyed the "levée" of the Wilsons.'[37] Ethel wrote to John Gray: 'What a lovely young woman she has become, & sometimes her beauty shines like a

star. She is so companionable, & we never laughed so much together ...
Our mutual joy in being together, & enjoying things together was
lovely.'[38] And to another: 'What a darling she is – so sincere, unaffected,
of deep affection, very intelligent, a woman of the world but artless too.
Since we have the same kind of sense of humour, natural hilarity, the
simplest, silliest things occur all the time ...'[39] Seeing Audrey again (it
had been nine years) reawakened in Ethel the desire for family, which
seemed to be getting stronger, not less, with the passing years. In Vancouver, she and Wallace took particular pleasure in the children of their
friends especially young men and women in their twenties and thirties.
These included their godchild, Erica Pepler, daughter of their friends
Betty and Eric Pepler, Mary McAlpine, the daughter of Helen Law, one
of Ethel's school friends, Beatrice Davidson, who was the daughter of a
distant cousin to Wallace, and Buchan McIntosh (known as Buck),
whose parents Wallace had attended at their wedding in London during
the First World War.

They went on to Portugal and again stayed at the Hotel Atlantico in
Estoril, where they had been so happy two years before and from which
they could easily make day trips to Lisbon, Cascais, and Coimbra. Ethel
was amazed that lodgings and meals were still only eight dollars a day
for two. During this trip, she set down her impressions of the country in
what would be her only formal piece of travel writing. It was titled 'On a
Portuguese Balcony' and published in the fall of 1956 in the first issue of
Tamarack Review. In my view, it is one of Wilson's least successful pieces
of writing. In contrast to her fiction, in which authorial intrusions add
an important dimension to the art of the story, Wilson's voice here has a
detached quality that identifies her, not just as a tourist, but as someone
who holds herself aloof and superior to the people and places she is
describing. There are a couple of disturbing moments in the text from a
later vantage point in time: the driver Antonio is belittled in terms of his
use of broken English, and he is stereotyped as a colourful local; but,
more disquieting, Wilson remarks of a tall, barefooted girl on the street
that she is 'very beautiful for a gypsy.' These are the kinds of attitudes to
class and race that Alice Munro feared she would find on revisiting Wilson's fiction, but didn't. It would be harder to exempt Wilson's travel
pieces from these charges. In another passage, she describes how aes-
thetically pleasing it is to see the peasant women in the country carrying
with skill and grace great burdens of food, firewood, or clothing on
their heads, but here she catches herself and recognizes that 'some sem-
blance of justice is not satisfied [when] you look, as on a picture, at your

sister.' We are relieved when she says her habit of moralizing intrudes and that she 'cannot see with a single eye.'

Mid-May the Wilsons flew from Lisbon to London, where they stayed for three weeks, apparently telling no one. Before they left, Ethel had written to John Gray saying they might not even go to England because there were too many friends and relatives there, including her in-laws, the Buckerfields, with their circle of affluent friends. Instead they visited places in the city they had not seen before, including the bombed church of St Mary the Virgin Aldermanbury, where Shakespeare's first editors and publishers, Condell and Heminge, worshipped and were buried. The taxi driver had trouble locating the church, but when they arrived at the ruined shell, the Wilsons were able to walk on the tended grass that grew around the church and absorb something of its historical meaning for the lovers of Shakespeare all over the world. When she returned to Canada, Wilson set down her thoughts on the church and its associations in what would be her best piece of non-fiction prose.[40] They also spent a morning observing at the Magistrate's Court on Bow Street, watching a sorry procession of convicted prostitutes (some looking like secretaries) paying their two pound fines. And they watched a case of 'possession of drugs.' But for Ethel the highlight of the trip was a visit to the Macmillan Company office, where she set aside her wheelchair and walked up the flight of steps to the office lounge and spent a very pleasant half hour with the president, Daniel Macmillan. He, in turn, introduced her to Lovat Dickson, the company's editor-in-chief, and they both complimented her enthusiastically on the manuscript for her next novel. She also met the man who designed their books' dust jackets, and he showed her three possibilities for the cover, one of which pleased her very much. She wrote to John Gray of her stay in England: 'The country is superlatively beautiful, London dearer (in every way) than ever.'[41]

The new book was *Love and Salt Water* and was more than three years in the making. It would be her last published novel. While she was still in the middle of revising *Swamp Angel* in 1953, she reported to John Gray from Bowen Island in August that she had 'unintentionally started another that flows like cream.'[42] That fall she sent him four chapters of this work in progress titled 'Miss Cuppy,' which has survived in typescript with her papers at UBC. Actually, on the title page is 'Herself When Young,' echoing Joyce Cary's *Herself Surprised,* but the first page of text is headed 'Miss Cuppy'[43] and that was the title Wilson used in her initial correspondence with John Gray. Written in the first person, this early draft is the story of Ellen Cuppy, a violinist living on the prairie who works for a Mr Platt and who is writing a novel based on her past life in Vancouver. There are scenes in Vancouver between Ellen and her sister, whose name at this point is Cora ('The Birds' is from this early draft of *Love and Salt Water*), and there are scenes in London, where Ellen serves as a WREN during the war. At the centre of the story is Ellen's love for Charles Tenner, who jilts her for another woman, her subsequent involvement with a middle-aged musician named Franz Lessing, and her marriage to Ralph Atchison, a man from Montreal she has been seeing for several years. In terms of action, the only connection between 'Miss Cuppy' and *Love and Salt Water* is the near drowning of Ellen's nephew Johnny and her scarring in the boat accident. There is a freshness to the voice in this first-person narrative, and, because Wilson never tried something like an artist's story in any of her other writings, one wishes she had been able to carry this project through. This is not, however, an artist's story in the *Kunstlerroman* tradition (the artist's personal struggle to achieve success within a chosen field); rather, this is a story about writing itself and some of the epistemological problems a writer faces when telling a story.

The manuscript is worth consideration here briefly for what, in the early 1950s, is its experimental nature. After beginning with a description of the new University Bridge over the river in Saskatoon, Ellen announces her project: 'It seems to be a good idea to write a book.' She knows herself to be observant but not particularly clever. However, she tackles with insight the problem of relativism that comes with every reconstruction of the past: 'It is difficult to be truthful about events, because no event stands alone but balances precariously on past and future and on the persons involved. Then as years pass, memory becomes full of holes, and events (but not persons) fall through.' She also questions what is important and what should be left out of her story, and draws the reader's attention to the fact she is digressing in places. She struggles with the tone of her narrating voice: 'I am sorry to speak in this stilted way. I think that writers ... must become familiar with paper and typewriter, but at present I do feel strange.' She is concerned with the mechanics of grammar: 'My sister Cora is six years older than me or is it I?' And in a self-reflexive, postmodern fashion, she describes herself rereading what she has written and finding fault with her manner of expression: 'I have read that paragraph over again and I am quite shocked to find out I have represented Cora as being hard ...

Nevertheless we are sisters and blood is thicker – No, in this book I will try not to say things like that.' She also gives us in some detail the physical circumstances of the writing task – a description of her desk by the window, interruptions by the telephone (asking the reader, what do 'real writers' do about the telephone?), the amount of time she has spent on a chapter. She opens one section saying, 'I will write only for a little while, and then relax and dress,' and concludes with a progress report for the reader: 'By the way, this thing of writing a book is becoming much easier than it was at the beginning. This week I am busy every evening and shall not be able to write my book, and I do not want to get out of the smoothness and ease and pleasure of writing this book, but the book is not important, and friends are and so is the orchestra.' Later she says her reason for writing the book ('though I dread writing it') is to come to terms with her aborted relationship with Charles Tenner, which ended more than ten years ago: 'I shall have purged my mind and my memory of something that has affected me far too deeply in my life; this is too long a time to be still concerned, even a little, with unhappy love.' Eventually she contemplates her book as an object for sale in the world, though she fears her realistic view of Canada (its need, for example, to become bilingual) will earn it bad reviews. But finally she concludes: 'The real reason why I am writing this book is that by this time I am enjoying the writing.' These became familiar strategies, conventions if you like, of storytelling in the late twentieth century, but were viewed as eccentric mannerisms in the context of the realistic novels being written during 1953–4.

John Gray held back from expressing an opinion while Ethel continued to work at the new book, though he queried the suitability of the name 'Cuppy,' which, in his opinion, sounded too much like Guppy. 'Yes,' Wilson wrote back, 'I might as well call Miss Cuppy Miss Fish,' but she felt at the same time that a character's name should have some jar to it if it's going to come alive.[44] When Gray had read the completed manuscript, he wrote in July 1954 an enthusiastic letter: 'I was completely captivated by the story of Miss Cuppy, and by the intricate art of this little symphony.'[45] He said there might be a few minor revisions to make, but on the whole he thought it was 'a lovely thing.' He had read it late into the night and finished it the next morning with coffee and the sun streaming through his study window. However, when he wrote again six weeks later to report for the readers at the press, he had to change both the tenor and substance of his response radically. 'With some hesitation I send you a report on "Miss Cuppy" giving the response of other readers. In spite of the memory of many beautiful and stimulating parts of the book, I think I must agree substantially with this comment.' He regrets that in his earlier letter he had been 'dangerously uncritical.'[46]

Two of the reports were harshly critical.[47] One said bluntly: '... this MS betrays no sign of forethought that I can detect ... [it lacks] either a story, or a central idea or sequence of ideas which could carry the reader along.' To this reader, who was dismayed by shifts in direction and 'otiose' digressions, the manuscript left an impression of a notebook into which plans and sketches for some essays and speeches had found their way. The other negative reader had similar complaints – that the story was unsatisfying and had no solidity, that there were too many digressions, 'irrelevant flights of fancy' and 'pensées.' These included disquisitions on the painter Canaletto, the English writer Samuel Butler, the arbutus tree, mayflies, etc. Unlike his past practice, John Gray scarcely toned down these comments in his cover report for Ethel. He began by linking the new manuscript with some of the disappointing reviews of *Swamp Angel*, and focused on her problems in telling a good story and her frequent failure to create convincing characters, giving Eddie Vardoe as an example. He pointed out that she was much admired as a stylist, but her lack of focus made her books difficult to read. The house readers would not criticize 'if the author could make us feel that she has a deeply-felt notion of what she is trying to do in the book,' but there was no evidence here that 'she had a firm grasp on her intention.' The metafictional aspect of this manuscript – the writing about writing – and its loose, experimental structure clearly baffled and dismayed the Macmillan house readers. They may also have balked at the friendship announced between Ellen Cuppy and Maggie Vardoe. Wilson's reply appears not to have survived. This was the most negative assessment Wilson had received of any of her manuscripts, and for a time she set the project aside.

But during the quiet months that followed Wallace's heart attack in 1954, she took up the novel again and completely rewrote it – this time in the third person, and with many changes to the structure and story-line. It was now chronologically a straightforward narrative, beginning with the deaths of Ellen Cuppy's parents when she is a teenager, a voyage by freighter through the Panama Canal to England, her relationship to her sister Nora Peake, who is married to a politician, then her engagement to Huw Peake and its annulment, followed by her years in Saskatoon working as a secretary for Mr Platt. Ellen is no longer a violinist or a writer, but her near drowning with her nephew Johnny in the

Gulf Islands remained, and the story was concluded with her marriage to a Montreal friend, George Gordon. The biggest change is in the relationship between Ellen and the man she is engaged to. In this version, Ellen grows tired of Huw, who is a bad-tempered war veteran, feeling strongly he is not the man she wants to marry. She is not romantically deceived by him, as she was by Charles Tenner. Wilson also deleted most of the digressions and the original epigraph from Thomas Browne's *Religio Medici*, which anticipated and justified the loose structure of 'Herself When Young.' It had read, in part, '... we carry with us the wonders we seek without us; There is all *Africa* and her prodigies in us.' She felt such an epigraph would be pretentious in the new, more conventionally told version of her story.[48]

John Gray wrote 15 February 1955 to say the rewritten manuscript had arrived, but he did not send a report until four months later. It began in very flattering terms, suggesting that this manuscript might turn out to be Ethel Wilson's most impressive work, and gave high praise to the new 'sea-boy' section. This incident itself, in which a boy sailor drowns in a storm at sea, the readers felt gave the book a power and magnificence that were missing from the earlier draft. Like good 'New Critics,' they praised its symbolic anticipation of the near drowning of Ellen and Johnny at the end of the story. But they still had much to complain of and felt the manuscript was far from ready to be published. Again they insisted the total effect was disjointed, and they were not happy to have Wilson's omniscient narrator intruding in the text. But they focused on her handling of character, especially George Gordon, Ellen's future husband, who did not seem developed as a character at all, but just an idea. And Ellen's experience of being in love they regarded as handled very badly. So once again there was still a great deal of work ahead to make the manuscript publishable.

But by 3 October 1955 Ethel sent the manuscript off to Toronto again, including an alternative ending and several suggestions for a title. In Ending B, wrote Wilson, 'to avoid the banality of a happy ending so detested by critics today,' Johnny does not survive the accident and Ellen drowns herself in the sea, unobserved unless by a seal 'who rose, looked with large inquisitive eyes, and sank, leaving not a ripple.'[49] Ellen's body is never found. At this point, Wilson had abandoned 'Herself When Young' and 'Miss Cuppy' as titles and sent five new ones for an opinion: 'The Younger Daughter' was the one she now affixed as the working title, but offered 'Love and the Salt Water,' 'Reflections in a Windy Pool,' 'Unimportant People,' and 'Nothing Is Safe' as other possibilities.[50] At some point that fall, she also sent in 'The Younger Sister' as a title. Wilson's perennial struggle with titles – almost every project, except *Hetty Dorval*, had half a dozen working titles – reveals that there was something provisional and tentative in her approach to her art, that writing itself was more important than the grand designs of character and plot. This was the original message in 'Herself When Young,' which focuses on the intimate process of writing, on the physical and mental conditions conducive to writing, the self-reflexive struggles with expression, the pleasures in finding words and phrases, and the pleasure in talking directly to the reader, dropping the mask or convention of the anonymous storyteller.

When she sent off the tragic ending, she wrote to Gray that it was not only a sad conclusion, but was beginning to suggest something obsessive in her writing: 'I nearly drowned Vera, & quite drowned the sea-boy, & Mort & his friend all by accident, not design (not to speak of a dog in the Fraser River).' She might also have mentioned Ernestine in *Hetty Dorval* and all the characters in her story 'From Flores.' 'I don't quite understand how the feeling of the sea is so dominant. I have never known anyone who was drowned.' But what is also suggestive here is that in the next sentence she points to another 'obsessive' pattern in her work: 'Although I never knew my mother (she died before I was two) & have no personal experience there, either, to draw on, the mother-child relationship occurs in nearly every story, either happy, normal and mutual, or softly possessive, or hard and devoted (Lilly) or negligent (Mrs Severance).'[51] We might observe that the absence of a mother as a firm anchor in life seems all too easily connected to the sea and drowning and a world where 'Nothing Is Safe.' On the back of the page on which Wilson lists the title suggestions, she wrote to Gray, '... for Heaven's Sake don't take it if it won't do. I couldn't bear that.'[52]

Reports were prepared quickly this time and both were fairly positive, although both felt the third section, titled 'A Scar,' remained problematic, especially in the presentation of character. One reader felt she had not rounded out Ellen's character sufficiently, and the other felt George Gordon was reported rather than rendered. This reader felt the book had limitations which could not be overcome but that it was nonetheless 'a beautiful little book,' perhaps Ethel Wilson's best. With these reports on file, John Gray took the manuscript with him to London in late November; but before leaving, he had written to Ethel to say that he didn't have full confidence in the manuscript, that he felt it was still uneven, but would leave it to the London company to make a final decision.[53] When Ethel received this letter, what little confidence she had in the manuscript completely vanished, and she wrote to Daniel Macmillan in London to stop proceedings.[54] But the London readers were of quite a different opinion from those in Toronto, and Daniel Macmillan wrote to Wilson 20 December 1955 that 'The Younger Daughter' was ready for publication, and he enclosed a contract urging her to reconsider her withdrawal.[55] He also reported that his readers believed the happy ending was the better one. Macmillan's letter was waiting for Ethel when she and Wallace returned from their Christmas in Victoria; she was delighted with the way Daniel Macmillan handled her with what she called a 'charming lordliness,'[56] and she sent back the contract signed. Except for the title (Macmillan London proposed *Love and Salt Water* without the definite article), there were no more changes made, and the book was published in September 1956.

In its final version, *Love and Salt Water* can be said almost to equal *The Innocent Traveller* in terms of autobiographical materials saved up and transmuted into fiction. In a talk she gave about the origins of her fictions,[57] Wilson said she had long wanted to write something about the coast, especially its lifelong association of summers which she had assimilated, and the possibility for a story came into focus one day when she was in Stanley Park and saw a mother, father, and little daughter 'walking together in health, companionship, and unusual physical beauty.' The happiness of this socially and economically privileged family, especially the lively bond between mother and daughter, fascinated the author, and she let her imagination ponder 'the dreadful private casualties of life [that] might or might not befall them.' In the novel, the mother's sudden death and the father's remarriage and death were, for Wilson, a retelling of her orphan story. When one of the characters says to herself, 'Do we always live on a brink, then?' (161), Wilson takes us, I believe, to the very heart of her imaginative world. The voyage Ellen takes with her father derives in many of its details, including Christmas celebration and the ship on a sandbank in the Scheldt River, from the Wilsons' passage to London on a freighter via the Panama Canal. Ellen's subsequent unhappy engagement to a man she really doesn't love is informed surely by Wilson's similar experience of breaking her commitment to marry J.P. Nicolls. Wilson had said then that she wanted to leave Vancouver and work in the interior, and she gives Ellen that opportunity, placing her in Saskatoon, a city Wilson found especially attractive and an area that had rich associations for her pioneering family. The book, in fact, is affectionately dedicated to her Uncle Harold Malkin, 'who was young Skookoonia-goose (North West Territories 1884).' She explained to John Gray that when translated the name meant 'Little White Rabbit' (a reference to Harold Malkin's diminutive stature and quickness) and was given to him by the Cree in that area of Saskatchewan, who permitted him to witness one of the last initiation of braves at a sun dance.[58] Wilson, orphaned and uprooted, was much concerned with creating history and connections to place, knowing at the same time that such rootings can be easily severed and lost. The story of Morgan Peake and his family connections was apparently based rather closely on Malkin family members (there is another fictional glimpse of Aunt Eliza Edge in the character of Miss Sneddon), but after she had finished writing the novel, she took great pains to alter the characters so that their prototypes would not be readily identifiable. Because *Love and Salt Water* is set in the social milieu in which Wilson herself lived, several people, including Mary McAlpine, have come forward to say they understand Ellen Cuppy to be based on themselves. Such a simple copying from life is not very likely. Details may be suggestive, but the core of this characterization almost certainly derives from an amalgam of the author's own experiences.

The reviews of *Love and Salt Water* were mixed but on the whole respectful of Wilson's reputation as a distinguished stylist. The brief notice in the *Evening Standard* was typical of the English reviews, describing *Love and Salt Water* as 'an excellent assured performance by Canada's best writer' with 'not a word out of place, and none too many.'[59] One English reviewer, less flattering, tried to place Wilson with a group of fiction writers, mostly women, whom he regarded as amateurs, writing as they like, with little regard for conventions. On the positive side, he says, their work is free from cliché but, on the other hand, their management of plot 'would make a professional's hair stand on end.' He cites Virginia Woolf, who thought this shift of focus was proper for women, and he points out that 'the very last thing one could call *Love and Salt Water* is a good story.' Nonetheless, he provides a suggestive metaphor: 'the story's gait is both musical and offhand, an indescribable compound of fireside chat and violin solo.'[60] What this description evokes is the loose, compendium structure of the novel's original conception in 'Herself When Young.' There were no American reviews because, in spite of heroic efforts, Ruth May had not been able to place the book with a publisher in the United States.

The *Edmonton Journal* called *Love and Salt Water* 'a ridiculous book' and 'a waste of time,'[61] but other Canadian reviews were fairly positive, including W.A. Deacon's piece in the *Globe and Mail*. Ethel would have been delighted with Eric Nicol's notice in the *Vancouver Province*, which praised her ability to capture the 'special tang' of the local waters and her almost 'telegraphic style,' her ability to convey in very few words the essence of things. He referred to her as the First Lady of Letters in Canada.[62] Probably the most flattering review was one by Harriet Hill that appeared in the *Montreal Gazette*. It praised Wilson's economy with words but drew attention as well to her mature philosophical outlook and the insights into human behaviour that flash throughout the story. Wilson's writing, says Hill, is a pleasure not to be gulped down but to be sipped like old brandy.[63] But Deacon's review is the most insightful and confirms the reputation he had developed as Canada's most important literary reviewer between the 1930s and 1961. He described *Love and Salt Water* accurately as a 'muted drama of repressed emotions' told in the 'chaste, restrained style for which Mrs Wilson is famous.' Although the characters, in his view, were anaemic and there could hardly be said to be any plot, Wilson managed to be acutely interesting in terms of atmosphere and observations, and he suggested that travel writing would suit her powers perfectly. But Deacon's most interesting observation is that Wilson is an analytical writer, not a novelist of great emotions, and that in her writings she has 'said things about the face of Canada that are poetic and true and inherently important.' Deacon's nationalism at last found things to commend in Ethel Wilson's work, especially her notion of the 'genius of place' as applied to the whole country, and her belief that 'the formidable power of geography determines the character and performance of a people' (89). He commended especially a passage from *Love and Salt Water* that traverses in imagination the breadth of the Dominion:

> No picture can show how wide the country is; no map convey ... Each time the interested traveller crosses the country by the northern route, by the southern route or by air, the country with its sleeping past, its awakened future, the gradual progress of discovery and habitation, the extravagant forests, prairies, lakes, and mountains, the great beauty, the isolated and sometimes collapsed shack that speaks of human effort and departure, the sudden appearance of a city in all that solitude (like an explosion) – the land enchants and speaks to him. The land is full of question. The journey disturbs and exhilarates. (87–8)

This was the kind of writing that fulfilled Deacon's program for a national literature, and he was delighted at this point in her career to laud Ethel Wilson as one of the country's most accomplished writers.[64]

There were, however, several Canadian reviewers who took the position that while *Love and Salt Water* was a beautifully written piece of fiction, as a story it was 'slight,' and altogether 'a lesser thing than its predecessors.' Poet Miriam Waddington tried to identify specifically why she felt it was a lesser book. She reviewed the novel in *Queen's Quarterly*, and while she praised the author's great gift with words and her magical skill in conveying character, she observed that the world of the novel was an affluent one, 'where people travel in airplanes, have no money problems, play badminton, and don't read much,' and that the reader 'instinctively likes this kind of world or not. And if not, one is alienated.'[65] In an incisive article which would have surprised and probably fascinated Wilson, Blanche H. Gelfant examines the reasons for that possible 'alienation' by looking at *Love and Salt Water* in terms of social and economic disparities or, put more bluntly, in terms of class and money.[66] She observes that Frank Cuppy, as an instrument of capitalism, supports his family by an unceasing quest for profit. His pursuit of potential oilfields makes him an absentee husband, and to compensate he gives his family expensive gifts: 'a nice new roadster for his wife,' and strange and beautiful presents that make his mind 'easier' about his children. He winds up living in New York City, where he is 'near to the heart of things,' meaning business. His success makes possible the privileged lives led by the rest of his family. Wilson, however, does not want to write a novel about business, argues Gelfant, and so her novel takes pains to disguise what would otherwise be a story of greed, pride, and avarice. The most obvious personification of the capitalistic will in this sense is Mr Platt, the miserly and impersonal businessman Ellen Cuppy goes to work for in Saskatoon, but he is made to appear such a Dickensian caricature that his effect is comic and the money theme remains curiously hidden. Some of the other characters, argues Gelfant, are also stock literary types (Mr Abednego, for example, a *deus ex machina* figure who rescues Ellen and her nephew from drowning in Active Pass) who distract the reader from the real working of this story, as does the novel's romance design. But what is evaded, she argues, is still present. The freighter's lower deck hides its crewmen from the passengers, the hotel hides its cooks so that guests will believe 'nobody works' (139), and a working-class family hides a brain-damaged child so that his wealthy mother can forget his existence, but the reader nonetheless knows they are there. Gelfant's essay would likely have fascinated Wilson because it illuminates the world of social privilege that she was often uneasy about, that complicated her friendly relations, for example, with Babe and Austin Taylor, chairman of the Home Oil Company, whose daughter was married to the highly visible young spokesman for American conservatism, William F. Buckley – and complicated relations closer to home, with her Malkin family and the Buckerfields.

A more conventional reading of *Love and Salt Water* views it as a 'romance' on the lines of Shakespeare's last plays, in which characters on a journey are tested through a series of misfortunes and misunderstandings before returning home and being reintegrated back into society. The journey motif is coupled with a symmetrical narrative design that takes Ellen Cuppy, the hero, from the unity of a happy family life to almost total isolation, and then back again into the larger fabric of the human community. As it was for Ethel Wilson, that journey is precipitated by a mother's death. When she finds her mother's body, Ellen's first instinct is not to tell anyone (as if this would prevent it from becoming true), and this impulse marks Ellen's gradual withdrawal from the confidences of other people. Her nickname is 'Gypsy,' and she becomes a wanderer, first on a freighter voyage to Europe during which a beautiful boy sailor is swept overboard like a leaf and lost at sea, and then during the war as a WREN. After the war and the breaking of an engagement, she goes to live in Saskatoon, where she works for Mr Platt, who boasts he has '"neether chick nor child"' and depersonalizes Ellen by calling her 'Miss Um.' In the romance plot, he represents the furthest point reached by Ellen in her withdrawal from human interaction. But while she is working for Mr Platt, she meets George Gordon, which is the turning point and the beginning of her return to social life and family. In the nature of romance, Ellen and George are tested before a marriage can take place. Ellen is responsible for the boating accident in which she and her nephew Johnny nearly drown, and she emerges with an ugly scar on one side of her face. Ellen's 'sea-change' becomes a test of love for George Gordon, and when she goes to the train station to meet him, she is prepared for his pity and rejection. But George's love for Ellen proves genuine, for we are told that though her disfigured cheek was repellent to him, he kissed her 'out of love and pity and delight.' The novel comes full circle as Ellen becomes part of the human family again, and she and George begin their 'happy chequered life together.'

Love and Salt Water may be the most conventional of Wilson's novels in terms of plot and characterization, but it contains some of the most

unconventional elements in her fiction. In the myriad gruesome accidents, maimings, and sudden deaths, it dramatizes more powerfully and
insistently than any of her other books her conviction that chaos lurks
beneath the smooth surface of events, that we always live 'on a brink.'
Sudden death carries away Ellen's mother, the beautiful boy-sailor, her
sister's first son, Aunt Maury Peake's son, Mr Platt in Saskatoon, and Miss
Sneddon in Vancouver; disfigurements and accidental maimings circum-
scribe the lives of Ellen's nephews (one is mentally retarded, the other
deaf), her friend Charles Cheney, whose hand was blown away in the war,
and Ellen herself, who will be permanently scarred by the boating accident. In this novel occurs that startling line '... you are walking along
through the grasses on the cliff top, admiring the pretty view, when –
crack crack' (128). The narrator observes unequivocally, '... most things
are dangerous. Nothing is safe' (68).

But being unsafe is not just a physical condition; it is something like a
philosophical one, as well. In this novel, the question is raised again:
what is truth? In all her writing, Wilson seems to say that to arrive 'somewhere near the truth' is to perceive or recognize in all experience a tension of opposites: her characters are 'repelled but pleased,' 'together yet
alone.' But in this novel, she reinforces another epistemological conviction – that truth is always relative to the perceiver. In the brief opening
chapter, Ellen wants to know what a virgin is, and she is told it is 'a
young girl,' a definition appropriate to a child, but one which suggests
that knowledge is always partial, and consists of both what is known and
what is not known. In the next chapter, 'truth' is defined specifically as
point of view. Mrs Cuppy and her two daughters watch a freighter coming into Vancouver harbour; the ship, which appeared long and elegant
in the distance, on the dividing line of sky and sea, became a large,
squat, black object in the harbour: 'it became a different ship.' Perception in Wilson's fiction is always conditional on light, and perhaps she
was, as Brent Thompson has suggested in his discussion of *Swamp Angel*,
influenced in some way by the talk of Einstein's theory of relativity, in
which movement and time are relative to the observer and the one constant is the speed of light. Perhaps directing us to this way of thinking,
she has Ellen conclude that the nature of reality was 'one (or almost
one) with the nature of light' (65). The narrator goes on to suggest that
'perhaps our whole existence, one with another, is a trick of light' (67).
As a metaphor for truth (for what is constant), light is the measure of
what is real in most of the novel's key sequences: Theatre under the
Stars (Einstein's way of measuring light), the absence of light during the

storm on the Atlantic, the Northern Lights on the prairie. Most dramatic is the absence and presence of light at the time of Mrs Cuppy's death. When Ellen comes back from the starlight theatre there is no light in her mother's bedroom. Next morning, as she comes to the realization that her mother is dead, the narrator keeps drawing the reader's attention to the morning light that pushes into the room around the edges of the blind, revealing the reality of what has happened. Later this becomes an ontological question: lying in bed and looking up at the rectangles of light and dark gliding across her ceiling, she asks what happens to them with the coming of dawn. 'Are they still there, but in the presence of light we do not see them? The thought alarmed her – what is around us?' (67)

These questions are usually viewed as being answered by Wilson in *Swamp Angel*, where she refers to a providential ordering and 'the everlasting web' of creation. In this light, Anjali Bhelande draws our attention to those strange tautological-sounding statements that flesh out such religious abstractions.[67] Struggling to save Johnny from drowning, Ellen thinks, 'She was Nora and Nora was herself' (148), just as earlier she had thought, 'I was a bird and the birds were I' (70). The far-reaching importance of this idea of 'being the other' is articulated at length in the first version of the novel, 'Herself When Young,' where Ellen is reflecting on her life in Saskatoon:

> I am looking now at the bridge and at the river going under the bridge. There are cars on the bridge and people walking along the narrow sidewalks. I shall never get used to certain moments of revelation that tell me that we are all one. Those people in the cars are I, and I am those people in the cars and those people walking. Oh look! There is the old Russian who wears high boots and a pith helmut, where does he get them? I am he, too, and he is me. It is rather frightening if one should think about it too long, this kinship. It is more than kinship, and might, if properly used, prevent wars.

But how does one propose a relationship in Wilson's writing between unpredictability and apparent disorder, on the one hand, and such universal designs, on the other? Blanche Gelfant suggests that when looking for a theoretical code to decipher meaning in Wilson's fictions, we might refer to chaos theory, which can translate themes of chance, providential order, and universal human values into terms that validate them in mathematical and scientific ways outside those provided by cultural codes. More than once in her fiction, Wilson describes something akin to the 'butterfly effect' of chaos theory, whereby the mere flapping of a butterfly's wings can alter weather patterns at a great distance.[68] In *Love and Salt Water*, for example, she connects (through a combination of events) a Mr Prendergast's becoming temporarily ill in Montreal with Ellen's near-fatal accident in Active Pass, British Columbia. As in the orderly disorder of chaos theory, random chance, accidents, and coincidence seem to signify a lack of purposeful design in Wilson's texts, yet order does emerge, nonetheless, as love prevails and the characters in this novel draw closer to each other after being tested by adversity. When she tells the reader about the consequences of Mr Prendergast's falling ill, the narrator says simply, '... the circle of life is extraordinary,' a seemingly trite statement, but one which in fact reflects both design ('the circle') and what is unpredictable (the 'extraordinary'). Shifting for a moment from a religious to something like a scientific view of Wilson's fictions is not meant to place the value of one reading above another, but to suggest rather the limitless possibilities for reading these theoretically accommodating texts.

In spite of valiant efforts, Ruth May Bendukov was unable to find an American publisher for *Love and Salt Water*. It has been reprinted only once, in the New Canadian Library in 1990 with the rest of Wilson's oeuvre. E.J. Hughes's painting of the sea at Qualicum with two figures in a rowboat seems an especially apt illustration for the cover. The afterword is by Anne Marriott, the Canadian poet who wrote so eloquently about the Saskatchewan dust storms in *The Wind Our Enemy* (1940). She reads Wilson's novel in a parallel fashion, in which salt water, like the wind, can quickly annihilate love and all human effort. She draws attention to the two endings Wilson wrote as proof of the unresolved tension in the novel between human love that binds individuals together and what Matthew Arnold in 'To Marguerite' called the 'unplumbed, salt, estranging sea.' If published in its original form, 'Herself When Young' might have enjoyed a vogue for those self-reflexive features so prized in late twentieth-century aesthetics, but its more conventional realization as *Love and Salt Water* made possible a philosophical distance for some of the author's summary views on art and life.

CHAPTER THIRTEEN

Mrs Golightly

1957–1961

Public speaker / 'The Vat and the Brew' / Creative writing /
Vile bodies / *Mrs Golightly and Other Stories*

Although Wallace had made a full recovery from the coronary thrombo-
sis in 1954, Ethel was never without anxiety. 'If Wallace *sneezes* even,' she
wrote John Gray, 'I see pneumonia.'[1] The increased sense that one
always lives on a brink, that one might be admiring a pretty view 'when –
crack crack,' is strikingly apparent if the first draft of *Love and Salt Water*,
titled 'Herself When Young, or Miss Cuppy' is compared to the published novel. It is only in the latter version that Wilson plumbs the
depths of physical and philosophical insecurities by portraying with
chilling poignancy the surprise death of Ellen Cuppy's mother and the
defection – through remarriage, then death – of her father. These
events are not dramatized in 'Herself When Young,' a manuscript that
had been completed in 1954 before Wallace's grave illness. Now ordinary happenings and large world events resonated with chaotic, even
apocalyptic, consequences for the author. In the fall of 1956, while
reviews of *Love and Salt Water* were coming in, the world's attention was,
as so often, on the Middle East and what came to be known as the Suez
Crisis, wherein Britain and France had joined forces and threatened to
ignite a third world war. Like many who protested the bombing of Iraq
during the Gulf War of the 1990s, Ethel was frightened and appalled by
European intervention in the Suez Canal:

> I have never been so unhappy about world and national affairs in my life –
> because always, before, whatever the anxieties & blows, I always felt that
> Britain was *right*, & this time I was, & am, shocked beyond measure. I feel I

never knew what 'shock' was before, that the U.K. (with France! indeed)
would land troops without notice & call it 'Police Action.' When W[allace]
returned from Toronto he said 'Wait, you don't know everything' & I said
'I know that the U.K. has shocked the world and the world's very shifty conscience, earned the hatred of the Moslem world, set a precedent of return
to bad old ways, etc.' ... Is it the inheritance of past stupidities and vacilla-
tions? Russia growls on nearer and nearer ...²

Ethel had never before doubted Britain, but she was now sixty-eight and
her world, it seemed, at every turn was growing shaky. From now on,
pleasures were circumscribed by apprehension, creativity curtailed by
doubt.

There were still pleasures in abundance, nonetheless, both personal
and professional. Christmas 1955 spent at the Empress Hotel, awash in
American tourists, had been somewhat grotesque in Ethel's opinion,
and so in 1956 they decided to try the quieter setting of the Island Hall
at Parksville on Vancouver Island. Wallace mildly protested that they
were becoming recluses, but he was apparently happy enough to make
up a packet of periodicals and books, including the ones for Christmas
sent by John Gray, and to spend a quiet week at the hotel reading in
Canadian history and walking the beach when skies were clear. The
highlight of the holiday was a drive north to Campbell River to have
lunch with Roderick and Anne Haig-Brown, an activity they would
repeat several times during the next few years. Ethel had met Haig-
Brown in 1954 when they participated on a panel together. His enthusiasm for the natural world and the landscapes of British Columbia struck
a sympathetic chord, and the two couples, though a generation apart in
age, formed a natural and easy bond. Wallace could converse readily
with anyone, but he found Roddy Haig-Brown an especially interesting
companion.

For Ethel, professional pleasure came in a new and surprising form –
that of public speaking. The shy and retiring persona that Wilson had
presented to the world all her life made room now for a gracious but
highly opinionated speaker on matters of literature and culture. Sally
Creighton, a Vancouver friend and critic, viewed her as truly a grande
dame – in appearance, training, and approach.³ Although she had said
repeatedly 'never again' after her appearance on television and at the
UBC conference on BC writing, she was persuaded nonetheless to give
several lectures and talks to the public. Bob Patchell convinced her to
speak on the radio again, this time on Joyce Cary for CBC radio's *Anthol-*

ogy, as a follow-up to an interview with Cary himself. She agreed to the request because she admired Cary's novels, because she heard he was terminally ill, and because there was the personal association of having met him at the Lynds nearly twenty years before. In the broadcast, she praised his ability to create so convincingly and compassionately the 'I' that resides in ordinary people, in the way that Defoe had done two centuries earlier. She also praised his ability to make the reader feel the anguish in difficult moral decisions, especially in deciding between two wrongs. And she praised his ability to evoke 'the important phenomena of light and colour.' She spoke of their meeting (which he was not likely to recall, she realized), and she remembered him as 'someone who was unimpressed [with] *himself* and was much more interested in other people and in *ideas*.' The talk was aired Wednesday evening, 22 January 1957.[4]

Two days later, she gave a lengthy talk in the Sedgewick Room, UBC Library, about the origin of her books. As the speaking engagement drew near, she questioned what she was doing, feeling intimidated once again by the fact that she did not have a university education. 'I must tell you,' she wrote John Gray 18 January 1957, 'that I feel keenly this business of expressing oneself at *a University*, amongst swells who have degrees and have studied these things,' and she referred again to the business of symbolism and the study of literary criticism. 'How pretentious of me [to speak], who have nothing but a very treasured *conferred* degree, & *know* nothing.'[5] Nonetheless, in her talk, which she titled 'Somewhere near the Truth,' she tackled some of the controversial topics of the day, giving her sceptical opinion on the extravagant attention to symbols in literary study and her equally sceptical reaction to the psychological pronouncement that all art is the product of inner conflict. She argued that everyone experiences conflict in their lives, but that art is born as well out of one's curiosity about the lives of others – 'identification with and compassion for our fellow human beings and not through our own conflicts alone' – though she conceded that the writer's experience of conflict may sharpen one's understanding of the human predicament. Equally, fiction is created, she argued, out of the 'sheer delight in writing – just as a person swims for the love of it – from a joy in and the selective use of our language.' This was the experience she gave to Ellen Cuppy as a writer in the manuscript 'Herself When Young.' Mixed in with theorizing were anecdotes about the inception and writing of her own books.[6]

At the close of her talk, she told the audience she was at work on 'a book with a real origin, a real anger, a real purpose,' something more akin to a tract than a novel. This was a reference to a manuscript which she started in January 1956 and which she sent off to John Gray on 27 March 1957. It was titled 'The Vat and the Brew' and carried the subtitle 'Written in Anger.'[7] It represented for Wilson a radical departure from anything she had done previously because it is an openly didactic tale with a specific moral lesson. The subject of the manuscript is juvenile delinquency in Vancouver, and the finger of blame is pointed at those parents who abandon responsibility for their children, specifically mothers who go out to work so that the family can acquire a bigger car, a fur coat, a television set. The vat is the uncaring family (and, by extension, society); the brew is delinquency. The manuscript focuses on the story of Dorine, the archetype of careless mothers, who gets her ideas and airy attitudes from cheap magazines with titles like 'Flames of Passion.' We are told in the narrator's angry, didactic voice that 'failing other mental and spiritual food, Dorothy [who changes her name to Dorine] flourished on and was nourished by this rubbish, which determined her very being.' Dorine abandons her small son Lennie to her older sister and moves to Vancouver, where she fantasizes living like a Hollywood starlet and where she flirts with men she picks up at bars. Dorine's sister eventually sends Lennie as a teenager to live with his mother in Vancouver, where, neglected, he becomes a juvenile delinquent, finally imprisoned for shooting a policeman. The lives of several other people affected by Lennie and his friends are described in detail, and the result is a grim picture of urban life in the 1950s. Wilson wrote a lengthy foreword pointing out that Vancouver, the city she has loved so dearly, had the greatest proportion of juvenile crime and drug addiction in all of Canada. 'I condemn us for our preoccupation with material things and for our lack of foresight,' she wrote, and stated that her story was an attempt to get at the causes of juvenile crime, 'the sources of infection.' She added pointedly that 'one is angry with those who, having a child, do not care for that child's well-being.'

When she sent the manuscript to Gray, she enclosed a note saying, '... one feels a huge preoccupation with this subject here ... shootings, robberies, knifings – & holdups ... beyond police control. The future, more than the present even, is so alarming.'[8] Gray replied with a readers report 30 April 1957, assuring her that one believes in the problem and its growing menace, but her manuscript, whether regarded as fiction or a tract, was not really convincing.[9]

Gray and his reader felt the project failed because she had not created in either Dorine or Lennie a centre of compassion. The result, judged Gray, was a group of characters whom one doesn't really know or love – or even care about – as people. The Macmillan reader did not feel comfortable with the narrator writing from Olympus, denouncing in shrill tones people who are ungifted and unloved. Her preaching, moreover, seemed directed at the wrong people, and the solution offered (mothers staying at home with their children) seemed too easy and pat. Both Gray and his reader felt Wilson's writing suffered: delicate perceptions were here supplanted by listings of sordid trivia; the language of backstreets and bars was sadly inept. They felt strongly that it would be a disservice to her reputation to publish this manuscript.

Although she was accustomed to strong criticism of her work from her editors, Wilson was probably disappointed, nonetheless, when she received Gray's letter because she felt so strongly about the subject. Her papers reveal that she had been keeping a large folder of newspaper cuttings about crime in the city,[10] and we know that she and Wallace had spent a morning at court when they were in London watching the prostitutes and drug pushers being sentenced and fined. But she wrote back to Gray on 4 May 1957 that probably everything he said about the manuscript was true and that she was not cut out to be a literary missionary,[11] and, except for arranging the return of the manuscript, they did not mention it again in their correspondence. This kind of writing ran directly counter to everything Wilson had said about the nature and function of the novel as an art form. In the CBC television interview, for example, she said that for the treatment of important social issues one does not turn to a novelist to better understand the problems and their possible solution but to a thinker like Bertrand Russell.

But she was not entirely finished with 'The Vat and the Brew.' She felt strongly that parts of the manuscript had social value and might be published in short-story form; when the manuscript came back, she rewrote a sequence about the senseless killing of a Chinese grocer and titled it 'Fog.' The story is very different from the incident in the novel-length manuscript because the old woman in the novel is a venomous busybody, a former friend of Dorine's and part of the 'vat,' who emerges unscathed from the hold-up in the grocery store. In the new version, she is a hapless victim of circumstances, a symbol of the elderly at risk in a city invaded by gangs of young criminals. Wilson sent the story to John Gray six months later, but his reaction was wholly negative and he discouraged her from sending it out for publication. He did not like the way point of view shifted in the story from the old lady, Mrs Bylow, to the author to the bystanders. As always in his criticism, he wanted more sympathetic character identification; he regarded Mrs Bylow as just 'a lump,' and the story accordingly without impact.[12] Attempts to find a publisher were unsuccessful, but Wilson had not lost faith in it and she included it with her story collection published in 1961. Since that time, 'Fog' has been one of Wilson's most frequently anthologized stories. Its power derives, as so often in Wilson's writing, from her rendering of the natural world as an intimate coordinate of the human one, the blinding fog in this story creating the condition in which violence will erupt. Wilson continued to rework one other segment of 'The Vat and the Brew,' the story of a widow who is run down by a car, stolen and driven by Lennie or one of his gang. She created a longish story in four parts titled 'The Life and Death of Mrs Grant,' subtitled 'A Didactic Tale, with Questions,' and sent it out for publication, but without any luck. Unlike 'Fog,' this story is probably not very successful; the metaphor of the vat and the brew is again rather crudely offered, and Mrs Grant's analysis of the ills of society, during a long sleepless night, is wholly lacking in dramatic interest. However, as a study of a widow's loneliness there is a poignant authenticity to the story, informed by the author's fear of the sundering of her 'perfect companionship' with Wallace. It appears in the scholarly volume of Wilson's previously unpublished short fiction. The origin of both stories – the killing of the grocer and the hit and run death of an elderly widow – can be found in the newspaper clippings Wilson had collected.

John Gray's decision not to encourage Wilson to go ahead with 'The Vat and the Brew' was probably the right one. Not only is the story burdened by an over-simplified didacticism, but the writing itself is weak, completely lacking in the kinds of perception and philosophical wisdom that characterizes Wilson's work. Reading the manuscript of 'The Vat and the Brew,' one is reminded of the characters in 'Tuesday and Wednesday,' many of whom are vain, illiterate people existing on the lowest rung of the economic order. But Dorine and Lennie are presented without humour, without any of the ironies that make Myrt and Mort part of the human community. Instead, the characters in 'The Vat and the Brew' are inhuman, cartoon-like figures meant to frighten the reader. The narrator's denouncements are shrill, her preaching terribly earnest but without compassion. Wilson's lifelong interest in and sympathy for working-class people seems to have vanished and been replaced by a fear of the grotesque denizens of a sub-human order. There are no Vicky Tritts in this novel, no beneficent Auntie Emblems, just drug pushers and killers and prostitutes, a criminal population created by mothers who abandon all responsibility for their children. As art this manuscript is pretty much a failure, but in terms of the author's biography, it has value for it illumines a dark centre in Ethel Wilson's imaginative world, a primal sense of chaos stemming from a mother's absence.

The writing project had been abortive, but otherwise the Wilsons enjoyed 1957 in their carefully circumscribed way. There may have been no humour in 'The Vat and the Brew,' but Ethel could still amuse her correspondents in describing the 'perils' of social life. She wrote to John Gray:

> My hand is red and purple from being bitten by a charming dog under the table a week ago. He understandably thought my hand was a pork chop. The lady of the home said with politeness, 'Oh yes, he bit someone else the other day ... but as I was saying ... etc.' He, the host, continued 'and we were the very first to fly machinery into New Guinea.' I did not flinch, wince nor cry aloud, but listened submissively while my hand went ping pong. The dog's aged teeth did not puncture – but, like lots of old men, his jaw was terrific.[13]

They spent most of August again at the Eldorado Arms in Kelowna, visiting the Crawleys several times at Penticton. At the end of their stay in Kelowna, with Wallace feeling fit and adventurous, they drove north to Lac Le Jeune for a couple of days of fishing, Wallace 'decanting' Ethel from wheelchair into rowboat, and then they drove further north into the Cariboo region, as far as Barkerville, the gold mining town that had been established in the mid-nineteenth century and was being reconstructed as a historical site.

That fall, Ethel gave a couple of dinner parties, including an obligatory one for her sister-in-law, Amy Buckerfield, who had returned to the city after living in London. It is the kind of party, she wrote John Gray, 'that still *terrifies* me.'[14] Her feelings about the Buckerfields would always be coloured by her strained relations with her mother-in-law during the first years of marriage, but they were also complicated by her feelings about wealth and class. Ernest Buckerfield had amassed a considerable amount of money through his feed and seed business, and his family lived in a way that Ethel deemed lavish. Ethel liked Amy, felt comfortable with her gentle nature ('her personal warmth and kindness is very real'),[15] but had no bond of sympathy with Ernest. Similarly, Ernest, who was very much a businessman, felt uneasy around Ethel. One

Christmas, at their home, she organized a musical skit based on the
story of Uncle Tom's cabin as adapted to Buckerfield's Seed and Feed,
with lines like 'Falling wheat, fading flour.' Ernest knew the humour was
at his expense and couldn't help feeling a distance between himself and
his accomplished sister-in-law. The Buckerfields, in turn, enjoyed an
affluent circle of friends, which intimidated Ethel.[16] Her deepest loyal-
ties remained with her Methodist father, who only left her a Bible, and
with her Bryant half-aunts, who had eked out a modest existence in London. She wrote, '... it has been brought home to me very forcefully that
the rich know the rich, & many of them care nothing at all about the
poor.'[17]

She felt much easier giving a talk to students at West Vancouver High
School.[18] It was based largely on a sequence culled from 'Somewhere
near the Truth,' and was designed to impress young students with the
importance of the sentence as the essential building block for every
kind of writing. Her observations are rich in metaphor:

> I have a reverence for the English sentence ... that is nearly worship. The
> sentence is a way of communication. It is a very humble bridge crossing a
> small stream; or it is the arch supporting the temple. It may be only a cul-
> vert or it may be a very great bridge connecting two distant shores. In its
> essence the sentence is a thing of beauty (always functional and strong)
> whether it appears frail or plain, or whether it is lavishly decorated. It has
> to carry its meaning. It is a shame to make an ugly bridge, tasteless in form
> and decoration, a bad sentence ... Whether a sentence is simple, as 'I see a
> star,' or whether it has the complex, formal, and curious construction that
> bears the mark of Henry James ... the sentence is a never-ceasing miracle
> and source of fascination. Time cannot exhaust the sentence.

Everything in her talk was subordinated to this idea that a piece of writing consists first and finally of sentences, which she urged her audience
to give thought to. She enjoyed speaking to the auditorium that was
filled with approximately two hundred students, and was amused by the
cheeky young male student who thanked her and said 'brashly and
engagingly, '"I am glad to see that Mrs Wilson is alive. I thought all
authors were dead."''[19]

In March of 1958, she gave a talk at UBC's School of Architecture,
and the university setting roused again her insecurities. She wrote to
John Gray: 'It seems preposterous for an uneducated person to stand up
and say what they think & believe, in front of scholars.'[20] But she hoped

that scholars would be patient and perhaps appreciate the pragmatic approach of the non-scholar. She opened the lecture by recalling her most powerful experience of architecture – viewing the Parthenon when she and Wallace and the Grahams visited Greece in 1930 – but the only idea she offered was that architecture, more than any other art, makes the observer aware of the passing of time. Instead she took the idea of structure, so obviously central to thinking about architecture, and reflected on its significance in the writing of fiction. Structure, she argued, plays an important role in the writing of short stories because this genre enforces 'economy of expression, the recognition of line and contour, and the opportunity for inference,' but the novel has no such restrictions. Thinking about *Tom Jones, Tristram Shandy, Moby Dick, Anna Karenina,* James's *The Wings of a Dove,* the novels of Virginia Woolf, Proust, or Cary's *The Horse's Mouth,* she could not identify any common laws of structure revealed, concluding instead that 'any structure in a novel partakes less of the structure of a building and more of the structure of a tree whose buds and branches grow.' Such structures are organic and fluid, and theories do not hold. On this basis, she urged any writers in the audience to undertake writing a novel in their own way and to be their own hardest critics.[21] By implication, she was saying that courses in creative writing could not help one write a novel. Earle Birney and Roy Daniells, two English teachers with strongly opposing views on this subject, were sitting in the audience.

 In November 1958, Wilson spoke again at UBC, this time in the prestigious Vancouver Institute series. Her talk was titled 'An Approach to Some Novels,' and she used this occasion to discuss her favourite writers and books, by now a familiar list including Defoe, Fielding, Trollope, and Forster.[22] What was of special interest to the audience was her discussion of the Canadian books she thought most distinguished. She pointed out first that there was no school of 'Canadian novel-writing,' such as the French novel *engagé* or the Group of Seven in painting, nor was one necessary. In her view there were simply novels written in Canada by Canadians without any prescribed formula for what constituted a Canadian novel, and, looking forward to the 1970s, she probably would have resisted the 'survival' thesis for identifying Canadian culture. (Interestingly, Atwood pretty much ignores Wilson in *Survival* because her books just don't fit the outline.)[23] She paid homage to her friends Earle Birney and Mazo de la Roche, made a list of the recent Canadian books she found impressive, which included Colin McDougall's *The Execution* and Adele Wiseman's *The Sacrifice,* and then went on to discuss the three Canadian books she thought stood out from all the others. They were Morley Callaghan's *Such Is My Beloved,* Sinclair Ross's *As for Me and My House,* and Robertson Davies' *A Mixture of Frailties.* In Callaghan and Ross, she praised spiritual qualities – faith and goodness and courage – and in Ross specifically his rendering of the Prairie climate, the constricted life of the false-fronted town, and the remarkable achievement of a man speaking through a woman's voice. Davies she praised for his wide learning and sense of the comic, though in a letter to Gray she said she did have a few misgivings about *A Mixture of Frailties,* particularly questioning the likelihood of a Jehovah's Witness girl becoming so very sophisticated in the arts.[24] There was a large audience on a rainy November evening to hear this lecture, which was probably Wilson's most distinguished appearance as a public speaker. Many of her friends were present, including Thea and Leon Koerner, Lawren and Bess Harris, Nan Cheney, and Margaret and Larry MacKenzie (he was still the president of the university). Roy Daniells hosted a party afterwards. Ethel enjoyed the experience enormously, and next morning, still elated by her hour on stage, she wrote to John Gray that 'she felt ten years younger' now that the lecture was over and she had achieved a success.[25] Only the portion of her lecture discussing Canadian writers has been published.

Ethel Wilson's rejection of a nationalist program for writers had become well known. She was strongly in favour of the Canada Council, but she cautioned against a narrow prescription that writing self-consciously identify itself as Canadian. Her engagement in the academic debates surrounding the arts, however, took a bolder step. As distressing to her as nationalism was the relatively recent introduction into Canada of creative writing courses at universities. In her opinion, they were a waste of time and money. She recalled on a number of occasions the young woman who contacted her after *Hetty Dorval* was published and asked for her help. The woman had taken a creative writing course at a university in New York and had written three novels, but they had been refused by publishers and she was in despair. Her writing teacher had used Thomas Wolfe as a model, and when Wilson looked at one of the manuscripts, she could see the influence sticking out on every page. Nonetheless, Wilson asked her editors at Macmillan to give the young woman's work a reading, which they reluctantly did. A year or so later, she met the woman again; the latter said Macmillan's readers had been very kind, but that she had given up all idea of writing and had gone into a business in which she was very happy.[26] This incident seemed to say a great deal to Wilson, and as time went by she began to speak out more and more often against creative writing classes. In the early 1950s, when sending Mazo de la Roche congratulations on an award she had won, she wrote, '... what gives me so much joy is that *you* did it. You had "the goods" ... no creative writing classes, no studying at the University of Iowa etc. Simply, you could write, and you did.'[27] She used the same phrase to indicate talent when she wrote to John Gray about a collection of interviews with writers that she had been reading: 'Doesn't it show that writers must have The Goods, & industry – nothing less will do, & we in Canada have had too often to substitute for the goods a "desire to write" which is a totally different & little thing.'[28] More colourfully in another letter, she points Gray to a 'sentence like a bright light' in Robertson Davies' *A Mixture of Frailties* and quotes, '"Nothing, nothing whatever really stands in the way of a creative artist except lack of talent,"' adding to Davies, 'Frighteningly true, and the goblins of "creative writing classes" go toppling down.'[29]

She quoted this same line from Davies in her Vancouver Institute talk, and in several of her other lectures pointed out that the writer must find his or her own way. At some point (there is no date on the typescript or mention in letters), she gave a talk to the Vancouver Soroptimists Club, and there she said that 'an aspiring writer could go to creative writing classes until he was black in the face, but if he has not a sound and critical knowledge of the construction and working power of the English sentence and the English language, he had better stay home. He will become muddled and waste his time, because he has not been given the basic tools.'[30] But her extended argument on this subject occurs in an essay coyly titled 'A Cat among the Falcons,' which appeared in the second issue of the newly formed journal *Canadian Literature*.[31] 'A Cat among the Falcons' is a summary collection of carefully measured, cultivated insights on the subject of literary creativity. In the first paragraph, she lays down the gauntlet by quoting the opening lines to *Love's Labour Lost* and says we hear all the winds of heaven blowing through these lines and no one taught Shakespeare how to do this. Rather, he was 'one of God's spies' and had what she calls 'The Gift,' without which creativity is impossible. As in some of her public talks, she argues here that a future writer must only have a good education in language, know about the construction and function of sentences and paragraphs, and must read widely in all kinds of literature. But thereafter he or she must be self-taught, for 'the conditions of privacy are the only conditions under which writing can be done.' She turns to a metaphor of light to describe the creative process: a synthesis, she says, takes place over which the artist has only partial control and there is 'an incandescence' from which meaning emerges. She gives Sheila Watson, who had just published *The Double Hook*, as an example of a 'lighted mind.' If this metaphor seems romantic and somewhat fuzzy, that is probably as it was intended because Wilson's point is that only a few have this mysterious gift and it cannot be acquired through teaching. One more point she makes is that a writer must feel a compulsion to follow this craft, and says of herself that just before the war she 'found it imperative to write.' 'Why' remains part of the mystery attendant on this somewhat romantic view of the artist. She does not say why she was compelled to write. In the final paragraph, she identifies herself on this subject, not as a cat among the pigeons, but as 'a country cat among [her] friends the falcons who are handsome, formidable and trained birds, equipped to detect and pounce on error.' Wilson in this last paragraph was referring almost certainly to her long friendship and argument with Earle Birney, whose teaching of creative writing at UBC had become mired in controversy and a thwarting of ambitions.

When the article appeared in December of 1959, Wilson wrote to Gray that she had long been concerned about the teaching of creative writing and felt the subject should be pondered and openly discussed. She was convinced the results of such classes would always be derivative, that good work was very personal and that only 'an ambitious mediocrity' was nurtured by the teaching of creative writing. But she had misgivings about making her opinions known in such a public way: 'Perhaps I have made a vast mistake – but [*Canadian Literature*] should be a journal of opinion & I think it is ... I cannot feel happy about it, yet I could not feel happy not to have taken that opportunity to express what I feel so strongly.'[32] Her misgivings were largely personal, because later that same day she wrote to Earle Birney: 'I have suffered a good deal of anguish in the process of writing my short piece in *Canadian Literature* current number ... While I think that *personal* help, which you have so often & willingly given, is wonderful – classes, as such, have increasingly disturbed me.' She restated her position that she had observed too often young aspirant writers emerging as imitators of Thomas Wolfe or Ernest Hemingway. Her letter concludes, 'I hope you can continue to have warm friendly feelings towards me as I have to you.'[33] But Birney, hard pressed at the university to defend his creation of a Department of Creative Writing, felt betrayed by his friend and eventually wrote back a month later in a mood of weary disillusionment:

I put your letter aside because I was angry, and wished to write when I was not. After a while it did not seem that there was any point in writing, except to rescue myself from the rudeness of failing to write. For now I am not angry but only oppressed with the futility of argument. You are not going to change your opinions for anything that I can say; if your mind were not already made up you would not have committed yourself to print without at least giving me a chance to argue with you first.[34]

He accused her of wanting to have her cake and eat it too, attacking him in public for his colleagues to see, but making a private peace with the founder of creative writing courses. He then went through her essay in detail, rebutting many of her points: he quotes '"Without [criticism] those of us who attempt to write would be poorer."' 'If this is so,' he argues, 'why are you so uneasy about the growth of creative writing classes. What do you imagine we do in them?' Wilson's reference to writing classes producing 'prentice comment which goes by the name of criticism' especially stirred his ire and he wrote, 'This is really too queenly an attitude even for you, Ethel.' He ended his letter bitterly: 'I could go on, but why ... I hope you and Wallace are well, and that you are working away at what you want to do. It must be pleasant to have time to write as much as one wants.' As there is no reply from Wilson in the Birney archive, we can conclude she did not write to him again. Birney, however, found an opportunity to go public with his side of the quarrel in a 1961 CBC radio broadcast, in which he and two of his creative writing students took apart 'A Cat among the Falcons,' just reprinted in A.J.M. Smith's *The Masks of Fiction.* She wrote to John Gray, 'Well, poor old Earle, how that has rankled!' and referred to his angry letter. 'But I didn't mind a bit,' she continued, determined to have the last word, if only in a private letter. 'Believe me, good old Earle couldn't make me angry – he's too damn sensitive.'[35] Yet it did rankle with Ethel, as well, because four years later she would write with only lightly veiled condescension: 'poor industrious egotistic ambitious Earle! kind to young hopefuls.'[36]

What do we make of this debate more than forty years later? Certainly, Wilson's refusal to self-consciously develop Canadian themes in her writing allies her work to that of writers in the twenty-first century, in a post-national era when outsiders, mingled homes, and migrancy have created new settings and themes for fiction. But in her quarrel with Earle Birney, I think she loses ground. Creative writing classes at UBC and University of Victoria have nurtured the talents of some of the province's most remarkable young writers: Eden Robinson, Christian Petersen, Madeleine Thien, and many others cite their university training as fundamental to what they have achieved. Ironically, both Robinson and Thien have won the 'Ethel Wilson Prize for Fiction.'

The Wilsons turned seventy in 1958, and physically they were feeling the weight of their years. Ethel's arthritis grew more painful, and her letters are full of references to her bad-tempered and irascible joints. She was now confined to a wheelchair whenever she left the apartment. She was also plagued with increasing deafness and hated to use the telephone, feeling she could not grasp the full text of any conversation. Increasingly, she wrote letters in lieu of phoning her friends, often three or four in a morning. But her personal problems were none as compared to her anxiety about Wallace. Most of 1958 passed smoothly for the Wilsons until late fall, when Wallace began having angina symptoms again, and until they eased up Ethel found the tension unbearable. Equally alarming and debilitating for Wallace was the onset of prostate gland problems, a series of infections that resisted antibiotics. There would be periods of remission when the problem seemed to have cleared, and then it would return more painful and limiting and humiliating than before. It reawakened the nightmare of 1948–50, when Wallace spent many months in hospital fighting mysterious infections that were in fact caused by antibiotics. The prostate problem led to five operations over the next few years and a further curtailing of their activities. Yet, in spite of physical miseries, Ethel could still write in that way that balanced the good and the bad: 'Vile bodies? Yes, they are, glorious & vile, & at present I loathe them & their ways, & love them.'[37]

When John Gray in 1957 rejected 'The Vat and the Brew,' he tried to offset Wilson's disappointment by suggesting she write more stories, so that some day they could publish a book of them.[38] Wilson didn't refer to this suggestion when she replied to his letter, but in March 1958 she did report that she had been working on two new stories, 'The Worlds of Mrs Forrester' and 'The Window,' and in November she questioned Gray whether he really thought a collection of stories was a feasible idea. She was especially interested in having 'Tuesday and Wednesday' reprinted, and, if the project were to go ahead, she wanted to make it the centrepiece of the collection. Gray urged her to proceed right away. Through most of 1959, Ethel was preoccupied with planning this collection – reworking some of her unpublished pieces, trying to put together a table of contents, and deciding on a title. Some of the stories Wilson listed in her letters to Gray create a mystery for the bibliographer because they have titles that appear nowhere else: 'Daily Bread,' 'Born to Sorrow,' 'The Comfort of Continuity,' 'Bobby Meroni,' and 'It's Best to Be Your Age.'[39] Of course, these may be working titles for otherwise familiar stories, just as 'Country Matters' was an early title for *Swamp Angel*. However, there are no further clues to stories that once bore these titles either in Wilson's correspondence or in her papers at the UBC Library. Typically, Wilson's confidence in the project waivered:[40] when John Gray visited with the Wilsons in late September 1959, he persuaded her to send her collection for a reading to the Macmillan office, and she complied; but by 23 October, she was writing to Gray saying NO to the project.[41] Wallace was going through another bad bout of infection, and she was too fatigued, she said, to take on any further work. Janice Patton, the reader in the Toronto office, was relieved that the project had been shelved because in her opinion the collection had too many soft spots and gaps. She was also offended by what she called 'a sort of superciliousness, perhaps a snobbery of taste' in the stories.[42]

What do these words imply when used to describe Ethel Wilson's style? 'Superciliousness' and 'snobbery' are cognate in association with terms like 'elegance' and 'patrician,' used frequently to describe Wilson's social qualities, and with Earle Birney's contemptuous reference to her queenly attitude. Wilson's critical success as a serious writer of fiction, her apparent self-confidence as a public speaker, and her studied elegance in social situations had by this time given her the reputation of being a grande dame, though interviewers were always at pains to point out how modest and unassuming she was in person. The aura of blue-blood society that hovered around Ethel Wilson was being transferred to her writing, and it obscured the reader's appreciation of her gift of sympathy for her characters and her powerful imaginative feeling for place. It would be more accurate, I think, to describe Wilson's perceptions as discriminating rather than snobbish, analytical and ironic rather than supercilious.

The most persuasive witness in Wilson's defence is Margaret Laurence. It was in 1960, while Wilson was planning her story collection, that they began a correspondence and established a loving friendship that lasted until Wilson's death. Although Wilson had been quite sceptical about the establishment of *Prism* (later *Prism International*), because it was closely associated with UBC's creative writing program, she was delighted by Margaret Laurence's African story 'The Merchant of Heaven,' which appeared in the second issue. Wilson sent praise to the magazine, and when Laurence wrote to thank her, she invited her to the apartment for tea. Ethel wrote to the Crawleys with an unusual sense of anticipation about this visit set for 15 January 1961: 'Over the telephone she sounds such a nice unaffected young woman, un-vain, natural. I am looking forward.' Later in the same letter, she referred again to her telephone conversation with Laurence: 'There was something immensely likeable & simple about her voice – but she is not "simple" in the ordinary meaning of the word. I hope she has a real future.'[43] The meeting and ensuing friendship probably meant more to Laurence than any other contact she would have within the literary community. She conveyed her excitement about coming to know Ethel Wilson in a letter to Adele Wiseman:

> She is so terrific I don't know how to describe her. She not only writes like an angel (in my opinion) but is, herself, a truly great lady – again, that probably sounds corny, but I don't know how else to express it. Her husband is a doctor (retired) and they live in an apartment overlooking English Bay. She is very badly crippled with arthritis, but she never mentions her health. She is poised in the true way – she never makes other people feel gauche. And she is absolutely straight in her speech – she has no pretensions, nor does she say anything she doesn't mean, and yet she has a kind of sympathetic tact.[44]

Many years later, Laurence would write publicly: 'A friendship [began] that I valued more than I can say. I was starved for the company of other writers, and here was an older woman whose work I admired so much, taking the time to talk with and encourage a young and unknown writer.'[45] They met frequently, discussing books and writers at great length, and when Laurence moved to England in 1962, they wrote to each other, Laurence preserving fifty letters which record the older writer's encouragement, faith, and great pride in the younger writer setting out on her career. Laurence's antipathy to anything elitist or false makes her estimate of Wilson's character especially valuable. In interviews, she would say, 'Ethel Wilson was regarded as a lady – for her reserve and dignity – but there was nothing phoney in this. Her modesty and sense of humility were the genuine article. She also had a sense of humour and proportion which gave scope and great subtlety to everything she wrote.'[46] What Laurence also appreciated in her meetings with Ethel Wilson was the way Wilson could always start a conversation with something of interest to both parties – go straight to the heart of any matter, but remain charming and gracious.[47] With such divergent social backgrounds, it was an unlikely friendship; yet they had both been orphaned in exactly the same way, made their way as writers unassisted, wrote of their characters with perception and compassion, and were not tied to a nationalist ideology, though Laurence's Manawaka novels would eventually be regarded as the very essence of Canadian writing. When *This Side Jordan* was published in 1960, Wilson wrote to the Crawleys that Margaret Laurence was 'a good writer, and a nice woman and doesn't follow anyone's "creative" lead ... she is someone to be very glad about, *and* she is self-critical and not self-important.'[48]

Laurence was inspired by Wilson's creative example and thought of it as a legacy to be passed down from one generation of writers to the next.[49] Alice Munro was similarly inspired by Wilson as a literary 'mother.' Looking back nearly thirty years, Munro remembered that Ethel Wilson was the only Canadian writer who impressed her as being an artist: 'I was *enormously* excited by her work because the style was such an enormous pleasure in itself ... It was important to me that a Canadian writer was using so elegant a style. You know I don't mean style in the superficial sense, but that a point of view so complex and ironic was possible in Canadian literature.'[50]

But inspiration may have worked in reverse, as well. Perhaps it was talking to Laurence about writing short stories that renewed Wilson's interest in putting together a collection, because on 20 May 1960 she wrote to John Gray reactivating the idea, though for a shorter volume, omitting 'Tuesday and Wednesday.'[51] She had also been receiving a number of requests for short fiction from both radio and magazines, and had been bowled over to receive $1,000 for the sale of 'From Flores.' With this expression of interest, she was encouraged to go forward, though she ruefully asked Gray, 'How many copies would you sell. Fifty?'[52] The new proposal, with a few exceptions, is close to the volume that was published. What is evident in this list is the author's experimental interest in the range of short-story writing stretching from non-fiction to complete fantasy. A few years before, she had composed two pieces of non-fiction based on experiences in London. She had not found Canadian publishers for 'The Corner of X and Y Streets,' her glimpse of Soho after the war, or for '"To Keep the Memory of So Worthy a Friend,"' her tribute to Condell and Heminge, the two actors who compiled the First Folio of Shakespeare's plays. She wanted them to be in this collection. Her interest in Canadian history, combined with her absorption in the water traffic visible from her apartment window, led her to write a piece about the *St Roch*, an ice-breaker that first navigated through the waters of the Canadian arctic. She placed these three pieces of non-fiction at the centre of the collection. At the other extreme was a short piece titled 'Simple Translation,' a fantasy that takes place in heaven. In between were action stories ('From Flores' and 'Hurry, Hurry,'), social comedies ('A Drink with Adolphus,' 'We Have to Sit Opposite'), sketches of scenery ('On Nimpish Lake'), comic dialogue ('God Help the Young Fishman'), diary-keeping ('Till Death Us Do Part'), and didactic narratives ('Fog' and 'The Life and Death of Mrs Grant'). There were others, and no one piece could be described as a conventional short story.

To get a different kind of reading for this substantially altered collection, Gray turned to Professor D.J. Conacher of Trinity College, University of Toronto. The latter's enthusiasm was very strong, and he praised the variety of forms, calling it an excellent collection.[53] His only recommendation was that 'Simple Translation' and 'The Life and Death of Mrs Grant' be dropped. The other readers were 'in house' and were both very positive. One wrote that the stories were superb and praised the author's 'light dry wit and quick insights into human folly,' pointing out as well that 'few writers have so lively a sense of place as Mrs Wilson.' The other reader wrote that some of the stories were magnificent, recommending especially the eerie effects in 'Haply the Soul of My Grandmother' and 'Mr Sleepwalker.' This reader, however, advised cutting 'God Help the Young Fishman' and particularly the two didactic stories from 'The Vat and the Brew,' suggesting that Ethel Wilson 'has an unacknowledged chip on her shoulder about other people's children. She has none, and wishes she had?' This reader judged her theory about juvenile delinquency as false in feeling and diagnosis, and 'as full of stale cliches as church social work.' There is no evidence that John Gray passed this biting judgment along to the author. The final published collection reveals that Wilson accepted the negative views of 'The Life and Death of Mrs Grant,' though she held firm in her positive feelings about 'Fog.' (Happily so, because this story about an unpleasant part of Mount Pleasant has become an anthology favourite.) She cut 'The St Roch' and 'Simple Translation'; otherwise the volume stands as she conceived it in 1960.

There were two more hurdles to pass. First that of finding a title.[54] Her first impulse, as so often, was to evoke place or geography, and she offered 'On Nimpish Lake and Other Stories' as a title. She also proposed 'From Flores and Other Stories,' and then withdrew that because it sounded 'too rhyming.' She listed 'Mrs Golightly and Other Stories' and 'The Window and Other Stories' as other possibilities, although she did not like the bleakness of 'The Window' in the main title; she said it sounded too much like 'The Pit,' 'The Trap,' 'The Snare,' 'The Door,' etc. She began to question the necessity of 'and other stories' in the title and came up with poetic phrases to encompass the book as a whole: from Edwin Muir, the titles 'A Difficult Country' and 'Ordinary People'; from John Donne, 'One Little Room,' 'Harmless Lovers,' 'Mutual Elements,' 'Riding Westward,' and 'Nothing Simple'; and from a poem by Keith Waddams she found in the *New Statesman and Nation,* 'A Measure of Contentment,' 'Unquiet Silences,' and 'Blind as Pennies.' I have recorded all these possible titles to show the extent of the author's perennial struggle with this aspect of writing and publishing, but also to record here some of the things she obviously felt her stories encompassed. John Gray, however, sounded confident when he selected 'Mrs Golightly,'[55] and Wilson acceded, feeling comfortable highlighting that story, which was a clear favourite with a wide variety of readers, and comfortable as well with the persona it created for the author herself.

The other hurdle concerned that old bugbear, punctuation. She had written to Kildare Dobbs at Macmillan, who had been assigned to take the manuscript through to publication, and had requested that there be a design on the jacket with shells – the kind one blows into because, in her words, 'this is particularly a voice-talking kind of book.'[56] Indeed, one more title she had suggested was 'Parts and Voices.' Some of the pieces in the collection were what she called talking stories, in which people 'race along in that fool-talking way without waiting for quotation marks,' and she was anxious to get that effect right. She knew her work often was at odds with the Macmillan house style and so gently reminded them of past experiences, adding that she would try of course to see their point of view, though she might be like Galileo. She was completely dismayed to open the galleys and find that her work had been repunctuated. She wrote at once to Dobbs, '... if it's a matter of expense ... I'd rather pay for fresh galley of *Golightly* in the form that I wrote it,' adding somewhat acerbically that she realized her punctuation had always been something of a problem for Macmillan, but she assumed at this point they were willing to let her unconventional practices stand. 'I have an awfully strong *feeling* for it as a form of modifying communication. To be used with care and a sparing eccentricity. Not like e.e. cumming[s].'[57] John Gray wrote back immediately, reassuring her that her punctuation would be interfered with as little as possible, though he knew Miss Eayrs would shake her head.[58] One other thing puzzled but did not really bother Wilson – Macmillan's decision to follow the French practice and use the lower case in the story titles.

Mrs Golightly and Other Stories was published in October to the best reviews that any of Wilson's books had received – reviews with headings like 'Short Stories Gripping,' 'Rich in Originality,' 'Medallist Ethel Wilson Displays Deft Writing,' 'Extraordinarily Compelling,' and 'Tour de Force: Mrs Golightly Humane, Witty AND Canadian.' Reviewers in Britain and the Commonwealth countries praised her connoisseur accomplishments in the short-story genre, especially her delicacy of perception, dry wit, and her ability to suggest so much more than was actually said. The reviews in Canada were of greater interest this time because there was no plot to summarize; rather, it was incumbent on the reviewers to convey the qualities of Wilson's writing. Ellen Stafford in the *Globe and Mail* recommended Wilson's rare sensibility and the exactness of her language, but especially her ability to engage the reader in conversation.[59] In the *Vancouver Sun*, Donald Stainsby wrote about Wilson's incisive curiosity, her exact sense of timing, and remarkable sense of place, and he argued that her accomplishment as a regional writer was a high quality of her art, not a limitation.[60] Robert Weaver, in the *Toronto Daily Star*, identified her writing as part of an English 'civilized and stylish' literary tradition, displaying a 'quiet intellectual toughness' and evading the Canadian stereotype of writing about childhood.[61] And in a fine summary statement, Lew Gloin in the *Hamilton Spectator* wrote that '[Wilson's] light, dry humour, conditioned by humility, experience and taste, has produced [fiction] keenly analytical but shaded by compassion.'[62] Interestingly, three reviews identified the stories as having a *New Yorker* quality, which must have struck the author as ironic because Ruth May Bendukov, her American agent, had over the years been unsuccessful in placing any of Wilson's stories with this elite magazine. Reviewers singled out for special praise 'Mrs Golightly and the First Convention,' 'We Have to Sit Opposite,' 'Mr Sleepwalker' (for its 'quality of fantastic imagination'), and 'A Drink with Adolphus.' At the same time, 'We Have to Sit Opposite' drew one of the few criticisms when Hilda Kirkwood in *Saturday Night* wrote that 'the anti-German sentiment is not worthy of so large-hearted a writer.'[63] Wilson had anticipated just this kind of comment about racial feeling and did not want to include the story in the collection, but Gray had assured her there would be no criticism of this kind. Other reviewers saw it as a political allegory about the Second World War and did not realize it was based on an experience from 1929.

The review of this book that Wilson valued most was a brief one that appeared in the *Times of India*, praising Wilson's 'remarkable human insight,' creation of mood, and 'splendid gift for the evocative word or phrase.'[64] Wilson felt this review revealed a common humanity. She was also thrilled to receive a letter from fiction writer Joyce Marshall, who had read the stories while living overseas and went to see St Mary the Virgin Aldermanbury for herself.[65]

In spite of excellent reviews, the book did not sell well, and copies were eventually remaindered. Nonetheless, Ethel Wilson is probably as well known today as a short-story writer as a novelist because her stories are an essential ingredient in anthologies of Canadian writing. Some, like 'The Birds,' 'Haply the Soul of My Grandmother,' and 'A Drink with Adolphus' are splendid examples of modernist prose – fragmented, allusive, and elliptical. By contrast, a story like 'Till Death Us Do Part,' in which a young shop clerk is keeping a diary, takes the postmodernist stance of the unpublished 'Herself When Young.' The diary-keeper records what she is able to deduce about an acquaintance named Kate, but foregrounded is the act of writing: the narrator says '[A] story has to end and this story hasn't ended yet and I don't know what the end will be.'

While Wilson was planning the book of stories, she was also writing some new ones, though she says very little about them in her letters. Other than a reference to sending it to Bob Weaver for publication in *Tamarack Review*, there is no mention of 'A Drink with Adolphus' in her correspondence, but the lame and aging Mrs Gormley is clearly an ironic self-portrait. In this story of a party, set on Capital Hill in Burnaby, Wilson has transformed certain aspects of her social life into a surrealistic comedy with a sinister twist at the end. 'A Drink with Adolphus' is one of her most important stories in that it illustrates vividly her apprehension that civilization is paper thin, or, as W.H. New has phrased it, 'a mere veneer over irrationality, uncertainty, and barbarism.'[66] The first part of the story gives an account of a party which is attended by art lovers and amusingly eccentric people, and proceeds through a series of misunderstandings in the best tradition of social comedy. In the story's second half, however, one of Adolphus's urbane guests gives an account of the party in his diary, which presents the social gathering in a wholly different light. Mr Leaper had found some of the guests, including his own wife, offensive and 'unintelligible' and was left disturbed and shaken rather than amused by the evening's events. But truly disturbing for the reader is Mr Leaper's fascination with a man he read about living in Illinois who was on trial for murdering his wife: 'The thing that impressed me,' he writes, 'was that he and his wife had seemed to live a devoted and harmonious life together.' That is Mr Leaper's concluding sentence in the published version of the story, but in a manuscript version, the story ends with the news that Mr Leaper in fact kills his wife.[67] Wilson's vision here, again quoting New, is that 'civilized individuals are susceptible to violence,' and civilized societies in turn '(even societies with rich traditions of art) are open to barbaric distortions of behaviour.' 'A Drink with Adolphus' shares this view of civilization with the earlier story, 'We Have to Sit Opposite.'

There is no mention in Wilson's letters of writing another story, one which is thematically similar in some respects to 'A Drink with Adolphus.' 'Beware the Jabberwock, My Son ... Beware the Jubjub Bird' is the story of a man who temporarily flees his incessantly talking wife, who finds his social life insupportable. This story includes a sequence at Lac Le Jeune (called by that name in this piece of fiction), where another character in the story describes the peace he achieves in his relationship to the natural world. There might be a mention of this story by another name in a letter to Wilson from John Gray in November 1957, in which he refers to a story she sent *Maclean's* titled 'Poor Felix.' Gray is sorry the magazine turned the story down (as they consistently did with all her fiction), because he likes it very much.[68] Felix may have been renamed Thomas Krispin, though there is no evidence other than a suggestion in the name, poor Felix, to prove this.

Wilson mentions 'The Window' in business correspondence with Bob Weaver (it was also published first in *Tamarack Review*), but again there is no account from the author of its composition or personal significance. Part of its meaning seems clear; the elderly man in the story, who has deliberately left his wife and all social life behind, is waiting for death, which comes in the form of an armed burglar lurking outside Mr Willy's picture window. But his time to die has not yet arrived, for the reflection in the window and the ringing of the telephone send the intruder back into the night, and Mr Willy is left to re-enter society and to contemplate further the meaning of life and the possibility of eternity. W.J. Keith writes well on this story, pointing out that windows are an important metaphor for vision in much of Wilson's writing, but that appearances are unreliable. The beautiful mountains as seen from Mr Willy's window are, as the story tells us, 'deceptive in their innocency, full of crags and crevasses and arêtes and danger' (197).[69] At the same time, in all three of these late stories, uneasy social relations and existential doubt are mitigated by landscape, however unreliable: by the 'ten cent's worth of view' Mrs Gormley pays her taxi driver on the way to Adolphus's party, by a retreat to Lac Le Jeune, 'heart's desire,' in 'Beware the Jabberwock,' and by that view of mountains and ocean from Mr Willy's picture window.

In an unpublished talk titled 'How Does the Writer Reach His Audience?' read on the CBC on 15 April 1956,[70] Wilson refers to a short but carefully written novel that she eventually abandoned. There is no other reference to this project, but one possibility is that it consisted of the stories she began writing in the 1940s about Lucy Lovat Forrester. There are six stories that can be linked around this character, spanning from 'In the Golden Days,' about Lucy's childhood in Vancouver,[71] to 'A Visit to the Frontier,' which describes the death of Lucy and her husband, Marcus, in a train crash. Lucy being courted as a young woman is described in 'The Mirage of Edward Pontifex,' and her travels abroad as a married woman in 'We Have to Sit Opposite' and 'Haply the Soul of My Grandmother.' The last story she wrote about Lucy is titled 'Truth and Mrs Forrester,' which appeared first in *Mrs Golightly and Other Stories,* though in this story she changed Lucy's name to Fanny Forrester. It records the anxious time for Ethel when Wallace was away for long stretches during the Second World War. ('Mr Sleepwalker,' about a woman's eerie relationship with a strange-smelling little man, is also occasioned by a wife's anxious separation from her husband during the war.)[72] In 'Truth and Mrs Forrester,' she asks one more time, 'What is truth?' and offers silence as a possible answer. Fanny and her husband experience such complete oneness in their union that words are not necessary between them. She says to her niece: '... truth is never distorted between your Uncle Mark and me, whether we talk ... [or] stay whole days silent like male and female happy Trappists. There is nothing that intervenes. There is just truth' (118). In this story, Wilson does fictional portraits of Audrey Butler (the adopted French-speaking niece Laura with whom Mrs Forrester has a perfectly sympathetic relationship) and Mrs Tufts as the garrulous housekeeper, Miss Riley. The story also provides one final glimpse of Wilson's view of social conversation as mostly false, yet necessary and funny. The inner thoughts of Mrs Forrester run counterpoint to her spoken words and reveal most of her conversation to be false, for as she says at the beginning of the story 'truth is so hard to tell, while fiction is the easiest thing in the world' (116). 'Truth and Mrs Forrester' is the last story Ethel Wilson wrote, an ironic farewell to her craft.

There was talk in literary circles that Ethel might receive the Governor General's Award for *Mrs Golightly*, but there were also rumours that it would go to Malcolm Lowry posthumously for *Hear Us O Lord from Heaven Thy Dwelling Place*. Some argued that Lowry's brief residence in Canada and his lack of citizenship disqualified him. Wilson at once deferred to Lowry's superior accomplishments, though earlier she had been surprised that Lowry was regarded as a Canadian writer: 'There is only one country that could have produced him, and it did.'[73] She could not bear being in the spotlight in this matter of awards. She was always amazed when any writer engaged in self-promotion, because it was so foreign to her instincts for privacy. She could not believe that Morley Callaghan would claim on radio that his stories were the best since Chekhov – 'Imagine *say*ing it, out loud!'[74] – and she squirmed to think of sitting like Roddy Haig-Brown signing copies of his books at Duthie's: 'My goodness, I'd hate that – I refused in pre-Duthie days – I'd feel awful.'[75] Yet there must have been a twinge of disappointment to see the award go elsewhere, knowing this would be her last book. She had been overlooked in the past in favour of writers with considerably less talent – writers like Philip Child, David Walker, and Igor Gouzenko – and she must have been puzzled by the list of previous winners filled with obscure names like Franklin D. McDowell, G. Herbert Sallans, and Winifred Bambrick. But no award was worth being made a spectacle of in public, and she fervently hoped there would be no discussion of the matter in the press. The award did indeed go to Malcolm Lowry.

Mrs Golightly and Other Stories was reprinted in paperback in the New Canadian Library series in 1990. (The story 'From Flores' was made into an animated short film by the National Film Board.) My introduction to the paperback points out that with one exception – *Hetty Dorval* – Ethel Wilson's novels began as short stories and that she believed that abbreviated forms of fiction suited her talent best. Hence the special place of the short story in her canon. After researching at length her biography, I would now draw attention to the peculiar poignancy in the epigraph she chose for the story collection. From Edwin Muir's collection of poems titled *The Difficult Land*, she constructed a simple line: 'Life "... is a difficult country, and our home."' Bringing together contraries, this line resonates with the experience of the orphan child taken to an alien land to be at home, where strangeness and familiarity, striving and rest, would always be combined. In this epigraph, we are reminded perhaps of Ethel Wilson's first seeing Vancouver as a child 'with an urgency that has remained in my heart ever since.' Her stories of women like Frankie Burnaby, Maggie Vardoe, or Ellen Cuppy, so sensitive to their environment, but who must move and make new homes, ask how one develops an identifying relationship between self and place when one is moved from one's 'home,' when place also means displacement.

Wilson's short stories are filled with such summary reflections and epistemological uncertainties. 'What is anybody like?' she puzzles in 'The Corner of X and Y Streets.' 'One never knows,' she concludes. Mrs Forrester confesses to her niece that her life is a masquerade. Mr Willy fears that life has no meaning at all. At the same time there are positive assertions in the stories: in her depiction of the natural world, the beauty of blue summer ocean and violet islands and snow-capped mountains is a solid value, and the order and purpose in a flight of wild geese or the splendour of a display of northern lights softens the harshness of their teleological mystery. Similarly there are positive assertions in the world of human affairs where truth, transcending words, can exist in the love between two individuals, where compassion heals injury, and where love and honour can bind men and women 'to keep the memory of so worthy a friend.'

CHAPTER FOURTEEN

Grande Dame
1961–1966

Canada Council Medal / 'In Defense of a Little Learning' / The rich /
Mrs Marshall / 'The Special One' / Margaret Laurence / Hospitals /
Killarney Manor / Death of Wallace

When Sally Creighton in 1967 described Ethel Wilson as a grande dame
in appearance and approach, she was summing up for radio listeners
Wilson's carefully cultivated social poise and her discriminating sense of
proportion in all things. But around that epithet there were accumulated many negative associations of power, class, and snobbery, which
had also become part of Wilson's public image. In the 1960s, with one
notable exception, she was in retreat from the world at large; the inca-
pacitating effects of arthritis and deafness and the ever-present anxiety
over her husband's physical condition meant shutting the door to most
social and professional opportunities. When she did appear in public,
her elegance and reticence were interpreted as hauteur and aloofness.
Ironically, as her self-confidence and self-esteem dwindled, she was
regarded increasingly as Canada's grande dame of the literary world.

While Ethel worked on the story collection, there were extended periods of physical misery and anxiety for the Wilsons, but life was also
sometimes good. Although they curtailed their social life further and
further each year, they still enjoyed a wide circle of personal friends who
were loyal to them in times of distress. A letter to the Crawleys in this
period reveals that they could still entertain on quite a scale; one day,
they were having eighteen for lunch (ham and Melton Mowbray pies),
but at the last minute everyone had to be cancelled because Wallace's
prostate problem flared up.[1] They still travelled, though cautiously.
They made their annual excursions to Kelowna, but Ethel would write to

John Gray: 'We came up gradually, my heart in my mouth a good part of the way.'[2] In the summer of 1960, Wallace in fact suffered a mild heart attack while they were vacationing in the Okanagan. That fall she wrote insightfully about herself: 'How much children we all remain! In Wallace's awfullest times, how alone I feel, loving friends or no, & need *him* to turn to, & he can't be there.'[3] Every time Wallace was sick and in hospital, she felt thrown back to her devastated condition when her father died. But when Wallace was recovered, he was eager, as always, to return to his committee work and the company of friends. Ethel held back socially: 'I always refuse, it's *so* hard on legs & eardrums, but I feel that Wallace is thereby deprived of wandering among his acquaintances.'[4] In 1961 she agreed to one special activity because it combined all the things she loved best – fly-fishing, the British Columbia landscape, and a group of good friends. In May of that year, the Wilsons were invited by the Haig-Browns to be part of a little fishing excursion north of Campbell River. In addition to Anne and Roddy Haig-Brown, their son Alan, and his wife, the party included Geoff and Margaret Andrew and Larry and Margaret MacKenzie. Their destination was Salmon River at Kelsey Bay. She described to John Gray her apprehension about making such a trip with no doctor or hospital nearer than sixty miles of rough roads. But on May 18 she could write to Mary McAlpine: 'Here we are on a lovely fly-fishing party composed of the most perfect component parts that ever went on a junket together';[5] and to John Gray: 'Little or no fishing for W, none for me, but simply to sit on a chair on a solitary green bank of a river with Margaret Andrew, talking and not talking, with W sitting on the grassy bank casting and not casting, was heaven with blue sky overhead ... and before, at, & after dinner such fun.'[6] Knitting was the only activity Ethel could now continue, but her pleasure in being on holiday was in no way diminished. On their way home, they stopped at Parksville's Island Hall, where they were joined for a couple of days by Nan Cheney and the Crawleys.

In 1961 Ethel had an experience that must have made her think again about Aunt Eliza, for she was presented to the Queen and Prince Philip in a small ceremony in Vancouver in which the wives of former CMA presidents were given a silver brooch for their services. She wrote about it to the Crawleys and to Mary McAlpine, saying that it was 'a lovely surprise,' and that she felt she had earned the honour for her year and a half's hard work. Nevertheless, she felt rather sorry for the Queen, 'poor lamb,' who surely must have been too busy for such a slight occasion.[7]

The other memorable event of 1961 came first in the form of a telegram dated 2 September from Claude Bissell, chairman of the Canada Council: there it was announced that along with nine other Canadians distinguished for their work in the arts, humanities, and social sciences, Ethel Wilson had been chosen to receive one of the newly created Canada Council Medals. A few days later, a cheque for $2,000 arrived in the mail. The following week there was an article in the *Vancouver Sun* congratulating the two local recipients of the award, Wilson and her painter friend Lawren Harris.[8] Other winners included the former governor general and Ethel's acquaintance, Vincent Massey, another painter from the Group of Seven, A.Y. Jackson, poet E.J. Pratt, composer Healey Willan, ethnologist Marius Barbeau, musician Wilfred Pelletier, Quebec historian and priest Lionel-Adolphe Groulx, and, posthumously, Brooke Claxton, distinguished lawyer and the Council's first chairman. All the winners were past seventy; Ethel was the only woman.

To celebrate this award and to give Book Week a special launch, the local Community Arts Council and Book Fair Committee hosted what was subsequently referred to as 'Ethel Wilson Night' at the B.C. Electric Auditorium on 10 November 1961. Ethel was reluctant to attend and wrote to the Crawleys that 'the picture of myself simpering on a platform while [others] spoke kindly, & then arising to make a "speech" myself – [is] quite terrible to me,'[9] and she only agreed to be there if she did not have to sit in front of the audience and if the talk focused on the Canada Council rather than on herself. But John Gray was flown out specially for the evening, and he gave a speech based on reading through their correspondence of the previous fifteen years. While Gray had never shown himself to be especially insightful when it came to editing Wilson's writing, he was nonetheless perfectly adept at nurturing her talent where it counted most, and this skill is evident in his account of their relationship. He began by pointing out that she had a well-honed talent when she first approached Macmillan with her stories – like someone who sits down to the piano for the first time and can play! What she lacked, however, that he as a publisher tried to supply her with, was self-confidence. He lamented that her books did not make her fortune, but their special qualities of insight into character, gentle irony, and love of B.C. landscape and the sea were not great crowd-pleasing effects. 'It is hard to interest people,' he observed disparagingly of Canadian culture, 'in the cool urbane subtleties of vin rosé when they have grown up on Red Eye.' He aptly summarized his little speech as 'a tribute of pride and pleasure in association – a testimony of affection and deep respect.'[10] Ethel, knowing in advance that John would be there, answered his tribute by calling theirs the ideal relationship between publisher and writer, pointing out that because she was a private, not a public, person, she was truly terrified always by public recognition and John Gray had been the perfect buffer. In her talk,[11] she also discussed how the Massey Commission had led to the Canada Council, and how these were stages in the development of a significant place for the arts in the country's life. She pointed out that when she was young, one bought a new hat, or new bicycle, but not a new book, and that had changed. She took this opportunity to refer publicly again to her favourite authors, including Shakespeare, Donne, Fielding, Trollope, James, Proust, Conrad, and Ivy Compton-Burnett, though in letters she often cited *Anna Karenina* as being in her opinion the greatest novel of all.[12] She also drew attention in this talk to the writing of Canadian exploration and history that absorbed her deeply, mentioning works like the *Journals and Letters of Simon Fraser*, Samuel Hearne's *Journey to the Northern Ocean*, the journal of Henry Kelsey, Margaret Ormsby's *History of British Columbia*, and Captain Walbran's *British Columbia Coast Names*. (Another local book which she frequently praised in letters was R.M. Patterson's *Dangerous River*.) Other special guests who spoke at 'Ethel Wilson Night' included Norman (Larry) MacKenzie from UBC and Donald Stainsby, the literary critic for the *Vancouver Sun*, whom Ethel had come to like. She was thrilled by so many friends in attendance, including Margaret and Jack Laurence, and especially by Lawren Harris being there, because he had become almost wholly reclusive. After speeches were concluded, the Wilsons were driven to the Georgian Club at the Ritz Hotel, where Isabel Tupper and Amy Buckerfield hosted a party in Ethel's honour. The whole evening was a very gratifying experience, professionally and personally. 'I rollicked unashamedly in love & praise,' she wrote to the Crawleys. 'It was a *heavenly* evening ... warm-hearted & happy.'[13]

But the Canada Council Medal also brought an invitation to Ottawa to receive the award at a special dinner ceremony on 19 February 1962. Aged seventy-four and severely crippled, Ethel did not think it was something she could manage. On her last trip to Ottawa, she had been humiliated at Rideau Hall by a massive nosebleed, and these had become more frequent and excessive.[14] But Wallace, always optimistic and adventurous, kept encouraging her to make the trip (they could visit their Toronto friends, he urged); and so she set about planning what to wear and what to take with her. Shopping for clothes was difficult in a wheelchair, and she now had a Haida dressmaker who made most of her clothes. The dressmaker, in fact, was Sophie Reid, mother of Bill Reid, who, Ethel noted, was becoming known for his jewelry-making and carving.[15] For the presentation dinner, she had Sophie take one of her old ball gowns and turn it into a dinner dress. 'I hope for the best,' she wrote to the Crawleys, and of her dressmaker, she added, 'She has the grandest *air* & pale blue hair, you'd think she was a social marquise. Where did she learn dressmaking?'[16]

The Wilsons flew first to Toronto, where once again they stayed at the Park Plaza Hotel on Bloor Street, and from there visited the Duncans and the Grays; and they had dinner with Mary McAlpine, who was now married to Kildare Dobbs, the writer and employee at Macmillan who had worked on *Mrs Golightly and Other Stories*. They travelled on to Ottawa, where they stayed at the Chateau Laurier, a CPR hotel reminiscent of the Hotel Frontenac at Quebec City, which had impressed itself indelibly on Ethel's sight sixty-four years before as the boat bringing the Malkin and Edge ladies to Canada made its way up the St Lawrence River. On the night of 19 February, they taxied out through streets banked high with snow to the Ottawa Country Club on Aylmer Road, Ethel in her newly fashioned dinner dress and Wallace in his dinner jacket, and after drinks and hors d'oeuvres sat down to dinner with approximately eighty guests.[17] Ethel saved the menu, which lists green turtle soup to begin, followed by sole meunière, braised beef tenderloin with vegetables and salad, and frozen rum mousse for dessert.[18] Some of the other medal winners were present, including Marius Barbeau, who had made Ethel feel so uncomfortable at Nan Cheney's house more than twenty years ago, and Vincent Massey, who had graciously hosted a luncheon for Ethel in 1956 when he was governor general. Their Vancouver friend Lawren Harris was ill and could not come to Ottawa, but Bess was there to accept the medal on his behalf. It was a grander occasion than 'Ethel Wilson Night,' and more intimidating for the author, but again a wholly gratifying one, though Wilson had humbly written to the Council's director, 'I only wish my attainments were greater & more pertinent.'[19] The Wilsons took the train home to Vancouver; it would be their last trip across the country, but, as McAlpine observes, they were very content.

Although Ethel Wilson was deeply gratified by the honours that came her way (and there was a further honour in the Lorne Pierce Medal from the Royal Society of Canada in 1964), she remained sceptical about the grants and fellowships that were being awarded to aspiring young artists. She wrote letters of reference to the Canada Council for ambitious young applicants like Mary McAlpine and Ronald Hambleton, though her enthusiasm for their apprentice work was guarded. She felt there was an important distinction between being encouraged to write and feeling within oneself compelled to do so. Her own apprenticeship was secret, and she sent out her work only when she felt she could sit down at the piano and play, and (to expand on John Gray's metaphor) she did not ask for money in order to take lessons. She gave a brief talk about Mazo de la Roche on the CBC in 1961 as part of a program eulogizing the late author. She admitted to the Crawleys that she found it difficult to read de la Roche's work, but that she wanted nonetheless 'to point out to listening smarties that ... at a time when grants & researches were not two a penny, at a time when young people were not served buttered toast & whiskey & encouragement, this young woman [de la Roche] went ahead *on her own*, & achieved a popularity & "success" that was amazing.'[20] Her response to the first collection of stories published by William McConnell's Klanak Press summed up her attitude: 'A legend has gone round among the younger writers in these parts that there is a tremendous amount of brilliant stuff with no outlet. I am inclined to think that brilliant stuff will find an outlet. If this is the best of what there is, it isn't very good.' She thought the production values for this volume were of very high quality; nonetheless, she concluded with unveiled sarcasm: 'a good coffin but a poor corpse.'[21] She kept wondering if the newly established Koerner Foundation in Vancouver, of which Wallace was a board member, would find sufficient first-class work to support. This thinking was an extension of her views on the teaching of creative writing.[22]

Closely connected was her view on the subject of education in general. She admired and supported the work of universities and had many friends who taught at UBC. In 1955 (after Wallace's first coronary), the Wilsons had donated Little Rock on Bowen Island to UBC for faculty to have a quiet recreational spot in which to work, and through that generous gift they made connections with several of the younger academics. One of these was the architect Arthur Erickson, whom they invited to dinner, and whose bourgeoning career they followed with great interest. When Northrop Frye received an honorary degree from UBC in June of 1963, they extended an invitation to Frye and his wife to dine at their place. What Ethel admired in both of these men was their academic creativity, though neither had a Ph.D. She was defensive at times about her own lack of post-secondary education, and when it came to the study of literature specifically, she promoted the values of being self-taught. Her account of discovering Donne, who would mean so much to her writing, is probably the best example of this attitude:

> Long before the return of John Donne to general favour, a chance word somewhere in one of the journals sent me in search of him. I cannot describe the fascination of discovery and exploration. I blundered on and on, dazzled but illuminated by that light that no one disclosed to me. It would be fine, I think now, to have been well taught about John Donne; there is so much to learn. But it was finest for me to discover him for myself, and then, after years, to search and enquire and find and read up and touch his marble toes in St. Paul's Cathedral.[23]

She also recommended discovering *Hamlet* for oneself – 'to see revealed ... the light and dark of the soul, without one warning, without one pre-conception.' Several readings, she observes, and you make bold with your own opinions and reach the conclusion that 'the Freudian guess is a shabby fabrication; the mystery is still there.' She suspects, in other words, that literature cannot be taught: 'Shakespeare shows it in thunder and lightning, but he does not explain.' The excitement of intellectual discovery is something that happens to the inquisitive, self-educated person who has a little learning; for that person there is a freshness of discovery that is never experienced by those who are 'taught.'

If there is a hint of 'crankiness' in these ideas, as Macmillan readers detected in her writing about juvenile delinquency in 'The Vat and the Brew,' it was an aspect of her character that was growing stronger with time. She was fully aware of this in social relations and wrote to the Crawleys in July 1962: 'I reproach myself that now, in age, I permit myself to dislike the company of some people ... One would feed & clothe them if needed & possible, & "love" in the Christian meaning of the term; but "liking" is different.'[24] It also emerged in her increasingly outspoken views on public affairs and the state of the world. She expressed openly her anti-Americanism in letters to friends, deploring the hiring of Americans to fill teaching posts at UBC in the early 1960s. She wrote to John Gray that she did not want to hear 'an American lecturer ... with two American degrees, shooting off his face about Canadian literature.' This was during the Cuban missile crisis, and she observed that, while she supported Kennedy, she could not help feeling that the 'U.S. is reaping the whirlwind for so many things ... from Hiroshima to the Bay of Pigs.'[25]

Her 'crankiness' was also evident in her views on wealth, which for
someone from her social stratum was a complicated matter. She
deplored the great gap between rich and poor: '... it maddens you when
you see so many too filthy rich people ... too great contrasts.'[26] What
especially maddened her was lack of self-awareness among the moneyed
class. She wrote ungenerously of her friend Ella Fell that 'rich people
don't even *know* they're rich, do they ... the feeling comes over one
quite often.'[27] That feeling was especially focused in her relations with
the Buckerfields, whose talk, she complained, was usually about 'multi-
millionaire business friends, expensive resorts.'[28] Her in-laws represented in her mind 'the ambitions and success and characteristics of
"the Establishment."'[29] In England they had connections with members
of the extended royal family (their daughter Mary had done a 'stately
homes' program and lunched with the Duke of Bedford). While very
supportive of the monarchy, Ethel was highly critical of the elite status
bestowed on any members of the royal family 'unless they are useful
people & un-snob.'[30] Overwhelmed by the materialism of Christmas celebrations in 1961, she wrote to the Crawleys, in the spirit of her Methodist forebears, that she viewed a desperate world avoiding 'the life & truth
of Christ whom presumably we celebrate with all this, and our departure
from his simple difficult truth which might really save us from mistrust,
and hate, and nonsense.'[31]

The Wilsons were not wealthy in the sense of having a personal fortune; their material well-being derived from Wallace's earnings as a doctor and from the investment of part of those earnings for retirement.
But they did have enough money to afford servants, which for Ethel was
the especially complicated part of having money. The master-servant
relationship, which in 'Lilly's Story' she prophetically saw could be just
as binding and oppressive from the point of view of the master, was
becoming a source of great personal difficulty for the Wilsons. With all
their physical problems, they had become increasingly dependent on
Mrs Marshall, who was an extraordinarily efficent housekeeper. Unlike
Mrs Tufts, who amused Ethel daily with her stories and anecdotes of
'ordinary working people,' Phyllis Marshall was a somewhat austere, reticent woman whose family and connections were very much middle-
class. Cleanliness and order in the apartment were her priorities. She
was a good cook, but she was 'allergic,' as Wilson several times phrased
it, to entertaining. As the Wilsons grew less able and willing to dine out,
they wanted to entertain friends for lunch and dinner at their apartment, but encountered various subtle forms of resistance on the part of

Mrs Marshall. The latter, according to Ethel's letters, was cooperative and cheerful one day, but sullen and refusing the next. In a letter to the Crawleys in 1961, she wrote, '... my schizophrenic arbiter has come twice into the bedroom with knit brows and baleful glum looks. I wish her moods weren't law to me.'[32] Ethel grew angry for allowing herself to be dominated in this relationship, but it continued, as a letter to Margaret Andrew of 10 February 1962 reveals: '... our Mrs Marshall has been not only difficult, but is a very sick woman, we think. I suppose we'll go on and on with this situation.'[33] Later that year, she complained bitterly that Mrs Marshall was making it impossible for them to have company at the apartment: 'Her passion is vacuuming, on hands and knees dusting, wall washing, cupboard & china washing ... I'd prefer it dirty than bad temper, & then so exhausted that getting our meal is a chore, & a guest is *too* much. I've tried to make it clear that we'd rather be happy & able to see the occasional friend, than so damn clean.'[34] By December they had hired an extra cleaning lady for every other Tuesday so that they could invite friends in for a meal occasionally 'without storms or apology.'[35] She wrote to Margaret Laurence in March 1963 that the winter had been hell – 'illness throughout. Mine doesn't matter, because it's not critical, but my darling W. was terribly ill over Christmas and New Years, then operation, then recovering, then laryngitis etc. ... and me flu, and an absolute withdrawal from life.'[36]

The difficult relations with Mrs Marshall came to a head in April, and Ethel described in detail to several friends the showdown with 'our dictator in the kitchen, our black fairy, with us 11 years.' The crisis erupted on a Monday afternoon when two Malkin relatives dropped by for tea. Mrs Marshall objected that it was 'wash day,' that company was not welcome, and threatened to leave. Ethel, knowing there was hardly any washing to be done, lost her temper and said, 'Yes, *do* & I'll make it as easy as possible for you.' She wrote to John Gray April 23rd: 'To my horror there were hysterics, & her "life is over" if she leaves. She was just bullying me as usual. So I read some riot acts – & now my word goes – but she is black with misery (I *wish* she'd go!) & the house most uncheerful. You see during W's many illnesses, her help & devotion made it impossible for me to say Go. She is a very unhappy woman & complicated, & sick, & it is very difficult.'[37]

But the confrontation apparently effected a change to everyone's benefit. Ethel wrote letters to several friends analysing the situation and what she recognized was her own uncharacteristic behaviour. To Margaret Andrew, she wrote on May 10: '... the kitchen atmosphere is [now] sweetened (gentle and humble apologies ... and was it ever needed!) I had been so tough eventually and that was good, but toughness is not my métier, & I think the many months of increased bullying and sulks on her part, & then my ultimate explosion has actually been bad for my arthritis.' Several pages later in this same letter, she went over the story again: 'Every room continually permeated with rudeness, passionate cleanliness, sulks & bad temper. The fact that I willingly accepted her leaving – which she never dreamed I would, was a shock that stunned her for some time, & then we teetered on a curious condition of stun & silence (I had urged her to go) – very unpleasant. W & I icy to her. Incredible. But gosh, how would I have coped, my joints being so criminal now, with establishing a new régime! Praise God from whom all blessings flow ... And it's a treat to see someone changed (as by fire) & mysteriously kind & happy. Long may it continue.'[38] In fact, Phyllis Marshall remained a loyal housekeeper and friend to the Wilsons for the rest of their lives. She told her friends that she could never leave them because they were so dependent on her and because she had such deep affection and regard for Wallace. She viewed Ethel's harsh reprimand as the result of all the medication she was taking for arthritis, but confided to close friends that Ethel had become a very difficult woman to work for, a grande dame indeed.

There is no question that Ethel now felt imprisoned by her physical condition, and letters in which she complains bitterly about the state of the world or the behaviour of acquaintances are invariably framed by references to 'irascible joints,' to knees, hands, wrists, and right hip that are 'diabolic.'[39] It occurs in her comments about Dorothy Livesay, who, she felt, had overstepped the boundaries of friendship on several occasions. Livesay worked for UNESCO in Zambia for four years from 1959 to 1963, and at one point she referred a young African to Wallace to be helped into a Canadian medical school. The young man had no qualifications or references, and, when he turned up in Winnipeg needing money, Wallace expended considerable effort to put him in contact with those who were in a position to advise and help. Ethel, who had fussed over this matter, was cross to learn that, on her return, Livesay could no longer remember the young man. Livesay had complained to mutual friends that she didn't like being back in Vancouver, and Ethel wrote to Nan Cheney: 'Oh dear, so Dorothy Livesay's back! I thought she was going to queen it in Africa for some time yet. If she hates Vancouver why doesn't she go to Victoria where there's a nice little university too. When I hear that whining voice over the telephone, if I do, I'll have the jim jams, as by this time I'm an old lady that has aches & pains & can't stand too imperceptive people.' She told Nan the story of the hopeful medical student and Livesay's presumption and insensitivity in such matters, adding reluctantly, '... but if I don't warm up to her she'll think I've gone snooty and Canada Council-Medally which is certainly not the case.'[40]

Ethel was equally impatient and outraged with a *Vancouver Sun* reporter, Mac Reynolds, who wrote an article about her for a series about previous winners of the Canada Council Medal that appeared in the *Toronto Star Weekly*, 4 April 1964. Reynolds interviewed her at the apartment early in the year, and she viewed him as 'a nice very he-man big person ... quiet, pleasant,' although she found it 'difficult to know what he wanted to know.'[41] To most readers, the article would have seemed like the man as Wilson describes him – 'quiet, pleasant' – but it deeply offended the author on several levels, and again she wrote to her friends about her disappointment. To John Gray and Margaret Andrew, she complained bitterly that Reynolds presented her as 'a writer of domestic trivia, & tittle-tattle without significance,'[42] that it showed poor judgment by the Canada Council 'to give so Victorian and conventional a person a medal for nothing at all.' She found the tone in the opening paragraph, where Reynolds described her as 'stately,' as unnecessarily insulting and went on to detail the errors in the article, what she called 'gratuitous inexactitudes': the reference to her pupils wrestling bears on the way to school, her books being published in Canada rather than England, the description of agents, in the plural, as her willing slaves, etc.[43] Gray wrote back tactfully on April 22nd suggesting that 'the things that bothered you will pretty well pass unnoticed' and suggested that Reynolds 'seems really to have intended respect and liking,'[44] but the letter she wrote to Margaret Andrew on May 8, angrily referring to Reynolds's 'assinine piece,' makes it clear she had not been placated. She told Margaret Laurence that she dropped her copy of the *Star Weekly* down the garbage chute.[45]

But Reynolds's article lost all importance when Wallace had another heart attack, his fourth, on 13 May 1964. That morning, Ethel had written to Desmond Pacey that they were about to leave for a trip to Vancouver Island to spend a holiday week at Parksville with the Crawleys: 'a precious time for all devoted to Alan, reading to him ... talking together, and all having a needed and health-giving lazy time.'[46] But later that day ('thank God it came before we left home'),[47] Wallace complained of chest pains and had to be taken to hospital. A week later, she wrote to Margaret Laurence, 'I did not think I could ever live through the sweat and misery of another. But apparently one can.'[48] And another week later, she wrote to Laurence again: 'These heart attacks of his *kill* me, there's no pretending. However, it is the least bad of all yet, but I am older, and arthritiker, and more anxious if possible every time.'[49]

Wilson's crankiness cannot be separated from the physical pain she was experiencing and her increasing anxiety about Wallace's condition. But perhaps it was also generated, in part, by her inability now to work on an extended piece of writing. She had told John Gray back in 1959 that, as she had intimated to him before, there was another novel she wanted to write, that it would be called 'The Special One,' and that she was tempted to 'roar into it,' but that at her age it was beyond possibility and she couldn't touch it – nonetheless, she added, 'what a story!'[50] We can only guess what that novel would have been about. She had contempt for novels about one's childhood and growing up, though, of course, she artfully refracted just such a story through a narrative about her great aunt in *The Innocent Traveller*. The title of the phantom novel suggests that it could have been about either her father (perhaps his life in South Africa, given the amount of work involved in its writing) or perhaps about Wallace. Gray's reply, which seems to be based on conversations they had had, is also suggestive: 'I do regret that the story which you really long to tell seems closed to you ... You have something important to say, some commentary on human relations. Can't it be told in some way that would not give pain?'[51] The reference to something painful about this story suggests perhaps a story about Wallace's immediate family, and her relations with his mother and with the Buckerfields. But speculation must stop at that point as there are no other references to this project, which Wilson apparently had held in her mind for a long time. Seemingly more manageable was a request from John Gray to write a history of Vancouver, to be illustrated by George Kuthan, but after writing three chapters she felt it was more than she could handle. One chapter was eventually published in 1967 as 'Young Vancouver Seen through the Eyes of Youth.'

The desire to write was still there and there was social pressure to do so; but that desire was repeatedly frustrated, and perhaps that is what gave rise to the essay 'Admissions, Seabirds, and People.'[52] In 1962 the Crawleys sent Ethel a copy of the *Montrealer* which contained a short story by Alice Munro titled 'The Office.' The story, among other things, explains how hard it is for a woman in a social gathering to claim that she is a writer. Ethel wrote back: 'What an *excellent* thing by Alice Munro. I don't know when I've read a short piece that so pleased me. Isn't she *good!*[53] It became the occasion for the essay, which begins with a nod to the story and Wilson's observation 'I have never before seen in print [this] admission of a frailty, a peculiarity, a folly, or an honesty which I share with her.' To 'women in minkery' at cocktail parties (she was thinking specifically of Babe Taylor and Ella Fell) who ask if she is a writer and what is she writing about, Wilson proposes replying, 'I am writing about an elephant,' as a way of getting rid of them. This comic proposal only thinly veils Ethel's painful earnestness in society and an anger that erupts when she finds herself, late in life, still unable to say she is a writer without feeling embarrassment:

> The most teasing comment to encounter is 'I do so envy you your writing – it's such a *lovely* hobby!' Curses rise within you – 'It's not a hobby, damn you, it's next but one to my life. If I were a man you'd never say that.' But you do not, or should not, utter those words. It is better to smile, or smirk if you cannot smile, and say No, it is not so lovely a hobby.

With almost no transition, Wilson concludes the essay with a description of various seabirds in flight, a celebration of nature, where hesitancies and ambiguities vanish. Whether this essay was given as a talk or intended for publication is not clear. It remained in manuscript until the 1987 publication of a selection of her stories, essays, and letters.

Wilson's interest and pleasure in young women writers in Canada was especially rewarded in her friendship with Margaret Laurence. There was nothing cranky or posturing in this relationship: she wrote to Laurence with the kind of affection she felt for Audrey Butler and for her godchildren, but with the additional excitement of being able to talk about literary craft and the life of the writer. What thrilled her at the outset was Laurence's imaginative scope – particularly her ability to write with insight and compassion about other parts of the world and about issues of race. After receiving from Laurence a copy of *The Tomorrow-Tamer*, her 1963 book of short stories set in Ghana, Wilson wrote: 'You have a remarkable awareness of that frightening difference in race, and of the continuous pitfalls, and of a need for an understanding which (I'm afraid) could be hardly human (try as hard as you will) but divine ... Relatively few human beings have compassed it.'[54] What also thrilled Wilson was what she called Laurence's 'natural gift,' the absence of posturing or imitation. Wilson never bestowed such high praise on a living writer as she did in these lines written to Laurence in November 1963: 'I have never known among what are called "our younger writers" – or our mature ones – anyone in whom I have not unwillingly detected an attitude or effort ... and towards whom I can pour out full admiration, with a kind of knowledge of belief in the power, resource, and resonance of their writing ... all natural, not studied and artful.'[55] And she continued to 'pour out' her admiration as long as she was able. When the next spring Laurence sent her a copy of *The Stone Angel*, she wrote breathlessly: 'Dear Margaret what a darling you are to send me the *glorious* book ... I simply can't say all I feel ... To me, this is a *great* book. I believe some people could not read it, because it is the very life of life, and they do not know life ... It has splendour ... the night in the cannery is terrific.'[56] She also called it a 'gorgeous' book, praising its production values, and thanked Laurence '1000 times' for the autographed copy. Then she did something she had never done before. She wrote a few lines for bookseller Bill Duthie to use for advertising: '*The Stone Angel* by Margaret Laurence is a magnificent book. After the first few pages this book mounts gradually into the beauties and terrors and follies of life and age. "Pride was my wilderness." Mrs Laurence's powerful use of language is natural to her, unforced, and is rare in our day and place. Some readers may find the book too painful, but it is worth the pain.'[57] Only one thing troubled her in the relation with Laurence – the latter's separation and eventual divorce from her husband. Jack Laurence visited the Wilsons in their apartment in the summer of 1964, and Ethel wrote fulsomely in praise of his engineer's experience of the world – Africa, Afghanistan, Pakistan – adding, 'May I say I do like him *terrifically!*' Indeed, she was so impressed with Margaret's husband, she said in a strangely old-fashioned postscript to her letter, that she feels somehow that she should address Margaret now as 'Mrs Jack Laurence.'[58] Seeing Margaret as a reasonable and very loving woman, she could not understand how she could want to live apart from her husband and felt helpless trying to reply to Margaret's announcement. Her letter, written sometime in 1965, began, 'I don't know what to say to you except how much I feel with you and it's not fair that you – and Jack – should have to face this thing.'[59] It was simply impossible for her to imagine this separation, and apart from saying that life can be cruel, she had little to say by way of comfort or advice, yet the fact of Margaret's divorce haunted their correspondence.

Although Wilson had almost completely stopped writing, she remained very much in the public eye in 1964, when three new pieces were published. Robert Weaver kept encouraging her to send stories and essays for *Tamarack Review*. The story that appeared, the last one published during her lifetime, was 'A Visit to the Frontier,' her frightening account of a couple's separation and death, which had been written during Wallace's lengthy illness in the late 1940s. It had appeared in one of the many tables of contents Wilson had drawn up for *Mrs Golightly and Other Stories* but was cut at an early stage in the planning. One reader found it implausible, and perhaps Wilson herself felt it would draw bad luck, but she sent it to Weaver, and since its appearance in the autumn 1964 issue of *Tamarack Review* it has become one of her more frequently anthologized pieces. Printed in the same issue was an essay titled 'Series of Combination of Events and Where Is John Goodwin?' The essay pays tribute to four people with little connection to each other in a format that might be described as digressive or, according to another poetics, as rhizomatic. The four people who appear in the essay are Tom Tokunaga, the Japanese student the Wilsons employed when they were first married, the Irish-born novelist Brian Moore, John Sutherland, the short-lived editor of *Northern Review*, and a high-school student by the name of John Goodwin. Tokunaga, describing the spill of a custard in the meat keeper as resulting from a 'series of combination of events,' provided the essay with part of its title. Wilson herself had been asked at the last minute to chair a reading by Brian Moore at the public library, but sitting at the front behind the speaker, she had been unable to hear his words. She did hear, however, *Northern Review*, and while Moore read from his book, her mind wandered back to her association with John Sutherland. Next day, she got out her back issues of the journal and found a note to herself directing her to reread the curious but promising little story by a West Vancouver high-school student by the name of John Goodwin. The story is reprinted within the essay, and the question 'Where is John Goodwin' brings Wilson's essay to a close. Not being able to hear Moore read, Wilson says that 'philosophy took over as usual,' and in this light I would suggest that the key sentence in the essay comes after Moore referred to *Northern Review* and she rehearsed in her mind her association with the deceased John Sutherland:

> The quick turn and glance of Brian Moore brought all these pictures through my mind rapidly as wind moves over sea and disturbs the waters, passes on, and when the thoughts had passed on, I looked up and – so quick it was – Brian Moore was answering the girl in red.

Perhaps the philosophy that Wilson alludes to here is something like chaos theory mentioned before and the 'butterfly effect,' whereby the mere flapping of a butterfly's wings can alter weather patterns at a great distance. In this philosophy, which reminds one of 'Tuesday and Wednesday' and *Love and Salt Water* especially, chance is supreme, and cause and effect are deemed irrational concepts for explaining human experience; nonetheless, it allows for self-organization and self-awareness in the form of the essay Wilson has written.

The other piece of writing that appeared in 1964 was a tribute to Alan Crawley, in *Canadian Literature*.[60] Once again it was an opportunity to celebrate the editors and writers who, like herself, worked on their own during the 1930s and 1940s – self-taught men and women who worked without the assistance of government grants or creative writing classes. The essay is important as literary history, providing a sketch of Crawley's pioneer family and his work as editor of *Contemporary Verse*, the literary magazine he founded with the assistance of his wife, Jean, and his business manager, Floris McLaren, and edited from 1941 to 1952. Because he was blind, all the submissions had to be read to him aloud, and he then typed them out in Braille for further reflection before replying to the authors of the poems. The essay is imbued with Wilson's enormous admiration for Crawley, his vision and courage. From among her contemporaries (Crawley was born in 1887), Wilson was closer to this man than to any other writer.

The year 1964 saw the steady accumulation of recognition for Wilson's work: the first graduate thesis on her fiction was completed that year by Helen Margaret Clarke at UBC, and Robertson Davies made his statement in *Holiday* magazine that 'Ethel Wilson produces fiction as elegantly fashioned as any that is written elsewhere.' Expressing many of her own views on the subject of literary art, Davies pointed out that Wilson was a stylist and that 'a lack of strong feeling for language is one of the principal weaknesses of Canadian prose writers.'[61] Wilson greatly admired Davies' comic novels about Salterton, especially *A Mixture of Frailties*, and so his high opinion of her work would have been very gratifying. Yet while to her admirers 1964 might have seemed a good year for Ethel Wilson, it was in fact a year of increasing problems. Wallace had seemed to recover from his heart trouble in May well enough that they decided to spend the month of August in Kelowna, as they had now done for at least ten years. Ethel cherished that time every year at the Eldorado Arms Hotel, where they were cut off from social obligations and could enjoy the warmth and relaxation of the lakeside resort. Being alone with Wallace and having his undivided attention and companionship still remained at the centre of her heart's desire. They knew it was risky to make the long trip through winding roads and canyons, and so they flew to Kelowna and arranged for the Whites (niece Mary Buckerfield and her husband, Victor) to drive their car up. But shortly after they arrived, Ethel fell and had to be taken to hospital; while she was being cared for, Wallace had another heart attack and was taken to hospital, as well. It was a prolonged, anxious time, not a holiday, and when they were well enough to travel again, they flew home, knowing they would never be able to journey to the interior of their beloved province again.

Then, on 20 December 1964, just hours before leaving to spend Christmas in Victoria, Wallace had another heart attack, his sixth, and the most damaging. His doctors knew that his life now could not be very long. 'It is hardly bearable,' Ethel wrote, 'to think that my dear Wallace is again in hospital, suffering in the oxygen tent, & the future uncertain.'[62] He remained in hospital over Christmas, and Ethel was taken by family and friends through a series of January snowstorms to visit him almost daily. His recovery was slow, almost glacial, complicated by other problems – diabetes, prostate, and the misery of bedsores. Shortly before suffering the heavy coronary, Wallace had fallen on the icy steps at the front of their Kensington apartment. The year before, Ethel had also fallen, despite the assistance of Wallace and a taximan. In despair, realizing they could no longer live in their apartment with such a dangerous entrance, Ethel cast around for another place to live while Wallace was recovering in hospital. Fortunately, an apartment became available in Killarney Manor, a gracious and imposing white building set back in lawn and trees on Point Grey Road, and while Wallace was in hospital, she and Mrs Marshall arranged for the move. It was an ideal location because, as Ethel later wrote to Margaret Laurence, 'light pours in on every side ... we sit beside a huge glass window-door opening on a simple and quite large balcony looking north and west over sea and mountain – and those things matter so much to us.'[63]

But 1965 was a hard year, nonetheless. Ethel suffered from an attack of shingles, followed by a period of such intense pain from arthritis that she was hospitalized for a long stretch of time. She described herself to Laurence as 'appallingly and painfully lame, hardly walkable,'[64] though her first concern, as always, was for Wallace, who had not gained his strength back this time. He sold his car and they were resigned now to both being invalids, though she dared to hope that they would have some fairly healthy days, months, even years, in the new place they loved so much.

But Ethel's hopes were fading when she wrote to John Gray that Wallace's illness was progressing terribly, that 'he has been very much on the brink.'[65] She refused any literary involvements. A John Rackliffe from Ontario wanted permission and assistance to tape some of Wilson's stories and to read them at literary gatherings, because he thought the aural pleasures of her style were comparable to Schubert,[66] but Ethel was too preoccupied with Wallace's condition and maintaining their fragile status quo to give attention to such requests. The doctor visited them daily, and they started a regimen of nurses around the clock. Ethel could not praise Mrs Marshall's goodness enough. Then suddenly on 19 January 1966 it was Ethel who suffered a physical blow with a stroke that paralyzed her left side. Wallace telephoned the news to John Gray and, a few days later, wrote to say that her mental state was hazy, her sight dim, and she had little mobility. It wasn't until 8 March that he could write with his more characteristic optimism that she was beginning to move her left arm and leg again and that her eyesight was coming back.[67] With daily therapy and Wallace's encouragement, Ethel slowly regained the use of her left arm and she was able to read again. She also regained full command of her speech, although her voice was now in a lower register (something she had wished a lifetime for) and words came more slowly. But when a full recovery finally seemed possible, the terrible event happened that Ethel had dreaded all her married life: Wallace died 12 March from a final fatal heart attack. On 13 March, Ethel penned two shaky lines to John Gray: 'My darling died yesterday. How glad I would be to join him.'[68]

CHAPTER FIFTEEN

Widow

1966–1980

We must be great boors to have made so little ... of a writer as fine as
Ethel Wilson. – Gabrielle Roy

Wallace's funeral / 'Unbearably sad' / A 'small finale' / Father /
'Dumb & muttery' / Order of Canada / Arbutus Private Hospital /
22 December 1980

Wallace's funeral took place at Christ Church Cathedral in downtown
Vancouver on Tuesday, March 16th.[1] The church was filled with citizens
who came to pay their respects to one of the country's most distinguished doctors and to the founder of several of the city's cultural and
charitable organizations. To many he was more than a great man who
commanded public respect; he was a friend valued for his loyalty, his
calm and wisdom, and, above all, for his conviviality and his sense of
humour. He was also a man of great public and private dignity. Ethel
was too incapacitated, emotionally and physically, to attend the service.
Mrs Marshall stayed in the apartment with her, and the two women did
not speak of the funeral taking place that day.[2]

There are almost no letters written by Ethel dated 1966. She had no
will to continue living, and in what few letters she did write that year, a
haunting refrain appears: 'I am very unbearably sad now'; [I am] 'so
awfully sad.'[3] Her wish, often repeated, was that she would soon die: '...
my heart aches to join him.'[4]

But when the shock of Wallace's death and the physical numbness she
felt had eased a little, she tried to find the courage to face life once
again. After reading Laurence's *A Jest of God* in the fall of 1966, she wrote

to Margaret to say that as a study in loneliness the book had intensified her sadness, but though she felt very low, she soon hoped to be braver, for that is what Wallace would want.[5] For a brief period – from late 1966 through 1967 – she let herself be drawn into literary projects once again. She was asked if she would contribute an article about the early days in Vancouver to *Habitat* magazine as part of the country's centennial celebrations. She had written three chapters of a personal history of the city back in the early 1960s at John Gray's suggestion, but had abandoned the project as her health grew worse and her anxiety over Wallace increased.[6] Now she took out the opening chapter and reworked it for the magazine with the circular title 'Young Vancouver Seen through the Eyes of Youth.' At the same time, the Alcuin Society in Vancouver had decided to publish a handsome, limited edition of *Hetty Dorval*, with engravings by Gus Reuter, and Ethel agreed to write a brief introductory essay. She also agreed to autograph all 375 copies, which took some time but helped to give shape to the days. This introduction to *Hetty Dorval* would be her last piece of writing. A few other literary interests remained active. Two days before her stroke in January 1966, John Gray had written with the idea of Macmillan publishing an 'Ethel Wilson Reader,' consisting of favourite short stories and passages from longer works.[7] Wallace had written back to Gray saying he thought it was a splendid idea and that it would be a good morale-boosting project for Ethel to work at while recovering from the cerebral haemorrhage.[8] Gray appears not to have proposed the reader again, but in February 1967 she wrote to him herself with the idea for a new book based on the manuscript titled 'Miss Cuppy,' which she had apparently retitled 'Herself When Young.' She knew that some sequences had been used in *Love and Salt Water*, and she was also aware that she no longer had the ability 'to re-write *en gros or en détail*,' but felt nonetheless that some of the manuscript was well written and that Gray might want to consider it. She said he could take a sword to it, that it might only yield a short story, and at the same time, in her old manner, reassured him that she had no ambition to be published.[9] Gray wrote back politely saying he would have a look at the manuscript, that nothing would please him more than a new title from Ethel Wilson, but that he felt it was one they had already seen and decided on.[10] There was no further correspondence on the subject.

Although there is no record of her response, she must have felt very flattered by a short piece written by Hugo McPherson and published in March 1967 in the Toronto *Telegram*.[11] McPherson identified Ethel Wilson as the matriarch and Sibyl of Canadian literature, 'a brilliant woman upon whose sensibility, in Henry James' phrase, nothing is lost.' He also described her as 'a great beauty – a woman of extraordinary physical presence, warmth and wit ... the reigning beauty of her generation in Vancouver.' In a more philosophical and critical vein, he observes shrewdly that in Wilson's fiction 'life is without plot, but full of meaning, and the "virtues" and "eternal verities" are not identical.' Similarly, that fall, she must have been pleased with a CBC radio production in which several people she knew and respected critically assessed her writing.[12] She must have been especially interested in and flattered by Margaret Laurence's claim that Ethel Wilson could create character in fewer words than almost any other writer. It happens almost instantly, says Laurence, because Wilson always implies so much more than she actually writes. On a more personal note, Laurence observes that one could never lie to Ethel Wilson because she would know instantly: she had 'an undeceived eye.' Roy Daniells also spoke about Wilson's extra-ordinary sensibility, so evident in her style. She was not so much a constructor of plots, he observes, as a stylist, but in this light he confesses a preference for the lucidity of *Hetty Dorval* to the more 'stylish' *Swamp Angel.* In a much more critical vein, Sally Creighton argues that Wilson was not able to sustain character for the full space of a novel, that this was her great limitation as a writer. Reflecting on Ethel Wilson, the person with whom she was acquainted, she points out accurately that Wilson believed privileged people owed volunteer service to other people, but that the dilemma for someone with Ethel's sensibility was how to do this service graciously. We can be pretty certain that even in her physically impaired condition, Ethel found this radio conversation stimulating, because she always found critical thinking much more invigorating than simple praise.

We know for certain that she was interested in what Desmond Pacey was writing about her in his forthcoming study in the Twayne series, though she was sceptical about his ability to convey anything like the true nature of what her life had been like. She wrote to her old friend Nan Cheney: 'I'm sure he'll make the best that can be made of such a quiet life as mine. The great thing of my life is Wallace & our great love. That makes a life, but does not necessarily make a *book* unless the writer knows the two people intimately, & he only saw us once, for a short evening.'[13]

But her determination to be brave for Wallace's sake faded as 1967 came to a close. Her letters filled again with despair. She wrote to Mary McAlpine: 'I never, never thought that the absence of my dear, accompanied by physical helplessness would be so unbearable – *and* so inexcusable. He planned everything for my happiness. I am just very stupid & ashamed, because it would be hard for him. But the days pass – "a day's march nearer home," that is incontrovertible ...' She continued in the same letter to deplore her inability to write: 'It enrages me that now that I have more spare time than ever in my life, I have no desire or ability to "write."' Her life now she said was '[a] bare desert, & nothing growing in it.'[14] She wrote to Margaret Laurence at Christmas that her piece in *Habitat* was her 'small finale.'[15]

Her emotional and physical longing for death grew stronger and permeated every letter she wrote, especially those to John Gray, her literary executor, whom she regarded now as a son. In the spring of 1969, she wrote to him in a mood of apology and confession: 'As I shouldn't have told you & probably did, I still long for real illness (e.g. heart) that would take me off & end this wearisome wasting condition, afflicted joints, annihilated memory, & perpetual longing for my Wallace. May you be spared anything like this, John – lost love, yet permanent.'[16] Looking out her apartment window, she wrote to Jean Crawley less openly but more poignantly, reporting that the swallows were returning: 'They have come in bridal couples, little husbands & wives, swerving & floating together ... Wallace & I always treasured them.'[17] As time slowly passed, her despair seemed to mount. She wrote to Gray: 'Never have I missed Wallace so distressingly. I beseech Heaven to take me, but I continue here in partial health & much inadequacy.'[18] Her grief was like physical torment. 'I should not speak of my loss,' she wrote to the Crawleys, 'but I suffer daily and nightly from it,'[19] a loss sometimes edged with metaphysical doubt as when she wrote to John Gray that some day she and Wallace would be together again, she '*hope[d]*.'[20] But to Audrey Butler, a devout Roman Catholic now working for the Church, she wrote with assurance: 'You say so truly that he is near to me in all but spoken word and that he is waiting for me in the unbelievable happiness of eternity ... In reading your wonderful letter, I can feel the marvelous sight of him. There was (and is) still the hard waiting and the undreamed of joy.'[21] In some of these letters, a telling confusion arises. To the Crawleys, referring to her apartment, she slips, then corrects herself: 'My dear house which my Father gave me, still serves me well. I say my "Father," & so he was, but he is my love & my husband. Everything to me.'[22] To visitors, she would sometimes point to Wallace's photographs on the wall and call him her Father in heaven, merging God, father, and husband, but those who knew about the minister's orphaned child would understand and not try to correct her.

Her wish to die remained urgent, but it was nearly fifteen years after Wallace's death before her wish was realized. The months and years passed slowly. At times she still found pleasure in reading: Shakespeare was an abiding companion, but her chief preference now was for travel writing. She marvelled that Mary Kingsley could make her journey through Africa. Perhaps thinking of her parents, she wrote to John Gray, 'It is incredible that a young woman voluntarily & almost alone travelled that formidable country with its alarming population.'[23] In a similar vein, she praised Forster's *A Passage to India* for its understanding of people of different races.[24] Picking up Simon Fraser's *Letters and Journals*, she wrote 'how vivid & fair is the account of that dangerous journey down, & the various encounters with the Indians.' She planned to read next *The Voyages of Alexander Mackenzie* and the writings of Daniel Harmon. But British Columbia travel writing made her keenly aware of Wallace's absence, and she hesitated: 'It makes me long more than ever to be with Wallace travelling up the Fraser towards the Chilcotin & all the superb fishing.'[25]

Her day's routine, much to her chagrin, centred around exercise to rehabilitate her limbs: 'It seems to me I do nothing but therapy exercises, walk clumsily with "walker" down the hall, & a few other things, each blotting out the other.'[26] At night she slept in a brace for comfort. In July 1970 she wrote to Geoff and Margaret Andrew that she was an old lady now at 82 and feeling like 102. 'I do feel old,' she continued, 'almost totally deaf, & no more memory ... I am very lame & my right leg & hip (long since cracked or broken) give me hell ... I am dumb & muttery.'[27] She was accurate in her assessment of memory loss, because just a few weeks later she wrote almost the same letter verbatim to the Andrews. Her old and pleasure-giving habit of letter writing persisted, even though she had little news to send her friends. She wrote short sad letters in a shaky scrawl, pouring out her grief: 'I try to exist without Wallace – it is terrible.'[28] To Nan Cheney: 'I long to see Wallace's special picture, & weep over it.'[29]

Usually the notes to Nan Cheney would beg for her to come and visit because she loved to see 'that lovely face & that gay radiant smile.'[30] Visitors – chiefly relatives – were the special part of the day. From the outset of Ethel's widowhood, the Malkin cousins, many of them retired and beginning to grow old themselves, were generous with their time. Lila Molson frequently took Ethel out for lunch and for a drive around Stanley Park. Ethel's Aunt Jo Malkin also lived at Killarney Manor, and Lila arranged with her aunt that cousin Ursula give a small concert for Ethel on Jo's grand piano: 'Chopin *Études*, Scarlatti,' Ethel wrote, '– heavenly, her stubby little fingers thrilling out those lovely little Chopin chords.'[31] Joseph Malkin and Lucile Parsons visited Wallace's gravesite at Ocean View Cemetery and reported to Ethel that it was being cared for perfectly. Her favourite family visitor was Aunt Jo, her close friend for more than sixty years, and the one remaining link to her youth and family, and when Jo died she felt keenly another severing with the past. With Wallace gone and Ethel in mourning, friends did not come to visit very often. Nan Cheney was the most faithful, sometimes bringing a bottle of dry sherry, and Leon Koerner, a widower, would bring flowers and have a drink with Ethel in the late afternoons – until his death in 1972. An 'agreeable' young academic brightened an afternoon in May 1969. W.H. New had tactfully not requested an interview, but instead brought 'masses of fragrant white lilac' from his garden. 'We had a pleasant brief afternoon visit & a glass of whiskey,' she wrote to John Gray. 'Much easier [than an interview].'[32] She had read and valued New's article about her titled 'The "Genius" of Place and Time: The Fiction of Ethel Wilson.' His article and one published earlier by Helen Sonthoff confirmed for her that her work was not likely to be forgotten, that it would live on as part of a developing continuum of Canadian literature.

In early May 1970, she received a letter from Gabrielle Roy, whose 1945 *Bonheur d'occasion* had been published in English as *The Tin Flute* in 1947, the same year as *Hetty Dorval.* The two writers had never met or corresponded, although Ethel had read some of Roy's books as they came along. Joyce Marshall created a link between them by sending Roy a copy of *Mrs Golightly and Other Stories*, which contained 'To Keep the Memory of So Worthy a Friend,' the piece she had found especially captivating. Now Gabrielle Roy found herself, in turn, captivated by the exquisiteness and 'rare charm' of this writer she had never read before and she wrote Wilson to convey her great delight in her work. Roy was saddened by Ethel's reply, and she wrote to Marshall: 'Poor soul, she does seem very ill, forlorn and diminished. Apparently my letter was an event in a life of sickness and loneliness. Sometimes we are truly inspired to send a letter at just the right moment, one might say. Perhaps I did just that, although I was merely acquitting myself of a debt of gratitude for so much pleasure given by her writing – at her best of a haunting quality.'[33] Regrettably the letters exchanged between Roy and Wilson have not survived. A few years later, Roy would write: 'It's not every day ... that one discovers an Ethel Wilson. We must be great boors to have made so little in a sense of a writer as fine as Ethel Wilson.'[34]

Ethel had been awarded an honorary doctorate, the Canada Council Medal, and the Lorne Pierce Medal, but there was one more honour waiting. In the spring of 1971, she was informed that she had been made a member of the Order of Canada, another medal of service bestowed for the body of her work. She was too frail, of course, to make a trip to Ottawa to be honoured in person at the annual ceremonies for the Order, but in August of that year the scroll and medal were presented to her in person by the Governor General, Roland Michener, at a brief ceremony in the Vancouver Hotel. Ethel enjoyed preparing for the occasion – choosing a dress to wear, thinking of a few words to say – and she enjoyed the pleasure it gave her Malkin cousins, who accompanied her to the little gathering; but the pleasure was fleeting and was soon overwhelmed and washed away again by the great sadness that perpetually engulfed her. In letters she wrote that spoke of the award, most of the space was given to detailing her daily and nightly suffering: 'My thoughts are always with my Love.'[35]

In May 1972, John Gray received a letter from an Idamay Martin, one of Ethel's day nurses, who wrote to say that Ethel had changed mentally in recent months, though she remained about the same physically. Nurse Martin suggested that Macmillan should now send any cheques or business letters directly to Canada Permanent Trust because Ethel could no longer comprehend or manage finances; such transactions, she wrote, confused and upset her for days – as she bluntly phrased it, 'it drives her frantic.' Sensing the special relation between Wilson and Gray, Martin reassured him that Ethel was a wonderful patient, 'one of, if not the best, I have ever had,' and she described the pleasure she and Mrs Marshall experienced taking Ethel to the Hudson's Bay store to shop for a dress and have lunch in the restaurant on the sixth floor. 'She was fascinated by the hordes ... and saw things we did not see. Sometimes she is a riot and so witty. It's so sad to see her deteriorating mentally. Yet at times she is as smart as a whip –'[36] Martin wrote on at length, like one of the garrulous characters from Ethel's fiction. She also reported that Ethel had been upset by a letter Gray had forwarded from the Committee for an Independent Canada, which urged that Canadian authors who published with international houses should switch to Canadian-owned companies.

Wilson's inability to grasp the intent of this letter and her confusion over money matters reflected a sharp decline in her mental capacities. The doctors who attended concluded that what had appeared to be a head cold in late winter had actually been another stroke. Her ability to read also declined sharply, and that summer she spent much of her time trying to write letters. To Nan Cheney she wrote almost every day, though the letters were not always finished. Mrs Marshall and the nurses would remind her that she had just written to Nan – and to others – but Ethel would press on trying to compose her communications, most often invitations begging for someone to visit her. Sometimes the caregivers would not post the notes Ethel had laboured over because they made little sense. The last letter she attempted to John Gray was dated 8 July 1972.

In the spring of 1974, the Wilsons' lawyer cousin, David Tupper (son of Isabel and Reg Tupper), to whom Ethel had delegated power of attorney, decided that, in her present condition and given the cost of the apartment and nurses around the clock, she should now be given institutional care. The Arbutus Private Hospital was selected, and the move took place at the beginning of June. Mary McAlpine writes that 'she astonished her nurses and friends, because she went without a murmur, perhaps still exercising the orphan's self-discipline.'[37] She took her photographs of Wallace and favourite books, and a few pieces of furniture which just barely fitted into the small room. For a time, the move seemed to rouse her from the lethargy and confusion into which she had sunk, and she composed fairly coherent, pithy letters once again. To Nan she wrote on June 18th:

> It has been a terrific time, getting into this 'Arbutus Private Hospital' & getting my various different possessions in. I just dressed myself today & have had such luck – I had the pleasure of seeing Bill Mowat, whom I'm so fond of, & Mr Walter Gage was here today & Buck McIntosh who partly built the house my dear Father & I lived in at Bowen Island – I hope to see him again. This place is full of aged women on wheels ... I can't describe to you how dear & good the nurses are.[38]

Mary McAlpine went to see Ethel shortly after she had moved, and her account of that visit makes clear that she still retained her sense of an occasion and her sense of humour:

> When I arrived, she was sitting in her wheelchair, meticulously groomed, watching the door. She beckoned to me, and smiled. The whisky and sherry decanters and two of her cut-glass whisky glasses were out, and there was fresh ice in her Chinese green bowl which they had always used for ice. We started to talk, and then I saw her eyes on the door, which was still open to the corridor. I turned to see what she was looking at and saw a very old

and thin woman who was peering, with oddly unseeing eyes, into the room. Our conversation stopped and we watched her, the unknowing intruder. Then the woman turned and started to walk away, her profile to us. As she went, her mouth opened, closed, opened ... 'Look,' [Ethel] said, 'a trout going upstream.'[39]

To Nan she wrote in August, 'I am spending an invalid life in a hospital, with much appreciation & boredom ... The population lives in armchairs. There is no dog or cat, alas. How I need my Father – I miss him daily.'[40] There were no further attempts to write letters.

Her days were spent in the company of a young, blondely attractive but motherly nurse-companion, Reilli Paachinen, who came in the morning after patients had been prepared for the day by hospital staff. (Another nurse fondly remembered by the family was Eileen Frost of West Vancouver.) There were visits from family members, including Amy Buckerfield and her daughter Mary, and from Phyllis Marshall, who remained faithful in attending to her former employer. But those who visited were aware now that she did not always recognize them. There were recurring small strokes that further diminished her hearing and her sight, though nothing took away her need to feel well dressed and properly turned out to greet the world that surrounded her.

On 21 December 1980 it was evident to the staff that Ethel was in severe pain; uncharacteristically, she cried out repeatedly like a small child who was frightened and in great physical distress. She was passing a kidney stone, and a doctor gave her an injection to ease the pain. She died the next day – at 7:30 A.M. on 22 December 1980, a month before her 93rd birthday.

Ethel Wilson's death was a small event locally and nationally; like Aunt Eliza's, it was overshadowed by the busy holiday season. There was a short piece in the *Vancouver Sun* that same day that listed her family connections and the titles of her six books, and quoted past praise by Seán O'Faoláin and Hugo McPherson. The only memorable line was her request that the death notice read that she had *died*, not 'passed away.' Margaret Laurence's personal tribute to 'a splendid writer and a great lady'. appeared a month later in the *Toronto Star* for 24 January 1981. In the meantime, a small funeral service was held at Christ Church Cathedral on December 27. Whereas nearly fifteen years earlier the church, had been filled to capacity to say farewell to Wallace, there were now scarcely forty people gathered to remember Ethel. Most of these were Buckerfields, Ethel's Malkin cousins and their children, and a small handful of teachers and students. The service was conducted in the chapel on the west side of the church, and 'Sheep May Safely Graze' and one of Elgar's 'Variations' were played clumsily on the organ, which likely would have both distressed and amused her. Retired Archbishop David Somerville, who had also conducted Wallace's funeral, read the service in a straightforward way, without a eulogy. Afterwards those in attendance crossed the street to a special room in the Vancouver Hotel for drinks or coffee and sandwiches. At the same time, her remains, with a cigar box containing Wallace's love letters, were being cremated as she had requested. Her ashes were placed beside his in Ocean View Cemetery.

But Ethel Wilson lives on, of course, in her work, and every few years its significance to Canadian culture is reconfirmed publicly. Four months after her death, from 24 to 26 April 1981, approximately fifty academics from across the country (and at least two from the United States) met at the University of Ottawa to appraise and celebrate the writing of Ethel Wilson. Those attending the symposium placed her squarely with the country's most important writers, praising her as feminist, philosopher, humanist, and stylist. In 1990 she became the first Canadian writer to have all of her works reissued in the New Canadian Library series, where they remain in print. More locally, British Columbians are annually reminded of her importance to their province, as the B.C. Book Prize for fiction is named in her honour. In the 1990s, two scholars outside of Canada wrote at length about her work: distinguished American critic Blanche H. Gelfant devoted a third of her Cambridge study on cross-cultural reading to Ethel Wilson, while Indian critic Anjali Bhelande, in a book-length analysis, examined Wilson in the light of Indian philosophical thought. *Swamp Angel* has become steady fare in college and university courses across the country, her short stories are the stuff of Canadian anthologies, and her works are read on the CBC.

Ethel Wilson is impossible to sum up; she is at once too obvious and too elusive, too full of doubt and too wise. Her compassion is too fortified with irony and wit to leave us feeling wholly comfortable; her eye and ear for beauty are too aware of natural ugliness to let us soar too high. We cannot easily sum her up, but we can praise what P.K. Page has called her 'incising, incisive eye,' her compassionate intelligence, and her ability to summon for us in landscapes and histories the 'genius' of our place.

Edge-Malkin Genealogy

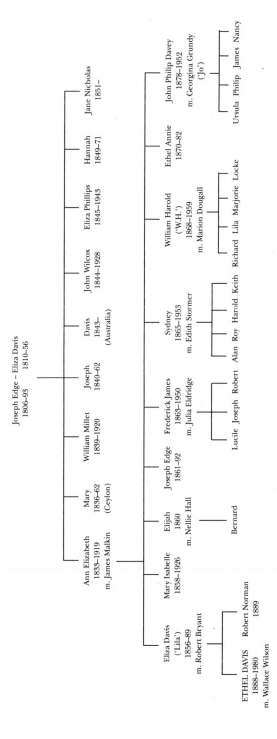

Joseph Edge – Eliza Davis
1806–93   1810–56

Ann Elizabeth
1833–1919
m. James Malkin

Mary
1836–62
(Ceylon)

William Millet
1839–1920

Joseph
1840–62

Davis
1843–
(Australia)

John Wilcox
1844–1928

Eliza Phillips
1845–1943

Hannah
1849–71

Jane Nicholas
1851–

Eliza Davis
('Lila')
1856–89
m. Robert Bryant

Mary Isabelle
1858–1926

Elijah
1860
m. Nellie Hall

Joseph Edge
1861–92

Frederick James
1863–1950
m. Julia Eldridge

Sydney
1865–1953
m. Edith Stormer

William Harold
('W.H.')
1868–1959
m. Marion Dougall

Ethel Annie
1870–82

John Philip Davey
1878–1952
m. Georgina Grundy
('Jo')

Robert Norman
1889

ETHEL DAVIS
1888–1980
m. Wallace Wilson

Bernard

Lucile Joseph Robert

Alan Roy Harold Keith

Richard Lila Marjorie Locke

Ursula Philip James Nancy

Notes

Abbreviations

CVA   City of Vancouver Archives
DMC   David Malkin Collection (private)
EABC   Ernest and Amy Buckerfield Collection (private)
EW:SEL   *Ethel Wilson: Stories, Essays, and Letters*
MUL   McMaster University Library
NAC   National Archives of Canada / Archives nationaux du Canada
QUL   Queen's University Library
TFRBL   Thomas Fisher Rare Book Library
UBCL   University of British Columbia Library
UCL   University of Calgary Library
YUL   York University Library

1. Child

1 See Barbara Wild, 'Piety, Propriety, and the Shaping of the Writer,' in McMullen, ed., *The Ethel Wilson Symposium*, 44.
2 See Ethel Wilson's untitled and unpublished 1958 address to the UBC Women's Undergraduate Society, UBCL, Wilson Papers, Box 10, Folder 9.
3 See 'Fountains in Italy, 1868,' in Stouck, ed., *EW:SEL*, 5–7.
4 This forms part of a collection of Malkin family papers put together by Lucile Parsons and placed in the City of Vancouver Archives. Ethel Wilson gave her own version of this story in a letter to her cousin David Malkin, 17 April 1953, and I have adopted some of her phrasings in my account here.
5 An account of the Edge family at Horton Hall can be found in J.F. Moxon, *The History of Horton Hall.*

6 See Wild, 'Piety, Propriety, and the Shaping of the Writer,' 29.

7 Mary McAlpine (*The Other Side of Silence*, 14) recounts Ursula Malkin's apt description of this photo.

8 See Wilson's 'My Father's Teacher,' 27.

9 Fred Macdonald was related to other famous members of the Macdonald family – brother-in-law and uncle respectively to the painter Edward Poynter and the politican Stanley Baldwin. For a full account of this interesting and distinguished family see A.W. Baldwin's *The Macdonald Sisters*.

10 This anecdote is from David Malkin, in correspondence, 25 Sept. 2001.

11 See letter from Fred Macdonald to Wilson, 2 Nov. 1904, which was later annotated by Wilson (UBCL, Wilson Papers, Box 12, Folder 1). In this letter, Macdonald writes to Wilson that he was the officiating minister at her parents' wedding, but this is at odds with an account of the marriage which appeared in North Staffordshire's *Evening Sentinel*, 16 April 1887, a copy of which is in the possession of David Malkin. According to this report, the service was performed by a Reverend Owen Watkyns.

12 According to Colin Graham Jr, who was curator of the Victoria Art Gallery for several years, the drawing proved to be a copy, though Ethel Wilson would not have known this (Colin Graham Jr, interviewed, 19 April 2000).

13 The description of the wedding given here is taken from the news item 'Marriage of Miss Malkin at Burslem,' which appeared in North Staffordshire's *Evening Sentinel*. See note 11 above.

14 McAlpine, *The Other Side of Silence*, 15. (Anthony Trollope was one of Wilson's favourite writers.)

15 Robert Bryant's African narrative is part of the Ethel Wilson Papers: UBCL, Box 12, Folders 6, 7.

16 See *Wesleyan Methodist Magazine* (1898): 71–4. Quoted by Wild, 33.

17 'Duchess' is published in McAlpine, *The Other Side of Silence*, 2–7. Much of the information about Wilson's early life is taken from this essay.

18 Early missionaries used the word 'Kaffir' to designate South Africans who had not converted to Christianity. (Even earlier, it was used by Muslims to indicate North Africans who had not converted to Islam.) It has long been a term of disparagement, like the American word 'Nigger,' and is now avoided as a racist epithet.

19 *The Innocent Traveller*, 27.

20 See Wilson's 'Reflections in a Pool,' 30.

21 See an unpublished talk Wilson gave to the girls of Crofton House School in UBCL, Wilson Papers, Box 10, Folder 4. The manuscript for the talk is undated.

22 Wilson interviewed by Ronald Hambleton, 1954. This unpublished interview is located in UBCL, Wilson Papers, Box 12, Folder 1.

23 *Wesleyan Methodist Magazine* (1898): 71–4. Quoted by Wild, 33.

24 'Reflections in a Pool,' 30.

25 'Duchess,' in McAlpine, *The Other Side of Silence*, 3.

26 'My Father's Teacher,' 27.

27 McAlpine, 'Ethel Wilson As I Knew Her,' 8.

28 'My Father's Teacher,' 27.

29 Stouck, ed., *EW:SEL*, 221.

30 'Duchess,' in McAlpine, *The Other Side of Silence*, 5.

31 Ibid. Mrs Moon, who is not mentioned in any other accounts, has not been identified. In 1962 Wilson gave another account of the days following her father's death in a letter to her friends Jean and Alan Crawley. See Stouck, ed., *EW:SEL*, 221.

32 See 'The Malkin Family,' CVA.

33 Letter to Wilson's cousin, H. Richardson Malkin, 23 Oct. 1960 (quoted in McAlpine, *The Other Side of Silence*, 18). Wilson would write many years later to one of Sydney's grandsons, David Malkin, that her male cousins 'were great friends & playmates,' but this more likely referred to the time when she was attending school in England as a teenager (Wilson to David Malkin, 21 Feb. 1963, DMC).

34 *The Equations of Love*, 228.

35 An obituary for William Harold Malkin in the *Vancouver Sun*, 13 Oct. 1959, p. 13, says that he came out to Saskatchewan to work for an uncle who was ranching there, but no family records refer to this relation. His mother's notes in a small book, which forms part of the Malkin Family collection in CVA, refer to her sons working at the Staff farm in Grenfell.

36 Isabelle Malkin to Jamie Malkin, 29 Nov. 1897, DMC.

2. Orphan

1 See Constance Mackay, 'Vancouver's New Novelist,' *Mayfair* (Nov. 1947): 67.

2 UBCL, Wilson Papers, Box 7, Folder 25.

3 'Young Vancouver Seen through the Eyes of Youth,' 138–9.

4 See 'The Malkin Family,' CVA, which includes an account of how the pioneering uncles were provisioned for their trip to Canada.

5 See Wilson's early notes for *The Innocent Traveller*, UBCL, Wilson Papers, Box 11, Folder 6.

6 Wilson to John Gray, 21 May 1955, UBCL, Macmillan Company Collection, Box 2, Folder 24.

7 *Vancouver Sun*, 31 Dec. 1929.

8 'Seen through Waves,' UBCL, Wilson Papers, Box 7, Folders 24–5.

9 *The Innocent Traveller*, 138.

10 Most of this information comes from Ethel Wilson's article 'This Was Miss Gordon's School in 1898,' written on the occasion of Crofton House School's fiftieth anniversary and published in the *Vancouver Province*, 5 Feb. 1948, p. 4.

11 See the Major Matthews Collection, CVA, Pamphlet 1905–1.

12 Information about Marion Martin Ward can be found in a letter written by her daughter, Vivien Maitland, dated 5 Aug. 1980, located in UBCL, Mary McAlpine Collection, Box 2, Folder 1.

13 This information is taken from an unpublished talk Wilson gave at Crofton House School. The manuscript for this undated talk is located in UBCL, Wilson Papers, Box 10, Folder 4.

14 Wilson tells about seeing the chain gang in 'Young Vancouver Seen through the Eyes of Youth,' 139, and in 'This Was Miss Gordon's School in 1898,' 4.

15 From a letter to H. Richardson Malkin, 23 Oct. 1960, quoted in McAlpine, *The Other Side of Silence*, 22.

16 There is a brief account of the church and the laying of the cornerstone in Rev. E.A. Davis, ed., *Commemorative Review of the Methodist, Presbyterian, and Congregational Churches in British Columbia* (1925).

17 See *Western Methodist Reader* (Jan. 1901): 5–6.

18 Irene Howard, 'Shockable and Unshockable Methodists in *The Innocent Traveller*,' 115.

19 Quoted in McAlpine, *The Other Side of Silence*, 30.

20 Howard's essay, 'Shockable and Unshockable Methodists in *The Innocent Traveller*,' is one of the best sources for this phase of Wilson's early life. This account of Eliza Edge is on pages 115–17.

21 *The Innocent Traveller*, 134.

22 Wilson, 'Young Vancouver Seen through the Eyes of Youth,' 139.

23 The 'Scandal' is summarized by Irene Howard in 'Shockable and Unshockable Methodists in *The Innocent Travellers*,' whose sources include M.G. Mackenzie, *Behind the Scenes in the W.C.T.U. of Vancouver, B.C.*, 5–7, 23; Vancouver Public Library clippings file; and J.S. Matthews, 'Early Vancouver,' CVA, TS, vol. 7, 54.

24 Wilson's account of the Gastown prostitutes occurs in 'Young Vancouver Seen through the Eyes of Youth,' 139, and 'Seen through Waves,' UBCL, Wilson Papers, Box 7, Folders 24–5. It is given fictional treatment in *The Innocent Traveller*, 141–2, and especially in the short story 'The Mirage of Edward Pontifex,' in Stouck, ed., *EW:SEL*, 42.

25 In an interview conducted by Irene Howard, Lucile Malkin Parsons said Yow caught her in a cubby hole and tried to kiss her. She struggled and got away,

but was afraid to tell her grandmother. Her father, on hearing this story, said, 'Next time scratch his eyes out,' but to the girl's dismay her father did nothing further (UBCL, Irene Howard Papers, Box 5, Folder 2). Lila Malkin Molson, daughter of Harold Malkin, also remembered her fear of that particular man, though she had high praise for other Chinese cooks in the families' employ (UBCL, Irene Howard Papers, Box 5, Folder 4).

26 See the 'W.H. Malkin File,' CVA.

27 UBCL, Wilson Papers, Box 10, Folder 9.

28 'Seen through Waves,' UBCL, Wilson Papers, Box 7, Folders 24–5.

29 This remembrance can be found in a piece of unpublished autobiographical fiction titled 'Herself When Young,' 119 (UBCL, Wilson Papers, Box 12, Folder 5).

30 UBCL, Wilson Papers, Box 3, Folder 16.

31 See Ethel Wilson, 'The Princess,' 61.

32 This account of Methodism as narrow and inducing a terrific sense of duty is contained in a letter Wilson wrote to Mazo de la Roche, 30 June 1955 (TFRBL, Mazo de la Roche Collection, Box 14, Folder 45).

33 See Irene Howard's 'Shockable and Unshockable Methodists in *The Innocent Traveller*,' 119–20.

3. Pupil

1 In an interview, July 1989, Phyllis Rochfort said that Wilson's childhood friend Laura Jukes was sometimes reluctant to spend time at the Barclay Street house because Aunt Eliza Edge interrupted the girls' games with her peculiar behaviour.

2 'Vancouver Child,' 2, EABC.

3 See McAlpine, *The Other Side of Silence*, 32–3.

4 'Vancouver Childhood,' 2, EABC.

5 See Wilson's unpublished essay 'In Defense of a Little Learning,' UBCL, Wilson Papers, Box 9, Folder 10.

6 Wilson to John Gray, 3 Oct. 1958, MUL, Macmillan Collection, Box 40, Folder 18.

7 UBCL, Mary McAlpine Collection, Box 4, Folder 5.

8 Information about the school comes chiefly from a final volume of *Trinity Hall School Magazine*, no. 87, especially the memoir by Lillian Cox, published in summer 1970, when the school, for financial reasons, was forced to close. For a good description of the school and Wilson's years there, see Christopher Armitage, 'Ethel Wilson's English Schooling and Its Echoes in Her Fiction,' in McMullen, ed., *The Ethel Wilson Symposium*, 19–26.

9 See Mac Reynolds, *[Toronto] Star Weekly*, 4 April 1964, p. 13.

10 Wilson, 'From the Farthest West,' *Trinity Hall School Magazine* (1951): 29.

11 'The Birds,' in *Mrs Golightly and Other Stories*, 67.

12 See Armitage, 'Ethel Wilson's English Schooling,' 23.

13 McAlpine, in *The Other Side of Silence*, 36–8, gives an account of Wilson's relations with her Burslem aunt and uncle that is presumably based on conversations with the author.

14 Wilson to Jean and Alan Crawley, in Stouck, ed., *EW:SEL*, 216.

15 McAlpine, *The Other Side of Silence*, 38.

16 Colin Graham Jr (interviewed 19 April 2000) remembered Sydney Malkin as 'a merry old grig,' but Aunt Edith as a very sober Puritan. Edith Malkin throughout her life observed strict Methodist practices. Wilson's youngest cousin, Nancy Malkin Rowell (interviewed 3 June 2000), remembered on a visit to Burslem in 1938 that Uncle Sydney warned her one Sunday to put away her knitting, as Aunt Edith did not permit work of any kind in her house on the Lord's Day.

17 McAlpine, *The Other Side of Silence*, 37. This account, however, has been challenged by David Malkin and Christine Malkin English (interviewed 30 July 2001), who insisted it was highly unlikely that their grandfather would have taken a drink.

18 Editorial signed 'I.J.' in the *Observer*, Feb. 1942.

19 Mackay, 'Vancouver's New Novelist,' 67.

20 Wilson refers to her father's three half-sisters in her published essay 'Reflections in a Pool,' 29–33.

21 In a travel diary for 1938 (UBCL, Wilson Papers, Box 13, Folder 4), Wilson says uncharacteristically that when she was young she 'detested' Aunt Elizabeth.

22 See Wilson's note on this matter, UBCL, Wilson Papers, Box 12, Folder 1. This is contradicted by the newspaper account of the Malkin-Bryant marriage, which lists Mrs Fred Macdonald in attendance at the wedding but describes the service as performed by Reverend Owen Watkyns (newspaper account from DMC). But in a printed eulogy to Lila Davis Bryant, Reverend Fred Macdonald refers to marrying the couple himself. See UBCL, Mary McAlpine Collection, Box 2, Folder 2.

23 Wilson, 'Reflections in a Pool,' 29–33.

24 McAlpine, *The Other Side of Silence*, 38.

25 A copy of this eulogy to Lila Davis Bryant, printed in Burslem, can be found in UBCL, Mary McAlpine Collection, Box 2, Folder 2.

26 Wilson, 'In Defense of a Little Learning,' UBCL, Wilson Papers, Box 9, Folder 10.

27 See 'A Ripple on the Ocean of Time,' in Stouck, ed., *EW:SEL*, 8.

28 Ibid., 9.

29 This information is on the back of a photograph of Lila Malkin (UBCL, Wilson Papers, Box 10, Folder 27).

30 Wilson to Jean and Alan Crawley (letter dated August 1962), in Stouck, ed., *EW:SEL*, 223.

31 The details about Monte Carlo appear in Cy Young's 'Shortcut to Success,' *Vancouver Sun*, 5 July 1952, p. 18.

32 Wilson, 'In Defense of a Little Learning,' UBCL, Wilson Papers, Box 9, Folder 10.

33 Wilson tells this story in a letter to Jean and Alan Crawley dated August 1962. See Stouck, ed., *EW:SEL*, 223–4.

34 Ibid., 224.

35 See Armitage, 'Ethel Wilson's English Schooling,' 23.

36 See McAlpine, *The Other Side of Silence*, 36, for a list of book prizes that Wilson won at Trinity Hall.

37 On Miss Peet, see Armitage, 'Ethel Wilson's English Schooling,' 22; and McAlpine, *The Other Side of Silence*, 35.

38 One of these watercolours can be found in UBCL, Wilson Papers, Box 11, Folder 6.

39 Wilson's accounts of Miss Mould can be found in the unpublished essays 'In Defense of a Little Learning,' UBCL, Wilson Papers, Box 9, Folder 10, and 'Seen through Waves,' UBCL, Wilson Papers, Box 7, Folders 24–5.

40 As there was more than one science teacher at Trinity Hall, one cannot be certain of her identity. Wilson describes her in a letter to John Gray dated 25 March 1956 (UBCL, Wilson Papers, Box 2, Folder 9).

41 Wilson to Jean and Alan Crawley (June 1961) in Stouck, ed., *EW:SEL*, 218.

42 *Swamp Angel*, 57.

43 'The Cigar and the Poor Young Girl,' *Echoes* (Autumn 1945): 11.

44 These views are taken from Wilson's 'Reflections in a Pool,' 33.

45 'The Mirage of Edward Pontifex' is collected in Stouck, ed., *EW:SEL*, 41–5.

4. Teacher

1 This description of Julia Malkin occurs in a letter Wilson wrote to Jean and Alan Crawley, 19 Oct. 1962, UBCL, Alan Crawley Papers.

2 Information about the Normal School and its teachers can be found in CVA, J.S. Matthews Collection, 'Normal School.'

3 Wilson's account of Principal Burns and other teachers at the Normal School appears in 'Seen through Waves,' UBCL, Wilson Papers, Box 7, Folder 25, 9–10.

4 In the notes to be found in the J.S. Matthews file labelled 'Normal School,' CVA, John Buchanan comes closest to this description. He taught several academic subjects.

5 McAlpine, *The Other Side of Silence*, 42.

6 See the 'Ethel Wilson' file, CVA.

7 See Dorothy Livesay, 'Ethel Wilson: West Coast Novelist,' *Saturday Night* 67 (26 July 1952): 20.

8 McAlpine, The Other Side of Silence, 44–5.

9 See undated letter from Wilson to John Gray, UBCL, Macmillan Company Collection, Box 2, Folder 9.

10 See especially 'In Defense of a Little Learning,' UBCL, Wilson Papers, Box 9, Folder 10.

11 See Mackay, 'Vancouver's New Novelist,' 67.

12 See Howard, 'Shockable and Unshockable Methodists,' 118.

13 Mackay, 67.

14 See Irene Howard's 'High Tea: Society in the Old West End,' 16–18, 45, and 'Shockable and Unshockable Methodists,' 113. In UBCL, Irene Howard Papers, Box 5, there are typed transcripts of the interviews Howard conducted with members of the Malkin family and other families living in Vancouver's West End in the early part of the twentieth century.

15 *The Innocent Traveller*, 180.

16 The best source of information about Wilson's Vancouver uncles is 'The Malkin Family' file, CVA.

17 Wilson's 'The Umbrella' forms part of the Ernest and Amy Buckerfield Collection.

18 See Livesay, 20.

19 Wilson to Jean and Alan Crawley (1962): UBCL, Alan Crawley Papers.

20 See the unpublished essay 'A Frail and Powerful Word,' UBCL, Wilson Papers, Box 7, Folder 15, 7–8.

21 CVA, J.S. Matthews Collection, BU.P. 561–567.

22 Much of this information is located in Irene Howard's *Bowen Island 1872–1972*, 60–82.

23 Wilson's photographs and photo albums are located in UBCL, Wilson Papers, Box 14, Folders 9–33, and the Mary McAlpine Collection, Box 6, Folders 5 and 6.

24 Caple's memories were recorded on tape in 1967 and form part of the Ronald Hambleton Collection, UBCL.

25 Wilson, 'Seen through Waves,' UBCL, Wilson Papers, Box 7, Folders 24–5. Only one art teacher is identified in J.S. Matthews's notes on the Normal School, CVA, and his name is William Blair.

26 This brief account of Wilson's art lessons from Emily Carr is taken from two references to them in Wilson's unpublished writings: in a 1960s address to the B.C. Society of Artists, UBCL, Wilson Papers, Box 10, Folder 7, n.d.; and, more interestingly, in some cancelled pages written in 1948 that became verso pages to a manuscript for *Swamp Angel* (UBCL, Wilson Papers, Box 4, Folder 2).

27 See Noel Robinson, 'History of the Art, Scientific and Historical Association,' 8–9, CVA.

28 Details about painting and music in early Vancouver are taken from 'Seen through Waves,' UBCL, Wilson Papers, Box 7, Folders 24–5, and 'Young Vancouver Seen through the Eyes of Youth,' 138–9.

29 *The Innocent Traveller*, 87.

30 Sources for this information include Irene Howard's interview with Lucile Malkin Parsons, UBCL, Irene Howard Papers, Box 5, Folder 2; McAlpine, *The Other Side of Silence*, 47 (though her sources are not cited); and an interview I conducted in Victoria in July 1989 with Phyllis Rochfort. J.P. Nicolls was the founder of the pioneer Vancouver real estate firm Macauley and Nicolls.

31 'Herself When Young,' 120, UBCL, Wilson Papers, Box 12, Folder 5.

32 'Seen through Waves,' Box 7, Folders 24–5.

33 Philip and Georgina Malkin's photo album is in the possession of their grandson, William Malkin, Burnaby, B.C.

34 UBCL, Wilson Papers, Box 14, Folder 3.

35 Wilson to Jean and Alan Crawley in Stouck, ed., *EW:SEL*, 224.

36 See the unpublished interview conducted by Ronald Hambleton, UBCL, Wilson Papers, Box 12, Folder 11.

37 Wilson's visit to the Woods home is described in a letter written by Marjorie Woods Crookston, 21 July 1980, UBCL, Mary McAlpine Collection, Box 2, Folder 1.

38 Wilson to Jean and Alan Crawley, 9 Feb. 1962, UBCL, Alan Crawley Papers.

39 See McAlpine, *The Other Side of Silence*, 47–9.

40 Bruce Robertson, interviewed January 1988.

41 Wilson to Mary McAlpine, 18 May 1961, UBCL, Mary McAlpine Collection, Box 2, Folder 2.

42 See McAlpine, *The Other Side of Silence*, 58. The diary belongs to Kathleen Graham's daughter, Joan Kenning, Victoria, B.C.

43 Wilson to Margaret Laurence, 1966, YUL, Margaret Laurence Collection.

44 Irene Howard, interview with Lucile Malkin, UBCL, Irene Howard Papers, Box 5, Folder 2. Ursula Malkin, Philip's older daughter, gave me a similar account in an interview at her home, February 1995.

45 See Howard, 'High Tea,' 21, 45.

46 One is tempted to identify Wilson as the artist because the illustrations are in much the same style as some of the sketches with her papers at UBCL.

47 See McAlpine, *The Other Side of Silence*, 64.

48 'Ethel Wilson,' *Profile*, CBC Television, August 1954.

49 'Herself When Young,' 120, UBCL, Wilson Papers, Box 12, Folder 5.

50 Wilson, 'Series of Combination of Events & Where Is John Goodwin?' 4.

51 McAlpine, *The Other Side of Silence*, 65.

5. Wife

1 'A Visit to the Frontier' in Stouck, ed., *EW:SEL*, 47–8.

2 *Swamp Angel*, 166.

3 Wilson to Margaret Laurence in Stouck, ed., *EW:SEL*, 246.

4 Wilson to Desmond Pacey, no date, NAC, Desmond Pacey Fonds, MG 30, D 339.

5 Reported in the *Vancouver World*, 25 May 1893, p. 3.

6 The anecdotes related here are taken from McAlpine, *The Other Side of Silence*, 53–4. McAlpine's source of information was chiefly Wallace Wilson's sister, Amy Buckerfield, but also his cousin, Alix Wilson Goolden.

7 McAlpine, *The Other Side of Silence*, 54.

8 Ibid., 61–2.

9 Wilson to Jean and Alan Crawley, 4 Jan. 1965, UBCL, Alan Crawley Papers.

10 *Vancouver Daily World*, 5 Jan. 1921, p. 6. A short piece appeared in the *Vancouver Sun*, 5 Jan. 1921, p. 8, and one in the *Province*, 5 Jan. 1921, p. 11.

11 McAlpine, *The Other Side of Silence*, 68.

12 See Wilson's essay 'Series of Combination of Events & Where Is John Goodwin?' 3.

13 McAlpine, *The Other Side of Silence*, 71.

14 Ibid., 53.

15 Some of these letters form part of the Ernest and Amy Buckerfield Collection.

16 Information here is taken from McAlpine, *The Other Side of Silence*, 71, and from interviews with Phyllis Rochfort, July 1989, and Mary Buckerfield White, 5 Feb. 2001.

17 'Beware the Jabberwock, My Son ... Beware the Jubjub Bird' (*Mrs Golightly and Other Stories*, 179).

18 Information about the fishing lodge can be found in Muriel Whitaker's 'Journeys to the Interior: The Wilsons at Lac Le Jeune,' in McMullen, ed., *The Ethel Wilson Symposium*, 13–18.

19 Wilson to John Gray, 2 Oct. 1957, UBCL, Macmillan Company Collection, Box 2, Folder 19.

20 Wilson's dislike of singing is probably best illustrated in her ridicule of a tenor she heard in Victoria. See Stouck, ed., *EW:SEL*, 192.

21 McAlpine, *The Other Side of Silence*, 71.

22 Amy Buckerfield to Bella Wilson, 16 Dec. 1921, EABC.

23 Alix Wilson in McAlpine, *The Other Side of Silence*, 72.

24 In an interview I conducted with Audrey Butler, October 1990, she explained that Ethel Wilson confided to her that she was unable to have children.

25 Described in a conversation with James Malkin, 8 March 2000.

26 McAlpine, *The Other Side of Silence*, 75.

27 In conversation with Phyllis Rochfort, July 1989, and with Theodora Dowsley, June 1992.

28 McAlpine, *The Other Side of Silence*, 80.

29 *The Innocent Traveller*, 193.

30 She was remembered this way in a taped interview by Kenneth Caple, UBCL, Ronald Hambleton Collection.

31 McAlpine, *The Other Side of Silence*, 81.

32 Wilson to Winifred Eayrs, copy editor at Macmillan, 13 Jan. 1947, UBCL, Macmillan Company Collection, Box 1, Folder 6.

33 McAlpine, *The Other Side of Silence*, 83.

34 Information about the Wilson and Graham friendship was collected in interviews with Colin Graham Jr, 19 April 2000, and his sister, Joan Graham Kenning, 20 April 2000.

35 Private Happiness,' 20, UBCL, Wilson Papers, Box 7, Folder 19. Mary McAlpine claims that after 1913 Ethel Wilson did not visit England for twenty-five years, but the reference to meeting her half-cousin in 1929 suggests that she and Wallace made a trip to England while he was studying in Vienna. This seems more than likely given the close connection maintained between the English and Canadian branches of the Malkin family.

36 See Cy Young, 'Shortcut to Success,' 18.

37 Wilson to Kildare Dobbs, 19 Feb. 1961, UBCL, Macmillan Company Collection, Box 2, Folder 6.

38 Letter to Mary Buckerfield, 19 March 1930, EABC.

39 Mention of their stop at this Arabian locale occurs in an undated letter to Earle Birney, TFRBL, Earle Birney Collection, Box 24, Folder 25.

40 'Words and Places,' UBCL, Wilson Papers, Box 7, Folder 3. Although Algiers is not mentioned in these travel sketches, Wilson made reference to it in the interview with Cy Young, 18.

41 Wilson to Mary McAlpine, 25 Oct. 1955, UBCL, Mary McAlpine Collection, Box 2, Folder 1.

42 'Herself When Young,' 67, UBCL, Wilson Papers, Box 12, Folder 4.

43 Wilson to John Gray, 30 Oct. 1968, UBCL, Macmillan Company Collection, Box 2, Folder 2.

6. Apprentice

1 Articles which helped to create this colourful story include Constance Mackay's 'Vancouver's New Novelist' and Wilson's talk titled 'Somewhere near the Truth,' in which she says that before 1946 she 'had never contemplated writing a book' (Stouck, ed., *EW:SEL*, 83). The story was made legend by her publisher John Gray in his talk 'An Evening with Ethel Wilson' (UBCL, Wilson Papers, Box 11, Folder 7). He says he once told Mrs Wilson he assumed she had always known that she had wanted to write and had practised, but her answer was a flat no – 'I never had, never wanted to.' He then compares her to someone who sits down at the piano for the first time and can play! Wilson gives the longest disclaimer to literary ambition in the 'Preface' she wrote in 1967 for the Alcuin Society edition of *Hetty Dorval*, 8–11.

2 See letters to the Macmillan Company published in Stouck, ed., *EW:SEL*, 118–23.

3 Wilson to John Gray, 14 June 1958, Macmillan Company Collection, Box 2, Folder 29.

4 These letters form part of the EABC.

5 UBCL, Wilson Papers, Box 11, Folder 6.

6 This information is from David Malkin, interviewed 30 July 2001.

7 James Malkin, interviewed 8 March 2000.

8 Wilson to Mary Buckerfield, 19 March 1930, EABC.

9 See Wilson's letter to Earle Birney, 29 Nov. 1955, which responds at some length to Birney's depiction of the 1930s in his novel *Down the Long Table* (TFRBL, Earle Birney Collection, Box 24, Folder 27).

10 *The Innocent Traveller*, 206.

11 'Herself When Young,' 64–5, UBCL, Wilson Papers, Box 12, Folder 4.

12 See 'Series of Combination of Events & Where Is John Goodwin?' 3–4.

13 See McAlpine, *The Other Side of Silence*, 103.

14 Wilson to Jean and Alan Crawley, 28 June 1961, UBCL, Alan Crawley Papers.

15 For an account of Wallace Wilson's career in the 1930s, see the annual issues of the *British Columbia Medical Journal* for 1963 and 1966, including the jour-

nal's special tributes to Wallace Wilson, 1888–1966. These are located in UBCL, Wilson Papers, Box 11, Folders 10–12.

16 Wilson to Jean and Alan Crawley, 9 Jan. 1961, UBCL, Alan Crawley Papers.

17 See especially Wilson to Amy Buckerfield, 16 May 1936, EABC.

18 Joy McDonagh, interviewed 20 June 1979 and 3 August 1984, was one of many who commented on this perception of the Wilsons. Nan Cheney, interviewed by telephone 23 May 1986, also described the enormous affection people had for Wallace and their uncertainty in response to Ethel's reserve.

19 See 'A Cat among the Falcons,' in Stouck, ed., *EW:SEL*, 101.

20 McAlpine, *The Other Side of Silence*, 93.

21 Bruce Robertson, interviewed January 1988.

22 Zipporah Woodward recounts this anecdote in a taped interview with Ronald Hambleton (Ronald Hambleton Collection, UBCL).

23 McAlpine, *The Other Side of Silence*, 93.

24 Mac Reynolds, 'Canada Council Medalists,' 13.

25 Butler to Stouck, 19 May 1986.

26 Amy Buckerfield to Wilson, 4 and 8 Aug. 1936, EABC.

27 James Malkin, interviewed 8 March 2000.

28 Unless otherwise indicated, quotations in the remainder of this chapter are from this document, located in UBCL, Wilson Papers, Box 13, Folder 4.

29 Amy Buckerfield to Wilson, 8 Oct. 1936, EABC.

30 Amy Buckerfield to Wilson, 8 Aug. 1936, EABC.

31 Ibid.

32 This reference to Priestley appears in Wilson's 1955 CBC Radio talk on Joyce Cary, transcribed and published in Stouck, ed., *EW:SEL*, 77–81.

33 Ibid., 81.

34 *Swamp Angel*, 95.

35 'Joyce Cary,' in Stouck, ed., *EW:SEL*, 80.

36 This description of Herbert Bryant appears in Wilson's brief memoir 'My Father's Teacher,' 28.

37 This story appears in 'Reflections in a Pool,' 32–3.

38 See 'My Father's Teacher.'

39 Wilson to George Woodcock, 10 Sept. [1965?], QUL, George Woodcock Papers.

40 From an 1887 newspaper account of the wedding provided by David Malkin.

41 There are two versions of Wilson's Charlie Peace anecdote: one in the travel diary, UBCL, Wilson Papers, Box 13, Folder 4; and the other in a letter to Jean and Alan Crawley, 28 Dec. 1960, in Stouck, ed., *EW:SEL*, 216.

42 Wilson's account of the Scandinavian cities appears in both her travel diary and in her 1952 interview with Cy Young.

43 'Hurry, Hurry,' *Mrs Golightly and Other Stories*, 111–15.
44 Wilson to Robert Weaver, 14 March 1951, NAC, MG 31, D 162, Vol. 5, File 25.

7. *The Innocent Traveller*

1 See Stouck, ed., *EW:SEL*, 101.
2 UBCL, Wilson Papers, Box 11, Folder 6.
3 Published in Stouck, ed., *EW:SEL*, 15–20.
4 John Gray, 'An Evening with Ethel Wilson,' UBCL, Wilson Papers, Box 11, Folder 7.
5 See Stouck, ed., *EW:SEL*, 118–23.
6 See Wilson to Ellen Elliott, 2 Nov. 1945, in Stouck, ed., *EW:SEL*, 122–3.
7 'Preface' to *Hetty Dorval* (Vancouver: The Alcuin Society, 1978), 8.
8 We know that on her father's death she remained at first with Maria Riggall, her father's aunt, then was taken to Staffordshire, staying briefly with Great-Uncle and Great-Aunt John Edge, then with Uncle Sydney and Aunt Edith Malkin and their four sons, and finally arriving in Vancouver a year after her father's death. In her essay 'Duchess,' she also refers to a Mrs Moon, which would be a fifth place where the orphan was given a home during that year, though it has not been possible to identify Mrs Moon.
9 McAlpine, *The Other Side of Silence*, 112.
10 Mackay, 'Vancouver's New Novelist,' 67.
11 Wilson's contributions to 'Vancouver Calling' are described by Mackay, 67.
12 Wilson describes this episode in a letter to Mazo de la Roche, 13 April 1957, TFRBL, Mazo de la Roche Collection, Box 14, Folder 47; and in a letter to John Gray, 17 Nov. 1961, UBCL, Macmillan Company Collection, Box 2, Folder 25.
13 This information is from an interview with Audrey Butler, October 1990.
14 Irene Howard, *Bowen Island 1872–1972*, 91–2.
15 See Stouck, ed., *EW:SEL*, 25–7.
16 Wilson to Mazo de la Roche, 22 Aug. 1955, TFRBL, Mazo de la Roche Collection, Box 14, Folder 46.
17 McAlpine, *The Other Side of Silence*, 118.
18 Stouck, ed., *EW:SEL*, 118.
19 Ibid., 119.
20 Anne Blochin to Wilson, 20 Dec. 1944, UBCL, Macmillan Company Collection, Box 1, Folder 2.
21 See Stouck, ed., *EW:SEL*, 120–1.
22 Blochin's and Blackstock's reports are located in UBCL, Macmillan Company Collection, Box 1, Folder 6.

23 Wilson to Ellen Elliott, 14 June 1945, UBCL, Macmillan Company Collection, Box 1, Folder 6.

24 Wilson to Anne Blochin, 10 Jan. 1945, UBCL, Macmillan Company Collection, Box 1, Folder 6.

25 Wilson to Ellen Elliott, 1 Aug. 1945, UBCL, Macmillan Company Collection, Box 1, Folder 6.

26 Ellen Elliott to Wilson, 13 Aug. 1945, UBCL, Macmillan Company Collection, Box 1, Folder 2.

27 See Stouck, ed., *EW:SEL*, 133–4.

28 Unfortunately, the lengthy correspondence between Wilson and Leiper appears not to have survived. The piece quoted here is from a letter Wilson wrote to Ellen Elliott, 28 April 1947, UBCL, Macmillan Company Collection, Box 1, Folder 6.

29 The Toronto reader's report dated 13 Aug. 1947 is located in UBCL, Macmillan Company Collection, Box 1, Folder 8.

30 The London report is described in a letter by Wilson to John Gray dated 4 April 1948 and is located in UBCL, Macmillan Company Collection, Box 1, Folder 15.

31 E.J.'s report is located in UBCL, Macmillan Company Collection, Box 1, Folder 8.

32 John Gray to Harold Latham, 17 May 1948, UBCL, Macmillan Company Collection, Box 1, Folder 10.

33 See Stouck, ed., *EW:SEL*, 144–5.

34 This information from Audrey Butler, interviewed Oct. 1990. In a letter to P.K. Page, 26 June 1990, Sandra Djwa wondered if the title might have been suggested by Page's poem 'Journey Home,' which appeared in *Canadian Forum*, Dec. 1944. The relevant lines are 'Hurry was in his veins / violence vaulted the loose box of his head; / hurry was hot in the straw / and snapped in the eyes / of the innocent traveller.' In the early 1940s, Wilson had a subscription to *Canadian Forum*, which had published her story 'On Nimpish Lake' in 1942.

35 The review in the *Province*, signed 'M.D.,' appeared 10 Sept. 1949 on page 6, and the review in the *Vancouver Sun*, titled 'Spinster Portrait' and signed G. Lane, appeared 17 Sept. 1949 on page 4.

36 'Immortal Topaz,' *Saturday Night* 65 (11 Oct. 1949): 46.

37 Claude Bissell, untitled review, *University of Toronto Quarterly* 19 (April 1950): 274–5.

38 American reviews: Mary Lamberton Becker, 'She Lived a Round Century,' *New York Herald Tribune Book Review*, 15 Jan. 1950, p. 6; Catherine Meredith Brown, 'Fiction Notes,' *Saturday Review of Books* 32 (10 Dec. 1949): 17; V.J.,

'The New Books,' *San Francisco Chronicle*, 13 Nov. 1949, p. 27; Ruth Chapin, 'Spinster on Wheels,' *Christian Science Monitor*, 21 Oct. 1949, p. 14.

39 '"Innocent Traveller" Is Latest from Author of "Hetty Dorval,"' *Toronto Daily Star*, 27 Aug. 1949, p. 18.

40 William Arthur Deacon, 'Victorian Gentlewoman Loved Young Vancouver,' *Globe and Mail*, 17 Sept. 1949, p. 12.

41 See Stouck, ed., *EW:SEL*, 154–5.

42 Mark G. Cohen, untitled review, *Canadian Forum* 29 (Dec. 1949): 214.

43 Wilhelmina Gordon, 'Among the New Books,' *Echoes* 197 (Winter 1949): 40.

44 *Times Literary Supplement*, 2 Sept. 1949, p. 575.

45 Wilson to Kathleen Graham, 20 July 1973, Joan Graham Kenning private collection.

46 *The Innocent Traveller*, 138.

47 Wilson to Kildare Dobbs, 12 March 1961, UBCL, Macmillan Company Collection, Box 2, Folder 16.

48 See W.H. New, 'The Irony of Order: Ethel Wilson's *The Innocent Traveller*,' *Critique: Studies in Modern Fiction* 10, no. 3 (1968): 22–30.

49 See Mary-Ann Stouck, 'Structure in Ethel Wilson's *The Innocent Traveller*,' *Canadian Literature* 109 (Summer 1986): 17–31.

50 See the chapter 'Ethel Wilson: Geography As Argument' in Arnold Harrichand Itwaru's *The Invention of Canada: Literary Text and the Immigrant Imaginary*, 31–44.

51 See Anjali Bhelande, *Self Beyond Self: Ethel Wilson and Indian Philosophical Thought*. For discussions specifically of *The Innocent Traveller*, see pages 10–11, 53, 69.

52 *The Innocent Traveller*, 221–2.

53 Ibid., 222.

54 P.K. Page, 'Afterword,' *The Innocent Traveller*, 238–43.

8. *Hetty Dorval*

1 Wilson to Desmond Pacey, 13 May 1964, NAC, Desmond Pacey Fonds, MG 30, D339.

2 Stouck, ed., *EW:SEL*, 83.

3 McAlpine, *The Other Side of Silence*, 125.

4 Stouck, ed., *EW:SEL*, 122.

5 These estimates are to be found in the 'Preface' to the Alcuin edition, 10; 'Somewhere near the Truth,' in Stouck, ed., *EW:SEL*, 84; a letter to Ellen Elliott, 8 March 1946 (uses the terms 'hokum' and 'illegitimate'), in Stouck,

ed., *EW:SEL*, 127–8; and an undated letter to Ellen Elliott that was probably written in May 1947 ('one very good sentence'), in Stouck, ed., *EW:SEL*, 134.

6 Anne Blochin's report is in UBCL, Macmillan Company Collection, Box 1, Folder 8.

7 Reader reports for *Hetty Dorval* are located in UBCL, Macmillan Company Collection, Box 1, Folder 1.

8 Ellen Elliott to Wilson, 16 Jan. 1946, UBCL, Macmillan Company Collection, Box 1, Folder 2.

9 Stouck, ed., *EW:SEL*, 124.

10 Ibid.

11 Robert Weaver, interviewed 20 April 1995.

12 Winifred Eayrs to Wilson, 19 March 1946, UBCL, Macmillan Company Collection, Box 1, Folder 2.

13 Wilson to Ellen Elliott, 24 Feb. 1946, UBCL, Macmillan Company Collection, Box 1 Folder 2.

14 Ibid.

15 Stouck, ed., *EW:SEL*, 126.

16 Ibid., 125.

17 Wilson to Ellen Elliott, 20 Jan. 1946, UBCL, Macmillan Company Collection, Box 1, Folder 6. One of Wilson's great-great-grandmothers was Ann Davis, née Millett. The Milletts were a family of some distinction in the seventeenth and eighteenth centuries, and included admirals and generals in their number. It was a family that prided itself in its breeding, although it had little money by the time Joseph Edge married Eliza Davis, the daughter of Ann Millett Davis. See 'The Malkin File,' CVA. According to an inscription on the back of a portrait in the possession of Nancy Malkin Rowell, Ann Millett's brother William married their cousin, whose name actually was Mary Millett.

18 Ellen Elliott to Wilson, 1 March 1946, UBCL, Macmillan Company Collection, Box 1, Folder 2.

19 Stouck, ed., *EW:SEL*, 127.

20 Wilson to Winifred Eayrs, 27 June 1946, UBCL, Macmillan Company Collection, Box 1, Folder 6.

21 Stouck, ed., *EW:SEL*, 131n.

22 Ibid., 127–8.

23 Ibid., 121.

24 Ibid., 132.

25 Ibid.

26 Stouck, ed., *EW:SEL*, 138–9.

27 McAlpine, *The Other Side of Silence*, 130.

28 This anecdote collected by Barbara Wild and reported April 1981.

29 Wilson to Ellen Elliott, 19 July 1946, UBCL, Macmillan Company Collection, Box 1, Folder 6.

30 Wilson to Mary McAlpine, UBCL, Mary McAlpine Papers, Box 3, Folder 11.

31 McAlpine, *The Other Side of Silence*, 129.

32 Wilson to Ellen Elliott and John Gray, both letters dated 25 Oct. 1946, UBCL, Macmillan Company Collection, Box 1, Folder 6.

33 Stouck, ed., *EW:SEL*, 135.

34 Wilson to Ellen Elliott, 7 April 1947, UBCL, Macmillan Company Collection, Box 1, Folder 6.

35 The publicity articles are by Georgie Lane (*Vancouver Sun*, 9 May 1947, p. 19), Pat Prowd (*Vancouver News-Herald*, 9 May 1947, p. 7), and Pat Wallace (*Vancouver Province*, 9 May 1947, p. 12).

36 W.J. Harlow, *Ottawa Evening Sun*, 21 June 1947, p. 24.

37 Edith James, *San Francisco Chronicle*, 31 Aug. 1947, p. 11.

38 Victor P. Hass, *Chicago Sunday Tribune*, 24 Aug. 1947.

39 *Halifax Daily Star*, 31 May 1947, p. 12.

40 Deacon's review appeared in the *Globe and Mail*, 17 May 1947, p. 12. Actually, this review is unsigned, and it is possible that it was not written by Deacon. However, since he was the literary editor for the newspaper, Wilson assumed he wrote the piece, or was at least responsible for its publication, and given his subsequent response to her work, it seems almost certain that he was the author.

41 Seymour Krim, 'As Visible As Green,' *New York Times Book Review*, 14 Sept. 1947, p. 16.

42 Daniel Macmillan to John Gray, 14 Feb. 1947, UBCL, Macmillan Company Collection, Box 1, Folder 4.

43 Daniel Macmillan to John Gray, 12 Aug. 1947, UBCL Macmillan Company Collection, Box 1, Folder 4.

44 'E.O.D.K,' *Punch*, 11 Aug. 1948, p. 135.

45 According to Bonnie M. McComb's bibliography, Elizabeth Bowen's review appeared in the *Tatler*, 11 Aug. 1948, n.pag., but a search does not confirm that information. To read the whole review, see UBCL, Wilson Papers, Box 10, Folder 16.

46 McAlpine, *The Other Side of Silence*, 131.

47 Letters exchanged on this matter are located in UBCL, Macmillan Company Collection, Box 1, Folder 3.

48 Wilson to John Gray, 10 Nov. 1947, UBCL, Macmillan Company Collection, Box 1, Folder 6.

49 John Gray to Wilson, 13 Nov. 1947, UBCL, Macmillan Company Collection, Box 1, Folder 3.

50 The Macmillan publication files at McMaster University Library record 3,900 copies of *Hetty Dorval* sold by 1961, as compared, for example, to 3,004 copies of *The Innocent Traveller* and 2,100 copies of *Swamp Angel.*

51 For example, when Ethel Wilson's name came up in a conversation I had with Sinclair Ross in May 1989, he said *Hetty Dorval* was the book he remembered best: 'wild geese flying over the sagebrush hills – one of the pure, powerful images in Canadian literature.'

52 Wilson's newspaper article, titled 'A Night in Lytton,' appeared in the *Vancouver Province Saturday Magazine,* 19 Oct. 1940, p. 6.

53 Stouck, ed., *EW:SEL,* 121. Wilson also refers to Hetty as 'thoroughly bad' in a letter to Frank Upjohn. See Stouck, ed., *EW:SEL,* 179.

54 See W.H. New, 'The "Genius" of Place and Time: The Fiction of Ethel Wilson,' 39–48.

55 *Hetty Dorval,* 65–6.

56 *Love and Salt Water,* 89.

57 Wilson to Margaret Andrew, no date, UBCL, Andrew Papers.

58 See, for example, Desmond Pacey, *Ethel Wilson,* 45–62.

59 See Wilson's unpublished essay 'Hunt the Symbol,' UBCL, Wilson Papers, Box 7, Folder 16.

60 The one exception is Beverley Mitchell, S.S.A., who argues in two articles, that 'at no point in the novel is there any real evidence against Hetty to warrant her condemnation.' She argues that it is all 'hear-say.' In one of her articles, Mitchell writes that Wilson herself confirmed this positive assessment of Hetty, but one must point out that the interview between Mitchell and Wilson took place in 1976, after Wilson had suffered a series of strokes and was no longer always able to recognize the members of her family much less take part in literary discussions. Mitchell's arguments are set forth in 'In Defense of *Hetty Dorval*' and 'The Right Word in the Right Place: Literary Techniques in the Fiction of Ethel Wilson.'

61 See Davies's article 'Lamia: The Allegorical Nature of Hetty Dorval.'

62 Frye's reading appears as an 'Afterword' to the New Canadian Library edition of *Hetty Dorval,* 105–8.

63 This mention appears in P.M. Hinchcliffe's '"To Keep the Memory of So Worthy a Friend": Ethel Wilson As an Elegist,' 65.

64 Jeannette Urbas, 'The Perquisites of Love,' 8.

65 See Robert Hare, *Without Conscience: The Disturbing World of the Psychopaths among Us.*

66 See R.D. MacDonald, 'Serious Whimsy.'

67 Stouck, ed., *EW:SEL*, 166.

9. *The Equations of Love*

1 Wilson to John Gray, 3 Oct. 1955, UBCL, Macmillan Company Collection, Box 2, Folder 9.
2 'Private Happiness,' quoted extensively here, is located in UBCL, Macmillan Company Collection, Box 7, Folder 19.
3 Daniel Macmillan to John Gray, 8 Sept. 1947, UBCL, Macmillan Company Collection, Box 1, Folder 4.
4 Wilson to John Gray, 14 Aug. 1947, UBCL, Macmillan Company Collection, Box 1, Folder 6.
5 Wilson to John Gray, 6 May 1957, UBCL, Macmillan Company Collection, Box 2, Folder 19.
6 In an interview in October 1990, Audrey Butler described this meeting for me, as well as providing the subsequent information about herself and the Wilsons.
7 Wilson to John Gray, 4 April 1948, UBCL, Macmillan Company Collection, Box 1, Folder 15.
8 Wilson to John Gray, 5 June 1948, UBCL, Macmillan Company Collection, Box 1, Folder 15.
9 See McAlpine, *The Other Side of Silence*, 142–3, for a description of Wallace's condition, including Ethel's stay with Alix and Massey Goolden. McAlpine, however, has dated the illness incorrectly, claiming that it started in October of 1947. Wilson's letters to John Gray make it clear that the dermatitis first appeared around the end of March 1948. See, for example, letters from Wilson to John Gray dated 4 April 1948 and 23 March 1949, UBCL, Macmillan Company Collection, Box 1, Folder 15.
10 Wilson to John Gray, 2 Sept. 1948, UBCL, Macmillan Company Collection, Box 1, Folder 15.
11 In an interview in June 1992, Theodora Dowsley remembered her doctor husband describing Ethel's emotional state at the hospital and the doctors' idea that the couple should be separated for Wallace's betterment. Phyllis Rochfort, in an interview in July 1989, also recalled vividly Ethel's acute anxiety over Wallace's condition and what seemed like an unnatural dependency on her husband.
12 McAlpine, *The Other Side of Silence*, 143.
13 Stouck, ed., *EW:SEL*, 146–8.
14 Ibid., 148–50.
15 Ibid.

16 'A Visit to the Frontier' was first published in *Tamarack Review* 33 (Autumn 1964): 55–65.

17 Wilson to Jean and Alan Crawley, 2 Jan. 1965, UBCL, Alan Crawley Papers.

18 See letter from Reginald Tupper to Wilson, 8 Feb. 1948, UBCL, Macmillan Company Collection, Box 2, Folder 26.

19 Wilson to John Gray, 21 March 1948, UBCL, Macmillan Company Collection, Box 2. Folder 1.

20 The reports are dated 7 and 27 April 1948 and are located in UBCL, Macmillan Company Collection, Box 1, Folder 17.

21 John Gray to Wilson, 25 May 1948, UBCL, Macmillan Company Collection, Box 1, Folder 19.

22 Stouck, ed., *EW:SEL*, 156.

23 Ibid., 156–8.

24 UBCL, Macmillan Company Collection, Box 1, Folder 17.

25 John Gray to Wilson, 23 Sept. 1950, UBCL, Macmillan Company Collection, Box 1, Folder 19.

26 Stouck, ed., *EW:SEL*, 158.

27 John Gray to Wilson, 10 Jan. 1951, UBCL, Macmillan Company Collection, Box 1, Folder 19.

28 Stouck, ed., *EW:SEL*, 162.

29 John Gray to Wilson, 29 Jan. 1951, UBCL, Macmillan Company Collection, Box 1, Folder 19.

30 Wilson to John Gray, 2 Feb. 1951, UBCL, Macmillan Company Collection, Box 2, Folder 1.

31 John Gray to Wilson, 5 March 1951, UBCL, Macmillan Company Collection, Box 1, Folder 19.

32 John Gray to Wilson, 8 June 1951, UBCL, Macmillan Company Collection, Box 1, Folder 19.

33 An undated letter (c. mid-June 1951) from Wilson to John Gray discussing possible titles is located in UBCL, Macmillan Company Collection, Box 2, Folder 1.

34 See letters from Wilson to John Gray, 19 July 1950 and 12 Jan. 1951, UBCL, Macmillan Company Collection, Box 2, Folder 1.

35 In a talk given to the Humanities Association, 12 Jan. 1960 (UBCL, Wilson Papers, Box 2, Folder 17), she put it this way: 'I had never seen and did not know the girl in question [Yow's white lady friend]. She did not exist in my knowledge any more than a fly in the next room, but I considered certain aspects and likelihoods ... characters multiplied, their outlines at first dim, later clear.'

36 See Wilson to John Gray, 26 Oct. 1950, UBCL, Macmillan Company Collection, Box 2, Folder 1.

37 Stouck, ed., *EW:SEL*, 157.

38 Ibid., 159.

39 'Why Two Women Lied' is the title of a positive review by Isabelle Hughes, which appeared in the *Globe and Mail*, 5 April 1952, p. 10. Wilson assumed now that she was beneath Deacon's notice.

40 Mr Keate was the editor and publisher of the *Daily Times*, Victoria, B.C., but his review actually appeared in the *New York Times Book Review*, 3 May 1953, pp. 5, 22.

41 See '"Equations of Love" Posed in Vancouver,' *Toronto Daily Star*, 29 March 1952, p. 7. The reviewer is not identified.

42 Gael Turnbull, *Northern Review* 6, no. 2 (June-July 1953): 36–40.

43 Bissell's review appeared in 'Letters in Canada: 1952,' *University of Toronto Quarterly* 22 (April 1953): 288–90, 292.

44 H.S. Latham to John Gray, 8 Oct. 1951, UBCL, Macmillan Company Collection, Box 1, Folder 20.

45 H.S. Latham to John Gray, 23 Oct. 1951, UBCL, Macmillan Company Collection, Box 1, Folder 20.

46 See the Ruth May correspondence in UBCL, Macmillan Company Collection, Box 1, Folder 18.

47 Elizabeth Lawrence at Harper's made some editorial suggestions, and Wilson says she 'threw out a shovelful of "ands."' There is a friendly correspondence consisting of eighteen letters from Wilson to Lawrence preserved in the archives at the University of Texas at Austin.

48 'Up from Skid Road' was the title of the review by Stuart Keate in the *New York Times Book Review*, 3 May 1953, pp. 5, 22; 'Humane Novel of Woman's Rise in the World' was the title of a review by Victor P. Hass in the *Chicago Sunday Tribune*, 3 May 1953, p. 2; 'uplifting story of the triumph of human character' appears in J.H. Jackson's review in the *San Francisco Chronicle*, 7 May 1953, p. 19.

49 'Superior Canadian Novel,' *Miami Herald*, 3 May 1953, p. 4F.

50 This statement appears in Sylvia Stallings's review, titled 'All for the Sake of Baby,' in the *New York Herald Tribune Book Review*, 3 May 1953, p. 4.

51 This brief unsigned review appeared in the *New Yorker* 29 (9 May 1953): 137.

52 Séan O'Faoláin's article 'New Novels' appeared in the *Listener* 47 (27 March 1952): 525. It was reprinted in the *Vancouver News-Herald*, 3 May 1952, p. 7. Séan O'Faoláin was himself especially distinguished as a short story writer.

53 Wilson to Margaret Andrew, n.d., UBCL, Andrew Papers. Marghanita Laski's review was excerpted for the *Vancouver News-Herald*, 24 April 1952, p. 7, with

the title 'Vancouver Author Wins London Praise.' Laski was a prominent English critic, well known for her studies of nineteenth-century women writers such as Jane Austen and George Eliot.

54 Wilson to John Gray, 28 March and 10 April 1952, UBCL, Macmillan Company Collection, Box 2, Folder 1.

55 Hannah Atkinson wrote to Wilson reporting on the BBC discussions of her books, 30 and 31 March 1952. The letters are located in UBCL, Wilson Papers, Box 3, Folder 1.

56 See Beverley Mitchell's 'Ulysses in Vancouver: A Critical Approach to Ethel Wilson's "Tuesday and Wednesday,"' 110–22.

57 See Blanche H. Gelfant, 'The Hidden Mines in Ethel Wilson's Landscape (or An American Cat among Canadian Falcons),' in McMullen, ed., *The Ethel Wilson Symposium*, 119–39. This essay has been reprinted at least three times, most recently in Gelfant's *Cross-Cultural Reckonings: A Triptych of Russian, American, and Canadian Texts* (New York: Cambridge University Press, 1995): 100–18.

58 'Ethel Wilson,' CBC *Profile*, August 1955.

59 *Love and Salt Water*, 128.

60 From Bowen Island, Ethel Wilson had described exactly this scene in a letter to A.J.M. Smith, written 19 July 1947: 'Today the return of the gulls, a deer in the veg. garden, crows after eagle, eagle after kitten, kitten after robin, robin after snake – nearly all in one moment. The only one who got anything was the robin, who at last took several tucks in the snake and flew off' (Stouck, ed., *EW:SEL*, 142–3).

61 Wilson to John Gray, 23 Nov. 1957, UBCL, Macmillan Company Collection, Box 2, Folder 24.

62 Stouck, ed., *EW:SEL*, 161.

63 Theo Tufts in conversation, 10 May 2002.

64 Stouck, ed., *EW:SEL*, 140.

65 Some of Wilson's motives for writing 'Tuesday and Wednesday' are presented in 'Somewhere near the Truth,' published in Stouck, ed., *EW:SEL*, 81–91, and in a talk she gave to the Vancouver Soroptimists Club, 'The Tool That Fits the Hand,' a typescript of which is located in UBCL, Wilson Papers, Box 2, Folder 13.

66 Stouck, ed., *EW:SEL*, 188

67 Undated letter to Nan Cheney, UBCL, Nan Cheney Collection, Box 4, Folder 24.

68 Stouck, ed., *EW:SEW*, 171.

69 'The Theory of Angels,' UBCL, Wilson Papers, Box 7, Folder 31.

70 See Helen Sonthoff, 'The Novels of Ethel Wilson.'

71 See UBCL, Macmillan Company Collection, Box 1, Folder 18.

10. Doyenne

1 Willa Cather to playwright Zoë Akins, 22 Dec. 1932, Huntington Library, Zoë Akins Collection.

2 Wilson wrote to John Gray, 5 Feb. 1953, to say she had recently turned down requests for stories from *Weekend Magazine*, a medical journal, and a couple of 'women's journals,' and had very reluctantly agreed to speak on two radio programs (UBCL, Wilson Papers, Box 3, Folder 7).

3 The letter to Dorothy Livesay is dated simply 30 January, but internal evidence, including a reference to the Wilsons' departure on a trip in March, makes clear that the year was 1953 (the Wilsons spent that month in the area of Palm Springs, California) (QUL, Dorothy Livesay Collection).

4 Information about this informal group was collected from interviews with Dorothy Livesay (5 Oct. 1977), Earle Birney (14 Oct. 1984), and William McConnell (26 July 1987).

5 Stouck, ed., *EW:SEL*, 152.

6 Wilson to John Gray, 12 Dec. 1947, UBCL, Macmillan Company Collection, Box 1, Folder 15.

7 Stouck, ed., *EW:SEL*, 153.

8 Ibid.

9 McAlpine, *The Other Side of Silence*, 154.

10 William McConnell, interviewed 26 July 1987.

11 Wilson to Earle Birney, 10 April 1942, TFRBL, Earle Birney Collection, Box 24, Folder 25.

12 Earle Birney to Wilson, 23 May 1942, TFRBL, Earle Birney Collection, Box 24, Folder 25.

13 Esther Birney interviewed 20 Oct. 1998.

14 See Stouck, ed., *EW:SEL*, 168–70.

15 Wilson to Dorothy Livesay, undated letter, QUL, Dorothy Livesay Collection.

16 Wilson to John Gray, 15 Nov. 1950, UBCL, Macmillan Company Collection, Box 2, Folder 1.

17 Wilson to John Gray, 10 Jan. 1952, UBCL, Macmillan Company Collection, Box 2, Folder 1.

18 Wilson to John Gray, 15 Nov. 1961, UBCL, Macmillan Company Collection, Box 2, Folder 1.

19 Wilson to Earle Birney, Oct. 1952 [no day], TFRBL, Earle Birney Collection, Box 24, Folder 25

20 See letter from Robert Weaver to Wilson, 8 Jan. 1953, NAC, Robert Weaver Fonds, MG 31, D162, Vol. 5, File 25.

21 Wilson to John Gray, 10 Jan. 1952, UBCL, Macmillan Company Collection, Box 2, Folder 1.

22 In Dorothy Livesay's article 'Ethel Wilson: West Coast Novelist,' *Saturday Night* 67 (26 July 1952): 20, 36, Wilson is quoted as saying that what her generation is doing is merely spadework: 'We are preparing the ground for that real roaring talent – that genius who will be here we hope; but who perhaps may choose to spring from some other commonwealth soil.' She saw new organizations like the Canada Council as doing much good for the arts, but cautioned in an undated latter to Geoffrey Andrew at UBC that 'all our geese are not swans' (UBCL, Andrew Papers).

23 Stouck, ed., *EW:SEL*, 145.

24 There is a useful summary on the report of this commission in 'The Writer and His Public (1920–1960),' by Desmond Pacey, in *Literary History of Canada*, 18–19.

25 See Stouck, ed., *EW:SEL*, 181–3.

26 The panel took place during Book Week, mid-November 1952.

27 *Queen's Quarterly* 60 (Summer 1953): 260.

28 Several references to this story appear in Wilson's correspondence with Robert Weaver. See, for example, his letter to Wilson dated 12 Dec. 1951 and hers dated 24 Sept. 1952. According to Weaver's notation on this letter, the story was broadcast 2 July 1952, but no story of that title has survived (NAC, Robert Weaver Fonds, MG 31, D162, Vol. 5, File 25). The only other reference to this story is in an undated letter Wilson wrote to Gray in which she says that 'Statistics' is just 'chit-chat' and not worth publishing (UBCL, Macmillan Company Collection, Box 2, Folder 1).

29 See letter from Helen Schull to John Gray, 1 Feb. 1953, UBCL, Macmillan Company Collection, Box 2, Folder 3.

30 See McAlpine, *The Other Side of Silence*, 159.

31 See Morley Callaghan, 'Writers and Critics: A Minor League,' *Saturday Night* 70 (6 Nov. 1953): 32–3.

32 Wilson to John Gray, 8 July 1953, UBCL, Macmillan Company Collection, Box 2, Folder 1.

33 The subject of 'Lilly's Story' and censorship came up again in the House of Commons in 1959 in a discussion of a bill to amend the Criminal Code that would provide a new definition of obscenity and create legal provisions for the seizure of obscene materials. Extracts from Hansard were published in *Quill and Quire* 25 (Aug.-Sept. 1959). See especially page 22.

34 Stouck, ed., *EW:SEL*, 126.

35 McAlpine has published Livesay's essay with Wilson's corrections on the left-hand margin. See McAlpine, *The Other Side of Silence*, 210–16.

36 Dorothy Livesay to Wilson, 18 April 1952, UBCL, Wilson Papers, Box 3, Folder 12.

37 Wilson singles this novel out for special attention in her talk titled 'An Approach to Some Novels,' delivered at the Vancouver Institute, 8 Nov. 1958. See Stouck, ed., *EW:SEL*, 93.

38 See Joan Givner, *Mazo de la Roche: The Hidden Life*, 210.

39 See Stouck, ed., *EW:SEL*, 92–3.

40 Wilson to Jean and Alan Crawley, July 1962, UBCL, Alan Crawley Papers. This letter is reprinted, in part, in McAlpine, *The Other Side of Silence*, 170–1.

41 See Stouck, ed., *EW:SEL*, 245.

42 Wilson to Jean and Alan Crawley, Dec. 1961, UBCL, Alan Crawley Papers.

43 Wilson to Jean and Alan Crawley, 2 Feb. 1965, UBCL, Alan Crawley Papers.

44 This anecdote appears in McAlpine, *The Other Side of Silence*, 106–7.

45 From an interview with Mary Buckerfield White, 5 Feb. 2001.

46 McAlpine, *The Other Side of Silence*, 161.

47 Ibid., 107.

48 Nan Cheney, interviewed by telephone, 15 May 1985.

49 In conversation with Dorothy Livesay, 5 June 1991.

50 Stouck, ed., *EW:SEL*, 120–1.

51 Ibid., 201.

52 Letter to Mazo de la Roche, 26 Feb. 1955, TFRBL, Mazo de la Roche Collection, Box 14, Folder 47.

53 Wilson to John Gray, 26 Feb. 1951, UBCL, Macmillan Company Collection, Box 2, Folder 1.

54 Wilson to Jean and Alan Crawley, 1 Dec. 1963, UBCL, Alan Crawley Papers.

55 Wilson to John Gray, 28 March 1952, UBCL, Macmillan Company Collection, Box 2, Folder 1.

56 Stouck, ed., *EW:SEL*, 173–4.

57 Ibid., 174–7.

58 Wilson to John Gray, 5 Feb. 1953, UBCL, Wilson Papers, Box 3, Folder 7.

59 Wilson to Audrey Butler. See Stouck, ed., *EW:SEL*, 192–3.

60 Stouck, ed., *EW:SEL*, 178.

61 Ibid., 180.

62 McAlpine, *The Other Side of Silence*, 163.

63 Wilson to Margaret Andrew, undated letter, UBCL, Andrew Papers.

64 Wilson to Earle Birney, 31 Dec. 1953, TFRBL, Earle Birney Collection, Box 24, Folder 26.

65 Mention of both Acton and Petersham are found in a letter from Wilson to the Buckerfields, 20 Jan. 1954, EABC.

66 Wilson to Earle Birney, 1 Feb. 1954, TFRBL, Earle Birney Collection, Box 24, Folder 26. The Portugal letters to the Buckerfields are undated. They form part of the Ernest and Amy Buckerfield Collection (EABC).

67 Wilson to John Gray, undated letter, UBCL, Wilson Papers, Box 11, Folder 22.

11. *Swamp Angel*

1 These materials are located in UBCL, Wilson Papers, Box 4, Folders 1–13.

2 Wilson to John Gray, 19 Dec. 1951, UBCL, Macmillan Company Collection, Box 2, Folder 1.

3 Wilson to John Gray, undated letter, UBCL, Macmillan Company Collection, Box 2, Folder 1.

4 Wilson to John Gray, 1 Nov. 1952, UBCL, Wilson Papers, Box 3, Folder 7.

5 Stouck, ed., *EW:SEL*, 172–3.

6 See Lester R. Peterson, *The Gibson's Landing Story*, 41.

7 In addition to the books mentioned here, there is an American children's book titled *Swamp Angel*, by Anne Isaacs (New York: Dutton, 1994). The dust jacket announces that 'when Angelica Longrider was born, there was little to suggest that she would become the greatest woodswoman in Tennessee, single-handedly saving settlers from the jaws of a fearsome bear.' Perhaps Isaacs, who has lived near the Canadian border, deliberately gave the nickname Swamp Angel to her character because of its association with the strong woman of Ethel Wilson's novel.

8 Stouck, ed., *EW:SEL*, 173.

9 Mrs Bell to Wilson, UBCL, Macmillan Company Collection, Box 2, Folder 28.

10 John Gray to Wilson, 16 March 1953, UBCL, Wilson Papers, Box 3, Folder 7.

11 Stouck, ed., *EW:SEL*, 173–4.

12 John Gray to Wilson, 31 March 1953, UBCL, Wilson Papers, Box 3, Folder 7.

13 Although Gray refers to readers in the plural, only the reports of one reader, signed 'L.H.,' have survived. They are dated 11 March 1953 and 19 Aug. 1953, and are located with Wilson's personal papers, not with the Macmillan Collection. See UBCL, Wilson Papers, Box 11, Folder 19.

14 UBCL, Wilson Papers, Box 4, Folder 12.

15 Stouck, ed., *EW:SEL*, 186.

16 Ibid.

17 Stouck, ed., *EW:SEL*, 172.

18 Ibid., 187.

19 John Gray to Wilson, 4 Aug. 1953, UBCL, Wilson Papers, Box 3, Folder 7.
20 John Gray to Wilson, 20 Aug. 1953, UBCL, Wilson Papers, Box 3, Folder 7.
21 Stouck, ed., *EW:SEL*, 193.
22 Ibid.
23 Stouck, ed., *EW:SEL*, 232–5.
24 'Ethel Wilson,' CBC *Profile*, August 1955.
25 Wilson to John Gray, UBCL, Macmillan Company Collection, Box 2, Folder 1. This letter is undated, but internal evidence indicates it was written almost certainly in July 1952.
26 Stouck, ed., *EW:SEL*, 193.
27 Wilson to Desmond Pacey, 11 June 1966, NAC, Desmond Pacey Fonds, MG 30, D339. In 'The Rival Editions of Ethel Wilson's *Swamp Angel*,' *Essays on Canadian Writing* 77 (Oct. 2002): 63–89, Li-Ping Geng has made a careful study of the two versions, showing how the novel may be read differently, depending on which edition one is reading.
28 See W.A. Deacon, 'Ethel Wilson Humanly Wise in Novel of Fishing Camp,' *Globe and Mail*, 21 Aug. 1954, p. 32.
29 Wilson to John Gray, 19 Aug. 1954, UBCL, Macmillan Company Collection, Box 2, Folder 1.
30 John Graham, 'Books,' *Vancouver Province B.C. Magazine*, 25 Sept. 1954, p. 13; J.H.S., 'A Strong Sensitive Statement,' *Winnipeg Tribune*, n.d., n.pag.; and 'Ethel Wilson's "Swamp Angel" Has British Columbia Locale' (unsigned), *Toronto Daily Star*, 21 Aug. 1954, p. 24.
31 *Canadian Forum* 34 (Feb. 1955): 263.
32 Coleman Rosenberger, 'Man's Fellow Creatures on the Earth,' *New York Herald Tribune Book Review*, 5 Sept. 1954, p. 4.
33 Pamela Taylor, 'Escape to the North,' *Saturday Review* 37 (4 Sept. 1954): 22; Stuart Keate, 'Cariboo Country,' *New York Times Book Review*, 29 Aug. 1954, p. 17.
34 'Symbolism and Simplicity' (unsigned), *Times Literary Supplement*, 27 Aug. 1954, p. 54.
35 Parry Idris, 'New Novels,' *Listener* 52 (19 Aug. 1954): 295.
36 Wilson to John Gray, 10 Sept. 1954, UBCL, Macmillan Company Collection, Box 2, Folder 9.
37 See letters from Wilson to John Gray, 29 Aug. and 1 Sept. 1954, UBCL, Macmillan Company Collection, Box 2, Folder 9.
38 'Ethel Wilson,' CBC *Profile*, August 1955.
39 Stouck, ed., *EW:SEL*, 234.
40 Pacey's readings of the novel referred to here are found in his review in *Queen's Quarterly* 61 (Winter 1955): 555–6, and in his introduction to the New

Canadian Library edition of *Swamp Angel* (Toronto: McClelland and Stewart, 1962): 5–10.

41 Wilson discusses Olivier's *Hamlet* in 'Ethel Wilson,' CBC *Profile*, August 1955.

42 UBCL, Wilson Papers, Box 7, Folder 16.

43 Stouck, ed., *EW:SEL*, 235n4.

44 Ibid., 235n5.

45 Wilson quotes this passage from the New Testament book of Galatians (6:2) in the CBC interview on *Profile*.

46 Paul Comeau, 'Ethel Wilson's Characters,' 32.

47 See Donna Smyth, 'Strong Women in the Web: Women's Work and Community in Ethel Wilson's Fiction, in McMullen, ed., *The Ethel Wilson Symposium*, 87–95; Blanche Gelfant, 'The Hidden Mines in Ethel Wilson's Landscape (or an American Cat among Canadian Falcons),' in McMullen, ed., *The Ethel Wilson Symposium*, 119–39; and Donna Smyth, 'Maggie's Lake,' in Moss, ed., *The Canadian Novel: Modern Times*, 159–65.

48 In 'Hunt the Symbol,' Wilson in fact refers to reading Fraser's *The Golden Bough*.

49 The two essays summarized and discussed here are Heather Murray's 'Metaphor and Metonymy, Language and Landscape in Ethel Wilson's *Swamp Angel*' and Brent Thompson's 'Ethel Wilson, Wary Mythologist.'

50 Stouck, ed., *EW:SEL*, 186.

51 Wilson to Frank Upjohn, 16 Sept. 1954, UBCL, Wilson Papers, Box 3, Folder 24.

52 John Moss, *Patterns of Isolation in English-Canadian Fiction*, passim.

53 Wilson was consistent in her high regard for 'Tuesday and Wednesday.' The most straightforward statement can be found in a letter to John Gray, 14 March 1955, where she writes, '"Tuesday and Wednesday" is to me ... the best thing I've done' (UBCL, Macmillan Company Collection, Box 2, Folder 2).

12. *Love and Salt Water*

1 Wilson to John Gray, 9 Aug. 1954, UBCL, Macmillan Company Collection, Box 2, Folder 9.

2 Wilson to Ronald Hambleton, 29 Sept. 1955, UBCL, Ronald Hambleton Collection.

3 Wilson to Margaret and Geoffrey Andrew, undated letter, UBCL, Andrew Papers. As this letter refers to her misgivings about the CBC radio broadcast, it was written sometime in the early fall of 1954.

4 McAlpine, *The Other Side of Silence*, 166.

5　Wilson to Earle Birney, 8 Nov. 1954, TFRBL, Earle Birney Collection, Box 24, Folder 26.

6　Wilson to John Gray, 8 Dec. 1954, UBCL, Macmillan Company Collection, Box 2, Folder 2.

7　McAlpine, *The Other Side of Silence*, 168.

8　Wilson to Margaret and Geoffrey Andrew, undated letter, UBCL, Andrew Papers. Internal evidence suggests this letter was written in 1955.

9　Unpublished manuscript titled 'At What Point Do I Grow Old?' UBCL, Ronald Hambleton Papers.

10　Wilson talks about their people-watching in the CBC television interview for *Profile* with Roy Daniells, filmed in June 1955.

11　Wilson to Mazo de la Roche, 20 April 1955, TFRBL, Mazo de la Roche Collection, Box 14, Folder 47.

12　Stouck, ed., *EW:SEL*, 194–6.

13　Wilson to John Gray, 14 April 1955, UBCL, Macmillan Company Collection, Box 2, Folder 24.

14　Wilson to John Gray, 18 May 1955, UBCL, Macmillan Company Collection, Box 2, Folder 24.

15　Stouck, ed., *EW:SEL*, 196–7.

16　Ibid.

17　Ibid.

18　Claude Bissell, letter to the *Globe and Mail*, 9 April 1955, p. 18.

19　Stouck, ed., *EW:SEL*, 197–9.

20　See Wilson's 'Series of Combination of Events and Where Is John Goodwin?' 6–7.

21　Stouck, ed., *EW:SEL*, 197–9.

22　Wilson to John Gray, 12 Aug. 1955, UBCL, Macmillan Company Collection, Box 2, Folder 2.

23　MUL, Macmillan Company Collection, Box 40, Wilson Folder.

24　Stouck, ed., *EW:SEL*, 202.

25　Wilson to Roy Daniells, 17 May 1948, UBCL, Roy Daniells Collection.

26　Although in this CBC film Roy Daniells appears to be a man with few opinions, he in fact had very strong views about Ethel Wilson. In a taped interview with Ronald Hambleton, he describes Wilson as a self-assured writer with a patrician background who situated herself in a window above street level and looked down on the world. Her motives and manners were pure, he suggested, and she was never a manipulator, but there was protective distance in the way she placed herself. See Ronald Hambleton Collection, UBCL.

27　Stouck, ed., *EW:SEL*, 196.

28　Ibid., 199–200.

29 Wilson to Mazo de la Roche, 22 Aug. 1955, TFRBL, Mazo de la Roche Collection, Box 14, Folder 47.

30 Ibid.

31 Wilson to John Gray, 19 Dec. 1955, UBCL, Macmillan Company Collection, Box 2, Folder 9.

32 These opinions were offered by Joy McDonagh, interviewed 20 June 1979 and 3 Aug. 1984; by Phyllis Marshall, interviewed briefly after the funeral service for Ethel Wilson, 27 Dec. 1980; by Phyllis Rochfort, interviewed August 1989, and by Theodora Dowsley, interviewed June 1992.

33 Wilson to John Gray, 28 Dec. 1955, UBCL, Macmillan Company Collection, Box 2, Folder 9.

34 Wilson titled her presentation 'The Writer and the Public.' There are four typescripts of this unpublished talk in UBCL, Wilson Papers, Box 9, Folders 5–8.

35 Wilson to Mary McAlpine, 4 Feb. 1956, UBCL, Mary McAlpine Collection, Box 1, Folder 5.

36 'The Writer and the Public,' UBCL, Wilson Papers, Box 9, Folders 5–8.

37 Letter from Audrey Butler, 21 Dec. 2000.

38 Wilson to John Gray, 19 April 1956, UBCL, Macmillan Company Collection, Box 2, Folder 24.

39 McAlpine, *The Other Side of Silence*, 178–9.

40 'To Keep the Memory of So Worthy a Friend' was first published in *Reporter* 15 (13 Dec. 1956): 35–6, and reprinted in *Mrs Golightly and Other Stories*.

41 Wilson to John Gray, 30 May 1956, UBCL, Macmillan Company Collection, Box 2, Folder 9.

42 Stouck, ed., *EW:SEL*, 190.

43 Manuscripts for this story are located in UBCL, Wilson Papers, Box 2, Folders 1–5; typescripts with the title 'Herself When Young' are located in UBCL, Wilson Papers, Box 12, Folders 4 and 5.

44 Wilson to John Gray, undated letter, UBCL, Macmillan Company Collection, Box 2, Folder 2.

45 John Gray to Wilson, 21 July 1954, UBCL, Macmillan Company Collection, Box 2, Folder 6.

46 John Gray to Wilson, 8 Sept. 1954, UBCL, Macmillan Company Collection, Box 2, Folder 6.

47 All the Macmillan reports on the different versions of *Love and Salt Water* are located in UBCL, Macmillan Company Collection, Box 2, Folder 4.

48 The epigraph and its withdrawal are in evidence in UBCL, Wilson Papers, Box 5, Folder 21.

49 Ending B is located in UBCL, Wilson Papers, Box 5, Folder 27.

50 Wilson to John Gray, undated letter, UBCL, Macmillan Company Collection, Box 2, Folder 9.

51 Wilson to John Gray, 3 Oct. 1955, UBCL, Macmillan Company Collection, Box 2, Folder 9.

52 Wilson to John Gray, undated letter, UBCL, Macmillan Company Collection, Box 2, Folder 9.

53 John Gray to Wilson, 17 Nov. 1955, UBCL, Macmillan Company Collection, Box 2, Folder 6.

54 Wilson to Daniel Macmillan, 30 Nov. 1955, UBCL, Macmillan Company Collection, Box 2, Folder 9.

55 Daniel Macmillan to Wilson, 20 Dec. 1955, UBCL, Macmillan Company Collection, Box 2, Folder 7.

56 Wilson to John Gray, 28 Dec. 1955, UBCL, Macmillan Company Collection, Box 2, Folder 9.

57 See 'Somewhere near the Truth,' published in Stouck, ed., *EW:SEL*, 81–91. Discussion of *Love and Salt Water* is on pages 89–90.

58 Wilson to John Gray, 21 May 1955, UBCL, Macmillan Company Collection, Box 2, Folder 24.

59 Philip Oakes's omnibus review, including mention of *Love and Salt Water*, is titled 'Long Wait for a Jackpot' and appeared in the *Evening Standard*, 18 Sept. 1956, p. 35.

60 Anonymous review titled 'Notes for the Novel-Reader,' *Illustrated London News*, 17 Nov. 1956, p. 864.

61 *Edmonton Journal*, 15 Dec. 1956.

62 Eric Nicol, 'Books,' *Vancouver Province Magazine*, 17 Nov. 1956, p. 16.

63 Harriet Hill, 'With Flashes of Insight,' *Montreal Gazette*, 13 Oct. 1956, p. 31.

64 W.A. Deacon, untitled review, *Globe and Mail*, 13 Oct. 1956, p. 29.

65 Miriam Waddington, 'Canadian Novelists,' *Queen's Quarterly* 64 (Spring 1957): 143–4.

66 See Blanche H. Gelfant, 'The Capitalistic Will: Women and Inheritance in *My Mortal Enemy* and *Love and Salt Water*,' in *Cross-Cultural Reckonings*, 119–81.

67 See Anjali Bhelande, 'Being the Other,' in *Self Beyond Self*, 36–76.

68 See Gelfant, *Cross-Cultural Reckonings*, 140, 178–9n60.

13. Mrs Golightly

1 Wilson to John Gray, 4 May 1955, UBCL, Macmillan Company Collection, Box 2, Folder 24.

2 McAlpine, *The Other Side of Silence*, 173–4.

3 Sally Creighton, interviewed by Ronald Hambleton, UBCL, Ronald Hambleton Collection.

4 Wilson's talk on Joyce Cary is published in Stouck, ed., *EW:SEL*, 77–81.

5 Wilson to John Gray, 18 Jan. 1957, UBCL, Macmillan Company Collection, Box 2, Folder 24.

6 See Stouck, ed., *EW:SEL*, 81–91.

7 There are two manuscripts for this novel in UBCL, Wilson Papers, Box 5, Folders 1–20.

8 Wilson to John Gray, 27 March 1957, UBCL, Macmillan Company Collection, Box 2, Folder 19.

9 John Gray to Wilson, 30 April 1957, UBCL, Macmillan Company Collection, Box 2, Folder 19. A report signed by 'ES' and dated 23 April 1957, upon which Gray draws, can be found in Macmillan Company Collection, Box 2, Folder 18.

10 UBCL, Wilson Papers, Box 11, Folder 4.

11 Wilson to John Gray, 4 May 1957, UBCL, Macmillan Company Collection, Box 2, Folder 19.

12 John Gray to Wilson, 7 Nov. 1957, UBCL, Macmillan Company Collection, Box 2, Folder 23.

13 Wilson to John Gray, 12 April 1957, UBCL, Macmillan Company Collection, Box 2, Folder 24.

14 Wilson to John Gray, 16 Nov. 1957, UBCL, Macmillan Company Collection, Box 2, Folder 24.

15 Wilson to McAlpine, letter dated 1956, UBCL, Mary McAlpine Collection, Box 1, Folder 5.

16 Anecdotes from an interview with Mary Buckerfield White, 5 Feb. 2001.

17 Wilson to John Gray, 10 April 1960, UBCL, Macmillan Company Collection, Box 2, Folder 25.

18 Three typescripts of this unpublished talk are located in UBCL, Wilson Papers, Box 9, Folders 20–2.

19 Wilson to John Gray, undated letter, UBCL, Macmillan Company Collection, Box 2, Folder 24.

20 Wilson to John Gray, 2 March 1958, UBCL, Macmillan Company Collection, Box 2, Folder 24.

21 This talk was published as 'An Address to the Students of the School of Architecture, U.B.C.,' *Royal Architectural Institute of Canada Journal* 36, no, 1 (April 1959): 130–3.

22 Three manuscripts and a typescript for this talk, delivered 8 Nov. 1958 at UBC, are located in UBCL, Wilson Papers, Box 9, Folders 1–4. A small portion of the lecture has been published in Stouck, ed., *EW:SEL*, 91–4.

23 The only mention of Wilson is a half-sentence reference to Nell Severance. See Margaret Atwood, *Survival*, 199.

24 Wilson to John Gray, 8 Nov. 1958, UBCL, Macmillan Company Collection, Box 2, Folder 24.

25 Wilson to John Gray, 9 Nov. 1958, UBCL, Macmillan Company Collection, Box 2, Folder 24.

26 The fullest account of this unidentified woman's experience occurs in a letter to Earle Birney, 9 Dec. 1959. See Stouck, ed., *EW:SEL*, 213–14.

27 Wilson to Mazo de la Roche, 5 Nov. No year is given, but the placement of this letter in the collection is with correspondence from 1953 (TFRBL, Mazo de la Roche Collection, Box 14, Folder 47).

28 Wilson to John Gray, 29 May 1958, UBCL, Macmillan Company Collection, Box 2, Folder 24.

29 Wilson to John Gray, 3 Oct. 1958, MUL, Macmillan Company Collection, Box 40, Folder 18.

30 A typescript for this talk titled 'The Tool That Fits the Hand' is located in UBCL, Wilson Papers, Box 2, Folder 13.

31 This essay was first published in *Canadian Literature* 2 (Autumn 1959): 10–19, and was reprinted in *The Masks of Fiction*, ed. A.J.M. Smith (Toronto: McClelland and Stewart, 1961): 23–32. See also Stouck, ed., *EW:SEL*, 94–103.

32 Wilson to John Gray, 9 Dec. 1959, UBCL, Macmillan Company Collection, Box 2, Folder 16.

33 Stouck, ed., *EW:SEL*, 213.

34 Earle Birney to Wilson, 9 Jan. 1960, TFRBL, Earle Birney Collection, Box 24, Folder 28.

35 Wilson to John Gray, 28 Dec. 1961, UBCL, Macmillan Company Collection, Box 2, Folder 25.

36 Wilson to Jean and Alan Crawley, 2 Feb. 1965, UBCL, Alan Crawley Papers.

37 Wilson to John Gray, 14 Jan. 1958, UBCL, Macmillan Company Collection, Box 2, Folder 29.

38 John Gray to Wilson, 19 Nov. 1957, UBCL, Macmillan Company Collection, Box 2, Folder 23.

39 To view *Mrs Golightly and Other Stories* in the planning stages with the many titles considered for this volume, see letters from Wilson to Gray dated 6 March 1958, UBCL, Macmillan Company Collection, Box 2, Folder 16, and 20 Nov. 1958, in Stouck, ed., *EW:SEL*, 212.

40 See the letter from Wilson to Gray dated 13 Sept. 1959, UBCL, Macmillan

Company Collection, Box 2, Folder 16. Here she says the stories are not good enough to publish, and that she is not being coy, just critical.

41 Wilson to John Gray, 23 Oct. 1959, UBCL, Macmillan Company Collection, Box 2, Folder 16.

42 Reader's report dated 29 Oct. 1959, UBCL, Macmillan Company Collection, Box 2, Folder 11.

43 Wilson to Jean and Alan Crawley, 9 Jan. 1961, UBCL, Alan Crawley Papers.

44 See James King, *The Life of Margaret Laurence*, 143.

45 Margaret Laurence, 'A Friend's Tribute to Ethel Wilson,' *Toronto Star*, 24 Jan. 1981, p. F7.

46 Margaret Laurence, interviewed June 1977 and June 1984.

47 Margaret Laurence, taped interview by Ronald Hambleton. See Ronald Hambleton Collection, UBCL.

48 Stouck, ed., *EW:SEL*, 218.

49 See letter from Margaret Laurence to Beverley Mitchell in Mitchell's 'Ethel Wilson (1888–1980),' 192. Nora Foster Stovel develops this idea in her essay titled 'Female Excalibur As Literary Legacy: Ethel Wison's *Swamp Angel* and Margaret Laurence's *The Fire-Dwellers*.'

50 J.R. (Tim) Struthers, 'The Real Material: An Interview with Alice Munro,' in MacKendrick, ed., *Probable Fictions: Alice Munro's Narrative Acts*, 18. Munro and Wilson never met, but Munro was present at the UBC conference on Canadian writing in 1956 and heard Wilson speak (Alice Munro to Mary McAlpine, 14 Oct. 1980, UBCL, Mary McAlpine Collection, Box 2, Folder 1).

51 Wilson to John Gray, 20 May 1960, UBCL, Macmillan Company Collection, Box 2, Folder 16.

52 Wilson to John Gray, 19 July 1960, UBCL, Macmillan Company Collection, Box 2, Folder 16.

53 Reader reports for *Mrs Golightly* are located in UBCL, Macmillan Company Collection, Box 2, Folder 16.

54 See Wilson to John Gray, undated letter, UBCL, Macmillan Company Collection, Box 2, Folder 16.

55 John Gray to Wilson, 14 Feb. 1961, UBCL, Macmillan Company Collection, Box 2. Folder 13.

56 Wilson to Kildare Dobbs, 12 March 1961, UBCL, Macmillan Company Collection, Box 2, Folder 16.

57 Wilson to Kildare Dobbs, 26 March 1961, UBCL, Macmillan Company Collection, Box 2, Folder 16.

58 John Gray to Wilson, 29 March 1961, UBCL, Macmillan Company Collection, Box 2, Folder 13.

59 Ellen Stafford, 'For Tired Taste-Buds: She Sees the Inner Worlds,' *Globe and Mail*, 21 Oct. 1961, p. 21.

60 Donald Stainsby, 'Delicate, Precise Prose Shines in Collection of Wilson Stories,' *Vancouver Sun*, 11 Oct. 1961, p. 5.

61 Robert Weaver, 'Tour de Force: Mrs Golightly Humane, Witty AND Canadian,' *Toronto Daily Star*, 9 Dec. 1961, p. 30.

62 Lew Gloin, 'Medallist Ethel Wilson Displays Deft Writing,' *Hamilton Spectator*, 23 Dec. 1961, p. 51.

63 Hilda Kirkwood, 'Realist with a Difference,' *Saturday Night* 76 (28 Oct. 1961): 41–2.

64 'Short Stories,' unsigned, *Times of India*, 27 May 1962, p. 11.

65 See Stouck, ed., *EW:SEL*, 228.

66 W.H. New, ed., *Canadian Short Fiction*, 150.

67 See Stouck, 'The Ethel Wilson Papers,' in McMullen, ed., *The Ethel Wilson Symposium*, 54. The manuscript for this story is located in UBCL, Wilson Papers, Box 6, Folder 18.

68 John Gray to Wilson, 7 Nov. 1957, UBCL, Macmillan Company Collection, Box 2, Folder 23.

69 See W.J. Keith, 'Overview: Ethel Wilson, Providence, and the Vocabulary of Vision,' in McMullen, ed., *The Ethel Wilson Symposium*, 105–18.

70 This variation on 'The Writer and the Public' can be found in UBCL, Wilson Papers, Box 9, Folder 8.

71 Published in Stouck, ed., *EW:SEL*, 31–41.

72 Wilson does mention writing this story in a letter dated 25 Jan. 1957 to R.E. Watters, who was selecting two of her stories for the provincial centennial volume, *B.C. Anthology*. She had sent 'Mr Sleepwalker' to Watters for his opinion but advises him that it is a 'nasty' tale, written for amusement not publication. She goes on to explain its writing this way: 'I did see such a person on a Winnipeg streetcar. He interested me enormously, & I really longed to know more about him. I thought he was quite awful. Of course I did not see him again, but as he reminded me so much of a fox or a very respectable weasel, he seemed to be a good thing to make a story about' (R.E. Watters Papers, UBCL, Box 1, Folder 30). There may also be a connection between this story and 'The Demon Lover,' an eerie and very popular story by Elizabeth Bowen, whom Wilson admired.

73 Stouck, ed., *EW:SEL*, 145.

74 Wilson to Jean and Alan Crawley, undated letter, UBCL, Alan Crawley Papers.

75 Wilson to Jean and Alan Crawley, 1962, UBCL, Alan Crawley Papers.

14. Grande Dame

1 Wilson to Jean and Alan Crawley, undated letter (internal evidence indicates early 1960s) UBCL, Alan Crawley Papers.

2 Wilson to John Gray, 11 Aug. 1959, UBCL, Macmillan Company Collection, Box 2, Folder 16.

3 Wilson to Mary McAlpine, 16 Oct. 1960, UBCL, Mary McAlpine Collection, Box 1, Folder 11.

4 Wilson to Jean and Alan Crawley, 26 June 1961, UBCL, Alan Crawley Papers.

5 Wilson to Mary McAlpine, 18 May 1961, UBCL, Mary McAlpine Collection, Box 1, Folder 8.

6 Wilson to John Gray, May 1961, UBCL, Macmillan Company Collection, Box 2, Folder 16.

7 See Wilson to Jean and Alan Crawley, 1961, UBCL, Alan Crawley Papers; and McAlpine, *The Other Side of Silence*, 202.

8 The article appeared 8 Sept. 1961, p. 23; a copy is located in UBCL, Wilson Papers, Box 11, Folder 7.

9 Wilson to Alan and Jean Crawley, 19 Oct. 1961, UBCL, Alan Crawley Papers.

10 A copy of John Gray's speech can be found in UBCL, Wilson Papers, Box 11, Folder 7.

11 A copy of Wilson's reply to John Gray is located in UBCL, Wilson Papers, Box 10, Folder 2.

12 See, for example, Wilson to Jean and Alan Crawley, July 1962, UBCL, Alan Crawley Papers. In an earlier letter to Mary McAlpine, simply dated 1956, she says that in her opinion *Anna Karenina* makes all other novels shrivel in comparison (UBCL, Mary McAlpine Collection, Box 1, Folder 5).

13 Wilson to Jean and Alan Crawley, 11 Nov. 1961, UBCL, Alan Crawley Papers.

14 In a letter dated October 1960, she relates to Mary McAlpine the necessity of waking Wallace at 7 A.M. to be driven to the hospital, where a cauterization procedure was necessary to stop a massive nasal haemorrhage (UBCL, Mary McAlpine Collection, Box 1, Folder 11).

15 The dressmaker is identified as the carver's mother in a letter to the Crawleys dated 30 Oct. 1962, UBCL, Alan Crawley Papers. She worked for Ethel Wilson for several years and is mentioned in two undated letters to the Crawleys, including one in which Mrs Reid is described as having fallen on the street and broken her hip: 'She must have lain there in the road, poor lamb, like a little white-haired doll.' Mrs Reid had written to Ethel from hospital. In a brief interview, 26 Nov. 1989, Bill Reid recalled sometimes driving his

mother to work for 'rich clients in the West End,' but he did not realize one
of these was the novelist, Ethel Wilson.

16 Wilson to Jean and Alan Crawley, 1962, UBCL, Alan Crawley Papers.

17 See McAlpine, *The Other Side of Silence*, 201.

18 See Wilson Papers, Box 10, Folder 2, UBCL.

19 McAlpine, *The Other Side of Silence*, 201.

20 Wilson to Jean and Alan Crawley, 1961, UBCL, Alan Crawley Papers.

21 Wilson to John Gray, 11 Aug. 1959, UBCL, Macmillan Company Collection,
    Box 2, Folder 16.

22 The Koerner Foundation was established in the mid-1950s to further the per-
    forming arts in British Columbia, and from the outset, Wilson questioned if
    there was enough genuine artistic enterprise and talent in the province to
    support. See, for example, her letter to John Gray as early as 27 Jan. 1956,
    UBCL, Macmillan Company Collection, Box 2, Folder 9.

23 'In Defense of a Little Learning,' 5–6, UBCL, Wilson Papers, Box 9, Folders
    9–10.

24 Wilson to Jean and Alan Crawley, July 1962, UBCL, Alan Crawley Papers.

25 Wilson to John Gray, 16 Feb. 1959, UBCL, Macmillan Company Collection,
    Box 2, Folder 16.

26 Wilson to Jean and Alan Crawley, 1962, UBCL, Alan Crawley Papers.

27 Ella Fell was a wealthy American woman who married Colonel James Fell, an
    English-born Canadian, and moved to Vancouver in the 1930s. She knew
    Ethel Wilson through mutual friends living in the Shaughnessy area of Van-
    couver. Wilson's comment on rich people lacking self-awareness is from a
    letter to Margaret Andrew, 27 Oct. 1962, UBCL, Andrew Papers.

28 Wilson to Jean and Alan Crawley, 28 Dec. 1960, UBCL, Alan Crawley Papers.

29 Wilson to Jean and Alan Crawley (two letters joined together and dated
    1961), UBCL, Alan Crawley Papers.

30 Wilson to Mary McAlpine, 9 Feb. 1964, UBCL, Mary McAlpine Collection,
    Box 1, Folder 9.

31 Wilson to Jean and Alan Crawley, 1961 (letter dated by archivist as 28 July,
    but Christmas reference makes this dating clearly inaccurate), UBCL, Alan
    Crawley Papers.

32 Wilson to Jean and Alan Crawley, 26 June 1961, UBCL, Alan Crawley Papers.

33 Wilson to Margaret Andrew, 10 Feb. 1962, UBCL, Andrew Papers.

34 Wilson to Jean and Alan Crawley, 1962, UBCL, Alan Crawley Papers.

35 Wilson to Jean and Alan Crawley, 3 Dec. 1962, UBCL, Alan Crawley Papers.

36 Stouck, ed., *EW:SEL*, 229–30.

37 Wilson to John Gray, 23 April 1963, UBCL, Macmillan Company Collection,
    Box 2, Folder 25.

38 Wilson to Margaret Andrew, 10 May 1963, UBCL, Andrew Papers.
39 Wilson to Margaret Andrew, 8 May and 10 May 1963, UBCL, Andrew Papers.
40 Wilson to Nan Cheney, undated letter, UBCL, Nan Cheney Papers.
41 Wilson to Margaret Andrew, 8 May 1964, UBCL, Andrew Papers.
42 Wilson to John Gray, 6 April 1964, UBCL, Macmillan Company Collection, Box 2, Folder 25.
43 Wilson to Margaret Andrew, 8 May 1964, UBCL, Andrew Papers.
44 John Gray to Wilson, 22 April 1964, UBCL, Macmillan Company Collection, Box 2, Folder 23.
45 Stouck, ed., *EW:SEL*, 240.
46 Ibid., 237.
47 Ibid., 239.
48 Wilson to Margaret Laurence, 20 May 1964, YUL, Margaret Laurence Collection.
49 Stouck, ed., *EW:SEL*, 239.
50 Wilson to John Gray, 1959, UBCL, Macmillan Company Collection, Box 2, Folder 24.
51 John Gray to Wilson, 21 Oct. 1959, UBCL, Macmillan Company Collection, Box 2, Folder 23.
52 Stouck, ed., *EW:SEL*, 110.
53 Wilson to Jean and Alan Crawley, 14 Oct. 1962, UBCL, Alan Crawley Papers.
54 Stouck, ed., *EW:SEL*, 231.
55 Ibid., 230.
56 Ibid., 239
57 Ibid., 242n2.
58 Ibid., 240, 242.
59 Ibid., 246–7.
60 'Of Alan Crawley,' *Canadian Literature* 19 (Winter 1964): 33–42.
61 Robertson Davies, *Holiday* (April 1964).
62 Wilson to Jean and Alan Crawley, Dec. 1964, UBCL, Alan Crawley Papers.
63 Stouck, ed., *EW:SEL*, 247.
64 Ibid., 245.
65 Wilson to John Gray, 11 Jan. 1966, UBCL, Macmillan Company Collection, Box 2, Folder 25.
66 John Rackliffe to John Gray, 5 May 1965, UBCL, Macmillan Company Collection, Box 2, Folder 17.
67 Wallace Wilson to John Gray, 8 March 1966, UBCL, Wilson Papers, Box 11, Folder 20.
68 Stouck, ed., *EW:SEL*, 248.

15. Widow

1 There were two articles in the *Vancouver Sun* about Wallace Wilson's death and funeral service. See the issues for 14 March 1966, p. 11, and 16 March 1966, p. 4.

2 McAlpine, *The Other Side of Silence*, 206.

3 Stouck, ed., *EW:SEL*, 248.

4 Wilson to Jean and Alan Crawley, undated letter, UBCL, Alan Crawley Papers.

5 Stouck, ed., *EW:SEL*, 249.

6 Donald Stainsby took over this project, which was published by Macmillan in 1962 as *Vancouver: Sights and Sounds*, with drawings by George Kuthan.

7 John Gray to Wilson, 19 Jan. 1966, UBCL, Macmillan Company Collection, Box 2, Folder 23.

8 Wallace Wilson to John Gray, 21 Jan. 1966, UBCL, Macmillan Company Collection, Box 2, Folder 26.

9 Wilson to John Gray, 4 Feb. 1967, UBCL, Macmillan Company Collection, Box 2, Folder 25.

10 John Gray to Wilson, 9 Feb. 1967, UBCL, Macmillan Company Collection, Box 2, Folder 23.

11 Hugo McPherson, *Telegram* [Toronto], 11 March 1967.

12 A copy of Ronald Hambleton's program, 'The Two Worlds of Ethel Wilson,' for *CBC Tuesday Night*, 28 Nov. 1967, is part of the Hambleton tape collection at UBCL.

13 Wilson to Nan Cheney, 20 Feb. 1967, UBCL, Nan Cheney Collection, Box 4, Folder 24. In fact, she wrote to Pacey 17 May 1968 to say the book gave her great pleasure, that it was 'full of taste, finesse, decision, & teaches me so much' (NAC, Desmond Pacey Fonds, MG 30, D339).

14 McAlpine, *The Other Side of Silence*, 207.

15 Wilson to Margaret Laurence, 25 Dec. 1967, YUL, Margaret Laurence Collection.

16 Wilson to John Gray, 4 April 1969, UBCL, Macmillan Company Collection, Box 2, Folder 25.

17 Wilson to Jean Crawley, 26 April 1969, UBCL, Alan Crawley Papers.

18 Wilson to John Gray, 12 June 1970, UBCL, Macmillan Company Collection, Box 2, Folder 25.

19 Wilson to Jean and Alan Crawley, 31 Aug. 1971, UBCL, Alan Crawley Papers.

20 Wilson to John Gray, 18 Oct. 1971, UBCL, Macmillan Company Collection, Box 2, Folder 25.

21 Stouck, ed., *EW:SEL*, 253–4.

22 Wilson to Jean and Alan Crawley, undated letter, UBCL, Alan Crawley Papers.

23 Wilson to John Gray, 10 April 1971, UBCL, Macmillan Company Collection, Box 2, Folder 25.

24 Wilson to George Woodcock, 19 May [1970?], QUL, George Woodcock Collection, Box 3, Folder 59.

25 Wilson to John Gray, 27 April 1969, UBCL, Macmillan Company Collection, Box 2, Folder 25.

26 Wilson to John Gray, 12 Dec. 1970, UBCL, Macmillan Company Collection, Box 2, Folder 25.

27 Wilson to Geoffrey and Margaret Andrew, 2 July 1970, UBCL, the Andrew Papers.

28 Wilson to Geoffrey and Margaret Andrew, undated letter, UBCL, the Andrew Papers.

29 Wilson to Nan Cheney, 7 July 1972, UBCL, Nan Cheney Collection, Box 4, Folder 21.

30 Wilson to Jean and Alan Crawley, undated letter, UBCL, Alan Crawley Papers.

31 Wilson to Nan Cheney, 3 Aug. 1966, UBCL, Nan Cheney Collection, Box 4, Folder 20.

32 Wilson to John Gray, 23 May 1969, UBCL, Macmillan Company Collection, Box 2, Folder 25; and Wilson to Jean Crawley, 25 May 1969, UBCL, Alan Crawley Papers.

33 Gabrielle Roy to Joyce Marshall, 10 May 1970, Fonds Gabrielle Roy, Montreal.

34 Gabrielle Roy to Joyce Marshall, 9 Feb. 1973, Fonds Gabrielle Roy, Montreal.

35 Wilson to Jean and Alan Crawley, 31 Aug. 1971, UBCL, Alan Crawley Papers.

36 Idamay Martin to John Gray, 23 May 1972, UBCL, Macmillan Company Collection, Box 2, Folder 25.

37 McAlpine, *The Other Side of Silence*, 207.

38 Wilson to Nan Cheney, 18 June 1974, UBCL, Nan Cheney Collection, Box 4, Folder 23.

39 This account is an amalgam of two pieces McAlpine wrote: 'Ethel Wilson As I Knew Her,' in McMullen, ed., *The Ethel Wilson Symposium*, 11; and *The Other Side of Silence*, 207–8.

40 Wilson to Nan Cheney, 24 Aug. 1974, UBCL, Nan Cheney Collection, Box 4, Folder 23.

Bibliography

A full account of primary and secondary sources until 1982 appears in Bonnie Martyn McComb's *Ethel Wilson: An Annotated Bibliography* (Downsview, ON: ECW Press, 1984). Given below is an abbreviated description of primary sources, an updated account of archival materials, and a selected list of secondary sources.

I. Ethel Wilson's Published Works

1. Books

For each title, the first edition is given and also the most recent edition, which has served as the source of quotations for this biography. Full accounts of editions, reprintings, and foreign translations of each book are given at the close of the chapters.

Hetty Dorval. Toronto: Macmillan, 1947. Toronto: McClelland and Stewart, 1990.

The Innocent Traveller. Toronto and London: Macmillan, 1949. Toronto: McClelland and Stewart, 1990.

The Equations of Love. Toronto and London: Macmillan, 1952. Toronto: McClelland and Stewart, 1990.

Swamp Angel. Toronto and London: Macmillan, 1954. Toronto: McClelland and Stewart, 1990.

Love and Salt Water. Toronto and London: Macmillan, 1956. Toronto: McClelland and Stewart, 1990.

Mrs Golightly and Other Stories. Toronto: Macmillan, 1961. Toronto: McClelland and Stewart, 1990.

Ethel Wilson: Stories, Essays, and Letters. Ed. David Stouck. Vancouver: University of British Columbia Press, 1987.

2. Short Stories

Listed here are first publications, with current printing in *Mrs Golightly and Other Stories* indicated as *MGOS*, and publication in *Ethel Wilson: Stories, Essays, and Letters*, as *EW:SEL*.

'The Surprising Adventures of Peter.' *Vancouver Province*, 1 March 1919 to 14 June 1919 (serialized on page 6 as an advertisement for 'Malkin's Best').

'I Just Love Dogs.' *New Statesman and Nation*, 4 Dec. 1937, pp. 929–30. *MGOS*, 85–9.

'I Have a Father in the Promised Land.' *New Statesman and Nation*, 4 Feb. 1939, pp. 167–9 (chapter 12 of *The Innocent Traveller*).

'Hurry, Hurry.' *New Statesman and Nation*, 25 Nov. 1939, pp. 754–5. *MGOS*, 111–15.

'On Nimpish Lake.' *Canadian Forum*, July 1942, pp. 119–20. *MGOS*, 36–40.

'We Have to Sit Opposite.' *Chatelaine*, May 1945, pp. 15, 46–7. *MGOS*, 56–66.

'The Cigar and the Poor Young Girl.' *Echoes*, Autumn 1945, pp. 11, 46.

'The Innumerable Laughter.' *Orion*, Autumn 1947, pp. 121–30 (chapter 17 of *The Innocent Traveller*).

'Down at English Bay.' *Here and Now* 1 (May 1948): 7–12 (chapter 14 of *The Innocent Traveller*).

'The Funeral Home.' *Northern Review* 4 (April-May 1951): 12–15 (chapter 4 of 'Tuesday and Wednesday' in *The Equations of Love*).

'Miss Tritt.' *Northern Review* 5 (Oct.-Nov. 1951): 11–19 (chapter 8 of 'Tuesday and Wednesday' in *The Equations of Love*).

'Mrs Golightly and the First Convention.' In *Canadian Short Stories*. Ed. Robert Weaver and Helen James. Toronto: Oxford University Press, 1952, 151–64. *MGOS*, 9–24.

'The Escape.' *Northern Review* 6 (June-July 1953): 2–7 (chapter 3 of *Swamp Angel*).

'Lilly's Story.' *B.C. Magazine* [*Vancouver Province*], 31 Oct. 1953, pp. 1–12 (from 'Lilly's Story' in *The Equations of Love*).

'The Birds.' *Northern Review* 7 (Oct.-Nov. 1954): 24–7. *MGOS*, 67–70.

'Swamp Angel.' *Queen's Quarterly* 60 (Winter 1954): 526–31 (from *Swamp Angel*).

'Haply the Soul of My Grandmother.' In *British Columbia: A Centennial Anthology*. Ed. R.E. Watters. Toronto: McClelland and Stewart, 1958, 560–70. *MGOS*, 25–35.

'The Window.' *Tamarack Review* 8 (Summer 1958): 3–16. *MGOS*, 196–211.

'A Drink with Adolphus.' *Tamarack Review* 16 (Summer 1960): 5–16. *MGOS*, 71–84.

'From Flores.' *MGOS*, 41–51.

'God Help the Young Fishman.' *MGOS*, 52–5.

'Fog.' *MGOS*, 102–10.

'Truth and Mrs Forrester.' *MGOS*, 116–30.

'Mr Sleepwalker.' *MGOS*, 131–50.

'Beware the Jabberwock, My Son ... Beware the Jubjub Bird.' *MGOS*, 151–84.

'Till Death Us Do Part.' *MGOS*, 185–95.

'Simple Translation.' *Saturday Night*, 23 Dec. 1961, p. 19. Abridged and reprinted
    as 'Journey to a Fair Land' in *Reader's Digest*, April 1962, pp. 143–4.

'A Visit to the Frontier.' *Tamarack Review* 33 (Autumn 1964): 55–65. *EW:SEL*,
    45–55.

'Fountains in Italy, 1868.' *EW:SEL*, 5–7.

'A Ripple on the Ocean of Time.' *EW:SEL*, 7–14.

'Lay Your Commands upon Her, Joseph.' *EW:SEL*, 15–20.

'The Very Ferocious Man.' *EW:SEL*, 20–5.

'In the Golden Days.' *EW:SEL*, 31–41.

'The Mirage of Edward Pontifex.' *EW:SEL*, 41–5.

'The Life and Death of Mrs Grant.' *EW:SEL*, 57–73.

3. Articles, Essays, Letters, and Reviews

'A Night in Lytton.' *Saturday Magazine* [*Vancouver Province*], 19 Oct. 1940, p. 6.

'This Was Miss Gordon's School in 1898.' *Vancouver Province*, 5 Feb. 1948, p. 4.

'From the Farthest West.' *Trinity Hall School Magazine* [Southport, England]
    (1951): 29–30.

'On a Portuguese Balcony.' *Tamarack Review* 1 (Autumn 1956): 7–17.

'To Keep the Memory of So Worthy a Friend.' *Reporter* [New York], 13 Dec. 1956,
    pp. 35–6. *MGOS*, 94–101.

'A Monologue to a Stranger.' *Community Arts Council of Vancouver, B.C.*, Summer
    1957, pp. 22–3.

'My Father's Teacher.' *Montrealer*, July 1958, pp. 27–8.

'An Address to the Students of the School of Architecture, U.B.C.' *Royal Architec-
    tural Institute of Canada Journal* 36 (April 1959): 130–3.

'A Cat among the Falcons: Reflections on the Writer's Craft.' *Canadian Literature*
    2 (Autumn 1959): 10–19.

Letter. *Prism* 1 (Winter 1959): 69.

'The Bridge or the Stokehold? Views of the Novelist's Art.' *Canadian Literature* 5
    (Summer 1960): 43–7.

'The Princess.' Rev. of *Legends of Vancouver*, by Pauline Johnson. *Canadian Litera-
    ture* 9 (Summer 1961): 60–1.

'The Corner of X and Y Streets.' *MGOS*, 90–3.

'Book Fair 1961.' *Arts Council News* 13, no. 7 (April 1962): 2–3.

'Reflections in a Pool.' *Canadian Literature* 19 (Autumn 1964): 29–33.

'Series of Combination of Events and Where Is John Goodwin?' *Tamarack Review* 33 (Autumn 1964): 3–9.

'Of Alan Crawley.' *Canadian Literature* 22 (Winter 1964), 33–42.

'Young Vancouver Seen through the Eyes of Youth.' *Habitat* 10 (1967): 138–9.

'Joyce Cary.' *EW:SEL*, 77–81.

'Somewhere near the Truth.' *EW:SEL*, 81–91.

'An Approach to Some Novels.' *EW:SEL*, 91–4.

'Admissions, Seabirds, and People.' *EW:SEL*, 107–11.

'Selected Correspondence, Nov. 1944-Mar. 1974.' *EW:SEL*, 115–253.

'Duchess.' In *The Other Side of Silence*, by Mary McAlpine, 2–7.

II. Archives and Unpublished Manuscripts

1. Archives

CVA: City of Vancouver Archives
   The Malkin File
   J.S. Matthews Collection
DMC: David Malkin Collection, Roswell, Georgia (private)
EABC: Ernest and Amy Buckerfield Collection, Vancouver, B.C. (private)
MUL: McMaster University Library
   The Macmillan Company (Canada) Papers
NAC: National Archives of Canada
   Desmond Pacey Collection
   Robert Weaver Collection
QUL: Queen's University Library
   Dorothy Livesay Papers
   George Woodcock Collection
TFRBL: Thomas Fisher Rare Book Library, University of Toronto
   Earle Birney Collection
   Mazo de la Roche Collection
   A.J.M. Smith Papers
   Anne Wilkinson Papers
UBCL: University of British Columbia Library, Rare Books and Special Collections
   Margaret and Geoffrey Andrew Papers
   Alan Crawley Papers
   Ronald Hambleton Collection

Irene Howard Papers
The Macmillan Company (Canada) Collection
Mary McAlpine Collection
R.E. Watters Papers
Ethel Wilson Papers
UCL: University of Calgary Library
Malcolm Ross Collection
UTA: University of Texas at Austin, Humanities Research Center
Harper Brothers Collection
YUL: York University Library
Margaret Laurence Archive

The largest archive of Wilson materials is housed at the University of British Columbia Library, Rare Books and Special Collections. The first two boxes of the Ethel Wilson Papers were deposited there by the author herself, the following eight by John Gray, friend and adviser, who was named in her will as literary executor, and the last three by her heirs after her death in 1980. The University of British Columbia holds the copyright to her unpublished as well as her published literary works.

Equally important are the Wilson papers that form part of the Macmillan Company of Canada Collection. This is an extensive correspondence between author and press that includes information about readers' reports, editorial revisions, jacket designs, publication, promotions, royalties, serializations, radio broadcasts, and film rights. Also included are copies of speeches, and published and unpublished articles. Some of these papers are at McMaster University Library, but most of them are at University of British Columbia Library. When they were transferred from the Macmillan Company, incoming and outgoing letters were attached together, so that one had a perfect record of the correspondence between Wilson and her Macmillan editors. Unfortunately, it was decided that the letters should be separated, Wilson's letters in separate folders from those of her correspondents at Macmillan. The letters are grouped according to book projects, but of course letters often discuss more than one project. The result is frustrating for the researcher, who has to search (sometimes for hours) to match the letters that address and respond to each other. McMaster University Library left their portion of the Wilson correspondence from Macmillan intact.

The researcher encounters a further source of frustration in the papers at UBC Library. In the Mary McAlpine Collection, Wilson's photograph albums have been damaged and pictures are missing. McAlpine explains it this way in a note she enclosed with the photo books: 'The cutting up of the albums was done by my publisher Howard White (or his employees) and not with my permission.'

2. Unpublished Fiction

These undated materials are listed alphabetically.

'From the Island.' UBCL, Wilson Papers, Box 6, Folder 18.
'Herself When Young' (or 'Miss Cuppy'). UBCL, Wilson Papers, Box 12, Folders 4–5.
'Poor Sydney.' UBCL, Wilson Papers, Box 6, Folder 29.
'The Umbrella.' EABC.
'Vancouver Child.' EABC.
'The Vat and the Brew.' UBCL, Wilson Papers, Box 5, Folders 1–20.

3. Unpublished Non-Fiction

The following are also listed alphabetically.

'At What Point Do I Grow Old?' UBCL, Ronald Hambleton Collection.
'B.C. Conference of Writers' (untitled talk). UBCL, Wilson Papers, Box 10, Folder 10.
'B.C. Society of Artists' (untitled talk). UBCL, Wilson Papers, Box 10, Folders 6–7.
'B.C. Writers.' UBCL, Wilson Papers, Box 10, Folder 5.
'Crofton House Library' (untitled talk). UBCL, Wilson Papers, Box 2, Folder 16; Box 10, Folder 4.
'The First Chief Justice.' UBCL, Wilson Papers, Box 7, Folders 13–14.
'A Frail and Powerful Word.' UBCL, Wilson Papers, Box 7, Folder 15.
'How Does the Writer Reach His Audience?' UBCL, Wilson Papers, Box 9, Folders 5–8.
'Hunt the Symbol.' UBCL, Wilson Papers, Box 7, Folder 16.
'In Defense of a Little Learning.' UBCL, Wilson Papers, Box 9, Folders 9–10.
'Mazo de la Roche.' UBCL, Wilson Papers, Box 10, Folder 8.
'A Meeting in Africa.' UBCL, Wilson Papers, Box 6, Folders 23–4.
'On Not Being Educated.' UBCL, Wilson Papers, Box 9, Folders 13–14.
'Private Happiness.' UBCL, Wilson Papers, Box 7, Folder 19.
'The Second Time of Voting.' UBCL, Wilson Papers, Box 7, Folder 23.
'Seen through Waves.' UBCL, Wilson Papers, Box 7, Folders 24–5.
'The St. Roch, 85 Tons.' UBCL, Wilson Papers, Box 7, Folders 28–30.

'Theory of Angels.' UBCL, Wilson Papers, Box 7, Folder 31.

'The Tool That Fits the Hand.' UBCL, Wilson Papers, Box 2, Folder 13; Box 9, Folder 19.

'UBC Women's Undergraduate Society Address' (untitled). UBCL, Wilson Papers, Box 10, Folder 9.

'West Vancouver High School' (untitled talk). UBCL, Wilson Papers, Box 2, Folder 15; Box 9, Folders 20–2.

'Words and Places.' UBCL, Wilson Papers, Box 7, Folders 3–4.

'The Writer and the Public.' UBCL, Wilson Papers, Box 2, Folder 14.

III. Secondary Sources: Selected Books and Articles

Armitage, Christopher M. 'Ethel Wilson's English Schooling and Its Echoes in Her Fiction.' In *The Ethel Wilson Symposium.* Ed. Lorraine McMullen. Ottawa: University of Ottawa Press, 1982. 19–26.

Atwood, Margaret. *Survival: A Thematic Guide to Canadian Literature.* Toronto: Anansi Press, 1972.

Baldwin, A.W. *The Macdonald Sisters.* London: Peter Davies, 1960.

Bhelande, Anjali. *Self Beyond Self: Ethel Wilson and Indian Philosophical Thought.* Mumbai: S.N.D.T. Women's University and Bharatiya Vidya Bhavan, 1996.

Birbalsingh, Frank. 'Ethel Wilson: Innocent Traveller.' *Canadian Literature* 49 (Summer 1971): 35–46.

Bowering, George. 'Afterword.' *Swamp Angel,* by Ethel Wilson. Toronto: McClelland and Stewart, 1990. 210–16.

Callaghan, Morley. 'Writers and Critics: A Minor League.' *Saturday Night* 70 (6 Nov. 1953): 32–3.

Comeau, Paul. 'Ethel Wilson's Characters.' *Studies in Canadian Literature* 6 (1981): 24–38.

Davies, Barrie. 'Lamia: The Allegorical Nature of Hetty Dorval.' *Studies in Canadian Literature* 1 (Winter 1976): 137–40.

Davis, Rev. E.A. *Commemorative Review of the Methodist, Presbyterian, and Congregational Churches in British Columbia.* [Publisher not identified], 1925.

Frye, Northrop. 'Afterword.' *Hetty Dorval,* by Ethel Wilson. Toronto: McClelland and Stewart, 1990. 105–8.

Gelfant, Blanche H. *Cross-Cultural Reckonings: A Triptych of Russian, American, and Canadian Texts.* New York: Cambridge University Press, 1995.

– 'Ethel Wilson's Absent City: A Personal View of Vancouver.' *Canadian Literature* 146 (Autumn 1995): 9–27.

– 'The Hidden Mines in Ethel Wilson's Landscape (or an American Cat among

Canadian Falcons).' In *The Ethel Wilson Symposium.* Ed. Lorraine McMullen. Ottawa: University of Ottawa Press, 1982. 119–39.

Geng, Li-Ping. 'The Rival Editions of Ethel Wilson's *Swamp Angel.*' *Essays on Canadian Writing* 77 (Oct. 2002): 63–89.

Givner, Joan. *Mazo de la Roche: The Hidden Life.* Toronto: Oxford University Press, 1989.

Hare, Robert. *Without Conscience: The Disturbing World of the Psychopaths among Us.* New York: Pocket Books, 1993.

Hinchcliffe, P.M. '"To Keep the Memory of So Worthy a Friend": Ethel Wilson as an Elegist.' *Journal of Canadian Fiction* 2 (Spring 1973): 62–6.

Howard, Irene. *Bowen Island 1872–1972.* Victoria: Morriss, 1973.

– 'High Tea: Society in the Old West End.' *Westworld* 5, no. 1 (Jan.-Feb. 1979): 16–18, 45.

– 'Shockable and Unshockable Methodists in *The Innocent Traveller.*' *Essays on Canadian Writing* 23 (Spring 1982): 107–34.

Itwaru, Arnold Harrichand. *The Invention of Canada: Literary Text and the Immigrant Imaginary.* Toronto: Tsar Publications, 1990.

Keith, W.J. 'Ethel Wilson.' In *A Sense of Style: Studies in the Art of Fiction in English-Speaking Canada.* Toronto: ECW Press, 1989. 40–60.

– 'Overview: Ethel Wilson, Providence, and the Vocabulary of Vision.' In *The Ethel Wilson Symposium.* Ed. Lorraine McMullen. Ottawa: University of Ottawa Press, 1982. 105–17.

King, James. *The Life of Margaret Laurence.* Toronto: McClelland and Stewart, 1996.

Laurence, Margaret. 'A Friend's Tribute to Ethel Wilson.' *Toronto Star,* 24 Jan. 1981, p. F7.

Livesay, Dorothy. 'Ethel Wilson: West Coast Novelist.' *Saturday Night* 67 (26 July 1952): 20, 36.

MacDonald, R.D. 'Serious Whimsy.' *Canadian Literature* 63 (Winter 1975): 40–51.

– 'Time in Ethel Wilson's *The Innocent Traveller* and *Swamp Angel.*' *Studies in Canadian Literature* 13 (1989): 64–79.

Mackay, Constance. 'Vancouver's New Novelist.' *Mayfair* (Nov. 1947): 67, 101.

Marriott, Anne. 'Afterword.' *Love and Salt Water,* by Ethel Wilson. Toronto: McClelland and Stewart, 1990. 173–7.

McAlpine, Mary. 'Ethel Wilson As I Knew Her.' In *The Ethel Wilson Symposium.* Ed. Lorraine McMullen. Ottawa: University of Ottawa Press, 1982.

– *The Other Side of Silence: A Life of Ethel Wilson.* Madeira Park, B.C.: Harbour Publishing, 1988.

McComb, Bonnie Martyn. *Ethel Wilson: An Annotated Bibliography.* Downsview, ON: ECW Press, 1984.

McLay, Catherine. 'Ethel Wilson's Lost Lady: *Hetty Dorval* and Willa Cather.' *Journal of Canadian Fiction* 33 (1981–2): 94–106.

McMullen, Lorraine, ed. *The Ethel Wilson Symposium.* Ottawa: University of Ottawa Press, 1982.

McPherson, Hugo. 'Fiction 1940–1960.' In *Literary History of Canada: Canadian Literature in English.* Gen. ed. Carl F. Klinck. Vol. 2. Toronto: University of Toronto Press, 1976. 205–33.

Mitchell, Beverley J. 'Ethel Wilson (1888–1980).' In *Canadian Writers and Their Works.* Fiction Series. Ed. Robert Lecker, Jack David, and Ellen Quigley. Vol. 6. Toronto: ECW Press, 1985. 183–238.

– 'In Defense of *Hetty Dorval.*' *Studies in Canadian Literature* 1 (Winter 1976): 26–48.

– 'The Right Word in the Right Place: Literary Techniques in the Fiction of Ethel Wilson.' In *The Ethel Wilson Symposium.* Ed. Lorraine McMullen. Ottawa: University of Ottawa Press, 1982. 73–85.

– 'Ulysses in Vancouver: A Critical Approach to Ethel Wilson's "Tuesday and Wednesday."' *Atlantis* 4 (Fall 1978): 110–22.

Moss, John, ed. *The Canadian Novel: Modern Times.* Toronto: NC Press, 1982.

– *Patterns of Isolation in English-Canadian Fiction.* Toronto: McClelland and Stewart, 1974.

Moxon, J.F. *The History of Horton Hall.* Leek, Staffordshire: Churnet Valley Books, 1997.

Munro, Alice. 'Afterword.' *The Equations of Love,* by Ethel Wilson. Toronto: McClelland and Stewart, 1990. 259–63.

Murray, Heather. 'Metaphor and Metonymy, Language and Landscape in Ethel Wilson's *Swamp Angel.*' *World Literature Written in English* 25, no. 1 (1985): 241–52.

New, W.H. 'The "Genius" of Place and Time: The Fiction of Ethel Wilson.' *Journal of Canadian Studies* 3 (Nov. 1968): 39–48.

– 'The Irony of Order: Ethel Wilson's *The Innocent Traveller.*' *Critique: Studies in Modern Fiction* 10, no. 3 (1968): 22–30.

– ed. *Canadian Short Fiction.* 2nd ed. Scarborough, ON: Prentice Hall Canada, 1997.

O'Faoláin, Seán. 'New Novels.' *Listener* 47 (27 March 1952): 535.

Pacey, Desmond. *Ethel Wilson.* New York: Twayne, 1967.

– 'Introduction.' *Swamp Angel,* by Ethel Wilson. Toronto: McClelland and Stewart, 1962. 5–10.

– 'The Writer and His Public (1920–1960).' In *Literary History of Canada: Canadian Literature in English.* Gen. ed. Carl F. Klinck. Vol. 2. Toronto: University of Toronto Press, 1976. 3–21.

Page, P.K. 'Afterword.' *The Innocent Traveller*, by Ethel Wilson. Toronto: McClelland and Stewart, 1990. 238–43.

Peterson, Lester R. *The Gibson's Landing Story.* Toronto: P. Martin Books, 1962.

Reynolds, Mac. 'Canada Council Medalists.' [*Toronto*] *Star Weekly*, 4 April 1964, p. 13.

Smyth, Donna. 'Maggie's Lake: The Vision of Female Power in *Swamp Angel.*' In *The Canadian Novel: Modern Times.* Ed. John Moss. Toronto: NC Press, 1982. 159–65.

– 'Strong Women in the Web: Women's Work and Community in Ethel Wilson's Fiction.' In *The Ethel Wilson Symposium.* Ed. Lorraine McMullen. Ottawa: University of Ottawa Press, 1982. 87–95.

Sonthoff, Helen W. 'The Novels of Ethel Wilson.' *Canadian Literature* 26 (Autumn 1965): 33–42.

Stouck, David. 'Afterword.' *Mrs Golightly and Other Stories*, by Ethel Wilson. Toronto: McClelland and Stewart, 1990. 212–16.

– 'Ethel Wilson's Novels.' *Canadian Literature* 74 (Autumn 1977): 74–88.

– ed. *Ethel Wilson: Stories, Essays, and Letters.* Vancouver: UBC Press, 1987.

Stouck, Mary-Ann. 'Structure in Ethel Wilson's *The Innocent Traveller.*' *Canadian Literature* 109 (Summer 1986): 17–31.

Stovel, Nora Foster. 'Female Excalibur As Literary Legacy: Ethel Wilson's *Swamp Angel* and Margaret Laurence's *The Fire-Dwellers.*' *International Fiction Review* 21 (1994): 25–31.

Struthers, J.R. (Tim). 'The Real Material: An Interview with Alice Munro.' In *Probable Fictions: Alice Munro's Narrative Acts.* Ed. Louis K. MacKendrick. Downsview, ON: ECW Press, 1983: 5–36.

Thompson, Brent. 'Ethel Wilson, Wary Mythologist.' *Canadian Literature* 102 (Autumn 1984): 20–32.

Urbas, Jeannette. 'The Perquisites of Love.' *Canadian Literature* 59 (Winter 1974): 6–15.

Whitaker, Muriel. 'Journeys to the Interior: The Wilsons at Lac Le Jeune.' In *The Ethel Wilson Symposium.* Ed. Lorraine McMullen. Ottawa: University of Ottawa Press, 1982. 13–18.

Wild, Barbara. 'Piety, Propriety, and the Shaping of the Writer.' In *The Ethel Wilson Symposium.* Ed. Lorraine McMullen. Ottawa: University of Ottawa Press, 1982. 27–46.

Woodcock, George. 'Ethel Wilson.' *Canadian Fiction Magazine* 15 (Autumn 1974): 44–9.

– 'Innocence and Solitude: The Fictions of Ethel Wilson.' In *The Canadian Novel: Modern Times.* Ed. John Moss. Toronto: NC Press, 1982. 166–91.

Young, Cy. 'Shortcut to Success.' *Vancouver Sun*, 5 July 1952, p. 18.

Illustration Credits

Special Collections, University of British Columbia: Robert and Lila Bryant en route to South Africa; Ethel Wilson's birthplace in South Africa; Lila and Ethel Bryant; Robert and Ethel Bryant; Ethel Bryant, ca. 1894; Ethel Bryant in early teens, ca. 1902; Wallace Wilson in WWI uniform; Ethel Wilson and Audrey Butler; Ethel Wilson, 1940s; Wallace Wilson in WWII uniform; Ethel Wilson's first publicity photo; John Gray; Canada Council Medalists; Wallace Wilson, Bill Reid, and Neal Harlow; Ethel and Wallace Wilson, ca. 1962 (photo by Nan Cheney)

City of Vancouver Archives: English Bay, CVA, BeP151N133; Malkin family, 1907, CVA 677–35; Ethel Bryant and cousins, CVA 373–6; Malkin family, 1935, CVA 373–12 (photo by G.L. Wadds)

Private Collections: Marriage of Lila Malkin and Robert Bryant (David Malkin Collection); Ethel Wilson, ca. 1921 (courtesy of Colin Graham, Jr); Ethel Wilson reading on a boat with in-laws (courtesy of Mary Buckerfield White); Ethel and Wallace Wilson fly-fishing (courtesy of Colin Graham, Jr); Kensington Place (photograph by Winnifred Stouck)

Index